Fodor's 2009

D0107387

MONTRÉAL &
QUÉBEC CITY

Where to Stay and Eat
for All Budgets

Must-See Sights
and Local Secrets

Ratings You Can Trust

Fodor's Travel Publications   New York, Toronto, London, Sydney, Auckland
www.fodors.com

FODOR'S MONTRÉAL & QUÉBEC CITY 2009

Editor: Rachel Klein

Editorial Contributors: Chris Barry, Eva Friede, Joanne Latimer, Anne Marie Marko, Brandon Presser, Julie Waters, Paul Waters

Production Editor: Tom Holton

Maps & Illustrations: David Lindroth, Mark Stroud, *cartographers*; Bob Blake, Rebecca Baer, *map editors;* William Wu, *information graphics*

Design: Fabrizio La Rocca, *creative director*; Guido Caroti, Siobhan O'Hare, *art directors;* Tina Malaney, Chie Ushio, Ann McBride, Jessica Walsh, *designers;* Melanie Marin, *senior picture editor*

Cover Photo: (place Jacques Cartier, Vieux Montréal): Bill Brooks, Masterfile

Production Manager: Angela L. McLean

ISBN 978–1–4000–0803–2

ISSN 1525–5867

SPECIAL SALES

This book is available at special discounts for bulk purchases for sales promotions or premiums. Special editions, including personalized covers, excerpts of existing books, and corporate imprints, can be created in large quantities for special needs. For more information, write to Special Markets/Premium Sales, 1745 Broadway, MD 6-2, New York, New York 10019, or e-mail specialmarkets@randomhouse.com.

AN IMPORTANT TIP & AN INVITATION

Although all prices, opening times, and other details in this book are based on information supplied to us at press time, changes occur all the time in the travel world, and Fodor's cannot accept responsibility for facts that become outdated or for inadvertent errors or omissions. So **always confirm information when it matters,** especially if you're making a detour to visit a specific place. Your experiences—positive and negative— matter to us. If we have missed or misstated something, **please write to us.** We follow up on all suggestions. Contact the Montréal & Québec City editor at editors@fodors.com or c/o Fodor's at 1745 Broadway, New York, NY 10019.

PRINTED IN THE UNITED STATES OF AMERICA

10 9 8 7 6 5 4 3 2 1

Be a Fodor's Correspondent

Your opinion matters. It matters to us. It matters to your fellow Fodor's travelers, too. And we'd like to hear it. In fact, we need to hear it.

When you share your experiences and opinions, you become an active member of the Fodor's community. That means we'll not only use your feedback to make our books better, but we'll publish your names and comments whenever possible. Throughout our guides, look for "Word of Mouth," excerpts of your unvarnished feedback.

Here's how you can help improve Fodor's for all of us.

Tell us when we're right. We rely on local writers to give you an insider's perspective. But our writers and staff editors—who are the best in the business—depend on you. Your positive feedback is a vote to renew our recommendations for the next edition.

Tell us when we're wrong. We're proud that we update most of our guides every year. But we're not perfect. Things change. Hotels cut services. Museums change hours. Charming cafés lose charm. If our writer didn't quite capture the essence of a place, tell us how you'd do it differently. If any of our descriptions are inaccurate or inadequate, we'll incorporate your changes in the next edition and will correct factual errors at fodors.com immediately.

Tell us what to include. You probably have had fantastic travel experiences that aren't yet in Fodor's. Why not share them with a community of like-minded travelers? Maybe you chanced upon a beach or bistro or B&B that you don't want to keep to yourself. Tell us why we should include it. And share your discoveries and experiences with everyone directly at fodors.com. Your input may lead us to add a new listing or highlight a place we cover with a "Highly Recommended" star or with our highest rating, "Fodor's Choice."

Give us your opinion instantly at our feedback center at www.fodors.com/feedback. You may also e-mail editors@fodors.com with the subject line "Montreal & Quebec City Editor." Or send your nominations, comments, and complaints by mail to Montreal & Quebec City Editor, Fodor's, 1745 Broadway, New York, NY 10019.

You and travelers like you are the heart of the Fodor's community. Make our community richer by sharing your experiences. Be a Fodor's correspondent.

Bon voyage!

Tim Jarrell, Publisher

CONTENTS

MAPS

ABOUT THIS BOOK

Our Ratings

Sometimes you find terrific travel experiences and sometimes they just find you. But usually the burden is on you to select the right combination of experiences. That's where our ratings come in.

As travelers we've all discovered a place so wonderful that its worthiness is obvious. And sometimes even superlatives don't do it justice: you just have to be there to know. These sights, properties, and experiences get our highest rating, **Fodor's Choice**, indicated by orange stars throughout this book.

Black stars highlight sights and properties we deem **Highly Recommended**, places that our writers, editors, and readers praise again and again for consistency and excellence.

By default, there's another category: any place we include in this book is by definition worth your time, unless we say otherwise. And we will.

Disagree with any of our choices? Care to nominate a place or suggest that we rate one more highly? Visit our feedback center at www.fodors.com/feedback.

Budget Well

Hotel and restaurant price categories from ¢ to $$$$ are defined in the Where to Stay and Where to Eat chapters. For attractions, we always give standard adult admission fees; reductions are usually available for children, students, and senior citizens. Want to pay with plastic? **AE, D, DC, MC, V** following restaurant and hotel listings indicate whether American Express, Discover, Diners Club, MasterCard, and Visa are accepted.

Restaurants

Unless we state otherwise, restaurants are open for lunch and dinner daily. We mention dress only when there's a specific requirement and reservations only when they're essential or not accepted—it's always best to book ahead.

Hotels

Hotels have private bath, phone, TV, and air-conditioning unless stated otherwise. They may operate on the European Plan (aka EP, meaning without meals), the Continental Plan (CP, with a Continental breakfast), Breakfast Plan (BP, with a full breakfast), or Modified American Plan (MAP, with breakfast and dinner). We always list

facilities but not whether you'll be charged an extra fee to use them, so when pricing accommodations, find out what's included.

Many Listings

★	Fodor's Choice
★	Highly recommended
⊠	Physical address
⊹	Directions
⬧	Mailing address
☎	Telephone
🖷	Fax
⊕	On the Web
✎	E-mail
🎫	Admission fee
☉	Open/closed times
Ⓜ	Metro stations
▭	Credit cards

Hotels & Restaurants

🏨	Hotel
⇱	Number of rooms
⛴	Facilities
⍾	Meal plans
✕	Restaurant
⚓	Reservations
⟍	Smoking
𝄡	BYOB
✕🏨	Hotel with restaurant that warrants a visit

Outdoors

🏌	Golf
⛺	Camping

Other

☺	Family-friendly
⇨	See also
⊠	Branch address
☞	Take note

1

Experience Montréal & Québec City

Cafe at night, Vieux Montréal.

WORD OF MOUTH

"In favor of Montréal and Québec City: lots of local festivals...the French flavor that makes it almost/sort of/partly like going overseas. Gourmet food, boutique hotels, excellent art museums..."

—BAK

www.fodors.com/forums

WHAT'S NEW IN MONTRÉAL & QUÉBEC CITY

Montréal remains the metropolis of Québec province and one of the most fascinating cities on the continent, but there's no doubt it's having a bit of an identity crisis these days.

For one thing, it's not as French as it used to be. Immigrants from the Middle East, Latin America, and South and East Asia have brought new vibrancy to the central city, as middle-class francophones have moved to the outer suburbs in search of more space and lower property taxes. But that's also left Montréal struggling with the challenge to preserve its role as the undisputed center of French culture in North America.

And the can-do spirit that gave the world Expo '67 and the '76 Olympics? It's long gone, as there's little public support or enthusiasm for new, large-scale projects. The loss of the Canada Grand Prix—North America's only Formula 1 race—in 2009 didn't help restore confidence. Montréal, however, never stays down long. There are signs of new vitality, most notably the new Quartier des Spectacles that should confirm the city's reputation as the party center of Canada.

Meanwhile, Québec City brims with new confidence. Flushed with the success of its 400th-anniversary celebrations in 2008, the province's political capital seems to have cast off the last vestiges of its reputation for stodgy provincialism.

Defending French
By most standards, the state of the French language in Québec has never been healthier. Government, courts, and even business are conducted almost exclusively in French, and a growing number of immigrants are choosing French as their primary language.

But the Québécois are still so anxious about language that just one bad number can overshadow any good news about French in the work place or immigrants joining the linguistic majority. Recent news from Statistics Canada revealed that the percentage of Montréal Island residents claiming French as their mother tongue had shrunk to just under 50 percent, which inspired much hand-wringing commentary on "whither French?"

It was in this atmosphere that the federal Parliament passed a motion recognizing the Québécois as a "nation within a united Canada." Even though the declaration was mostly symbolic, it was hugely popular in Québec. When you're a French-speaking minnow in a vast English-speaking sea, you need all the reassurance you can get.

Hockey Resurgent
After 15 years in the doldrums, the Montréal Canadiens have come back with a bang in more ways than one. When last season the team finished the National Hockey League season on top of its division, the whole province rejoiced. But when they eliminated the Boston Bruins in the first round of the Stanley Cup play-offs, fans went wild, laying waste to shop windows on rue Ste-Catherine and burning a few police cruisers for good measure. Understandably, downtown merchants were secretly relieved when the Philadelphia Flyers eliminated the Canadiens in the next round, and remain ambivalent, at best, about the resurgent Canadiens. Still, the team that's been cupless since 1993 is back in contention. And in a province where hockey is practically a national religion, that means something.

Soaring Loonie

A soaring Canadian dollar reignited old cross-border shopping traditions, with cavalcades of jubilant Québécois heading south to the malls of Vermont and northern New York with their suddenly desirable currency.

The trouble for the province is that north-heading traffic shrank to a trickle as American tourists, accustomed for decades to an automatic 20- and even 30-percent discount on everything, stayed home in droves. A strong buck, it turns out, is great for Maine beach resorts, but not so good for the merchants and innkeepers at home. Québec, unfortunately, is no longer quite the bargain it was just a couple of years ago—at least not for Americans.

Racing Blues

Montréal has had to make some difficult cultural adjustments in its time, but none more challenging than the one forced on it in 2008 when the Fédération Internationale de l'Automobile, the body that governs the elite world of Formula 1 racing, cancelled the 2009 Canadian Grand Prix and gave the city's favorite race date to Turkey. That wiped out a summer tradition that dates back to 1978, when Montréal welcomed its first Formula 1 crowd. At the time it seemed a match made in heaven. Formula 1 racing attracts the kind of fans who wash their windshields with Evian water, order champagne by the magnum, and pay scandalous sums for scandalously small bits of clothing. They filled every high-end hotel room in town for a week and kept all the nightspots humming, much to the delight of ogling locals.

But all is not lost. NASCAR—which is to Formula 1 as sirloin is to hamburger—had an experimental run on the city's race track in 2008, and all seemed to go well. The beer-and-burger crowd stock-car racing attracts might not have had the same eye-appeal for Montréalers as the Formula 1 crowd, but they seemed friendly enough and, like most visitors to the city, had a really good time.

Smokeless at Last

Québec was Canada's last holdout against the anti-smoking crusade. As recently as early 2007, long after the rest of Canada had outlawed smoking just about everywhere, the province's restaurants and bars were still blue with smoke. Some predicted that Québec would never kick the habit. But by the spring of 2008, when the last phase of the provincial Government's draconian health measures went into effect in spite of the protests of a small but vocal lobby, Québec finally became smoke-free. The rule of thumb: Don't light up anywhere there's a roof over your head, even if it's just the umbrella over your table at a sidewalk café.

New Downtown Theatre District

Montréal is hoping to cement its status as the festival capital of Canada by transforming a huge chunk of its downtown into an entertainment district and calling it the Quartier des Spectacles. The first phase of the project, to be ready in time for the city's annual jazz festival in June 2009, is a 70-acre park with stages for outdoor concerts and an underground control room to monitor the sound systems. By the time the $132 million project is completed in 2012, it will be home to nearly 30 venues for dance, music, theatre, and art displays.

WHAT'S WHERE

1 Montréal. Montréal and the island on which it stands takes its name from Mont-Royal, a stubby plug of tree-covered igneous rock that rises high above the surrounding cityscape. It's a bustling, multiethnic city of neighborhoods, from the historic Old City to the hip Plâteau.

2 Québec City. The capital of Québec Province is widely considered to be the most French city in North America. Vieux-Québec (Old Québec) is split into two tiers, separated by steep rock against which are more than 25 *escaliers* (staircases) and a funicular. The surrounding cluster of small, low-rise neighborhoods each have their own charm and flavor.

3 The Laurentians. The Laurentians (les Laurentides) encompass thousands of miles of wilderness, but for many people the draw is Mont-Tremblant and its world-class slopes. At just 1½–2 hours from Montréal, the area has become a favorite weekend ski destination.

4 The Eastern Townships. If being 3,150 feet high doesn't make you feel close enough to the heavens, you can turn your attention to the stars at the Mont-Mégantic observatory in the Eastern Townships. Also known as les Cantons de l'Est, the Townships have the architecture and rolling hills of the New England countryside to their south.

5 Île d'Orléans. Île d'Orléans is called the "Garden of Québec," as it provides many area restaurants with local produce. Made up of six small villages, this charming island has B&Bs, crafts, and wineries.

6 Côte de Beaupré. The coast hugged by the St. Lawrence River is opposite the north shore of Île d'Orléans, and features the thundering Montmorency Falls and the impressive Ste-Anne de Beaupré.

7 Charlevoix. Valleys and plateaus, cliffs cut by waterfalls, and mountains that brush the St. Lawrence River characterize the Charlevoix region. This "Switzerland of Québec" has infused the art of painters, poets, and musicians for generations.

La Mauricie
National Park

THE LAURENTIANS

Lac
Saint-Pierre

Berthierville

Saint-Joseph-
de-Sorel

St Jérôme   Le Gardeur

Boisbriand   Douville

Oka   **Montréal**   Beloeil

Mercier   Candiac

Salaberry-   Iberville
de-Valleyfield MONTÉRÉGIE

CANADA
UNITED STATES

NEW YORK

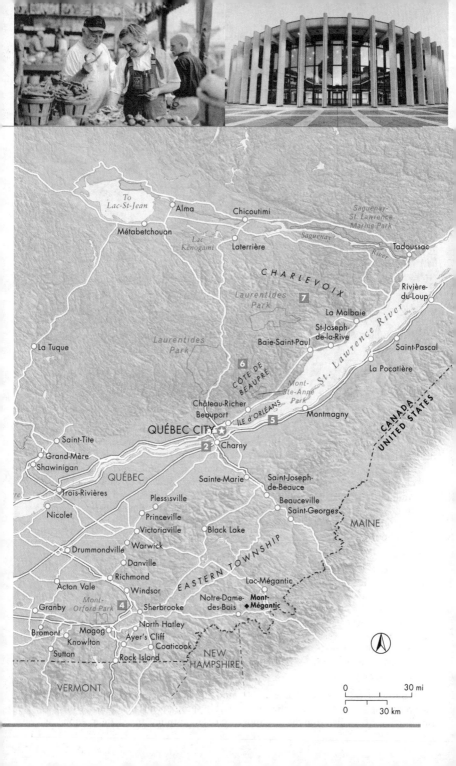

TOP MONTRÉAL & QUÉBEC CITY ATTRACTIONS

Mont-Tremblant

(B) Take a mountain with a 2,870-foot vertical drop and 600 acres of skiable terrain, plus state-of-the-art snowmaking and chairlifts, first-class hotels and condos, and an on-slope village full of bars, restaurants, and nightclubs, and you end up with one of the finest ski resorts in North America.

Tadoussac

(C) This old trading-post village has become the place to whale-watch in the region. You may see mink, finback, and even blue whales, but more commonly the southernmost colony of beluga whales that shelter year-round beneath the soaring cliffs of the Saguenay Fjord. Watch them from the shore, or sign up for a cruise to get a closer look.

Basilique Notre-Dame-de-Montréal

(A) Everything about Montréal's first parish church is overscale, from the 228-foot twin steeples to the 7,000-pipe organ in the loft. The thousands of stars spattered across the vaulted blue ceiling are 24-carat gold and were painstakingly applied by hand. To catch a bit of traditional Catholic pomp and hear the organ roar, consider attending the 11 AM solemn mass on Sunday.

Vieux-Port-de-Montréal

(D) Until the 1980s, Montréal's old port was an industrial slum, full of rusted rail sidings and crumbling warehouses. Now it's one of the city's favorite parks, a place to cycle, stroll, or take a boat ride on the Lachine Rapids—plus has excellent restaurants and nightlife.

Parc Mont-Royal

The "mountain" that gives Montréal its name, just over 760 feet high, rises above the 500-acre park where the city-weary flirt in spring, picnic in summer, enjoy colors of autumn, and skate in winter.

Musée des Beaux-Arts de Montréal

(E) Canada's oldest art museum has one of the world's finest collections of Canadian art, from Paul Kane's portrayals of pioneer life to Paul-Émile Borduas's dazzling abstractions. The permanent collection includes works by such world masters as Rembrandt, Renoir, and Picasso.

La Citadelle

(H) The star-shaped fortress just outside the walls of Vieux-Québec is the largest fortified base in North America still occupied by troops, and it's a fascinating place to explore.

La Citadelle was built in 1832 to protect the city from a feared American invasion that never came, and now home to Canada's Royal 22e Régiment. Every summer morning at 10, the regiment turns out in scarlet tunics and bearskin caps, along with their mascot, Batisse the Goat, for the ceremonial changing of the guard.

Château Frontenac

(F) The Hôtel Château Frontenac towers above Vieux-Québec the way Cinderella's castle towers over DisneyWorld—except the Château is real, as are the 18th- and 19th-century homes and shops that huddle in its shadow. At its base is Dufferin Terrace, a wide boardwalk with sweeping views of the St. Lawrence River and the Laurentians.

Plains of Abraham

(G) It's a peaceful city park now, full of winding walking paths and bicycle trails, and a favorite in winter of local cross-country skiers. But on Sept. 13, 1759, it was anything but peaceful, when British troops routed the flower of New France and changed North American history forever.

TOP MONTRÉAL & QUÉBEC CITY EXPERIENCES

A la Française

One of the very best reasons to visit Québec is to experience its unique culture. Steeped in traditions inherited from its former mother country France, the province remains distinctly North American, yet is unlike anything else to be found on this side of the pond. Where else in America can you relax on a terrace, sipping café au laits while listening to the artist couple beside you debate politics in the language of Molière? Or treat your taste buds to that perfect foie gras, or crème brûlée, pleasantly served up by a French-speaking waiter who probably couldn't indulge you in your own language even if he wanted to?

Québec truly is like the European country next door, the France you can drive to in less than a day from your home in, say, Ohio, or New Jersey, yet separated by a million miles of difference from anything like it just south, or north, or east, or west, of its borders. The people who reside in this relatively laid-back part of the world, both French and English, share an approach to life that is uniquely Québécois, a work-to-live attitude as opposed to the live-to-work ethic found in most North American cities. It's a truly wonderful thing to experience, and the inhabitants of Québec, warm, intriguing, by all accounts a distinct society, are as interesting a people as they are gracious hosts. From the magnificent architecture of the grand basilicas to the trendy terraces lining the bohemian enclaves of Montréal's Plateau district, the French face of Québec is delightfully ubiquitous, and one of the most charming elements of this most charming of destinations.

Savor Local Cuisine

It would be an understatement to say that Québec has a wide variety of unique food tastes to sample. Of course, Québécois take their French food very seriously, and traveling through most towns you won't have to look too hard to find a fab restaurant serving traditional French fare and regional specialties. Some of the best meals in the province can be had at the inns and dining rooms of the tourist-heavy regions outside the major urban centers.

A far cry from fine dining is the time-honored and much-cherished *casse croûte*. Sure, on the surface a casse croûte doesn't seem like much more than your run-of-the-mill hot dog and hamburger joint—although hot chicken and green-pea sandwich plates are a staple of any self-respecting casse-croûte operation. Among the foods the region is famous for are poutine and smoked meats.

Another Québécois institution anyone with a sweet tooth will certainly appreciate are the traditional *cabanes à sucre* (maple-sugaring shacks), which open every spring come the maple syrup harvest. Québec is one of the largest maple syrup producers in the world, and there's no better way to sample the province's wares than by stopping by one of these rural establishments for a home-cooked meal that may include ham and pea soup, syrup-soaked pudding, and maple syrup with beans, eggs, pickles, ham, and little strips of crispy pig skin called "les oreilles du Crisse," or Christ's ears. The resulting sugar rush will keep you wide awake until you get home. Many cabanes à sucre can be found within a short range of Montréal and Québec City.

Romp in Snow

Québécois have little choice but to embrace the winter season. After all, from early December until mid-April the province is covered in snow, with subarctic temperatures the rule rather than the exception in the bitterly cold months of January and February.

With much of the landscape covered in the white stuff five months of the year, it's not surprising that Québec has taken great pains to nurture its reputation as one of the top winter vacation destinations in North America. In the Eastern Townships region alpine skiers can enjoy a day on the slopes at the strikingly beautiful Owl's Head ski resort for a mere C$36, with even better promotional rates during the week. Compare that to Colorado or the resorts just over the border in nearby Vermont, where a day of downhill skiing will easily run you upwards of US$65, and you realize just how good a deal Québec is when it comes to winter activities.

Of course there's more to winter in Québec than simply skiing, snowshoeing, ice-skating, or sipping cognac by the fireplace in the dining area of your 150-year-old rural inn. One activity steadily growing in popularity is dogsledding, and several operators around the province, like Globe-Trotter Aventure Canada Tours (☎888/598–7688 ⊕www.aventurecanada.com), offer backwoods dogsledding excursions lasting from a few hours to a full seven days. Cold as it may sound, most operators will provide the appropriate protective clothing upon request, and the faint of heart can take comfort in the knowledge that evenings are always spent sleeping and dining in cozy, heated cabins.

Shop for Fur & Crafts

People have traveled to Canada to look for furs ever since the beginning of the 17th century, and this is still very much the place to come. The fur industry remains an important part of the country's economic picture, contributing about $800 million to the GDP and employing about 60,000 trappers and 5,000 fur farmers, manufacturers, craftspeople, and retailers. Mink, fox, and chinchilla are the most commonly farmed fur-bearing animals, but trappers supply the market with beaver, raccoon, muskrat, otter, bear, and wolf pelts among others. Note that conservation and humane rules for both farmers and trappers are very strict.

In Montréal, the best place to look for quality furs in the region is the cluster of stores along rue Mayor and boulevard de Maisonneuve between rues de Bleury and Alymer. In Québec City, try Fourrures Richard Robitaille in Lower Town or Fourrures Sola in Upper Town.

It was the fur trade that allowed many native Canadians—the country's First Nations—to live on the land according to the traditions of their ancestors, which explains why Canada has such a rich heritage of native crafts. Québec's best-known traditional crafts are woodcarving, weaving, pine cabinetry and furniture, and canoe making. For the best price and guaranteed authenticity, buy items in the province where they originate, and look for the Canadian government's igloo symbol.

LIKE A LOCAL

Visiting Montréal and Québec City is like stumbling upon a little piece of Europe in North America. Soak up the rich French culture by sampling local cuisine, catching a hockey game at a bar, or finding yourself in the midst of some fabulous all-night party.

Try Some Poutine

The legend is that sometime in 1957 a customer walked into Le Café Idéal in the little village of Warwick, Québec, and asked owner Fernand Lachance to add a handful of cheese curds to his order of frites. He shoved the result in front of his customer and muttered "Quel poutine"—which could be roughly translated as "What a mess."

And so was born what has become Québec's favorite fast food. Poutine is everywhere. But it's no longer just hot french fries topped with a ladleful of thick brown gravy, as dozens of high- and low-brow variations have sprung up.

You might want to try poutine Michigan, for example, which replaces the gravy with spaghetti sauce, or poutine poulet, which adds chunks of barbecued chicken to the mix. Some of the province's top chefs have come up with their own gourmet versions, made with duck gravy instead of the usual tinned goop, or blue cheese instead of curds, and sometimes even foie gras.

Have Hockey Night

What soccer is to Brazilians and baseball is to Americans, hockey is to the Québécois. It's not a game, it's a religion, and its winter-long rites are celebrated in hundreds of arenas across the province.

In the morning, bleary-eyed parents hunker down in the stands watching their children practice. At 10 PM the beer leagues take over the ice—men (and increasingly women) with full-time jobs as lawyers, accountants, and lab technicians, who strap on the skates and pads just for the fun of it.

If you can afford the scalpers' prices (or if you have a friend with connections), then get a ticket to a game at the Centre Bell. The Montréal Canadiens—the province's only National Hockey League team—haven't won a Stanley Cup since 1993—but a night at the Bell is an experience to savor.

Attend a Cinq-à-sept

If someone invites you to what sounds like a "sank-a-sett," it has nothing to do with swimming or tennis. It's a cocktail party that's supposed to happen between 5 and 7 PM, but which rarely starts before 6 PM and usually ends around 8 or 8:30 PM.

The true 5-à-7 is not to be confused with the vulgar happy hour. It does not involve thirsty hordes packing away as many cheap drinks as they can before heading home. It's a more refined affair, at which conversation is at least as important as the drinks.

One of the most essential skills you should master before attending your first 5-à-7 is the two-cheek kiss. The secret to perfecting this Québec-style greeting is to find a middle ground between the air-kiss and the enthusiastic smack of long-separated lovers. Something that expresses delight without possession is just about right.

Learn to Say "Eh"

Canada's "eh" is like France's "zut, alors," except in Canada, people actually say "eh," and say it all the time. Master this verbal tic and you'll fit in here in

French-speaking Québec. The wonderful thing about "eh" is its versatility. There's the interrogatory "eh" ("You want to go to a movie, eh?"), the consensus-seeking "eh" ("This is good sugar pie, eh?"), the inquisitive "eh" ("She's got a new boyfriend, eh?"), the solo "eh," which means "Repeat please," and the simple punctuation "eh" that can be dropped randomly into long narratives to reassure the listener that it's a dialogue, not a soliloquy.

And then, there's the conciliatory "eh"—perhaps the oddest one of all. Canadians drop it in at the end of insults to change a command like "Take off" or "Beat it" (or worse) into more of a suggestion than a command. And really, it does take the edge off, eh?

Order a "Large Double-Double"
Nothing says Canada more clearly than a maple-glazed donut and a "large double-double" (large coffee with two creams and two sugars) at Tim Hortons, and dozens upon dozens of Timmy's brown-and-yellow shops line the highways and stand on street corners in the Provence of Québec.

Timmy's is Canada's meeting place—despite the fact that the chain is now owned by an American conglomerate and that most people under 40 have forgotten that its founder was hockey great Tim Horton of the Toronto Maple Leafs.

There will always be those who won't stray from deep-seeded tradition, but if you're craving a coffee a little fancier than a regular cup of Joe, you can still take part in the Timmy's experience. Those lines out the door when the weather warms up are most likely for what may become the new most popular order—their fantastic iced lattes.

Drink Some Beer
Timmy's coffee isn't the only beverage that fuels Canadians. Not so long ago, a pint of Ex (Molson's Export Ale) or a tin of Blue (Labatt's Pilsner) would have been a more appropriate liquid symbol for this nation of beer-drinkers. But things have changed in the Canadian beer world, as microbreweries have entered the beer scene. In Québec, brewers tend to choose apocalyptic names like Maudite (Damned) and Le Fin du Monde (End of the World), and even the smallest mircobrews are finding their way on tap in the cities' best bars. Bottoms up, eh.

Linger at Sidewalk Cafés
There's something about surviving one of the harshest winters on the planet that makes it particularly sweet to spend long summer evenings sipping drinks under the open sky. And make no mistake: despite global warming, Québec still endures a fierce and unforgiving winter.

Alfresco dining begins in the southern part of the province as early as May or even late April—when it can still be quite chilly, especially at night. But if you've been cooped up eating indoors for months, a few buds on the trees or a few crocuses in the garden are enough to bring out the tables.

Restaurants and snack bars pack as many tables as they can on the sidewalks. Some have elaborate terraces— fenced-in patios often with retractable awnings—perfect for one of the great treats of dining or drinking outside: watching the passing show.

WITH KIDS

There's no shortage of fantastic activities in Montréal and Québec City for kids. Here's just a sampling of what the little ones might enjoy during a visit.

Montréal

Kids bored with the churches and museums of **Vieux-Montréal**, for example, can find dozens of ways to expend pent up energy at the Vieux-Port, with boats to pedal, a clock tower to climb, and a maze to lose themselves in. For the more culturally adventurous, there are outdoor dance and theater presentations at **Parc Lafontaine**, while the biologically inclined can explore the mysteries of bonsai trees and Chinese gardens at the **Jardin Botanique** (as well as drop into the on-site **Insectarium** to see the world's largest collection of bugs).

The island **Parc Jean-Drapeau** offers 18th-century military drills at the **Stewart Museum at the Old Fort**, swimming at the Plage de l'Île Notre-Dame, painless lessons in environmental science at the **Biosphère**, and thrills and chills at the **La Ronde** amusement park. But no Montréal visit is complete without a climb up **Parc Mont-Royal** for exhilarating views of the city and a picnic by **Lac-aux-Castors**.

The **Centre des Sciences**' Imax movies and hands-on experiments at will keep your little scientists happy, as will the mummies and dinosaurs of McGill University's delightfully eclectic **Redpath Museum**. For something more historical, take a cycle ride to the **Lachine Canal Historic Site** to learn about 19th-century navigation, or drop into **Musée McCord de l'Histoire Canadienne** for a glimpse into the lives of Montréalers of times past.

Nothing beats a Saturday-morning visit to **Marché Jean-Talon**, the city's best open market, for a mouthwatering taste of cultural diversity.

Québec City

Ice-cream stands, street performers, and (in winter) a thrilling toboggan run, make **Terrasse Dufferin** as entertaining for children as for adults, as do the **Plains of Abraham's** open spaces. **Place Royale** in Basse-Ville brings the 17th and 18th centuries to life for even the youngest children. Polar bears, seals, and walrus are the stars of the city's **Parc Aquarium**.

La Citadelle's changing-of-the-guard ceremony, complete with the Royal 22e Régiment's mascot, Batisse the Goat, has lots of kid appeal, as do the hands-on exhibits at the **Musée de la Civilisation** and a visit to the 19th-century jail cells preserved in the **Musée de Québec**.

Excursions from Montréal & Québec City

In the Laurentians the gentle rides of the **Pays des Merveilles** and the **Village du Père Noël** (Santa's Village) are perfect for younger children, while those looking for a little more excitement will find plenty of thrills at the water parks at Mont-St-Sauveur in the Laurentians and Bromont in the Eastern Townships.

Montmorency Falls, on the Côte de Beapré, aren't as grand as Niagara, but they are higher, and crossing the suspension bridge above them is a thrill that almost matches an up-close encounter with a minke or finback whale on an excursion from Tadoussac.

GREAT ITINERARIES

Montréal and Québec City are the perfect destinations for long weekend trips, although if you'd like to see both areas, you could easily spend a week.

Essential Montréal in a Day

If it's your first time in Montréal and you're spending a long weekend but don't want to play tourist too much, you can catch all the major sites in one day, or split them up between two half days.

Any visit should start with the peak of Mont-Royal, the city's most enduring symbol. Afterward, wander down to avenue des Pins and then through McGill University to downtown, to take a stroll along bustling St. Catherine. While in the area, visit the Musée des Beaux-Arts de Montréal and St. Patrick's Basilica.

In the late afternoon, head down to Vieux-Montréal, and pop into the Basilique Notre-Dame-de-Montréal before getting in some nightlife—as the Old City has become the most popular place to party. There are dozens of restaurants to choose from, as well as clubs and bars.

Montréal's Day Trips & Overnights

If you have only a couple of days for a visit, you need to concentrate on one area, and the Laurentians are a good choice. This resort area has recreational options (depending on the season) that include golf, hiking, and great skiing.

Pick a resort town to stay in, whether it's St-Sauveur-des-Monts, Ste-Adèle, or Mont-Tremblant near the vast Parc du Mont-Tremblant, and use that as a base for visiting some of the surrounding towns. There's good eating and shopping here.

You can combine a taste of the Eastern Townships with a two-day visit to the Laurentians. Get a feel for the Laurentians by staying overnight in St-Sauveur-des-Monts or Ste-Adèle and exploring surrounding towns such as St-Jérôme and Morin Heights. Then head back south of Montréal to the Townships, which extend to the east along the border with New England. Overnight in Granby or Bromont: Granby has a zoo, and Bromont is known for golf and its water park.

The next day, you can shop in pretty Knowlton (look for signs to Lac Brome) and explore regional history in such towns as Valcourt. Spend a night or two in the appealing resort town of Magog, along Lac Memphrémagog, or in the quieter North Hatley, on Lac Massawippi. You'll have good dining in either. Save some time for something outdoors, whether it's golfing, skiing, biking, or hiking.

Essential Québec City in a Day

It's best to start your day in Lower Town, which is the earliest site of French civilization in North America, before heading to Upper Town. Stroll along the narrow streets of the Quartier Petit-Champlain, visit the Maison Chevalier and browse the craft stores and boutiques.

From there, head to Place Royale, making a stop at the Église Notre-Dame-des-Victoires and continue on to Terrasse Dufferin. In the afternoon, when the crowds thin out, check out the Musée National des Beaux-Arts du Québec or the Musée de la Civilisation.

Catch a gorgeous sunset on the Plains of Abraham, site of the battle that ended France's colonial dreams in North America and marked the beginning of British rule in Canada, before dining anywhere on Rue St-Jean, the best street in the city for restaurants and nightlife.

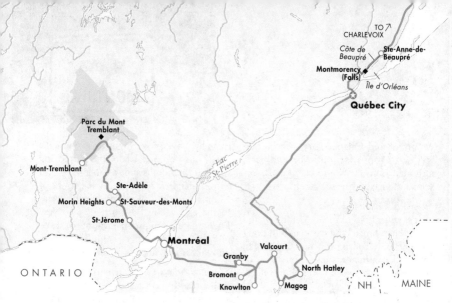

Québec City's Day Trips & Overnights

If you just want to get out of Québec City for the day, head the Côte de Beaupré or Île d'Orléans. You can drive along the Côte de Beaupré, stop at Montmorency Falls if you wish, then continue on toward Ste-Anne-de-Beaupré to visit the shrine.

Head back along boulevard Ste-Anne to Île d'Orléans. From here you can either return to the city or spend the night at one of the cozy B&Bs on the river's edge. In the morning, explore the island's farms, boutiques, galleries, and restaurants, where you can taste local produce.

If you're here for more time, you can head to Charlevoix and Tadoussac for a long day trip, but because these areas are several hours north of the city, they're better suited for overnights.

In Charlevoix, see Baie-St-Paul's local crafts and galleries, and spend the night in an inn or B&B. Spend the morning of the fourth day seeing more of Baie-St-Paul, or take a drive to St-Joseph-de-la-Rive for a tour of the Maritime Museum (Exposition Maritime). In winter you can see dogsled races here.

Tadoussac sits on the Saguenay River and is best known for whale-watching in summer, when small, white beluga whales breed in the lower part of the river. Stop in the town of La Malbaie for lunch or for some time at the casino, or the Musée de Charlevoix. You can easily tack on a stop at Côte de Beaupré or Île d'Orléans on the way there or while heading back.

FREE & ALMOST FREE

There might be no such thing as a free lunch in Montréal or Québec, but plenty of other things are free, or nearly so.

Art

Admission to the permanent collections of Montréal's Musée des Beaux-Arts (⊕*www.mbam.qc.ca*) and Québec City's Musée Nationale des Beaux-Arts (⊕*www.mnba.qc.ca*) is always free. Every summer the city of Montréal mounts an outdoor exhibit of art or photographs on the sidewalks of avenue McGill College betweens rues Ste-Catherine and Sherbrooke.

Concerts

Montréal Christ Church Cathedral (⊠*635 Rue Ste-Catherine Ouest* ☎*514/843–6577*) and Oratoire St-Joseph (⊠*3800 Chemin Queen-Mary* ☎*514/733–8211*) offer frequent free organ recitals throughout the year. And Les Petits Chanteurs du Mont-Royal, one of the finest boys' choirs in North America, sing the 11 am solemn mass at the Oratoire every Sunday from March to Dec. 24. They also perform several free concerts through the year.

Time your summer visit right to the Basilique Notre-Dame de Montréal (⊠*110 Rue Notre-Dame Ouest* ☎*514/842–2925*), and you can catch the Orchéstre Symphonique de Montréal rehearsing its summer program.

Montréal's Festival Internationale de Jazz every June and Québec City's Festival d'Été in July have dozens of free, open-air concerts.

Every Wednesday from mid-June to mid-August, Financière Sun Life sponsors a series of noon-time concerts in Square Dorchester at just across the street from the Tourisme Québec's main information office at 1255 Rue Peel, offering every-thing from jazz and blues to country and traditional Québécois.

Fireworks

Every Saturday from late June to early August, fireworks teams from around the world compete in L'Internationale des Feux Loto-Québec. You can pay for a seat at La Ronde amusement park or join thousands of Montrealers in the Vieux-Port, on the Jacques Cartier Bridge, and in Parc Champlain on the South Shore watching for free.

Politics

Political junkies can arrange to get free passes to the Visitors' Gallery in North America's only French-speaking legislature, the Assemblée Nationale du Québec. Write to: Information Division, Hôtel du Parlement, 1045 Rue des Parlementaires, Bureau 0.190, Québec QC G1A 1A3; or email: responsable.contenu@assnat.qc.ca.

Science

McGill University's Redpath Museum's eclectic collection of dinosaur skeletons, seashells, fossils, minerals, Egyptian mummies, and Stone Age tools (all housed in a beautiful 19th-century building) is open to the public Monday to Friday from 9 AM to 5 PM and on Sundays from 1 PM to 5 PM. The museum also offers free lectures. ⊠*859 Rue Sherbrooke Ouest* ☎*514/398–4086*.

Sightseeing

For great views of Québec City, take the ferry across the St. Lawrence River to Lévy and back Cost, just $3 (⊠*10 Rue des Traversiers*, ☎*418/643–8420*). Or for just $1.75, ride the Funiculaire, the antiquated elevator that creaks up the cliff from Basse-Ville to Haute-Ville (⊠*16 Rue Petit-Champlain*, ☎*418/692–1132*).

MONTRÉAL & QUÉBEC CITY LOVE TO FÊTE!

People living in Montréal and Québec City have always found good reason to party. Québec City celebrates one of the world's most brutal winters with a carnival that includes a boat race across an ice-choked river. Throughout the province, the rest of the year is full of festivals celebrating jazz, international folklore, film, classical music, fireworks, comedy, and hot-air balloons. The provincial tourist board has more information about these and other festivals.

January & February

Québec City's **Carnaval de Québec** (⊕*www. carnaval.qc.ca*), a festival of winter-sports competitions, ice-sculpture contests, and parades, spans three weekends. The Plains of Abraham are the main stage.

La Fête des Neiges (⊕*www.fetedesneiges. com*) is Winter Carnival in Montréal. It lasts about two weeks and takes place at Parc Jean Drapeau on the river, in the east end of the city.

Montréal en Lumière (*Montréal Highlights* ☎*514/288–9955 or 888/477–9955* ⊕*www.montrealenlumiere.com*) brightens the bleak days of February. For every event, experts artfully illuminate a few historic buildings. Such leading chefs as Paul Bocuse of France come to town to give demonstrations and to take over the kitchens of leading restaurants. Concerts, ice-sculpture displays, plays, dance recitals, and other cultural events take place during the festival.

April

Sugaring-off parties celebrate the maple-syrup season throughout the province, but especially north and east of Montréal. **The Blue Metropolis Montréal International Literary Festival** (⊕*www.blue-met-bleu.com*) presents more than 200 writers for readings, discussions, and other events in English, French, and other languages.

June

FrancoFolies (☎*514/876–8989* ⊕*www. francofolies.com*) celebrates the art of French songwriting. Such major French stars as Isabelle Boulay, Paul Piché, and Michel Rivard play at packed concert halls, while lesser-known artists play free outdoor concerts. More than 1,000 musicians perform in dozens of styles, including rock, hip-hop, jazz, funk, and Latin. The festival usually starts in late July and lasts through early August.

The Fringe Festival (⊕*www.montreal fringe.ca*) brings world-renowned playwrights, acting troupes, dancers, and musicians to Montréal.

For five days every June, the **Mondiale de la Bière** (☎*514/722–9640* ⊕*www.festival-mondialbiere.qc.ca*) transforms the glass-roofed concourse of the Gare Windsor into a giant beer garden offering visitors a chance to sample more than 350 ales, lagers, and ciders from nearly 100 microbreweries. Snacks such as grilled meat, kippered herrings, Belgian chocolates, quail eggs, and an almost infinite variety of Québec cheeses are also available.

July

Teams from around the world compete in the **Concours d'Art International Pyrotechnique** (*International Fireworks Competition* ☎*514/397–2000, 514/790–1245, 800/361–4595 in Canada, 800/678–5440 in the U.S.* ⊕*www.montrealfeux.com*), held in late June and July (mostly on weekends). Their launch site is La Ronde, on Île Ste-Hélène. A ticket includes an amusement-park pass and a reserved seat with a view, but thousands fill the Jacques-Cartier Bridge to watch the show

for free, and hundreds more head to the Vieux-Port.

Festival d'Été International de Québec (*Québec City Summer Festival*), an annual highlight in mid-July, is Québec City's Summer Festival—an exuberant, 11-day music festival with rock, folk, hip-hop, and more—also world sounds. The main concerts take place each evening on three outdoor stages in or near the Old City, including one on the Plains of Abraham. A button (AC$30; C$20 *if purchased in advance*) admits you to all events throughout the festival; the Web site has a detailed program. Book lodging several months in advance if you plan to attend this popular event. ☎418/523–4540 or 888/992–5200 ⊕www.infofestival.com.

The **Festival International de Jazz de Montréal** (*Montréal International Jazz Festival* ☎514/790–1245, 800/361–4595 in Canada, 800/678–5440 in the U.S. ⊕www.montrealjazzfest.com) brings together more than 1,000 musicians for more than 400 concerts over a period of nearly two weeks, from the end of June to the beginning of July. Past stars have included Count Basie, Ella Fitzgerald, Lauryn Hill, Wynton Marsalis, Chick Corea, Dave Brubeck, and Canada's most famed singer-pianist, Diana Krall. About three-fourths of the concerts are presented free on outdoor stages. You can also hear blues, Latin rhythms, gospel, Cajun, and world music. Contact **Bell Info-Jazz** (☎514/871–1881 or 888/515–0515) for information about the festival and travel packages.

Festival OFF is a sidekick of the Festival d'Été. Most of the shows are free and take place in offbeat spaces—in front of Église St-Jean-Baptiste, Bar Le Sacrilèe,

and Musée de l'Amérique Française, just to name a few. People of all ages check out this more alternative scene. Folk, alternative, experimental, and everything in between is what you'll find. The Festival OFF takes to the stage in July at the same time as its big brother. ☎418/692–1008 ⊕www.quebecoff.org.

Montréal's world-famous **Juste pour Rire** ([Just for Laughs] ☎514/845–2322 ⊕ www.hahaha.com) comedy festival hosts international comics, in French and English, from the second through third weeks of July.

World Outgames Montréal (☎514/252–5858 ⊕ www.montreal2009.org), is a weeklong series of sports and cultural activities that begins in late July, celebrates individuals of all backgrounds, orientations, and abilities.

August

International stars show up for the **Festival International des Films du Monde** (*World Film Festival* ☎514/848–3883 ⊕www.ffm-montreal.org), from late August to early September, which usually screens about 400 films in a dozen venues.

During **Fêtes de la Nouvelle France** (*New France Festival*), the streets of the Lower Town are transported back in time for this five-day festival in early to mid-August. Events, ranging from an old-time farmers' market to games, music, demonstrations, and spontaneous skits, are held throughout the Old City, and you'll see people in period costume everywhere you look. ☎418/694–3311 ⊕www.nouvellefrance.qc.ca.

MONTRÉAL & QUÉBEC CITY LOVE TO FÊTE!

The streets of Old Québec resound with military airs during the **Québec City International Festival of Military Bands** in mid-August. Bands from several countries participate in the four-day festival, which includes a gala parade. Shows—most of them free—are held in Vieux-Québec or just outside the walls. ☎418/694–5757.

St-Jean-sur-Richelieu's Hot-Air Balloon Festival (☎450/347–9555 ⊕*www.montgolfieres. com*) is the largest gathering of hot-air balloons in Canada.

September

The **Gatineau Hot-Air Balloon Festival** (⊕*www.montgolfieresgatineau.com*), held Labor Day weekend, brings together hot-air balloons from across Canada, the United States, and Europe.

October

The **Black and Blue Festival** (☎*514/875–7026* ⊕*www.bbcm.org*), a weeklong string of parties hosted by BBCM (Bad Boy Club Montréal), began in 1991 and is now held annually in October. Proceeds are donated to AIDS support organizations.

Farmers' markets, arts-and-crafts fairs, and activities such as weekend hikes are part of the **Festival of Colors**, which celebrates autumn throughout the province of Québec.

Exploring
Montréal

Quais du Vieux, Port de Montréal.

WORD OF MOUTH

"Locals do what tourists do, as far as the festivals and activities and museums go; we walk around different areas and eat at outdoor spots. We walk up Mt. Royal trails to the chalet. Walk and shop on St-Denis street for a more local French Canadian feel."

—mitchdesja

WELCOME TO MONTRÉAL

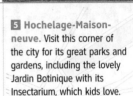

TOP REASONS TO GO

★ **Public Markets:** Marche Atwater, one of the city's oldest public markets, and the sprawling, bustling Marché Jean-Talon, north of downtown in Little Italy, are two places to dedicate extra time to see.

★ **Hot, Hot, Nightlife:** There's a strong history of late-night revelry in this city. To find the spot of-the-moment, stoll along rue St-Denis or rue Crescent and look for the place with the longest line.

★ **Multiculturalism:** Montréal is a melting pot of world culture, yours to experience by strolling through multi-ethnic neighborhoods and sampling cuisine.

★ **Jazz Fest:** Montréal's biggest party happens every July—and if Jazz is your thing it's not to be missed. Hotels book up nearly a year in advance, so reserve early.

★ **Vieux-Montréal:** The Old City has it all—cobblestone streets, a great waterfront for recreation, top-notch restaurants and charming B&Bs, and a small but vibrant dose of nightlife.

1 Vieux-Montréal & the Old Port. This is the oldest part of the city, rife with historical buildings, horse-drawn carriages, street performers, and charming restaurants with terraces to enjoy meals in warm weather.

2 Downtown & Chinatown. Montréal's center for hustle and bustle, where you can shop with the masses on Ste. Catherine, get a huge bowl of Pho for $10 at lunch, check out museums' newest exhibitions, then head back to your hotel for a nap before hitting the town again.

3 The Plateau & Environs. Come to the cozy Plateau and bordering neighborhoods Mile-End and Outremont for Sunday brunch, upscale boutiques, funky resale shops, art galleries, and, of course, people-watching.

4 Mont-Royal & Environs. Home of the mountain that gave Montréal its name, this is where city dwellers come for refuge—and for some of the city's best world cuisine in the Cote-des-Neiges neighborhood.

5 Hochelage-Maison-neuve. Visit this corner of the city for its great parks and gardens, including the lovely Jardin Botinique with its Insectarium, which kids love.

2

Olympic Park

6 The Islands. Once home to Expo '67 and the '76 Olympics, Île St-Helene and Île Notre-Dame are now a vast playground in several ways—from La Ronde amusement park, to Parc Jean-Drapeau, to Casino de Montréal.

GETTING ORIENTED

Montréal is divided by a grid of streets roughly aligned east–west and north–south. North–south street numbers begin at the St. Lawrence River and increase as you head north; east–west street numbers begin at boulevard St-Laurent, which divides Montréal into east and west halves.

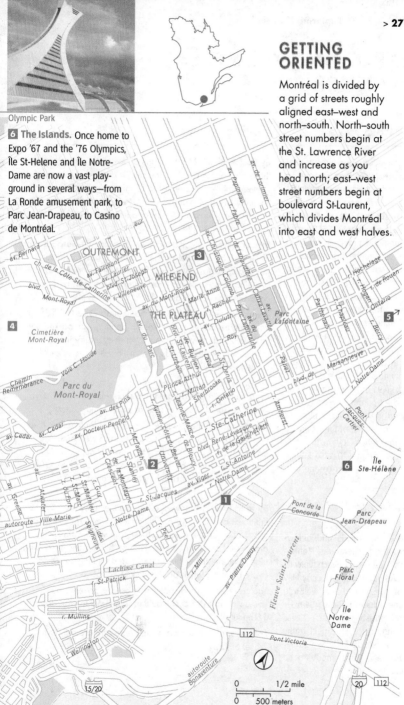

EXPLORING MONTRÉAL PLANNER

Getting Here

Montréal's Trudeau International Airport (also often referred to by its previous name, Dorval) is about 15 mi west of the city. The easiest way to get in is to take a cab for about C$35, unless your hotel provides transportation. Another less expensive alternative is Le Quebécoise shuttles, which cost about C$15 one-way and C$25 for a round-trip ticket, and run every 25 minutes or so from 4 AM to 11 PM. Once you're on your way, plan on it taking about a half-hour outside rush hour to get downtown. If you're driving in, take I–91 or I–89 from Vermont, and I–87 from New York. It's a good idea to have a plan for parking ahead of time. Coming from Québec City, you'll be taking Autoroute 20, also known as Autoroute Jean-Lesage.

When to Go

To avoid crowds and below-freezing temperatures, Montréal's short spring, which typically starts in late April or early May but doesn't end until well into June, is ideal. Fall is gorgeous—and touristy—when the leaves change color, so expect traffic on weekends. Early September after Labor Day is another good time to visit.

Getting Around

By Bus: Although Montréal has an excellent metro system, there are certain areas of the city worth visiting that are not conveniently located within a 15-minute walk of a station. As such, bus routes and schedules are worth checking out in advance. The same tickets and transfers are valid on either service.

By Car: Having a car downtown is not ideal—garages are expensive on on-street parking can be a hassle. The city has a diligent tow-away and fine system for double-parking or sitting in no-stopping zones during rush hour, and tickets costs between C$42 and C$100.

If your car gets towed, it's an additional C$62 to C$88. In winter, street plows are ruthless in dealing with parked cars in their way. If they don't tow them, they'll bury them. In residential neighborhoods, beware of alternate-side-of-the-street-parking rules.

By Metro: The Montréal métro is clean, quiet, and safe, but as in any metropolitan area you should be alert and attentive to personal property such as purses and wallets.

Métro hours on the Orange, Green, Blue, and Yellow lines are weekdays 5:30 AM to 12:30 AM and weekends 5:30 AM to 12:30, 1, or 1:30 AM (it varies by line). Trains run every three minutes or so on the most crowded lines—Orange and Green—at rush hours. Rates are C$2.75 for a single ticket.

By Taxi: Taxis in Montréal all run on the same rate: $3.15 minimum and C$1.45 per kilometer (½ mi). They're usually easy to hail on the street, outside train stations, in shopping areas, and at major hotels, although finding one on a rainy night after the métro has closed can be difficult. A taxi is available if the white or orange plastic rooftop light is on.

You can also call a dispatcher to send a driver to pick you up at no extra cost (you'll usually have to wait about 15 minutes).

For more information on getting here and around, turn to Travel Smart.

Making the Most of Your Time

Put Vieux-Montréal and the Old Port at the top of your sightseeing list. Spend a full day walking around this area, head back to your hotel for a late-day break, and return for dinner. Aside from several notable restaurants here, City Hall, Marché Bonsecours, and other charming buildings are illuminated at night. Also dedicate a full day to wandering around downtown to visit museums, check out rue Ste-Catherine, and explore Chinatown. Visit the Latin Quarter as well as the area around McGill University—both have vibrant student life, but shouldn't be dismissed as places where only under-20s frequent. Even if you're too tired to go out on the town, take a walk down Crescent Street and St-Denis for a taste of the city's *joie de vivre*.

For browsing, shopping, and dining out, explore Outremont, Mile-End, The Plateau, and Westmount. For kid-friendly activities, check out Hochelage-Maisonneuve and The Island for the Biôdôme, La Ronde, and the Jardin Botanique. If it's a culinary tour you're after, hit the Côte-des-Neiges neighborhood, as well as Little Italy.

Dining & Lodging

Dining choices are seemingly endless in Montréal. Dive into some of the best French cuisine outside France, or opt for one of dozens of eateries offering everything from Brazilian to Korean to Modern Canadian.

Where you stay makes or breaks a trip. You'll find several types of lodging here—swanky hotels are downtown, and the Old City has many B&Bs and boutique hotels.

For more information on Where to Eat, see chapter 6; for more on Where to Stay, see chapter 7.

DINING & LODGING PRICES IN CANADIAN DOLLARS

	$	$$	$$$	$$$$
Restaurants				
Under C$8	C$8–C$12	C$13–C$20	C$21–C$30	Over C$30
Hotels				
Under C$75	C$75–C$125	C$126–C$175	C$176–C$250	Over C$250

Restaurant prices are per person for a main course at dinner, excluding tax. Hotel prices are for a standard double room in high season, excluding tax.

Money-Saving Tips

Visiting Montréal isn't as inexpensive as it once was, as the Canadian and American dollars vied for the top spot in terms of their worth for most of 2008. But even if you happen to visit when the U.S. dollar is down, there are several ways to save money during your trip.

If you'll be visiting three or more of the city's museums, consider buying a museum pass. It's available for C$45 for three days, but an even better deal is to purchase a C$50 pass, which also entitles you to unlimited access to Montréal's transportation system, including the métro and busses.

Other transportation discounts are worth considering. A booklet of six tickets is available for C$12. Tourist passes also may be worth your while; one-day passes are C$9, three-day passes are C$17, and weekly passes are C$19.25.

Take advantage of Montréal's fabulous markets, including Marché Jean-Talon and Marché Atwater, to grab provisions for picnics or for snacks to take back to your hotel room. Hitting the town earlier in the evening is a good way to save as well, by taking advantage of drink and food specials offered during cinq-à-sept (5-to-7), Montréal's happy hour.

Updated by
Paul and Julie
Waters

CANADA'S MOST DIVERSE METROPOLIS, MONTREAL, is an island city that favors grace and elegance over order and even prosperity, a city where past and present intrude on each other daily. In some ways it resembles Vienna—well beyond its peak of power and glory, perhaps, yet still vibrant and beautiful.

But don't get the wrong idea. Montréal's always had a bit of an edge. During Prohibition, thirsty Americans headed north to the city on the St. Lawrence for booze, jazz, and a good time, and people still come for the same things. Festivals all summer long celebrate everything from comedy and French songs to beer and fireworks, and, of course, jazz. And on those rare weeks when there isn't a planned event, the party continues. Clubs and sidewalk cafés are abuzz from late afternoon to the early hours of the morning. More extraordinarily, Montréal is a city that knows how to mix it up even when it's 20 below zero. Rue St-Denis is almost as lively on a Saturday night in January as it is in July, and the festival Montréal en Lumière, or Montréal Highlights, enlivens the dreary days of February with concerts, balls, and gourmet food.

Montréal is the only French-speaking city in North America and the second-largest French-speaking city in the Western world, but it's not only Francophone culture that thrives here. About 14% of the 3.3 million people who call Montréal home claim English as their mother tongue. The two cultures, however, are not as separate as they were. Chatter in the bars and bistros of rue St-Denis east of boulevard St-Laurent still tends to be French, and crowds in clubs and restaurants on rue Crescent downtown speak, argue, and court in English. But the lines have definitely blurred.

Both major linguistic groups have had to come to grips with no longer being the only players on the field. So called *allophones*—people whose mother tongue is neither French nor English—make up fully 19% of the city's population, and to them the old, French–English quarrels are close to meaningless. Some—Jews, Italians, Greeks, and Portuguese—have been here for generations, while others—Arabs, Haitians, Vietnamese, and Latin Americans—are more recent arrivals. But together they've changed the very nature of the city, and are still doing so.

EXPLORING MONTRÉAL

The best way to see Montréal is to walk and take public transportation. Streets, subways (Métro), and bus lines are clearly marked. You can also rent a bike, in-line skates (murder on cobblestones, but fine along the waterfront), hire a horse-drawn calèche.

VIEUX-MONTRÉAL

A walk through the cobbled streets of Vieux-Montréal is a lot more than a privileged stroll through history; it's also an encounter with a very lively present—especially in summer, when the restaurants and bistros spill out onto the sidewalks; jugglers, musicians, and magi-

Montréal History

CLOSE UP

The first European settlement on Montréal island was Ville-Marie, founded in 1642 by 54 pious men and women under the leadership of Paul de Chomedey, Sieur de Maisonneuve, and Jeanne Mance, a French noble-woman, who hoped to create a new Christian society.

But piety wasn't Ville-Marie's only raison d'être. The settlement's location on the banks of the St. Lawrence and Ottawa rivers meant a lucrative trade in beaver pelts, as the fur was a staple of European hat fashion for nearly a century.

The French regime in Canada ended with the Seven Years' War—what Americans call the French and Indian War. The Treaty of Paris ceded all of New France to Britain in 1763. American troops under generals Richard Montgomery and Benedict Arnold occupied the city during their 1775–76 campaign to conquer Canada, but their efforts failed and the troops withdrew. Soon invaders of another kind—English and Scottish settlers, traders, and merchants—poured into Montréal. By 1832 the city became a leading colonial capital. But 1837 brought anti-British rebellions, and the unrest led to Canada's becoming a self-governing dominion in 1867.

The city's ports continued to bustle until the St. Lawrence Seaway opened in 1957, allowing ships to sail from the Atlantic to the Great Lakes without having to stop in Montréal to transfer cargo.

The opening of the Métro in 1966 changed the way Montrealers lived, and the next year the city hosted the World's Fair. But the rise of Québec separatism in the late 1960s under the charismatic René Lévesque created political uncertainty, and many major businesses moved to Toronto. By the time Lévesque's separatist Parti Québécois won power in Québec in 1976—the same year the summer Olympics came to the city—Montréal was clearly No. 2.

Uncertainty continued through the 1980s and '90s, with the separatist Parti Québécois and the federalist Liberals alternating in power in Québec City. Since 1980 the city has endured four referenda on the future of Québec and Canada. In the most recent—the cliff-hanger of 1995—just 50.58% of Québécois voted to remain part of Canada. Montréal bucked the separatist trend and voted nearly 70% against independence.

---

cians jostle for performance space on the public squares and along the riverfront in the Vieux-Port; and visitors and locals alike crowd the district to drink, to dine, to party, take in a show, and maybe even go to church.

Vieux-Montréal, which was once enclosed by thick stone walls, is the oldest part of the city. It runs roughly from the waterfront in the south to ruelle des-Fortifications in the north and from rue McGill in the west to rue Berri in the east. The churches and chapels here stand as testament to the religious fervor that inspired the French settlers who landed here in 1642 to build a "Christian commonwealth" under the leadership of Paul de Chomedy, Sieur de Maisonneuve, and the indomitable Jeanne Mance. Stone warehouses and residences are reminders of how quickly the fur trade commercialized that lofty ideal and made the city one of the most prosperous in 18th-century Nouvelle France. And finally, the financial houses along rue St-Jacques, bristling with Victorian ornamentation, recall the days when Montrealers controlled virtually all the wealth of the young Dominion of Canada.

History and good looks aside, however, Vieux-Montréal still works for a living. Stockbrokers and shipping companies continue to operate out of the old financial district. The city's largest newspaper, La Presse, has its offices here. Lawyers in black gowns hurry through the streets to plead cases at the Palais de Justice or the Cour d'Appel, the City Council meets in the Second Empire City Hall on rue Notre-Dame, and local shoppers hunt for deals in the bargain clothing stores just off rue McGill.

MAIN ATTRACTIONS

3 Basilique Notre-Dame-de-Montréal *(Our Lady of Montréal Basilica).*
FodorśChoice   Few churches in North America are as wow-inducing as Notre-Dame.
★   Everything about the place, which opened in 1829, seems designed to make you gasp—from the 228-foot twin towers out front to the tens of thousands of 24-karat gold stars that stud the soaring blue ceiling. Nothing in a city renowned for churches matches Notre-Dame for sheer grandeur—or noisemaking capacity: its 12-ton bass bell is the largest in North America, and its 7,000-pipe Casavant organ can make the walls tremble. The pulpit is a work of art in itself, with an intricately curving staircase and fierce figures of Ezekiel and Jeremiah crouching at its base. The whole place is so overwhelming it's easy to miss such lesser features as the stained-glass windows from Limoges and the side altars dedicated to St. Marguerite d'Youville, Canada's first native-born saint; St. Marguerite Bourgeoys, Canada's first schoolteacher; and a group of Sulpician priests martyred in Paris during the French Revolution. For a peek at the magnificent baptistery, decorated with frescoes by Ozias Leduc, you'll have to tiptoe through the glassed-off prayer room in the northwest corner of the church. Every year dozens of brides march up the aisle of **Chapelle Notre-Dame-du-Sacré-Coeur** (Our Lady of the Sacred Heart Chapel), behind the main altar, to exchange vows with their grooms before a huge modern bronze sculpture that you either love or hate.

In the evening, the nave of the main church is darkened for "La Lumière Fut" ("There Was Light"), a light-and-sound show that depicts the history of Montréal and showcases the church's extraordinary art.

Notre-Dame is an active house of worship, so dress accordingly (i.e., no shorts or bare midriffs). The main church is closed to tours on Sunday during the 9:30 AM, 11 AM, and 5 PM masses. The chapel can't be viewed weekdays during the 12:15 PM and 5 PM masses, and is often closed Saturday for weddings.

The stone residence on the west side of the basilica is the **Vieux Séminaire** (Old Seminary ✉ *116 rue Notre-Dame Ouest, behind wall west of Basilique Notre-Dame-de-Montréal, Vieux-Montréal* Ⓜ *Place-d'Armes.*), Montréal's oldest building. It was built in 1685 as a headquarters for

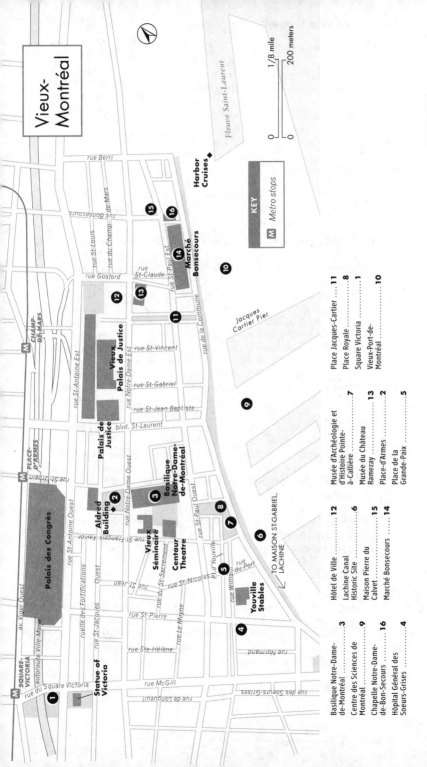

Vieux-Montréal

Basilique Notre-Dame-
de-Montréal **3**
Centre des Sciences de
Montréal **9**
Chapelle Notre-Dame-
de-Bon-Secours **16**
Hôpital Général des
Soeurs-Grises **4**

Hôtel de Ville **12**
Lachine Canal
Historic Site **6**
Maison Pierre du
Calvet **15**
Marché Bonsecours **14**

Musée d'Archéologie et
d'Histoire Pointe-
à-Callière **7**
Musée du Château
Ramezay **13**
Place-d'Armes **2**
Place de la
Grande-Paix **5**

Place Jacques-Cartier **11**
Place Royale **8**
Square Victoria **1**
Vieux-Port-de-
Montréal **10**

KEY

M Metro stops

0 ———— 1/8 mile
0 ———— 200 meters

2

the Sulpician priests who owned the island of Montréal until 1854. It's still a residence for the Sulpicians who administer the basilica. The clock on the roof over the main doorway is the oldest (pre-1701) public timepiece in North America. ✉ *110 rue Notre-Dame Ouest, Vieux-Montréal* ☎ *514/842–2925 or 866/842–2925* ⊕ *www.basiliquenddm.org* ✍ *C$5, including guided tour; La Lumière Fut C$10* ☉ *Daily 7–5; 20-min tours in French and English every ½ hr July–Sept., weekdays 8–4:30, Sat. 8–3:15, Sun. 12:30–3:15; every 2 hrs (or by prior arrangement) Oct.–June* Ⓜ *Place-d'Armes.*

⑯ **Chapelle Notre-Dame-de-Bon-Secours** *(Our Lady of Perpetual Help Cha-*
★ *pel).* Mariners have been popping into Notre-Dame-de-Bon-Secours for centuries to kneel before a little 17th-century statue of the Virgin Mary and pray for a safe passage—or give thanks for one. Often, they've expressed their gratitude by leaving votive lamps in the shape of small ships, many of which still hang from the barrel-vaulted ceiling. This is why most Montrealers call the chapel the Église des Matelots (the Sailors' Church), and why many still stop by to say a prayer and light a candle before leaving on a long trip. These days, the statue of Our Lady of Perpetual Help guards the remains of St. Marguerite Bourgeoys, who had the original chapel built in 1657 and is entombed in the side altar next to the east wall of the chapel. The current chapel dates from 1771; a renovation project in 1998 revealed some beautiful 18th-century murals that had been hidden under layers of paint. The steep climb to the top of the steeple is worth the effort for the glorious view of the harbor, as is the equally steep climb down to the archaeological excavations under the chapel for a glimpse into the chapel's history and the neighborhood. The dig is accessible through the adjacent **Musée Marguerite Bourgeoys,** which also has exhibits on the life of St. Marguerite and the daily lives of the colonists she served. The chapel is closed mid-January through February except for the 10:30 AM mass on Sunday. ✉ *400 rue St-Paul Est, Vieux-Montréal* ☎ *514/282–8670* ⊕ *www.marguerite-bourgeoys.com* ✍ *Museum C$6, museum plus archaeology site with guide C$8* ☉ *May–Oct., Tues.–Sun. 10–5:30; Nov.–mid-Jan., Tues.–Sun. 11–3:30; Mar. and Apr., Tues.–Sun. 11–3:30* Ⓜ *Champ-de-Mars.*

OFF THE
BEATEN
PATH

Fodor'sChoice
★

Maison St-Gabriel. This little island of New France is well off the beaten path, deep in the working-class Pointe St-Charles neighborhood, but it's certainly worth the 10-minute taxi ride from Vieux-Montréal. Walk into the big, low-ceiling kitchen of the Maison St-Gabriel, close your eyes, and you can almost hear the squeals and giggles of the *filles du roy* (king's daughters) as they learn the niceties of 17th-century home management. The filles du roy were young women without family or money but plenty of spunk who volunteered to cross the Atlantic on

Art in the Métro

Operating since 1966, the Métro is among the most architecturally distinctive subway systems in the world, with each of its 65 stations individually designed and decorated. The largest of these is Berri-UQAM, a cross-shaped station with many corridors filled with artworks. The most memorable pieces include a huge black granite bench; three Expo '67 murals depicting science, culture, and recreation; a 25th-anniversary plaque and time capsule; a statue of Montréal heroine Mother Émilie Gamelin, a 19th-century nun who worked with the poor; and a vibrant red-and-blue stained-glass mural depicting three founders of Montréal.

The newer stations along the Blue Line are all worth a visit as well, particularly Outremont, with a glass-block design from 1988. Even Place-d'Armes, one of the least visually remarkable stations in the system, includes a treasure: look for the small exhibit of archaeological artifacts representing each of Montréal's four historical eras (Aboriginal, French, English, and multicultural).

2

leaky wooden boats to become the wives and mothers of New France. At the Maison, they learned from St. Marguerite Bourgeoys and her religious order how to cook and clean, how to pray and read, and how to survive the rigors of colonial life. It can't have been easy—long hours, hard little beds, and cold stone walls—but it had its rewards, and the prize at the end was a respectable, settled life. St. Marguerite also had some state-of-the-art domestic equipment—the latest in looms and butter churns, labor-saving spit turners for roasting meat, and an ingenious granite sink with a drainage system that piped water straight out to the garden. ⊠*2146 pl. Dublin, Pointe St-Charles* 🕾*514/935–8136* ⊕*www.maisonsaint-gabriel.qc.ca* ⊠*C$8* ⊗*June 25–early Sept., Tues.–Sun. 11–6 (guided tours every hr); early Sept.–mid-Dec. and late Apr.–June 24, Tues.–Sun. 1–5* Ⓜ*Charlevoix, 57 bus.*

❼ Musée d'Archéologie et d'Histoire Pointe-à-Callière *(Pointe-à-Callière*
Fodor'sChoice   *Archaeology and History Museum).* The modern glass building is
★   impressive, and the audiovisual show is a breezy romp through Montréal's history from the Ice Age to the present, but the real reason to visit the city's most ambitious archaeological museum is to take the elevator ride down to the 17th century. It's dark down there, and just a little creepy thanks to the 350-year-old tombstones teetering in the gloom, but it's worth the trip. This is a serious archaeological dig that takes you to the very foundations of the city. You begin on the banks of the long-vanished Rivière St-Pierre, where the first settlers built their homes and traded with the Native American inhabitants. From there you climb up toward the present, past the stone foundations of an 18th-century tavern and a 19th-century insurance building. Along the way, filmed figures representing past inhabitants appear on ghostly screens to chat to you about their lives and times. A more lighthearted exhibit explores life and love in multicultural Montréal. For a spectacular view of the Vieux-Port, the river, and the islands, ride the elevator to the top of the tower, or stop for lunch in the museum's glass-fronted café.

In summer there are re-creations of period fairs and festivals on the grounds near the museum. ⊠ *350 pl. Royale, Vieux-Montréal* ☎ *514/872–9150* ⊕ *www.pacmuseum.qc.ca* ☜ *C$13* ⊙ *July and Aug., weekdays 10–6, weekends 11–6; Sept.–June, Tues.–Fri. 10–5, weekends 11–5* Ⓜ *Place-d'Armes.*

⓫ **Place Jacques-Cartier.** The cobbled square at the heart of Vieux-Montréal
★ is part carnival, part flower market, and part sheer fun. You can pause here to have your portrait painted or to buy an ice cream or to watch the street performers. If you have more time, try to get a table at one of the sidewalk cafés, order a beer or a glass of wine, and watch the passing parade. The 1809 monument honoring Lord Nelson's victory over Napoléon Bonaparte's French navy at Trafalgar angers some modern-day Québec nationalists, but the campaign to raise money for it was led by the Sulpician priests, who were engaged in delicate land negotiations with the British government at the time and were eager to show what good subjects they were. ⊠ *Bordered by rues Notre-Dame Est and de la Commune, Vieux-Montréal* Ⓜ *Champ-de-Mars.*

⓾ **Vieux-Port-de-Montréal** *(Old Port of Montréal).* Montréal's favor-
☾ ite waterfront park is your ideal gateway to the St. Lawrence River.
★ Rent a pedal boat, take a ferry to **Île Ste-Hélène,** sign up for a dinner cruise, or, if you're really adventurous, ride a raft through the turbulent Lachine Rapids. If you're determined to stay ashore, however, there's still plenty to do. You can rent a bicycle or a pair of in-line skates at one of the shops along rue de la Commune and explore the waterfront at your leisure. If it's raining, the Centre des Sciences de Montréal on **King Edward Pier** will keep you dry and entertained, and if your lungs are in good shape you can climb the 192 steps to the top of the **Clock Tower** for a good view of the waterfront and the islands; it was erected at the eastern end of the waterfront in memory of merchant mariners killed during World War I. You can, quite literally, lose the kids in Shed 16's Labyrinthe, a maze of alleys, surprises, and obstacles built inside an old waterfront warehouse. Every couple of years or so Montréal's Cirque du Soleil comes home to pitch its blue-and-yellow tent in the Vieux-Port. But be warned: when the circus is in town, the tickets sell faster than water in a drought. ⊠ *Vieux-Montréal* ☎ *514/496–7678 or 800/971–7678* ⊕ *www.quaysoftheoldport.com* Ⓜ *Place-d'Armes or Champ-de-Mars.*

ALSO WORTH SEEING

⓽ **Centre des Sciences de Montréal.** You—or more likely, your kids—can
☾ design an energy-efficient bike, create a television news report, explore the impact that manufacturing one T-shirt has on the environment, find out what it's like to ride a unicycle 20 feet above the ground, create an animated film, or just watch an IMAX movie on a giant screen at Montréal's interactive science center. Games, puzzles, and hands-on experiments make it an ideal place for rainy days or even fair ones. The center also has a bistro serving lights meals, a coffee and pastry shop (with the disturbing name Café Arsenik), and a food court. ⊠ *Quai King Edward, Vieux-Montréal* ☎ *514/496–4724 or 877/496–4724* ⊕ *www.isci.ca* ☜ *Exhibit halls C$12, IMAX C$12, combined ticket*

C$20–C$23 ⊙ *May 10–Sept. 16, daily 9–9; Sept. 16–May 10, weekdays 8:30–4, weekends 9:30–5* Ⓜ *Place-d'Armes.*

WORD OF MOUTH

"While in Montréal, spend some time in Old Montréal where you'll discover several tourists sites, including the Old Port, monuments, religious and government buildings, tourist shops, and a host of good French restaurants, distinctly Quebecois in flavor."

—zola

❹ **Hôpital Général des Soeurs-Grises** *(General Hospital of the Gray Nuns).* A few jagged stone walls are all that's left of Montréal's first general hospital. The ruins—which once formed the west wing and the transept of the chapel—have been preserved as a memorial to Canada's first native-born saint, Marguerite d'Youville (1701–71), who took over the hospital in 1747 and ran it until a fire destroyed the building in 1765. The gold script on the wall facing the street is a copy of the letters patent signed by Louis XIV establishing the hospital. St. Marguerite's life was no walk in the park, as you'll find out if you visit the **Maison de Mère d'Youville** next door to the ruins. Marguerite started looking after the city's down-and-outs after the death of her abusive and disreputable husband. Amused that the widow of a whiskey trader should be helping the town drunks, locals took to calling Marguerite and her Soeurs de la Charité (Sisters of Charity) the Soeurs Grises (Gray Nuns), slang for "tipsy nuns." The Maison has some remarkable reminders of her life, such as the kitchen where she worked, with its enormous fireplace and stone sink. Call ahead for tours of the house (ask for Sister Thérèse Pelletier or Sister Marguerite Daoust). ⊠ *138 rue St-Pierre, Vieux-Montréal* ⊠ *Free* ⊙ *By appointment only, Tues.–Sun. 9–4* ☎ *514/842–9411* Ⓜ *Square-Victoria.*

⑫ **Hôtel de Ville** *(City Hall).* President Charles de Gaulle of France marked Canada's centennial celebrations in 1967 by standing on the central balcony of Montréal's ornate city hall on July 24 and shouting "*Vive le Québec libre*" ("Long live free Québec"), much to the delight of the separatist movement and to the horror of the federal government that had invited him over in the first place. Perhaps he got carried away because he felt so at home: the Second Empire–style city hall, built in 1878, is modeled after the one in Tours, France. Free guided tours are available daily 9–5 in June, July, and August. ⊠ *275 rue Notre-Dame Est, Vieux-Montréal* ☎ *514/872–3355* ⊠ *Free* ⊙ *Daily 9–5* Ⓜ *Champ-de-Mars.*

❻ **Lachine Canal Historic Site.** If you want to work up an appetite for lunch—
ℭ or just get some exercise—rent a bike on rue de la Commune and ride
★ west along the 14-km (9-mi) Lachine Canal through what used to be Montréal's industrial heartland. You could stop at the Marché Atwater to buy some cheese, bread, wine, and maybe a little pâté for a picnic in the lakefront park at the end of the trail. If that sounds too energetic, hop aboard an excursion boat and dine more formally in one of the century-old homes that line the waterfront.

The Lachine Canal is all about leisure now, but it wasn't always so. It was built in 1825 to get boats and cargo around the treacherous Lachine Rapids, and quickly became a magnet for all sorts of industries. That lasted until 1959, when the St. Lawrence Seaway opened and large cargo ships were

> **CALÈCHE-CATCHING?**
>
> The best place to find a calèche for a horse-drawn tour of the Old City is on the south side of Place-d'Armes. And be careful what you pay. Fares are set by the city.

able to go straight from the Atlantic to the Great Lakes without stopping in Montréal. The Lachine Canal was subsequently closed to navigation and became an illicit dumping ground for old cars and the victims of underworld killings, while the area around it degenerated into an industrial slum.

The federal government rescued the place in 1988. Lawns and trees along the old canal were planted, and it was transformed into a long, thin park. The abandoned canneries, sugar refineries, and steelworks have since been converted into desirable residential and commercial condominiums. The bicycle path, which in winter hosts cross-country skiers, is the first link in the more than 97 km (60 mi) of bike trails that make up the **Pôle des Rapides** (☎514/364–4490 ⊕*www.poledes rapides.com*). A permanent exhibit at the **Lachine Canal Interpretation Centre** explains the history and construction of the canal. The center, on the western end of the canal, is open daily (except Monday morning) mid-May through August, 9:30–12:30 and 1–5. ⊠*Lachine* ☎*514/637–7433* ⊕*www.parkscanada.gc.ca* ☜*Free* ☉*Sunrise–sunset* Ⓜ*Square-Victoria (at the eastern end)*.

⑮ Maison Pierre du Calvet. Merchant Pierre du Calvet was everything Roman Catholic, British-ruled Montréal didn't like—a notorious republican, an admirer of Voltaire, a pal of Benjamin Franklin, and a fierce supporter of the American Revolution. But he was also prosperous enough in 1725 to build a fine residence with thick stone walls and multipane casement windows. His home now houses a restaurant and a small but opulent bed-and-breakfast (called Pierre du Calvet AD 1725), where you can enjoy the same hospitality Franklin did in the mid-18th century. ⊠*405 rue Bonsecours, Vieux-Montréal* ☎*514/282–1725* ⊕*www.pierreducalvet.ca* Ⓜ*Champ-de-Mars*.

⑭ Marché Bonsecours *(Bonsecours Market).* You can't buy fruits and vegetables in the Marché Bonsecours anymore, but you can shop for local fashions and crafts in the row of upscale boutiques that fill its main hall, or lunch in one of several restaurants opening onto the Vieux-Port or rue St-Paul. But the Marché is best admired from the outside. Built in the 1840s as the city's main market, it is possibly the most beautifully proportioned neoclassical building in Montréal, with its six cast-iron Doric columns and two rows of meticulously even sashed windows, all topped with a silvery dome. In fact, the Marché was always too elegant to be just a farmers' market. It was also Montréal's premier gathering place for balls and galas, and served as city hall for 25 years. The parliament of Canada even met briefly in the market's upper hall in the

MONTRÉAL'S BEST WALKING TOURS

You can walk through various historic, cultural, or architecturally diverse areas of the city with a costumed guide, courtesy of Guidatour. Popular tours include Old Montréal, the red-light district, and the elite 19th-century neighborhood known as the Golden Square Mile.

From mid-April to mid-November, Circuit des Fantômes du Vieux-Montréal has walking tours through the old city where a host of spirits are said to still haunt the streets. Kaleidoscope has a wide selection of guided walking tours through Montréal's many culturally diverse neighborhoods.

Contacts Circuit des Fantômes du Vieux-Montréal (*Old Montréal Ghost Trail* ✉ *469 rue St-François-Xavier, Vieux-Montréal* ☎ *514/868–0303 or 877/868–0303* ⊕ *www.fantommontreal.com* Ⓜ *Champ-de-Mars*). **Guidatour** (✉ *477 rue St-François-Xavier, Suite 300, Vieux-Montréal* ☎ *514/844–4021 or 800/363–4021* ⊕ *www.guidatour.qc.ca* Ⓜ *Place-d'Armes*). **Kaleidoscope** (✉ *6592 Châteaubriand, Villeray* ☎ *514/990–1872* 🖷 *514/277–4630* ⊕ *www.tourskaleidoscope.com* Ⓜ *Beaubien*)

late 1800s. ✉ *350 rue St-Paul Est, Vieux-Montréal* ☎ *514/872–7730* ⊕ *www.marchebonsecours.qc.ca* Ⓜ *Champ-de-Mars*.

⑬ **Musée du Château Ramezay.** Claude de Ramezay, the city's 11th governor, was probably daydreaming of home when he built his Montréal residence. Its thick stone walls, dormer windows, and steeply pitched roof make it look like a little bit of 18th-century Normandy dropped into the middle of North America—although the round, squat tower is a 19th-century addition. The extravagant mahogany paneling in the Salon de Nantes was installed when Louis XV was still king of France. The British used the château as headquarters after their conquest in 1760, and so did the American commanders Richard Montgomery and Benedict Arnold. Benjamin Franklin, who came north in a failed attempt to persuade the Québécois to join the American Revolution, stayed here during that winter adventure. Most of the château's exhibits are a little staid—guns, uniforms, and documents on the main floor and tableaux depicting colonial life in the cellars—but they include some unexpected little eccentricities that make it worth the visit. One of its prized possessions is a bright-red automobile the De Dion-Bouton Co. produced at the turn of the 20th century for the city's first motorist. ✉ *280 rue Notre-Dame Est, Vieux-Montréal* ☎ *514/861–3708* ⊕ *www.chateauramezay.qc.ca* 🖷 *C$8* ☉ *June–mid-Oct., daily 10–6; Oct.–May, Tues.–Sun. 10–4:30* Ⓜ *Champ-de-Mars*.

NEED A BREAK? Step out the back door of the **Musée du Château Ramezay** and into 18th-century tranquillity. The *jardins* are laid out just as formally as Mme. de Ramezay might have wished, with a *potager* for vegetables and a little *verger*, or orchard. You can sit on a bench in the sun, admire the flowers, and inhale the sage-scented air from the herb garden.

❷ Place-d'Armes. When Montréal was under attack, citizens and soldiers would rally at Place-d'Armes, but these days the only rallying is done by tourists, lunching office workers, calèche drivers, and flocks of voracious pigeons. The pigeons are particularly fond of the triumphant statue of Montréal's founder, Paul de Chomedey, with his lance upraised, perched above the fountain in the middle of the cobblestone square. He slew an Iroquois chief in a battle here in 1644 and was wounded in return. Tunnels beneath the square protected the colonists from the winter weather and provided an escape route; unfortunately, they are too small and dangerous to visit. ✉ *Bordered by rues Notre-Dame Ouest, St-Jacques, and St-Sulpice, Vieux-Montréal* Ⓜ *Place-d'Armes.*

> **WORD OF MOUTH**
>
> "In Old Montréal there is a strip of nice galleries between St. Sulpice and St. Laurent Street."
>
> —mitchdesi

❺ Place de la Grande-Paix. If you're looking for peace and quiet, the narrow strip of grass and trees on Place d'Youville just east of Place Royale is an appropriate place to find it. It was here, after all, that the French signed a major peace treaty with dozens of aboriginal nations in 1702. It was also here that the first French colonists landed their four boats on May 17, 1642. An obelisk records the names of the settlers. ✉ *Between pl. d'Youville and rue William, Vieux-Montréal* Ⓜ *Place-d'Armes.*

❽ Place Royale. The oldest public square in Montréal, dating to the 17th century, was a market during the French regime and later became a Victorian garden. The neoclassical Vielle Douane (Old Customs House) on its south side serves as the gift shop for the Musée d'Archéologie et d'Histoire Pointe-à-Callière. ✉ *Bordered by rues St-Paul Ouest and de la Commune, Vieux-Montréal* Ⓜ *Place-d'Armes.*

❶ Square Victoria. The perfect Montréal mix: an 1872 statue of Queen Victoria on one side and an authentic Parisian Métro entrance on the other. Both are framed by a two-block stretch of trees, benches, and fountains that makes a great place to relax and admire the handsome 1920s business buildings on the east side. The art nouveau Métro entrance, incidentally, was a gift from the French capital's transit commission. ✉ *Rue Square Victoria, between rues Viger and St-Jacques, Vieux-Montréal* Ⓜ *Square-Victoria.*

DOWNTOWN & CHINATOWN

Rue Ste-Catherine—and the Métro line that runs under it—is the main cord that binds together the disparate, sprawling neighborhoods that comprise Montréal's **downtown,** or *centre-ville.* It's a long, boisterous, sometimes seedy, and sometimes elegant street that runs from rue Claremont in Westmount to rue d'Iberville in the east end. The downtown stretch—usually clogged with traffic and lined with department stores, boutiques, bars, restaurants, strip clubs, amusement arcades, theaters, cinemas, art galleries, bookstores, and even a few churches—is considerably shorter, running from avenue Atwater to boulevard St-Laurent, where downtown morphs into the Quartier Latin and the Village, the center of Montréal's gay and lesbian community.

But vibrant as the street is, much of the downtown action happens on such cross streets as rues Crescent, Bishop, de la Montagne, and Peel, which are packed with some of the district's best clubs, restaurants, and boutiques. If you're looking for a little nighttime excitement, you won't find a livelier block in the city than the stretch of rue Crescent between rue Ste-Catherine and boulevard de Maisonneuve.

Walk even farther north on rue Crescent to the lower slopes of Mont-Royal and you come to what used to be the most exclusive neighborhood in Canada—the Golden Square Mile. During the boom years of the mid-1800s, the families who lived in the area—most of them Scottish and Protestant—controlled about 70% of the country's wealth. Their baronial homes and handsome churches covered the mountain north of rue Sherbrooke roughly between avenue Côte-des-Neiges and rue University. Incidentally, the descendants of those old families always call the neighborhood simply the Square Mile, and sneer at the extra adjective. Many of the old homes are gone—replaced by highrises or modern town houses—but there are still plenty of architectural treasures for you to admire, even if most of them are now foreign consulates or university institutes.

At the other end of the downtown area is **Chinatown,** an 18-block area between boulevard René-Lévesque and avenue Viger to the north and south, and near rue de Bleury and avenue Hôtel de Ville on the west and east. Chinese people first came to Montréal in large numbers after 1880, following the construction of the transcontinental railroad. Their legacy is a shrinking but lively neighborhood of mainly Chinese and Southeast Asian restaurants, food stores, and gift shops.

MAIN ATTRACTIONS

❾ Cathédrale Marie-Reine-du-Monde (*Mary Queen of the World Cathedral*). The best reason to visit this cathedral is that it's a quarter-scale replica of St. Peter's Basilica, complete with a magnificent reproduction of Bernini's ornate baldachin (canopy) over the main altar and an ornately coffered ceiling. When Bishop Ignace Bourget (1799–1885) decided to build his cathedral in the heart of the city's Protestant-dominated commercial quarter, many fellow Catholics thought he was crazy. But the bishop was determined to assert the Church's authority—and its loyalty to Rome—in the British-ruled city. Bourget didn't live to see the cathedral dedicated in 1894, but his tomb holds place of honor among those of his successors in the burial chapel on the east side of the nave. ⊠*1085 rue de la Cathédrale (enter through main doors on blvd. René-Lévesque), Downtown* ☎*514/866–1661* ⊕*www.cathedralecatholiquedemontreal. org* 🎫*Free* ☉ *Weekdays 6:30 AM–6:30 PM, Sat. 7 AM–6:30 PM, Sun. 7 AM–6:30 PM* Ⓜ*Bonaventure or Peel.*

❹ Christ Church Cathedral. This cathedral offers a series of free noontime concerts and organ recitals that are very popular with downtowners and visitors alike, and offers a bit of a respite from Ste-Catherine's crowds.

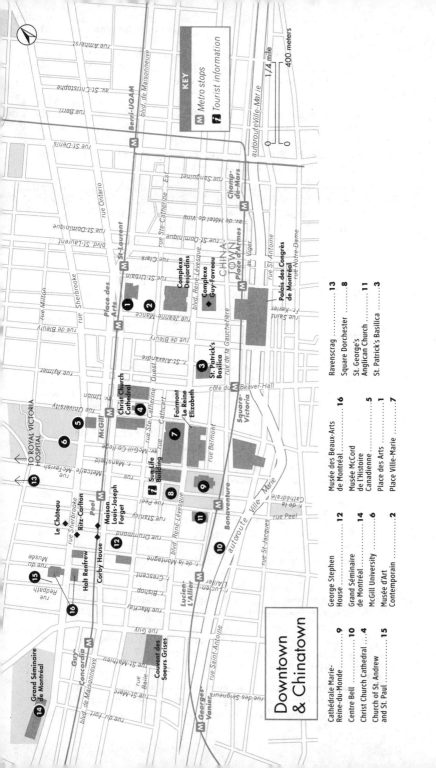

Downtown
& Chinatown

Cathédrale Marie-
Reine-du-Monde **9**
Centre Bell **10**
Christ Church Cathedral **4**
Church of St. Andrew
and St. Paul **15**

George Stephen
House **12**
Grand Séminaire
de Montréal **14**
McGill University **6**
Musée d'Art
Contemporain **2**

Musée des Beaux-Arts
de Montréal **16**
Musée McCord
de l'Histoire
Canadienne **5**
Place des Arts **1**
Place Ville-Marie **7**

Ravenscrag **13**
Square Dorchester **8**
St. George's
Anglican Church **11**
St. Patrick's Basilica **3**

KEY
Ⓜ Metro stops
🛈 Tourist information

0 ————— 1/4 mile
0 ————— 400 meters

The Other "Downtown"

When Place Ville-Marie, the cruciform skyscraper designed by I.M. Pei, opened in the heart of downtown in 1962, the tallest structure of the time also signaled the beginning of Montréal's subterranean city. Montréalers were skeptical that anyone would want to shop or even walk around in the new "down" town, but more than four decades later they can't live without it. About half a million people use the 30-km (19-mi) underground pedestrian network daily. The tunnels link 10 Métro stations, 7 hotels, 200 restaurants, 1,700 boutiques, and 60 office buildings—not to mention movie theaters, concert halls, convention complexes, the Bell Centre, two universities and a college, and subway, commuter rail, and bus stations. Montrealers who live in one of more than 2,000 apartments connected to the Underground City can pop out to buy a liter of milk on a February day and never have to change out of shirtsleeves and house slippers.

Most of the Underground City parallels the Métro lines. The six-block sector of continuous shopping between La Baie (east of the McGill station) and Les Cours Montréal (west of the Peel station) is perhaps the densest portion of the network. Montréal was ahead of the curve in requiring all construction in the Métro system to include an art component, resulting in such dramatic works as Frédéric Back's mural of the history of music in Place-des-Arts and the dramatically swirling stained-glass windows by Marcelle Ferron in Champs-de-Mars. The art nouveau entrance to the Square-Victoria station, a gift from the city of Paris, is the only original piece of Hector Guimard's architectural-design work outside the City of Light.

–By Patricia Harris and David Lyon

Built in 1859, the cathedral is modeled on Snettisham Parish Church in Norfolk, England, with some distinctly Canadian touches. The steeple, for example, is made with aluminum plates molded to simulate stone, and inside, the Gothic arches are crowned with carvings of the types of foliage growing on Mont-Royal when the church was built. The stained-glass windows behind the main altar, installed in the early 1920s as a memorial to the dead of World War I, show scenes from the life of Christ. On the wall just above and to the left of the pulpit is the Coventry Cross; it's made of nails taken from the ruins of Britain's Coventry Cathedral, destroyed by bombing in 1940. ⊠*635 rue Ste-Catherine Ouest, Downtown* ☎*514/843–6577* ⊕*www.montreal.anglican.org/cathedral* ⊠*Free* ⊗*Daily 10–6* Ⓜ*McGill.*

② **Musée d'Art Contemporain** *(Museum of Contemporary Art).* If you have
★ a taste for pastoral landscapes and formal portraits, you might want to stick with the Musée des Beaux-Arts. But for a walk on the wild side of art, see what you can make of the jagged splashes of color that cover the canvases of the "Automatistes," as Québec's rebellious artists of the 1930s styled themselves. Their works form the core of this museum's collection of 5,000 pieces. One of the leaders of the movement, Jean-Paul Riopelle (1923–2002), often tossed his brushes and palette knives aside and just squeezed the paint directly on to the canvas—sometimes several tubes at a time. In 1948, Riopelle and his friends fired the first

shot in Québec's Quiet Revolution by signing *Le Refus Global*, a manifesto that renounced the political and religious establishment of the day and revolutionized art in the province. The museum often has weekend programs and art workshops, some of which are geared toward children, and almost all

are free. And for a little romance and music with your art, try the Vendredi Nocturnes every Friday evening with live music, bar service, and guided tours of the exhibits. Hours for guided tours vary. ⊠ *185 rue Ste-Catherine Ouest, Downtown* ☎ *514/847–6226* ⊕ *www.macm. org* ⊠ *C$8, free Wed. after 6* PM ☉ *Mid-June–Labor Day, Mon.–Tues. 11–6, Wed. 11–9, Thurs.–Sun. 11–6; closed Mondays the rest of the year* Ⓜ *Place-des-Arts.*

⑯ Musée des Beaux-Arts de Montréal *(Montréal Museum of Fine Arts).* Canada's oldest museum has been accumulating art from all over the world since 1860. The permanent collection includes everyone from Rembrandt to Renoir, and not surprisingly, one of the best assemblies of Canadian art anywhere, with works by such luminaries as Paul Kane, the Group of Seven, and Paul-Émile Borduas. If landscapes are your thing, the collected works of Québec artist Marc-Aurèle Fortin were recently acquired.

Fodor'sChoice ★

Trace the country's history from New France to New Age through the decorative art, painting, and sculpture collections, and don't miss the Musée des Arts Décoratifs, where you can take a look at some fanciful bentwood furniture designed by Frank Gehry, a marvelous collection of 18th-century English porcelain, and 3,000—count 'em—Japanese snuffboxes collected by, of all people, Georges Clémenceau, France's prime minister during World War I. All this is housed in two buildings linked by an underground tunnel—the older, neoclassical **Michal and Renata Hornstein Pavilion** on the north side of rue Sherbrooke, and the glittering, glass-fronted **Jean-Noël-Desmarais Pavilion** across the street. The museum also has a gift shop, a bookstore, a restaurant, a cafeteria, and a gallery where you can buy or even rent paintings by local artists. ⊠ *1380 rue Sherbrooke Ouest, Square Mile* ☎ *514/285–2000* ⊕ *www. mmfa.qc.ca* ⊠ *Permanent collection free, special exhibits C$15, C$7.50 Wed.* ☉ *Tues.–Fri. 11–9, weekends 10–6* Ⓜ *Guy-Concordia.*

❺ Musée McCord de l'Histoire Canadienne *(McCord Museum of Canadian History).* David Ross McCord (1844–1930) was a wealthy pack rat with a passion for anything that had to do with Montréal and its history. His collection of paintings, costumes, toys, tools, drawings, and housewares provides a glimpse of what city life was like for all classes in the 19th century. If you're interested in the lifestyles of the elite, however, you'll love the photographs that William Notman (1826–91) took of the rich at play. One series portrays members of the posh Montréal Athletic Association posing in snowshoes on the slopes of Mont-Royal, all decked out in Hudson Bay coats and woolen hats. Each of the hundreds of portraits was shot individually in a studio and then painstakingly mounted on a picture of the snowy mountain to give the impression of a winter outing. There are guided tours (call for schedule), a reading room, a documentation center, a gift shop, a bookstore, and a café. ✉*690 rue Sherbrooke Ouest, Square Mile* ☎*514/398-7100* ⊕*www.mccord-museum.qc.ca* 🎟*C$12* ⊙*June 25–early Sept., Mon. and weekends 10–5, Tues.–Fri. 10–6; early Sept.–June 24, Tues.–Fri. 10–6, weekends 10–5* Ⓜ*McGill.*

❸ **St. Patrick's Basilica.** St. Pat's—as most of its parishioners call it—is to
★ Montréal's Anglophone Catholics what the Basilique Notre-Dame is to their French-speaking brethren—the mother church and a monument to faith and courage. One of the joys of visiting the place is that you'll probably be the only tourist there, so you'll have plenty of time to check out the old pulpit and the huge lamp decorated with six 6-foot-tall angels hanging over the main altar. And if you're named after some obscure saint like Scholastica or Aeden of Fleury, you can search for your namesake's portrait among the 170 painted panels on the walls of the nave. The church was built in 1847, and is also one of the purest examples of the Gothic Revival style in Canada, with a high vaulted ceiling glowing with green and gold mosaics. The tall, slender columns are actually pine logs lashed together and decorated to look like marble, so that if you stand in one of the back corners and look toward the altar you really do feel as if you're peering at the sacred through a grove of trees. ✉*454 blvd. René-Lévesque Ouest, Downtown* ☎*514/866–7379* ⊕*www.stpatricksmtl.ca* 🎟*Free* ⊙*Daily 8:30–6* Ⓜ*Square-Victoria.*

NEED A BREAK? On the west side of **St. Patrick's Basilica** (✉ **460 blvd. René-Lévesque Ouest, Downtown** Ⓜ **Square-Victoria**) is a small but delightful green space with picnic tables and shady trees. The Van Houtte coffee shop in the nearby office tower has a patio that opens on to the park, so refreshments are available.

ALSO WORTH SEEING

❿ **Centre Bell.** There was a time when the Montréal Canadiens almost seemed to own the National Hockey League's Stanley Cup. After each winning season in the 1960s and '70s, city hall would put out a press release announcing the "Stanley Cup parade will follow the usual route." Those days are long gone. *Les Glorieux* (or "the glorious ones"), as the fans call the team, haven't won a cup since 1993, and the superstitious blame it on their 1996 move from the hallowed Forum to the brown-brick Centre Bell, although things started looking up in 2008 when the Habs—as locals call their favorite team—finished the season on top of the eastern division, only to be knocked out in round two of the playoffs. Guided tours usually include a visit to the Canadiens' dressing room. ✉*1260 rue de la Gauchetière Ouest, Downtown* ☎*800/363–3723 or 514/989–2841 tours, 514/987–2841 tickets* ⊕*www.canadiens.com* 🎟*Tour C$8* ⊙*Tours daily at 11:15 and 2:45 in English, 9:45 and 1:15 in French* Ⓜ*Bonaventure.*

⓯ **Church of St. Andrew and St. Paul.** If you want to see the inside of Montréal's largest Presbyterian church—sometimes affectionately called the

Underground City Know-How

To get the optimum use of the whole network of tunnels, shops, and Métro lines that make up the Underground City, buy a Métro pass. Daily and weekly passes are available. Start at Place Ville-Marie. This was the first link in the system and is still part of the main hub. From here you could cover most of the main sites—from the Centre Bell to Place des Arts—without ever coming up and without having to take the Métro. But the network is so large, you'll want to use the subway system to save time, energy, and wear and tear on your feet. You might also want to explore some of the Underground City's more remote centers—the Grande Bibliothèque or Westmount Square, for example. Remember: it's easy to get lost. There are no landmarks, and routes are seldom direct, so keep your eyes on the signs (a Métro map helps), and if you start to feel panicky, come up for air.

A&P—you'll have to call the secretary and make arrangements, or simply show up for Sunday services. Either way, it's worth the effort, if only to see the glorious stained-glass window of the risen Christ that dominates the sanctuary behind the white-stone communion table. It's a memorial to members of the Royal Highland Regiment of Canada (the Black Watch) who were killed in World War I. One of the advantages of showing up for the Sunday service is that you get a chance to hear the church's fine, 6,911-pipe Cassavant organ and its 50-voice choir. ☒*Rue Sherbrooke Ouest at rue Redpath, Square Mile* ☎*514/842–3431* ⊕*www.standrewstpaul.com* ☒*Free* ⊗*Sun. service at 11* AM, *other times by arrangement* Ⓜ*Guy-Concordia.*

OFF THE BEATEN PATH

Exporail. You can rattle around Canada's largest railway museum in a vintage tram specially built in the 1950s for sightseeing tours in Montréal when the city still had a streetcar system. The museum has more than 150 locomotives, but if you're a steam buff, you won't want to miss CPR 5935, the largest steam locomotive built in Canada, and CNR 4100, the most powerful in the British Empire when it was built in 1924. To see how the rich and powerful traveled, take a look at Sir William Van Horne's luxurious private car. Of special interest to the kids will be the car that served as a mobile classroom. The museum is south of the city in the town of St-Constant. On several summer Saturdays, rail buffs can take the Museum Express, which leaves from the Lucien-L'Allier suburban train station, in the west end of Centre Bell. Trains depart at 11 AM and return at 4 PM. ☒*110 rue St-Pierre, St-Constant* ☎*450/632–2410* ⊕*www.exporail.org* ☒*C$14, with Museum Express excursion C$32* ⊗*Mid-June–mid-Sept., daily 10–6; early Sept.–Oct., Wed.–Sun. 10–5; Nov.–mid-May, weekends 10–5.*

⑫ **George Stephen House.** Scottish-born Sir George Stephen (1829–1921) was in his way as grandiose as Donald Trump is today. He founded the Canadian Pacific Railway, and in 1882 he spent C$600,000—an almost unimaginable sum at the time—to build a suitable home for himself and his family. He imported artisans from all over the world to panel its ceilings with Cuban mahogany, Indian lemon tree, and English oak and to cover its walls in marble, onyx, and gold. It's now a private club, but you can get a glimpse of all this grandeur on Saturday evening when the dining room, now open year-round, welcomes the public for dinner (C$40 for three courses, C$70 for seven) and on Sunday for brunch and music (C$42, including a guided tour). Warning: The dress code for dinner is semi-formal, which means a jacket and tie for men, something dressy for women, and jeans (of any colour) for no one. ⊠ *1440 rue Drummond, Square Mile* ☎ *514/849–7338* ⊕ *www.clubmountstephen.net* ⚑ *Reservations essential* Ⓜ *Peel or Guy-Concordia.*

⑭ **Grand Séminaire de Montréal.** Education goes way back at the Grand Séminaire. In the mid-1600s, St. Marguerite Bourgeoys used one of the two stone towers in the garden as a school for First Nations (Native American) girls while she and her nuns lived in the other. The 1860 seminary buildings behind the towers are now used by men studying for the priesthood. In summer there are free guided tours of the towers, the extensive gardens, and the college's beautiful Romanesque chapel. The chapel is open for Sunday mass from September through June. ⊠ *2065 rue Sherbrooke Ouest, Square Mile* ☎ *514/935–7775 Ext. 239* 🖷 *514/935–5497* ⊕ *www.gsdm.qc.ca* 🖙 *By donation* ⊙ *Guided tours June–Aug., Tues.–Sat. at 1 and 3; mass Sept.–June, Sun. at 10:30* AM Ⓜ *Guy-Concordia.*

➏ **McGill University.** Merchant and fur trader James McGill would probably be horrified to know that the university that he helped found in 1828 has developed an international reputation as one of North America's best party schools. The administration isn't too happy about it, either. But there's no real cause for alarm. McGill is still one of the two or three best English-language universities in Canada, and certainly one of the prettiest. Its campus is an island of grass and trees in a sea of traffic and skyscrapers. If you take the time to stroll up the drive that leads from the Greek Revival Roddick Gates to the austere neoclassical Arts Building, keep an eye out to your right for the life-size statue of McGill himself, hurrying across campus clutching his tricorn hat. If you have an hour or so, drop into the templelike **Redpath Museum of Natural History** to browse its eclectic collection of dinosaur bones, old coins, African art, and shrunken heads. ⊠ *859 rue Sherbrooke Ouest, Square Mile* ☎ *514/398–4455, 514/398–4094 tours, 514/398–4086 museum* ⊕ *www.mcgill.ca* 🖙 *Free* ⊙ *Museum weekdays 9–5, Sun. 1–5 (June–Aug., closed Fri.)* Ⓜ *McGill.*

NEED A BREAK?

Sit in the shade of one of the 100-year-old maples at McGill University (⊠ *859 rue Sherbrooke Ouest, Square Mile* ☎ *514/398–4455* Ⓜ *McGill*) and read a chapter or two of a Montréal classic like Hugh MacLennan's *Two Solitudes,* or just let the world drift by.

➊ **Place des Arts.** The vast plaza in front of this venue becomes a real summertime magnet for visitors and locals alike—especially during the Montréal Jazz Festival, when it's crammed with music lovers for the free concerts. Montréal's primary performing-arts center was built in

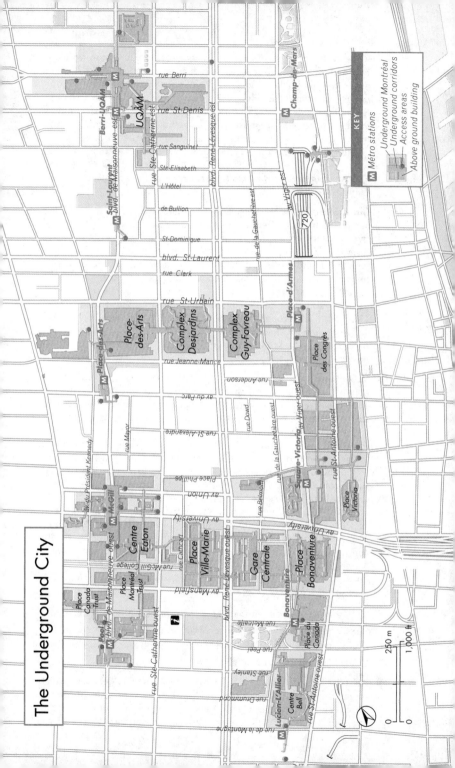

the 1960s, when sleek mausoleum-like buildings and vast stark plazas were all the rage. Sadly, the complex no longer offers backstage tours of its five theaters and auditoriums. ⊠ *175 rue Ste-Catherine Ouest, Downtown* ☏ *514/842–2112 tickets, 514/285–4270 information* ⊕ *www.pda.qc.ca* Ⓜ *Place-des-Arts.*

❼ **Place Ville-Marie.** The cross-shaped 1962 office tower was Montréal's first modern skyscraper; the mall complex underneath it was the first link in the Underground City. The wide expanse of the building's plaza, just upstairs from the mall, makes a fine place to relax with coffee or a snack from the food court below. Benches, potted greenery, and fine views of Mont-Royal make it popular with walkers, tourists, and office workers. ⊠ *Bordered by blvd. René-Lévesque and rues Mansfield, Cathcart, and University, Downtown* ☏ *514/866–6666* Ⓜ *McGill or Bonaventure.*

⓭ **Ravenscrag.** If you're up for a bit of a climb, walk up rue Peel to avenue des Pins for a look at a grand example of the kind of palaces Montréal's industrial barons built for themselves in the 19th century. From Ravenscrag's lofty perch, Sir Hugh Allan—who pretty much controlled Canada's transatlantic transport—could watch his ships come and go. The 60-room mansion, which looks like Tuscany dropped onto the slopes of Mont-Royal, is one of the finest bits of neo-Renaissance architecture in North America. ⊠ *1025 av. des Pins, Square Mile* Ⓜ *Peel.*

❽ **Square Dorchester.** On sunny summer days you can join the office workers, store clerks, and downtown shoppers who gather in Square Dorchester to eat lunch under the trees and perhaps listen to an open-air concert. If there are no vacant benches or picnic tables, you can still find a place to sit on the steps at the base of the dramatic monument to the dead of the Boer War. Other statues honor Scottish poet Robert Burns (1759–96) and Sir Wilfrid Laurier (1841–1919), Canada's first French-speaking prime minister. The buildings surrounding the square represent a fine cross-section of the city's architectural styles, from Scottish baronial and Gothic through neo-classical and Renaissance to starkly modern. ⊠ *Bordered by blvd. René-Lévesque and rues Peel, Metcalfe, and McTavish, Downtown* Ⓜ *Bonaventure or Peel.*

⓫ **St. George's Anglican Church.** St. George's is possibly the prettiest Anglican (Episcopalian) church in Montréal. Step into its dim, candle-scented interior and you'll feel you've been transported to some prosperous market town in East Anglia. The double hammer-beam roof, the rich stained-glass windows, and the Lady Chapel on the east side of the main altar all add to the effect. It certainly seems a world away from Centre Bell, the modern temple to professional hockey just across the street. On the other hand, several prominent National Hockey League players and game announcers regularly drop in for a few minutes of quiet meditation before joining the action on the ice. ⊠ *1101 rue Stanley, Downtown* ☏ *514/866–7113* ⊕ *www.st-georges.org* ⊠ *Free* ⊙ *Tues.–Sun. 9–4; Sun. services at 9 and 10:30* AM Ⓜ *Bonaventure.*

THE PLATEAU & ENVIRONS

Plateau Mont-Royal—or simply The Plateau as it's more commonly called these days—is still home to a vibrant Portuguese community, but much of the housing originally built for factory workers has been bought up and renovated by professionals, artists, performers, and academics eager to find houses that are also close to all the action. The **Quartier Latin** or Latin Quarter just south of the Plateau has been drawing the young since the 1700s, when Université de Montréal students gave the area its name. Both the Quartier Latin and the Plateau have rows of French and ethnic restaurants, bistros, coffee shops, designer boutiques, antiques shops, and art galleries. When night falls these streets are full of omnilingual hordes—young and not so young, rich and poor, established and still studying.

The gentrification of the Plateau inevitably pushed up rents and drove students, immigrant families, and single young graduates just starting out farther north to **Mile-End,** an old working-class neighborhood that is now full of inexpensive restaurants and funky little shops selling handicrafts and secondhand clothes. Farther north is **Little Italy,** which is still home base to Montréal's enormous Italian community. Families of Italian descent live all over the greater Montréal area now, but many come back here every week or so to shop, eat out, or visit family and friends.

The lively strip of rue Ste-Catherine running east of the Quartier Latin is the backbone of the **Village**—Montréal's main gay community. Its restaurants, antiques shops (on rue Amherst), and bars make it a popular destination for visitors of all persuasions.

Many of the older residences in these neighborhoods have the graceful wrought-iron balconies and twisting staircases that are typical of Montréal. The stairs and balconies, treacherous in winter, are often full of families and couples gossiping, picnicking, and partying come summer. If Montrealers tell you they spend the summer in Balconville, they mean they don't have the money or the time to leave town and won't get any farther than their balconies.

MAIN ATTRACTIONS

❷ **Boulevard St-Laurent.** A walk along boulevard St-Laurent is like a walk through Montréal's cultural history. The shops and restaurants, synagogues and churches that line the 10-block stretch north of rue Sherbrooke reflect the various waves of immigrants that have called it home. Keep your eyes open and you'll see Jewish delis, Hungarian sausage shops, Chinese grocery stores, Portuguese favelas, Italian coffee bars, Greek restaurants, Vietnamese sandwich shops, and Peruvian snack bars. You'll also spot some of the city's trendiest restaurants and nightclubs. The first immigrants to move into the area in the 1880s were Jews escaping pogroms in Eastern Europe. It was they who called the street "the Main," as in Main Street—a nickname that endures to this day. Even Francophone Montrealers sometimes call it "Le Main." Ⓜ*St-Laurent, Sherbrooke, or Mont-Royal.*

The Plateau
& Environs

Parc Sir Wilfrid Laurier

rue Laurier
boul St-Joseph est
rue Fabre
rue Garnier
rue de Lanaudière
rue Chambord
rue de Brébeuf
rue de la Roche
rue St-André
av Christophe
rue Boyer

av Papineau
rue Cartier
rue Marquette
av du Mont-Royal est
rue Marie-Anne est
rue Bureau
rue Rachel est

rue de Rouen
av de Lorimier
rue Dorion

Laurier Ⓜ

Ⓜ **7–9**

rue Bienville
rue Resther
rue Fontiac

Ⓜ **Mont-Royal**

6
Parc Lafontaine

Université de Québec à Montréal

rue Sherbrooke est
av Papineau
rue de Champlain
rue Plessis
rue Panet
rue de la Visitation
rue Beaudry
rue de Montcalm
rue Wolfe
rue Amherst
rue la fontaine

TO MILE END & LITTLE ITALY

PLATEAU MONT-ROYAL

335

rue Drolet
rue St-Denis
rue Berri
rue St-Hubert
rue St-André
av Parc Lafontaine
rue Roy est

THE VILLAGE

rue Logan

Beaudry est Ⓜ

Parc du Portugal
rue de Bullion
rue Coloniale
rue St-Dominique
boul St-Laurent
rue Clark

av Duluth est
av Laval

rue Cherrier

Ⓜ **Sherbrooke**

QUARTIER LATIN

de Maisonneuve est

rue Ste-Catherine est

Parc Jeanne-Mance

av du Parc

2
The Main
1

3

5
rue Sherbrooke est
rue Berri

av Ontario est

rue St-Denis

Ⓜ

boul de Maisonneuve

Berri-UQÀM Ⓜ
4

Parc Mont-Royal

0   1/4 mi
0   1/4 km

av des Pins
rue St-Urbain
rue Clark

rue Prince-Arthur
rue Ste-Elisabeth
rue Jeanne-Mance
av du Parc
rue Hutchison
rue Durocher
rue Aylmer
rue University

St-Laurent Ⓜ

rue Sanguinet
Ste-Elisabeth
L'Hôtel
de Bullion
rue St-Dominique
boul René-Lévesque est

Champ-de-Mars Ⓜ

av Viger est
Autoroute Ville-Marie
720

DOWNTOWN

138

Place des Arts Ⓜ

CHINATOWN

Neighborhood Focus: Mile-End

Historically the home to Montréal's working-class Jewish community, in recent years the Mile-End section of the Plateau Mont-Royal has become one of the hippest neighborhoods in town. By day it's a great place to take a stroll or simply hang out on the terraces of its numerous cafés to watch the colorful mix of locals—artsy bohemians, Hasidic Jews, Greeks, and rock and rollers—pass by. The closest Métro to Mile-End is Laurier.

Lingering testaments to the still considerable Jewish population include **Wilensky's** (✉ 34 Fairmount Ouest), whose highly celebrated salami sandwiches were immortalized in Mordecai Richler's novel The Apprenticeship of Duddy Kravitz, as well as the **Fairmount** (✉ 74 Fairmount Ouest) and **St-Viateur** (✉ 263 St-Viateur Ouest) bagel emporiums. Baked in wood ovens, Montréal's bagels are as unique, if not as famous, as its smoked-meat sandwiches, and locals will insist you've never really eaten a bagel until you've tried one from either of these culinary institutions.

At night Mile-End comes alive with the sound of rock and roll, with **Casa del Popolo** (✉ 873 St-Laurent), the **Playhouse** (✉ 5656 av. Park), the **Main Hall** (✉ 5390 St-Laurent), and the **Green Room** (✉ 5386 St-Laurent) all hosting local and international indie bands most nights of the week. Montréal's indie music scene has been booming for several years now, and if you spend a little time in any of these venues you might get a glimpse of why the New York Times and Spin magazine (among others) have recently championed Montréal as "the new Seattle," i.e., the latest mecca for aspiring indie rock sensations. It's also, without question, the best neighborhood in town for reasonably priced Greek food, with **le Coin Grec** (✉ 4903 av. Park) and **Arahova** (✉ 256 St-Viateur Ouest) being choice favorites among discerning Mile-End-ers.

❹ Chapelle Notre-Dame-de-Lourdes *(Our Lady of Lourdes Chapel)*. Artist and architect Napoléon Bourassa called the Chapelle Notre-Dame-des-Lourdes *l'oeuvre de mes amours*, or a labor of love—and it shows. He designed the little Byzantine-style building himself and set about decorating it with the exuberance of an eight-year-old making a Mother's Day card. He covered the walls with murals and encrusted the altar and pillars with gilt and ornamental carving. It's not Montréal's biggest monument to the Virgin Mary, but it's the most unabashedly sentimental. ✉ 430 rue Ste-Catherine Est, Quartier Latin 🎫 Free ⊗ Mon.–Sat. 7:30–6, Sun. 9–6:30 Ⓜ Berri-UQAM.

❼ Chiesa della Madonna della Difesa. If you look up at the cupola behind the main altar of Little Italy's most famous church, you'll spot Montréal's most infamous piece of ecclesiastical portraiture. Yes, indeed, that lantern-jaw fellow on horseback who looks so pleased with himself is Benito Mussolini, the dictator who led Italy into World War II on the wrong side. In fairness, though, the mural, by Guido Nincheri (1885–1973), was completed long before the war and commemorates the signing of the Lateran Pact with Pope Pius XI, one of Il Duce's few lasting achievements. The controversy shouldn't distract you from the beauties of the rest of the richly decorated church. ⊠6800 av. Henri-Julien, Little Italy ☎514/277–6522 ✆Free ⊙Daily 10 AM–6 PM Ⓜ Beaubien or Jean-Talon.

OFF THE
BEATEN
PATH

8 **Église de la Visitation de la Bienheureuse Vierge Marie.** You have to ride the Métro to its northern terminus at the Henri-Bourassa station, and then walk for 15–20 minutes through some pretty ordinary neighborhoods to reach the Church of the Visitation of the Blessed Virgin Mary, but it's worth the trek to see the oldest church on the island. Its stone walls were raised in the 1750s, and the beautifully proportioned Palladian front was added in 1850. Decorating lasted from 1764 until 1837, with stunning results. The altar and the pulpit are as ornate as wedding cakes but still delicate. The church's most notable treasure is a rendering of the Visitation attributed to Pierre Mignard, a painter at the 17th-century court of Louis XIV. Parkland surrounds the church, and the nearby Îles de la Visitation (reachable by footbridge) make for a very good walk. ⊠1847 blvd. Gouin Est, Sault-au-Récollet ☎514/388–4050 ✆Free ⊙Daily 8–noon and 1–4 Ⓜ Henri-Bourassa.

> WORD OF MOUTH
>
> "The Plateau/Quartier Latin—to me this is the 'real' Montréal. Very French, very lively. Lots of outdoor cafés, small shops, byob restaurants, ethnic neighborhoods. It gets a bit run down as you get into the lower end, near St. Catherine, but much of it is quiet tree-lined streets."
>
> —zootsi

9 **Marché Jean-Talon.** If you're trying to stick to a diet, stay away: the smells of grilling sausages, roasting chestnuts, and fresh pastries will almost certainly crack your resolve. And if they don't, there are dozens of tiny shops full of Québec cheeses, Lebanese sweets, country pâtés, local wines, and handmade chocolates that will. Less threatening to the waistline are the huge mounds of peas, beans, apples, carrots, pears, garlic, and other produce on sale at the open-air stalls. On Saturday mornings in particular, it feels as if all Montréal has come out to shop. ⊠7070 rue Henri-Julien, Little Italy ☎514/277–1588 Ⓜ Jean-Talon.

3 **Rue Prince-Arthur.** In the 1960s rue Prince-Arthur was the Haight-Ashbury of Montréal, full of shops selling leather vests, tie-dyed T-shirts, recycled clothes, and drug paraphernalia. It still retains a little of that raffish attitude, but it's much tamer and more commercial these days. The blocks between avenue Laval and boulevard St-Laurent are a pedestrian mall, and the hippie shops have metamorphosed into inexpensive Greek, Vietnamese, Italian, Polish, and Chinese restaurants and neighborhood bars. So grab a table, order a coffee or an *apéro,* and watch the passing parade. Ⓜ Sherbrooke.

1 **Square St-Louis.** The prosperous bourgeois families who built their comfortable homes around Square St-Louis's fountain and trees in the late 1870s would probably be dismayed to see the kind of people who congregate in their little park these days. It's difficult to walk through the place without dodging a skateboarder or a panhandler, or without

Neighborhood Focus: Little Italy

At first glance, you'll have a hard time differentiating Montréal's Little Italy from other working-class neighborhoods in the city's north end—a few little parks, a shopping strip, and rows of brick buildings with outdoor staircases and two or three flats each. But just glance at the gardens and you'll know where you are. Those tiny patches of soil full of tomato plants, fruit trees, and—wonder of wonders in this semifrozen city—grapevines, are a dead giveaway.

You'll see, hear, and smell plenty of other signs of the area's heritage, as well: the sausages and tins of olive oil in the windows of Milano's supermarket, the occasional Ferrari rumbling in the stalled traffic along rue Jean-Talon, the tang of pizza and sharp cheese, the Italian voices in the trat-toria, and of course, the heady smell of espresso from the dozens of little cafés along rue Dante and boulevard St-Laurent.

The best time to visit the neighborhood is on the weekend, when hundreds of Italian-Canadians "come home" to visit family, to sip coffee or dine with friends, and to shop for produce and cheese at the Marché Jean-Talon. If you're lucky you'll spot a young couple getting married at the Madonna della Difesa church (whose frescoes include a portrait of Benito Mussolini).

Montréal's Italian community—at nearly a quarter of a million people—might have outgrown Little Italy, but those 30-odd blocks bounded by rues Jean-Talon, St-Zotique, Marconi, and Drolet remain its heart and soul.

being offered a sip of something from a bottle in a paper bag. But they're generally a friendly bunch, and the square is still worth a visit just to see the elegant Second Empire–style homes that surround it. ✉ *Bordered by av. Laval and rue St-Denis between rue Sherbrooke Est and av. des Pins Est, Quartier Latin* Ⓜ *Sherbrooke.*

ALSO WORTH SEEING

❺ Musée des Hospitalières de l'Hôtel-Dieu. The nuns of the Religieuses Hospitalières de St-Joseph ran Montréal's Hôpital Hôtel-Dieu for more than 300 years until the province and the Université de Montréal took it over in the 1970s. The first sisters—girls of good families caught up in the religious fervor of the age—came to New France with Jeanne Mance in the mid-1600s to look after the poor, the sick, and the dying. The order's museum—tucked away in a corner of the hospital the nuns built but no longer run—captures the spirit of that age with a series of meticulously bilingual exhibits. Just reading the excerpts from the letters and diaries of those young women helps you to understand the zeal that drove them to abandon the comforts of home for the hardships of the colonies. The museum also traces the history of medicine and nursing in Montréal. ✉ *201 av. des Pins Ouest, Plateau Mont-Royal* ☎ *514/849–2919* ⊕ *www.museedeshospitalieres.qc.ca* ✆ *C$6* ◯ *Mid-June–mid-Oct., Tues.–Fri. 10–5, weekends 1–5; mid-Oct.–mid-June, Wed.–Sun. 1–5* Ⓜ *Sherbrooke.*

⑥ Parc Lafontaine. You could say that Parc Lafontaine is a microcosm of Montréal: the eastern half is French, with paths, gardens, and lawns laid out in geometric shapes; the western half is English, with meandering paths and irregularly shaped ponds that follow the natural contours of the land. In summer you can take advantage of bowling greens, tennis courts, an open-air theater (Théâtre de Verdure) where there are free arts events, and two artificial lakes with paddleboats. In winter one lake becomes a large skating rink. The park is named for Sir Louis-Hippolyte Lafontaine (1807–64), a pioneer of responsible government in Canada. His statue graces a plot on the park's southwestern edge. ✉ *3933 av. Parc Lafontaine, Plateau Mont-Royal* ☎ *514/872–9800* ⊙ *Daily 9* AM–10 PM Ⓜ *Sherbrooke or Mont-Royal.*

MONT-ROYAL & ENVIRONS

Fodor'sChoice ★ In geological terms, **Mont-Royal** is a mere bump—a plug of basaltlike rock that has been worn down by several ice ages to a mere 760 feet. But in the affections of Montrealers it's a Matterhorn. Without a trace of irony, they call it simply *la Montagne* or "the Mountain," and it's easy to see why it's so well loved. For Montrealers it's a refuge in the middle of the city, a semitamed wilderness you can get to by bus or, if you have the lungs for the climb, simply by walking. It's where you go to get away from it all—to walk, to jog, to ski, to feed the squirrels, and to admire the view—and sometimes to fall in love. And even when you can't get away, you can see the mountain glimmering beyond the skyscrapers and the high-rises—green in summer, gray and white in winter, and gold and crimson in fall.

The heart of all this is Parc Mont-Royal itself—nearly 500 acres of forests and meadows laid out by Frederick Law Olmsted (1822–1903), the man responsible for New York City's Central Park. Olmsted believed that communion with nature could cure body and soul, so much of the park has been left as wild as possible, with narrow paths meandering through tall stands of maples and red oaks. In summer it's full of picnicking families and strolling couples; in winter cross-country skiers and snowshoers take over, while families skate at Lac aux Castors and ride sleds and inner tubes down groomed slopes. If you want to explore with minimum effort, you can hire the services of a horse-drawn carriage (or sleigh in winter).

Just outside the park's northern boundaries are the city's two biggest cemeteries, and beyond that the campus of the Université de Montréal. Not far away from the park and perched on a neighboring crest of the

Neighborhood Focus: The Village

Formerly known as the Gay Village, the area bordering rue Ste-Catherine Est from Amherst to de Lorimier, and on the north–south axis from René-Lévesque to Sherbrooke, is a thriving part of town, replete with restaurants, bars, bathhouses, boutiques, and cafés. Montréal has one of the most vibrant gay communities in the world, widely supported by residents of this proudly liberal, open-minded city. In recent years the municipal, federal, and provincial governments have taken it upon themselves to aggressively promote the Village and Montréal's gay-friendly climate as a reason for tourists to visit, including those who wish to wed. In recognition of the Village's importance to the city, the downtown borough of Ville-Marie hangs a rainbow flag in its council chambers, and the recently rebuilt entrance to the Beaudry Métro station, essentially the gateway to the neighborhood, is now adorned with rainbow pillars.

The best way to explore the area is on foot, getting off at the Beaudry Métro station and heading east along rue Ste-Catherine. No trip to the Village would be complete without stopping by **Le Drugstore** (⊠ *1366 rue Ste-Catherine Est*), the largest gay entertainment complex in the world, or

Cabaret Mado (⊠ *1115 rue Ste-Catherine Est*), which, operated by legendary local drag queen Mado, regularly plays host to the city's swankiest drag entertainers.

same mountain is the Oratoire St-Joseph, a shrine that draws millions every year. North of the oratory is the busy **Côte-des-Neiges** neighborhood, teeming with shops and restaurants—Thai, Russian, Korean, Indian, Peruvian, and Filipino, to name a few. South of the oratory, on the other side of the mountain, is **Westmount,** one of the wealthiest Anglophone neighborhoods on the island. Its Francophone twin—the equally prosperous **Outremont**—skirts the mountain's northeastern slopes. While there, be sure to take a walk along Rue Bernard, lined with great well-priced restaurants and sidewalk cafés.

MAIN ATTRACTIONS

4 **Chalet du Mont-Royal.** No trip to Montréal is complete without a visit
★ to the terrace in front of the Chalet du Mont-Royal. It's not the only place to go to get an overview of the city, the river, and the countryside beyond, but it's the most spectacular. On clear days you can see not just the downtown skyscrapers, but Mont-Royal's sister mountains—Monts St-Bruno, St-Hilaire, and St-Grégoire—as well. These isolated peaks, called the Montérégies, or Mountains of the King, rise dramatically from the flat countryside. Beyond them, you might be able to see the northern reaches of the Appalachians. Be sure to take a look inside the chalet, especially at the murals depicting scenes from Canadian history. There's a snack bar in the back. ⊠ *Off voie Camillien-Houde, Plateau Mont-Royal* ☎ *No phone* ⊡ *Free* ⊙ *Daily 9–5* Ⓜ *Mont-Royal.*

10 **Oratoire St-Joseph** *(St. Joseph's Oratory).* Two million people from all
★ over North America and beyond visit St. Joseph's Oratory yearly. The most devout Catholics climb the 99 steps to its front door on their

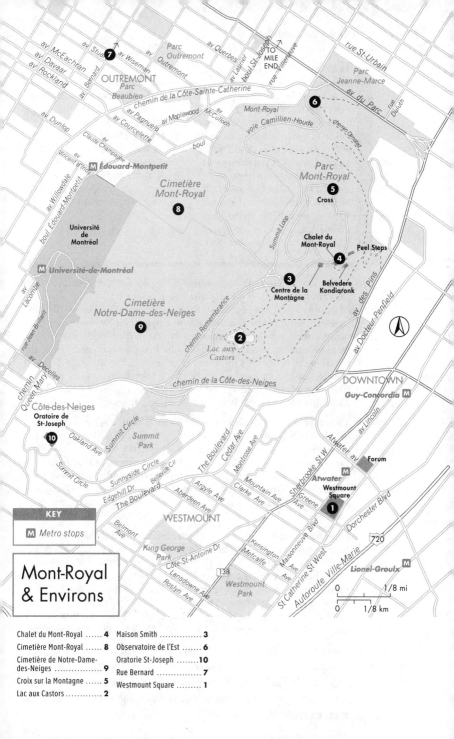

KEY

Ⓜ Metro stops

Mont-Royal & Environs

The Story of Oratoire St-Joseph

By worldly standards Brother André didn't have much going for him, but he had a deep devotion to St. Joseph and an iron will. In 1870 he joined the Holy Cross religious order, and was assigned to work as a doorkeeper at the classical college the order operated just north of Mont-Royal. In 1904 he began building a little chapel to honor his favorite saint on the mountainside across the road, and the rest is history. Thanks to reports of miracu-lous cures attributed to St. Joseph's intercession, donations started to pour in, and Brother André was able to start work replacing his modest little shrine with something more substantial. The result, which wasn't completed until after his death, is one of the most triumphal pieces of church architecture in North America.

knees. It is the world's largest and most popular shrine dedicated to the earthly father of Jesus (Canada's patron saint), and it's all the work of a man named Brother André Besette (1845–1937). The oratory and its extensive gardens dominate Mont-Royal's northwestern slope. Its octagonal copper dome—one of the largest in the world—can be seen from miles away in all directions. Under that dome, the interior of the main church is equally grand, but its austerity is almost frigid. The best time to visit it is on Sunday for the 11 AM solemn mass, when the sanctuary is brightly lighted and the sweet voices of Les Petits Chanteurs de Mont-Royal—the city's best boys' choir—fill the nave with music.

The crypt is shabbier than its big brother upstairs but more welcoming. In a long, narrow room behind the crypt, 10,000 votive candles glitter before a dozen carved murals extolling the virtues of St. Joseph; the walls are hung with crutches discarded by those said to have been cured. Just beyond is the simple tomb of Brother André, who was beatified in 1982. His preserved heart is displayed in a glass case upstairs in one of the several layers of galleries sandwiched between the crypt and the main church.

High on the mountain, east of the main church, is a beautiful garden commemorating the Passion of Christ, with life-size representations of the 14 traditional stations of the cross. On the west side of the church is Brother André's original chapel, with pressed-tin ceilings and plaster saints that is, in many ways, more moving than the church that overshadows it. ✉ *3800 chemin Queen Mary, Côte-des-Neiges* ☎ *514/733–8211* ∰ *www.saint-joseph.org* ✇ *Free* ⊘ *Mid-Sept.–mid-May, daily 7 AM–8:30 PM; mid-May–mid-Sept., daily 7 AM–9 PM* Ⓜ *Côte-des-Neiges.*

NEED A BREAK? A sinfully light croissant or decadent pastry from the **Duc de Lorraine** (✉ *5002 Côte-des-Neiges* ☎ *514/731–4128* Ⓜ *Côte-des-Neiges*) is just the antidote to the sanctity of the **Oratoire St-Joseph**. If it's lunchtime, try one of the Duc's meat pies or a quiche, followed by coffee and a scoop of homemade ice cream.

2

❼ **Rue Bernard.** If your taste runs to chic and fashionable rather than bohe-
★ mian and eccentric, there is simply no better street for people-watching than rue Bernard. Its wide sidewalks and shady trees make it ideal
for the kind of outdoor cafés that attract the bright and the beautiful.
✉ *Outremont* Ⓜ *Outremont.*

ALSO WORTH SEEING

❽ **Cimetière Mont-Royal.** If you find yourself humming *Getting to Know
You* as you explore Mont-Royal Cemetery's 165 acres, blame it on
the graveyard's most famous permanent guest, Anna Leonowens
(1834–1915). She was the real-life model for the heroine of the musical *The King and I.* The cemetery—established in 1852 by the Anglican, Presbyterian, Unitarian, and Baptist churches—is laid out like a
terraced garden, with footpaths that meander between crab apple trees
and past Japanese lilacs. ✉ *1297 chemin de la Forêt, Côte-des-Neiges* ☎ *514/279–7358* ⊕ *www.mountroyalcem.com* ⊘ *Mon.–Fri. 8–5,
weekends and holidays 8–4* Ⓜ *Edouard-Montpetit.*

❾ **Cimetière de Notre-Dame-des-Neiges** *(Our Lady of the Snows Cemetery).*
At 343 acres, Canada's largest cemetery is not much smaller than the
neighboring **Parc Mont-Royal,** and as long as you just count the living,
it's usually a lot less crowded. You don't have to be morbid to wander
the graveyard's 55 km (34 mi) of tree-shaded paths and roadways past
the tombs of hundreds of prominent artists, poets, intellectuals, politicians, and clerics. Among them is Calixa Lavallée (1842–91), who
wrote "O Canada," the country's national anthem. Many of the monuments are the work of such leading Québécois artists as Louis-Philippe
Hébert and Alfred Laliberité. The cemetery offers some guided tours in
summer. Phone ahead for details. ✉ *4601 chemin de la Côte-des-Neiges, Plateau Mont-Royal* ☎ *514/735–1361* ⊕ *www.cimetierenddn.org*
⊘ *Daily 8–7* Ⓜ *Université-de-Montréal.*

**OFF THE
BEATEN
PATH**

Cosmodome. Replicas of rockets and spaceships and a full-size mock-
up of the space shuttle *Endeavor* are among the kid-pleasing exhibits
that make the 30-minute drive to the Cosmodome in suburban Laval
a worthwhile trek for families—especially on a rainy day. There are
also films, demonstrations, and games. Next door to the Cosmodome
is the **Space Camp** (☎ *800/565–2267*), a training center for amateur
astronauts age nine or older. It is affiliated with the U.S. Space Camp in
Georgia. ✉ *2150 autoroute des Laurentides, Laval* ☎ *450/978–3600*
⊕ *www.cosmodome.org* ☞ *C$11.50* ⊘ *Late June–Aug., daily 10–6;
Sept.–late June, Tues.–Sun. 10–6.*

❺ **Croix sur la Montagne.** The 102-foot-high steel cross at the top of Mont-
Royal has been a city landmark since it was erected in 1924, largely
with money raised through the efforts of 85,000 high-school students.
In 1993 the 249 bulbs used to light the cross were replaced with an
ultramodern fiber-optic system.

❷ **Lac aux Castors** *(Beaver Lake).* Mont-Royal's single body of water is
actually a reclaimed bog, but it's a great place for kids to float model
boats in the summertime or take a ride on a pedal boat. In winter,
the lake's frozen surface attracts whole families of skaters, and nearby

Neighborhood Focus: Westmount & Outremont

On the Island of Montréal the names "Westmount" and "Outremont" are synonymous with wealth and power. If—as some people say—the neighborhoods are two sides of the same coin, that coin has to be a gold one.

The similarities between the two places are obvious. Both have grand homes, tree-shaded streets, and perfectly groomed parks. Both are built on the slopes of Mont-Royal—Westmount on the southwest and Outremont on the northeast—and both are close to the city center. Each has its own trendy—or, in Outremont, branché—area for shopping, dining, and sipping lattes. Westmount's is concentrated along avenue Greene and Outremont's is centered on the western ends of rues Laurier and Bernard. Less well known, perhaps, is that both places are not uniformly wealthy. The southern stretch of Westmount is full

of immigrant, working-class families, and the eastern fringes of Outremont are home to Montréal's thriving Hasidic community.

The two neighborhoods may appear mirror images of each other, but they have one essential difference. Although the barriers between Francophones and Anglophones in the city might be eroding, Westmount remains stubbornly English—right down to its neo-Gothic churches and lawn-bowling club—and Outremont is stubbornly French, with a distinct preference for Second Empire homes.

If you want to get a feel for what novelist Hugh MacLennan called Montréal's "two solitudes," there's no more pleasant way to do it than to take a stroll down avenue Green on one afternoon and then go shopping on rue Laurier the next. Vive la difference.

there's a groomed slope where kids of all ages can ride inner tubes. The city recently refurbished the glass-fronted Beaver Lake Pavilion, turning part of it into a very pleasant bistro that serves lunch and dinner. Skate and cross-country-ski rentals are available downstairs. ⊠ *Off chemin Remembrance, Plateau Mont-Royal* Ⓜ *Edouard-Montpetit.*

❸ **Maison Smith.** If you need a map of Mont-Royal's extensive hiking trails or want to know about the more than 150 kinds of birds here, the old park keeper's residence is the place to go. It's also a good for getting a snack, drink, or souvenir. The pretty little stone house—built in 1858—is the headquarters of Les Amis de la Montagne (The Friends of the Mountain), an organization that offers various guided walks on the mountain and in nearby areas. ⊠ *1260 chemin Remembrance, Plateau Mont-Royal* ☎ *514/843–8240* ⊕ *www.lemontroyal.qc.ca* ⊙ *Late June–early Sept., weekdays 9–6, weekends 9–8; early Sept.–late June, weekdays 9–5, weekends 9–6* Ⓜ *Mont-Royal.*

❻ **Observatoire de l'Est.** If you're just driving across the mountain, be sure to stop at least briefly at the mountain's eastern lookout for a spectacular view of the Stade Olympique and the east end of the city. Snacks are available. ⊠ *Voie Camillien-Houde, Plateau Mont-Royal* Ⓜ *Mont-Royal.*

① **Westmount Square.** You be the judge: were the skylights cut into the terrace of Westmount Square in 1990 a desecration, as the architectural community claimed at the time, or a necessary step to bring some light into the gloomy, high-end shopping mall beneath? What infuriated the architects is that the square—a complex of three towers, a two-story office building, and a shopping concourse—was the work of the sainted Ludwig Mies Van der Rohe and should be left untouched by mere mortals lest Van der Rohe's vision of pure forms rising from a flat plain be blighted. But Van der Rohe himself showed some flexibility in the design of this building. For one thing, he clothed it in dark granite instead of his beloved travertine marble—a sensible concession to Montréal's harsh climate. ⊠*Corner of av. Wood and blvd. de Maisonneuve, Westmount* ☎*514/932–0211* ☞*Free* Ⓜ*Atwater.*

> **AN EATING FRENZY**
>
> If you're looking for an exotic lunch, the Côte-des-Neiges neighborhood north of Mont-Royal is a maze of world-cuisine restaurants.

HOCHELAGA-MAISONNEUVE

The Stade Olympique that played host to the 1976 Summer Olympics and the leaning tower that supports the stadium's roof dominate the skyline of Hochelaga-Maisonneuve. But there's much more to the area than the stadium complex, including the Jardin Botanique (Botanical Garden); the Insectarium, which houses the world's largest collection of bugs; and Parc Maisonneuve, an ideal place for a stroll or a picnic. The rest of the area is largely working-class residential, but there are some good restaurants and little shops along rue Ontario Est.

Until 1918, when it was annexed by Montréal, the east-end district of Maisonneuve was a city unto itself, a booming, prosperous industrial center full of factories making everything from shoes to cheese. The neighborhood was also packed with houses for the almost entirely French-Canadian workers who kept the whole machine humming.

Maisonneuve was also the site of one of Canada's earliest experiments in urban planning. The Dufresne brothers, a pair of prosperous shoe manufacturers, built a series of grand civic buildings along rue Morgan, including a theater, public baths, and a bustling market, all of which you can still see today. The Dufresne administration also opened Parc Maisonneuve, a 155-acre green space that is now home to the Jardin Botanique de Montréal and a municipal golf course. All this was supposed to make working-class life more bearable, but World War I put an end to the brothers' plans and Maisonneuve became part of Montréal, twinned with the east-end district of Hochelaga.

MAIN ATTRACTIONS

⑥ **Insectarium.** If you're a little squeamish about beetles and roaches, you ⓒ might want to give the bug-shaped building in the middle of the **Jardin Botanique** a pass, but kids especially seem to love it. Most of the more

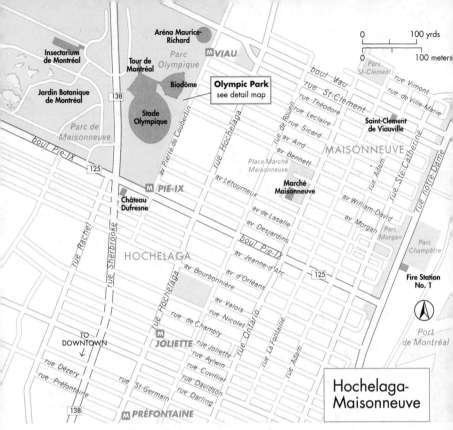

than 250,000 insects in the Insectarium's collection are either mounted or behind panes of glass thick enough to minimize the shudder factor—a good thing when you're looking at a tree roach the size of a wrestler's thumb. There is, however, a room full of free-flying butterflies, and in February and May the Insectarium releases thousands of butterflies and moths into the Jardin Botanique's main greenhouse. At varying times during the year the Insectarium brings in chefs to prepare such delicacies as deep-fried bumblebees and chocolate-dipped locusts—protein-rich treats that most adults seem able to resist. ⊠ *4581 rue Sherbrooke Est, Hochelaga-Maisonneuve* ☎ *514/872–1400* ⊕ *www.ville.montreal. qc.ca/insectarium* 🎫 *May–Oct. C$16, Nov.–Apr. C$13.50 (includes Jardin Botanique)* ☉ *May–Aug., daily 9–6; Sept. and Oct., daily 9–9; Nov.–Apr., Tues.–Sun. 9–5* Ⓜ *Pie-IX or Viau.*

❺ Jardin Botanique *(Botanical Garden).* Creating one of the world's great botanical gardens in a city with a winter as harsh as Montréal's was no mean feat, and the result is that no matter how brutal it gets in January there's one corner of the city where it's always summer. With 181 acres of plantings in summer and 10 greenhouses open all year, Montréal's Jardin Botanique is the second-largest attraction of its kind in the world (after England's Kew Gardens). It grows more than 26,000 species of plants, and among its 30 thematic gardens are a rose garden, an alpine garden, and—a favorite with the kids—a poisonous-plant garden. You can attend traditional tea ceremonies in the Japanese Garden, which has one of the best bonsai collections in the West, or wander among the native birches and maples of the Jardin des Premières-Nations (First Nations Garden). The Jardin de Chine (Chinese Garden), with its pagoda and waterfall, will transport you back to the Ming Dynasty. Another highlight is the **Insectarium.** ✉*4101 rue Sherbrooke Est, Hochelaga-Maisonneuve* ☎*514/872-1400* ⊕*www.*

ville.montreal.qc.ca/jardin ☎*May–Oct. C$16, Nov.–Apr. C$11.50 (includes Insectarium)* ⊙*May–Aug., daily 9–6; Sept. and Oct., daily 9–9; Nov.–Apr., Tues.–Sun. 9–5* Ⓜ*Pie-IX.*

② **Stade Olympique.** Montrealers finished paying for their Olympic stadium in the spring of 2006—30 years after the games it was built for—but they still call it the Big Owe, and not very affectionately, either. It certainly looks dramatic, squatting like a giant flying saucer in the middle of the east end. But the place is hard to heat, it's falling apart, and the saga of the retractable roof—it worked precisely three times—is a running joke for local comics. Abandoned by the baseball and football teams it was supposed to house, the stadium is now used mostly for trade shows that are housed under the stands as the crumbling roof makes the actual playing field too dangerous to use. Daily guided tours of the complex in French and English leave from **Tourist Hall** (☎*514/252-8687*) in the base of the Tour Olympique every hour on the hour between 11 and 4 from September to June and 10 and 5 from June to September. ✉*4141 av. Pierre-de-Coubertin, Hochelaga-Maisonneuve* ☎*514/252-8687* ☎*Tour of Olympic complex C$13* ⊕*www.rio.gouv.qc.ca* Ⓜ*Pie-IX or Viau.*

③ **Tour Olympique.** The world's tallest tilting structure—eat your heart out, Pisa—is the 890-foot tower that was supposed to hold the Stade Olympique's retractable roof. It looked great on paper, but never worked in practice. If you want a great view of the city, however, ride one of the cable cars that slide up the outside of the tower to the observatory at the top. On a clear day you can see up to 80 km (50 mi). ✉*4141 av. Pierre-de-Coubertin, Hochelaga-Maisonneuve* ☎*514/252-4141 Ext. 5246* ☎*Observation deck $14; Observation deck and guided tour of Olympic complex $17.75* ⊙*Mid-June–Labor Day, daily 9–7; Labor Day–mid-June, 9–5* Ⓜ*Pie-IX or Viau.*

ALSO WORTH SEEING

④ **Biodôme.** Not everyone thought it was a great idea to transform an Olympic bicycle-racing stadium into a natural-history exhibit, but the result is one of the city's most popular attractions, albeit one that's

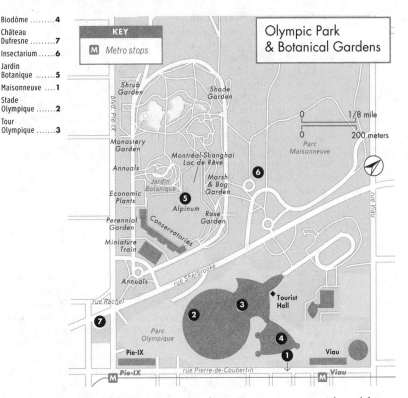

begun to show some wear and tear. Four ecosystems—a boreal forest, a tropical forest, a polar landscape, and the St. Lawrence River—are under one climate-controlled dome. You follow protected pathways through each environment, observing indigenous flora and fauna. A word of warning: the tropical forest is as hot and humid as the real thing, and the Québec and arctic exhibits can be quite frigid. If you want to stay comfortable, dress in layers. ⊠4777 av. Pierre-de-Coubertin, Hochelaga-Maisonneuve ☎514/868–3000 ⊕www.biodome. qc.ca ⊠C$16 ⊙Late June–early Sept., daily 9–6; early Sept.–late June, Tues.–Sun. and holiday Mondays 9–5 Ⓜ Viau.

⑦ Château Dufresne. The adjoining homes of a pair of shoe manufacturers, Oscar and Marius Dufresne, provide a revealing glimpse into the lives of Montréal's Francophone bourgeoisie in the early 20th century. The brothers built their Beaux-Arts palace in 1916 along the lines of the Petit-Trianon in Paris, and lived in it with their families—Oscar in the eastern half and Marius in the western half. Worth searching out are the delicate domestic scenes on the walls of the Petit Salon, where Oscar's wife entertained her friends. Her brother-in-law relaxed with his male friends in a smoking room decked out like a Turkish lounge. During the house's incarnation as a boys' school in the 1950s, the Eudist priests, who ran the place, covered the room's frieze of frolicking nymphs and satyrs with a modest curtain that their charges lifted at every opportunity. ⊠*2929 rue Jeanne-d'Arc, Hochelaga-Maisonneuve* ☎*514/259–9201* ⊕*www.chateaudufresne.qc.com* ⊠*C$7* ⊙*Thurs.–Sun. 10–5* Ⓜ*Viau.*

❶ **Maisonneuve.** At the beginning of the 20th century, civic leaders wanted to transform this industrial center into a model city with broad boulevards, grandiose public buildings, and fine homes. World War I and the Depression killed those plans, but a few fine fragments of the grand dream survive, just three blocks south of the Olympic site. The magnificent Beaux-Arts public market, which has a 20-foot-tall bronze statue of a farm woman, stands at the northern end of tree-lined avenue Morgan. Farmers and butchers have moved into a modern building next door; the old market is now a community center and the site of summer shows and concerts. Monumental staircases and a heroic rooftop sculpture embellish the public baths across the street. The **Théâtre Denise Pelletier**, at the corner of rue Ste-Catherine Est and rue Morgan, has a lavish Italianate interior; **Fire Station No. 1**, at 4300 rue Notre-Dame Est, was inspired by Frank Lloyd Wright's Unity Temple in suburban Chicago; and the sumptuously decorated **Église Très-Saint-Nom-de-Jésus** has one of the most powerful organs in North America. The 60-acre **Parc Maisonneuve**, stretching north of the botanical garden, is a lovely place for a stroll. Ⓜ*Pie-IX or Viau.*

NEED A BREAK?

If you're feeling a bit peckish and want to soak up a little neighborhood ambience, drop into the cash-only **Chez Clo** (⊠ *3199 rue Ontario Est, Hochelaga-Maisonneuve* ☎*514/522–5348* Ⓜ *Pie-IX or Viau*) for a bowl of the best pea soup in the city, followed—if you have the room for it—by a slab of *tourtière* (meat pie) with homemade ketchup. The dessert specialty is *pudding au chomeur* (literally, pudding for the unemployed), a kind of shortcake smothered in a thick brown-sugar sauce. The service is noisy and friendly, and the clientele mostly local, but there are often lines.

THE ISLANDS

Expo '67—the World's Fair staged to celebrate the centennial of the Canadian federation—was the biggest party in Montréal's history, and it marked a defining moment in the city's evolution as a modern metropolis. That party was held on two islands in the middle of the St. Lawrence River—Île Ste-Hélène, formed by nature, and Île Notre-Dame, created with the stone rubble excavated from the construction of Montréal's Métro. Both are very accessible. You can drive to them via the Pont de la Concorde or the Pont Jacques-Cartier, or take the Métro from the Berri-UQAM station.

MAIN ATTRACTIONS

❸ **Biosphère.** Nothing captures the exuberance of Expo '67 better than the geodesic dome designed by Buckminster Fuller (1895–1983) as the American Pavilion. It's only a skeleton now—the polymer panels that protected the U.S. exhibits from the elements were burned out in a fire long ago—but it's still an eye-catching sight, like something plucked from a science-fiction film. Science of a non-fictional kind, however, is the specialty of environmental center the federal government has built in the middle of the dome. It focuses on the challenges of preserving the Great Lakes and St. Lawrence River system, but it has lively and interactive exhibits on climate change, sustainable energy, and air pollution. Visitors of all ages—especially kids—can use games and interactive displays arranged around a large model of the waterway to explore how shipping, tourism, water supplies, and hydroelectric power are affected. ⊠ *160 chemin Tour-de-l'Île, Île Ste-Hélène* ☎ *514/283–5000* ⊕ *www.biosphere.ec.gc.ca* ▣ *C$10* ⊙ *June–Sept., daily 10–6; Oct.–May, Tues.–Fri. noon–5* Ⓜ *Jean-Drapeau.*

❹ Casino de Montréal. You have to be at least 18 to visit Montréal's government-owned casino, but you don't have to be a gambler. You can come for the bilingual cabaret theater or to sip a martini in the Cheval bar or to dine in Nuances, where the prices are almost as spectacular as the views of the city across the river. You can even come just to look at the architecture—the main building was the French pavilion at Expo '67. But if you do want to risk the family fortune, there are more than 3,200 slot machines, a keno lounge, a high-stakes gaming area, and 120 tables for playing blackjack, baccarat, roulette, craps, and various types of poker. ⊠ *1 av. du Casino, H3C 4W7, Île Notre-Dame* ☎ *514/392–2746 or 800/665–2274* ⊕ *www.casino-de-montreal.com* Ⓜ *Jean-Drapeau (then Bus 167).*

❺ Parc Jean-Drapeau. Île Ste-Hélène and Île Notre-Dame now constitute a single park named, fittingly enough, for Jean Drapeau (1916–99), the visionary (and spendthrift) mayor who built the Métro and brought the city both the 1967 World's Fair and the 1976 Olympics. The park includes a major amusement park, acres of flower gardens, a beach with filtered water, and the Casino de Montréal. There's history, too, at the Old Fort, where soldiers in colonial uniforms display the military methods used in ancient wars. In winter you can skate on the old Olympic rowing basin or slide down iced trails on an inner tube. ☎ *514/872–6120* ⊕ *www.parcjeandrapeau.com/en* Ⓜ *Jean-Drapeau.*

FodorsChoice
★

❷ Stewart Museum at the Fort. Each summer the grassy parade square of the Old Fort comes alive with the crackle of colonial muskets and the skirl of bagpipes. The French are represented by the Compagnie Franche de la Marine and the British by the kilted 78th Fraser Highlanders, one of the regiments that participated in the conquest of Québec in 1759. The two companies of colonial soldiers raise the flag every day at 11 AM, practice maneuvers at 1 PM, put on a combined display of precision drilling and musket fire at 3 PM, and lower the flag at 4:30 PM. Children are encouraged to take part. The fort itself, built between 1820 and 1824 to protect Montréal from an American invasion that never came, is now a museum that tells the story of colonial life in the city through displays of old firearms, maps, and uniforms. ⊠ *West of Pont Jacques-Cartier, Île Ste-Hélène* ☎ *514/861–6701* ⊕ *www.stewart-museum.org* ▣ *C$10* ⊙ *Early May–mid-Oct., daily 10–5; mid-Oct.–early May, Wed.–Mon. 10–4:30* Ⓜ *Jean-Drapeau, plus 10-min walk.*

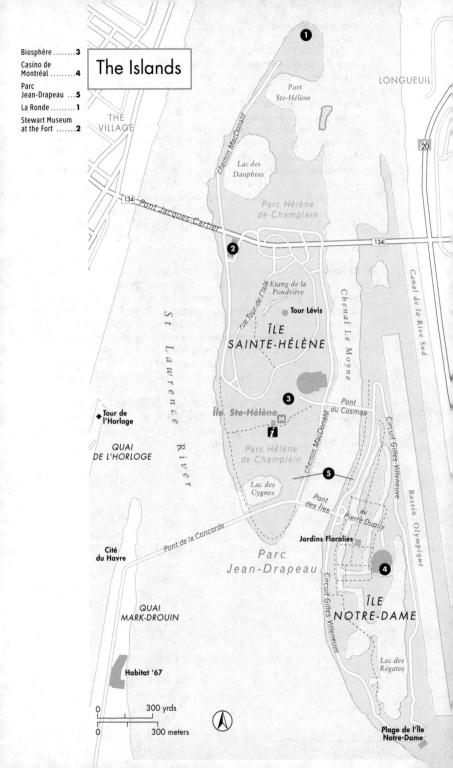

The Islands

LONGUEUIL

THE
VILLAGE

Port
Ste-Hélène

chemin MacDonald

Lac des
Dauphins

20

134

Pont Jacques-Cartier

Parc Hélène
de-Champlain

134

Étang de la
Poudrière

rue Tour-de-l'Isle

Tour Lévis

ÎLE
SAINTE-HÉLÈNE

Chenal Le Moyne

Canal de la Rive Sud

St Lawrence River

Tour de
l'Horloge

QUAI
DE L'HORLOGE

Île Ste-Hélène

M

Pont
du Cosmos

chemin MacDonald

Parc Hélène
de-Champlain

Lac des
Cygnes

Circuit Gilles-Villeneuve

Bassin
Olympique

Cité
du Havre

Pont de la Concorde

Pont
des Îles

av
Pierre Dupuy

Jardins Floralies

Parc
Jean-Drapeau

QUAI
MARK-DROUIN

Circuit Gilles-Villeneuve

ÎLE
NOTRE-DAME

Habitat '67

Lac des
Régates

0   300 yrds

0   300 meters

Plage de l'Île
Notre-Dame

ALSO WORTH SEEING

🐚 **Plage de l'Île Notre-Dame** *(Île Notre-Dame Beach)*. The dress code at the neighboring **Casino de Montréal** might ban camisoles and strapless tops, but here anything seems to go on warm summer days, when the beach is a sea of oiled bodies. You get the distinct impression that

> **ISLAND TRIP TIP**
>
> A ferry carries foot passengers and their bikes from the Bassin Jacques-Cartier in the Vieux-Port to Île Ste-Hélène—the nicest way to get to the islands.

swimming is not uppermost on the minds of many of the scantily clad hordes. If you do want to go in, however, the water is filtered and closely monitored for contamination, and there are lifeguards on duty to protect you from other hazards. A shop rents swimming and boating paraphernalia, and there are picnic areas and a restaurant. ⊠ *West side of Île Notre-Dame, Île Notre-Dame* ☎ *514/872–4537* 🎟 *C$7.50* 🕐 *Late June–Aug., daily 10–7* Ⓜ *Jean-Drapeau.*

❶ **La Ronde.** Every year, it seems, La Ronde adds some new and mon-
🐚 strous way to scare the living daylights (and perhaps your lunch as well) out of you. The most recent addition is the Goliath, a giant steel roller coaster that opened in the summer of 2006. It dwarfs the previous favorites—the aptly named Vampire and Monstre—in both height and speed. But if the idea of hurtling along a narrow steel track at 110 KPH (68 MPH) doesn't appeal to you, you might prefer the boat rides or the Ferris wheel. The popular **International Fireworks Competition** is held here weekends and a couple of weeknights in late June and July. ⊠ *Eastern end of Île Ste-Hélène, Île Ste-Hélène* ☎ *514/397–2000 or 800/361–4595* 🌐 *www.laronde.com/en* 🎟 *C$30* 🕐 *Late May, weekends 10–8; early June–late June, daily 10–8; late June–late Aug., daily 10 AM–10:30 PM; Sept., weekends 10–7; Oct., Fri. 5 PM–9 PM, Sat. noon–9, Sun. noon–8* Ⓜ *Jean-Drapeau.*

Nightlife & the Arts

Theater du Nouveau Monde, Downtown Montréal.

WORD OF MOUTH

"Montréal has excellent nightlife and a strong arts scene. It's all about eating and drinking and strolling around enjoying the sights and the neighborhoods."

—Carmanah

NIGHTLIFE & THE ARTS PLANNER

Where to Get Information

Nightlife magazine offers a city-centric guide to the various goings-on about town, MAG33 is also worth a look. *Le Mirror* (⊕ *www.montrealmirror.com*) and French-language *Le Voir* (⊕ *www.voir.ca*) also list events, and are distributed free at restaurants and other public places. Have a look at the following Web sites for comprehensive information about Montréal's nightlife scene: www.montreal.tv; www.montreal-clubs.com; www.madeinmtl.com; www.bestclubsinmontreal.com; and www.toutmontreal.com.

The "Friday Preview" section of the *Gazette* (⊕ *www.montrealgazette.com*), the English-language daily paper, has a thorough list of events at the city's concert halls, theaters, clubs, dance spaces, and movie houses.

Hours

The bars stop serving around 3 AM and close shortly thereafter (with the exception of sanctioned "after hour" haunts), and on the weekends expect them to be packed to the gills until then. The club scene picks up right after, and extends until dawn.

Where to Get Tickets

For tickets to major pop and rock concerts, shows, festivals, and hockey, soccer, and football games, you can go to the individual box offices or contact **Admission** (☎ *514/790–1245 or 800/361–4595* ⊕ *www.admission.com*).

Tickets to Théâtre St-Denis and other venues are available through **Ticketmaster** (☎ *514/790–1111* ⊕ *www.ticketmaster.ca*).

What to Wear

If you have a daring outfit in your closet that you've hesitated wearing, bring it. Montréalers get absolutely decked to go out on the town to bars and clubs—even if the temperature is below freezing.

Men will wear slick black pants, a sharp button-down and even a tie. Women wear anything from jeans, but only if they're fitted and dark, with fitted matching tops, to a cocktail dress with stockings and heels. Certain clubs have dress codes, so check ahead.

For a music or dance performance you can tone it down a bit, but orchestra- and opera-goers favor slacks and skirts over jeans. If in doubt, err on the dressier side and you'll fit right in.

Best Bar Bets

Best for music: Casa del Popolo
Best kitsch: Gogo Lounge
Best water view: Café des Eclusiers
Best martini: Jello Bar
Best for hockey games: Le Pistol
Best off-the-beaten path: Le Sainte-Elisabeth
Best for a date: Wunderbar
Best outdoor patio: Saint-Sulpice
Best for expense accounts: Suite 701
Best no-frills: Peel Pub

Updated
by Brandon
Presser

IF NIGHTLIFE IN MONTRÉAL COULD BE DISTILLED into a cocktail, it would be one part sophisticated New York club scene (with the accompanying pretension), one part Parisian joie-de-vivre (and again, a dash of snobbery), and one part Barcelonan stamina, which keeps the clubs booming 'til dawn. Due to the diverse nature of club-goers, most places house trendy tables, slippery DJs, and a bouncing dance floor all wrapped up into one über-venue.

As the largest city in the province, Montréal's arts scene is just as lively as its nightlife. It's where Cirque du Soleil was founded in the '80s, and is indeed a *spectacle* Québéquois-style. Along with several well-known dance troupes and theaters, there's the fabulous Orchestre Symphonique de Montréal, as well as the Orchestre Métropolitain du Grand Montréal.

NIGHTLIFE

Hot spots are peppered throughout the city, with compact clusters along rue Crescent, boulevard St-Laurent, boulevard Mont-Royal, and rue St-Denis. Prominent rue Ste-Catherine plows through town, connecting most of these nighttime niches, and farther east, near Beaudry Métro station, it becomes the main drag for the Gay Village. The Old Port is Montréal's upcoming neighborhood, with a steady stream of venues opening all the time in this cobblestone district.

BARS & LOUNGES

There's certainly no shortage of places to go drinking in Montréal. The sheer volume of options promises satisfaction for every taste and persuasion. During the warmer months, French café culture exerts its influence as local watering holes spill onto the street, letting patrons recline on terrasses along the cobblestone streets.

Bifteck. Throughout the 1990s this busy no-frills Plateau nightspot, the former workplace of Hole bassist and celebrated local luminary Melissa Auf der Maur, was the center of the indie music scene and a choice location for those looking to mingle with visiting rock stars. Although not quite as vibrant as it was in its heyday, the Bif, as it's often referred to, still packs 'em in most nights with a clientele comprised of beer-guzzling university students and local rock musicians. ✉*3702 blvd. St-Laurent, Plateau Mont-Royal* ☎*514/844–6211* Ⓜ*Sherbrooke or St-Laurent.*

Brutopia. Homemade concoctions like Raspberry Blond Beer, or the Scotch Ale attract locals and tourists alike. In addition to the unique brews, check out the sprawling outdoor seating, the art gallery on the third floor, and frequent live music. ✉*1215 rue Crescent, Downtown* ☎*514/393–9277* Ⓜ*Guy-Concordia.*

Bily Kun. A hipster fave tucked deep within the Plateau, Bily Kun serves up a mix of DJ-ed and live beats amid darkwood panels, taxidermic emus, and pseudo-intellectual chatter. ✉*354 av. du Mont-Royal, Plateau* ☎*514/845–5392* Ⓜ*Mont Royal.*

Bu. The hip wine bar, drenched in luscious green, offers over 500 types of wine and the melodious clang of trumpet jazz. ✉ *5245 blvd. St-Laurent, Mile-End* ☎ *514/276–0249* Ⓜ *Laurier.*

Café des Eclusiers. When spring rolls around there's no better place to get a tan and a buzz before dinner. Perched along the water in the picturesque Old Port district, it's no wonder that the lines are gruesome, in fact the ambience is so enjoyable that regulars easily forgive the use of plastic cups. ✉ *400 rue de la Commune, Ouest, Old Port* ☎ *514/496–0109* Ⓜ *Place d'Armes.*

Café Souvenir. Nestled among a row of street-side cafés, this gem has offbeat projections in the evenings and the menus are fashioned out of photo albums. ✉ *1261 rue Bernard Ouest, Outremont* ☎ *514/948–5259* Ⓜ *Outremont.*

Casa del Popolo. Undoubtedly one of the city's top venues for indie rock music, this scruffy bar is ideal if you want to hear up-and-coming local acts. Casa—as it's commonly known—also books out-of-town bands. While you enjoy the music, take a look at the original art and sample some of the tasty, reasonably priced grub. ✉ *4873 blvd. St-Laurent, Plateau Mont-Royal* ☎ *514/284–0122* Ⓜ *Mont-Royal.*

Foufounes Electriques. Foufs, as it's locally known, is the oldest alternative rock venue in the city, having played host to everyone from Nirvana to the Dickies. Enter under the googly eyes of an arachnoid creature and join the mishmash of leather and big hair—perhaps the only thing more bizarre is the name, which roughly translates to "electric buttocks." ✉ *87 rue Ste-Catherine Est, Downtown* ☎ *514/844–5539* Ⓜ *St-Laurent.*

Gogo Lounge. Funky, colorful decor and a retro-café feel attract twenty- and thirtysomethings to sip kitschy-named martinis like Hello Kitty, and Yellow Submarine. ✉ *3682 blvd. St-Laurent, Plateau Mont-Royal* ☎ *514/286–0882* Ⓜ *Sherbrooke.*

Hurley's Irish Pub. A sprawling Irish pub with dangling antique lamps and a stage for live music. Slink to the back and find the awesome stone cloister brimming with tiki torches and a private bar. ✉ *1225 rue Crescent, Downtown* ☎ *514/861–4111* Ⓜ *Guy-Concordia.*

Jello Bar. Lava lamps, love seats, more than 50 different martinis, a '60s feel, and assorted live music almost every night make this happenin' spot just that much more happenin'. They've perfected the classic martini. ✉ *151 rue Ontario Est, Quartier Latin* ☎ *514/285–9193* Ⓜ *Berri-UQAM.*

Mile-End Bar. Although the days as the toast of the town are somewhat fading, the Mile-End remains a favorite spot for lunchtime drinks and late-night romps under the lavish chandelier on the second floor. ✉ *5322 blvd. St-Laurent, Mile-End* ☎ *514/279–0200* Ⓜ *Laurier.*

Old Dublin. This lively and friendly Montréal institution located at the back of a parking lot offers live music every night of the week. The joint is surprisingly busy at lunch due to the tasty pub menu with the notable inclusion of a few first-rate Indian dishes. ✉ *1219A rue University, Downtown* ☎ *514/861–4448* Ⓜ *McGill.*

Peel Pub. Cheap pub grub and a wall full of televisions lure weary students for a rowdy time. Escape to the second-floor balcony for '80s beats and cheap drinks. ✉ *1196 rue Peel, Downtown* ☎ *514/844–7296* Ⓜ *Peel.*

Le Pistol. Packed with swarms of hipsters and McGill students, it's often impossible to get a seat on weekend nights thanks to the sophisticated yet unpretentious atmosphere. Catch the latest hockey game on one of the snazzy plasma TVs. ✉ *3723 blvd. St-Laurent, Mile-End* ☎ *514/847–2222* Ⓜ *Sherbrooke.*

Le Sainte-Elisabeth. Situated in one of the arguably seedier sections of the downtown core, a stone's throw from the heart of the city's traditional red-light district, the Sainte-Elisabeth retains one of the nicest backyard terraces in town. The service is friendly, a good selection of domestic and imported beers is yours to choose from, and the crowd is primarily comprised of French twentysomethings and students from the nearby UQAM campus. Great patio. ✉ *1412 rue Ste-Elisabeth, Downtown* ☎ *514/286–4302* Ⓜ *St-Laurent.*

Saint-Sulpice. The four-floor palace fits over 1,500 buzz-hungry visitors, and its usually at capacity due to the winning outdoor terrace considered to be the best in town. ✉ *1680 blvd. St-Denis, Village* ☎ *514/844–9458* Ⓜ *Berri-UQAM.*

Le Social. Set in an old manse, the stone turret, dark-wood paneling, and Gothic stained-glass window make this house of hooch a new favorite among young professionals seeking classier digs. ✉ *1445 rue Bishop, Downtown* ☎ *514/849–8585* Ⓜ *Guy-Concordia.*

Stogie's Lounge. If the surprisingly swish interior and views of rue Crescent below aren't reason enough to swing by, then check out the conspicuous glass humidor housing a seemingly infinite supply of imported cigars. ✉ *2015 rue Crescent, Downtown* ☎ *514/848–0069* Ⓜ *Guy-Concordia.*

Suite 701. Come drop the big bucks with sundry young professionals who slide through the enormous glass doors for handcrafted cocktails. ✉ *701 Côte de la Place d'Armes, Old Port* ☎ *514/904–1201* Ⓜ *Place-d'Armes.*

Vol de Nuit. A premier watering hole for McGill students, the best thing about Vol de Nuit, besides the continuous two-for-one drink special, is their large terrace on the Prince Arthur street pedestrian mall. Come the warm weather, this is one of the best people-watching terraces in the city—if you're lucky enough to find a vacant seat. ✉ *14 rue Prince Arthur Est, Plateau Mont-Royal* ☎ *514/845–6253* Ⓜ *Sherbrooke.*

Whiskey Café. Sip one of the 70 kinds of Scotch at the granite countertop and absorb the decidedly adult atmosphere amid imported artifacts like a stone Romanesque horse head. ✉ *5800 blvd. St-Laurent, Plateau Mont-Royal* ☎ *514/278–2646* Ⓜ *Rosemont.*

Winnie. Relax among a sea of red-leather chairs and enjoy the second floor's old-school redbrick interior. Note the obligatory portrait of Sir Winston Churchill, for whom the bar is named. ✉ *1455 rue Crescent, Downtown* ☎ *514/288–3814* Ⓜ *Guy-Concordia.*

Wunderbar. The place is so small it can barely fit the bouncer's ego; however, it's one of the premier haunts in town, with seductive black walls that are shinier than a hooker's boots. ✉ *901 Square Victoria, Old Port* ☎ *514/395–3190* Ⓜ *Square-Victoria.*

SUPPERCLUBS

Over the last few years, a sleek hybrid has evolved known as the supperclub (also known as a resto-bar): a savvy combustion of gourmet recipes, trendy decor, and designer cocktails.

Buenanotte. A pleasure-plex meticulously engineered to delight the senses: gourmet food, extensive wine bar, trippy beats, and smooth decor. This primo resto-bar has lured myriad celebs from George Clooney to Giselle. ⊠*3518 blvd. St-Laurent, Mile End* ☎*514/276–0249* Ⓜ*Mont-Royal.*

Cavalli. Join the resto-bar's purple haze of urban socialites and dripping chandeliers for avant-garde cuisine or after-dinner drinks. Thursdays are particularly packed with the see-and-be-seen types. ⊠*2040 rue Peel, Downtown* ☎*514/843–5100* Ⓜ*Peel.*

Garde Manger. The heart of the Old Port beats anew with the outpost of haute cuisine at Garde Manger. Although the name refers to the pre-revolutionary French tradition of preparing and presenting cold foods, customers will enjoy subtle twists on traditional fare, making the entire dining experience decidedly avant-garde. ⊠*408 rue Saint-Francois Xavier, Old Port* ☎*514/678–5044* Ⓜ*Place-d'Armes.*

Newtown. The tri-level supper club, named for Formula 1 racer Jacques Villeneuve, is easy on the eyes and ears. Super-sleek window treatments, and a smooth wooden interior have converted this older mansion into one of the chicest spots in town. Reserve early for the private tables outside on the terrace.

Pub St. James. This popular hangout in the Old Port strikes an elegant balance between modern austerity and traditional Victorian design. ⊠*380 rue St-Jacques Ouest, Old Port* ☎*514/849–6978* Ⓜ*Square-Victoria.*

Time Supper Club. Timeless Time Supper Club offers dining and dancing in equal measure. Tasty French favorites are matched with a wide selection of wines from the cellar, and the swish art deco atmosphere transports socialites back to the '40s. ⊠*997 St-Jacques, Old Port* ☎*514/392–9292* Ⓜ*Bonaventure.*

NIGHTCLUBS

Clubbing is, to say the least, huge in Montréal. Back at the height of the disco era in the 1970s, Montréal was considered one of the top five cities in the world for both the trendsetting dance music it produced, and also for the sheer volume of discotheques found around town. The legacy continues today, with an impressive armada of local DJs and frequent visits from artists on the international circuit. The demand for dance venues has increased so much in the last few years that restaurants are installing discotheques in their basements. Club covers can range from $5 to $25, depending on the night of the week and the notoriety of the DJ.

Aria. Take a disco nap in the afternoon because it's worth staying up late to check out Montréal's most established after-hours club, which caters to an urban crowd with local and international DJs. Doors open at 1:30 AM on weekends. ⊠*1280 rue St-Denis, Quartier Latin* ☎*514/987–6712* Ⓜ*Berri-UQAM.*

Cactus. Thursday through Saturday, the dance floor is always packed with patrons enjoying the rigorously authentic Latin music. ✉4461 rue St-Denis, Plateau Mont-Royal ☎514/849–0349 Ⓜ Mont-Royal.

Coda. A favorite among hipster locals (membership fees are a mere $25), slick Coda is the perfect way to end the evening. ✉4119 rue St-Laurent, St-Laurent ☎No phone Ⓜ St-Laurent.

Club 737. A sweeping panoramic view and a rooftop terrace are two of the outstanding features of this multilevel dance club. It also does the weekend disco thing and is very popular with the mid-twenties to mid-thirties office crowd. ✉1 pl. Ville-Marie, Downtown ☎514/397–0737 Ⓜ Bonaventure.

Club Exit. This lively Plateau dance hall is a temple for hip-hop worshippers. ✉3553 blvd. St-Laurent, Plateau Mont-Royal ☎514/285–2223 Ⓜ Sherbrooke or St-Laurent.

Electric Avenue. Where the DJs are unapologetically nostalgic for the 1980s and the clientele bops amid pulsing post-modern cubes. Open Thursday to Saturday from 10 PM until last call. ✉1469 rue Crescent, Downtown ☎514/285–8885 Ⓜ Guy-Concordia. ✉2145 rue Crescent, Downtown ☎514/284–9119 Ⓜ Guy-Concordia.

Opera. Bump and grind in this extensive club to a healthy mix of live music and DJs. It's a great place to get down on Sunday nights. ✉32 rue Ste-Catherine Ouest, Ville-Marie ☎514/842–2836 Ⓜ St-Laurent.

Playhouse. This former strip club in Mile-End is now a stage-centric cabaret featuring a steady diet of local indie bands. Despite the change in entertainment policy, Playhouse still manages to maintain that strip-club vibe—in a good way, of course. ✉5656 av. du Parc, Mile-End ☎514/276–0594 Ⓜ Laurier.

Salsathèque. If you can get past the blinking lights at the entrance without having a seizure, you'll find a kitschy Latin paradise decked with beach paraphernalia. Check out the old-school salsa competitions on Friday nights, or enjoy raggaeton, Latin, and Top 40 beats on other evenings. ✉1220 rue Peel, Downtown ☎514/875–0016 Ⓜ Peel.

Saphir. Offering an eclectic cross section of underground subcultures and music, Saphir's first floor leans more towards goth, punk, and glam, while upstairs the sounds are urban and electronica. Drinks are cheap, and the clientele relatively unassuming. ✉3699 blvd. St-Laurent, Plateau Mont-Royal ☎514/284–5093 Ⓜ Sherbrooke or St-Laurent.

Thursdays/Les Beaux Jeudis. This massive venue is reminiscent of '80s Vegas, with hotel carpet patterns, vested security guards, slot machines, and a bumping discotheque. Thursday evenings are swamped (surprise) with an older crowd: think Grey Goose and grey hair. ✉1449 rue Crescent, Downtown ☎514/288–5656 Ⓜ Guy-Concordia.

Tokyo Bar. A traditional Montréal discotheque located in the heart of the action: the music is loud, pumping, and either house, hip-hop, disco, or '80s retro, depending on the night. If the music gets too loud, head up to the rooftop terrace and watch the gong show down below on colorful boulevard St-Laurent. ✉3709 blvd. St-Laurent, Plateau Mont-Royal ☎514/842–6838 Ⓜ St-Laurent.

Tribe Hyperclub. Tribe is as alluring as it is pretentious. Once you've passed the choosy bouncers, settle in for an evening of space-age furniture and well-dressed socialite wannabes. ✉ *1445 rue Bishop, Downtown* ☎ *514/849–8585* Ⓜ *Guy-Concordia.*

GAY & LESBIAN NIGHTLIFE

The Scissor Sisters' anthem "Filthy Gorgeous" pretty much defines this section of town. Colorful drag theatres, brilliant discotheques, and steaming bathhouses fill up the one-time warehouses around the Beaudry Métro station. Gay or straight, a night in the "Gay Village" will surely be a memorable one. *Fugues* (☎ *514/848–1854* ⊕ *www. fugues.com*) is a gay publication written mostly in French that is geared toward news and events in Québec (the Web site offers English translation). All of the clubs with dance floors charge a cover fee ranging from $5 to $25, depending on the night of the week and the notoriety of the DJ.

Agora. An intimate and casual gay and lesbian hangout in the middle of downtown, Agora is usually quiet and perfect for intimate conversation—apart, of course, from Saturday karaoke nights. ✉ *1160 rue Mackay, Downtown* ☎ *514/934–1428* Ⓜ *Guy-Concordia.*

Cabaret Mado. Pass Madame Simone and her drag-tastic hats to enter the quirky cabaret-theme club where drag queen extraordinaire Mado holds court and encourages patrons to get involved in the weekly karaoke and improv nights. ✉ *1115 rue Ste-Catherine Est, Village* ☎ *514/525–7566* ⊕ *www.mado.qc.ca* Ⓜ *Beaudry.*

Club Bolo. Country-and-western dancing and ambience attract both men and women to this Village club staffed partly by country-lovin' volunteers. ✉ *960 rue Amherst, Village* ☎ *514/849–4777* Ⓜ *Berri-UQAM.*

Club Date Piano Bar. Think Billy Joel plus Elton John—Club Date caters to a mixed clientele and has karaoke competitions almost every night. ✉ *1218 rue Ste-Catherine Est, Village* ☎ *514/521–1242* Ⓜ *Beaudry.*

Club Parking. In the heart of the Village, Parking serves an interesting mix of older guys and young hipsters. The vast dance floor, equipped with giant orbiting disco balls, hosts some of the best (and sweatiest) parties. The upstairs bar, where the music is mostly from the '80s, has a reputation for being one of the best meeting spots in town. ✉ *1296 rue Amherst, Village* ☎ *514/282–1199* Ⓜ *Beaudry.*

Club Sandwich. This epic café is open 24 hours and makes a perfect place to re-juice at the end of a nightlong clubbing adventure. ✉ *1578 rue Ste-Catherine, Village* ☎ *514/523–4679* Ⓜ *Beaudry.*

Club Unity. Unity is the third avatar in this location (note the flame-like lettering in the signage paying homage to Unity 2, which was tragically incinerated). Small, semiprivate lounges are scattered throughout the two-story complex, and the beautiful rooftop terrace is one of the finest in the Gay Village. ✉ *1171 rue Ste-Catherine Est, Village* ☎ *514/523–2777* Ⓜ *Beaudry or Berri-UQAM.*

Le Drugstore. This mammoth warehouse, featuring numerous dance floors, lounges, and billiards, has become an institution of the city's gay scene and a veritable treasure trove of random urban artifacts like vintage subway signs and stop lights. Although the factory-like complex teems with crowds of all kinds, it's most popular with lesbians. ✉ *1360 rue Ste-Catherine Est, Village* ☎ *514/524–1960* Ⓜ *Beaudry.*

Sky Pub/Sky Club. This Sky complex is one of the most popular places for the twentysomething gay population. The dance floor on the second level is the fave, although the pièce de résistance is the beachlike roof deck with city views and a hot tub. Other features include a bar and stage on the ground level, and a smaller dance floor on the third story with grind-friendly beats. ⊠*1474 rue Ste-Catherine Est, Village* ☎*514/529–6969* Ⓜ*Beaudry.*

Stereo. Some of the most beautiful cross-dressers in the city gather here to bust a move on the huge dance floor of this converted theater. It's popular with both men and women. Things get started late, so don't even bother arriving before midnight. ⊠*858 rue Ste-Catherine Est, Village* ☎*514/286–0325* Ⓜ*Beaudry or Berri-UQAM.*

Le Stud. Le Stud is loud, leather-filled, and legendary as a men-only hangout that's open until the wee hours. ⊠*1812 rue Ste-Catherine Est, Village* ☎*514/598–8243* Ⓜ*Papineau.*

LIVE MUSIC

Barfly. Fans of blues, punk rock, country, and bluegrass jam into this tiny but tasteful hole-in-the-wall with some of the cheapest drink prices to be found anywhere on the Main (St-Laurent). ⊠*4062A blvd. St-Laurent, Plateau Mont-Royal* ☎*514/284–6665* Ⓜ*Sherbrooke.*

Club Soda. The granddaddy of city rock clubs, Club Soda is a tall, narrow concert hall with high-tech design and 500 seats—all of them good. The club is open only for shows; phone the box office to find out what's playing. ⊠*1225 blvd. St-Laurent, Downtown* ☎*514/286–1010 Ext. 200* ⊕*www.clubsoda.ca* Ⓜ*St-Laurent.*

House of Jazz. This is a great spot to catch live performances and chow down on some tasty ribs and chicken, too. ⊠*2060 rue Aylmer, Downtown* ☎*514/842–8656* Ⓜ*McGill.*

McKibbin's Irish Pub. A giant Irish flag on the facade warmly welcomes thirsty patrons for pints of beer and non-stop live music from Celtic fiddlers to Clapton cover bands. ⊠*1426 rue Bishop, Downtown* ☎*514/288–1580* Ⓜ*Guy-Concordia.*

Upstairs Jazz Club. Local and imported jazz musicians take the stage seven nights a week and for frequent jam sessions. ⊠*1254 rue Mackay, Downtown* ☎*514/931–6808* ⊕*www.upstairsjazz.com* Ⓜ*Guy-Concordia.*

Yellow Door. A Montréal folk-music institution since the 1960s and Canada's longest-running coffeehouse, the Yellow Door is an alcohol-free basement club in the heart of the McGill University student ghetto. It is a showcase for both local and international folk-music acts. ⊠*3625 rue Aylmer, Downtown* ☎*514/398–6243* Ⓜ*McGill.*

COMEDY

The Montréal Just For Laughs comedy festival, which takes place every July, has been the largest such festival in the world since its inception back in 1983. But Montrealers don't have to wait until summer every year to get their comedy fix, as there are several downtown clubs catering exclusively to all things funny.

Comedy Nest. This modest, unassuming club hosts established Canadian and international comedians, but is also an excellent spot to catch some of the city's funniest up-and-comers. Dinner-and-show packages are available. ✉ *Pepsi Forum, 2313 rue Ste-Catherine Ouest, 3rd fl., Downtown* ☎ *514/932–6378* ⊕ *www.thecomedynest.com* Ⓜ *Atwater.*

Comedyworks. Comedyworks is a popular room at the back of an Irish pub that books both amateur and established comics and has a reputation for offering fairly risqué fare on occasion. ✉ *1238 rue Bishop, Downtown* ☎ *514/398–9661* ⊕ *www.comedyworks.com* Ⓜ *Guy-Concordia.*

CASINO

Although there are several casinos within striking distance of Montréal, the most popular local gaming institution by far is le Casino de Montréal, which is conveniently located on Île Notre-Dame, only a few minutes by car, bicycle, or Métro from the city's downtown core.

Casino de Montréal. One of the world's largest gaming rooms, the casino has more than 3,000 slot machines and 120 tables for baccarat, craps, blackjack, and roulette. There are some quirks for those used to Vegas-style gambling: no drinking on the floor, and no tipping the croupiers. Winners may want to spend some of their gains at Nuances or one of the casino's three other restaurants. The Cabaret de Casino offers some of the best shows in town. To get to the casino, which is open around the clock, you can take a C$10 cab ride from downtown, drive (parking is free), or take the Métro to the Jean-Drapeau station and then board Bus 167, which will deliver you right to the doorstep. ✉ *1 av. du Casino, Île Notre-Dame* ☎ *514/392–2746 or 800/665–2274* ⊕ *www. casino-de-montreal.com* Ⓜ *Jean-Drapeau.*

THE ARTS

It's hardly surprising that North America's largest French-speaking metropolis should be the continent's capital of French theater. Montréal is the home of nearly a dozen professional companies and several important theater schools. But the city also has a lively English-language theater scene and one of the few Yiddish theaters in North America. Add a couple of world-renowned orchestras and some bold dance companies to the mix, and you have a rich cultural stew that has something to appeal to everyone.

CIRCUS

Fodor'sChoice **Cirque du Soleil.** This amazing circus is one of Montréal's great success stories. The company—founded in 1984 by a pair of street Z performers—has revolutionized the ancient art of circus. Its shows, now an international phenomenon, use no lions, tigers, or animals of any kind. Instead, colorful acrobatics flirt with the absurd through the use of music, humor, dance, and glorious (and often risqué) costumes. The cirque has four resident companies in Las Vegas, one in Orlando, but none in Montréal. However, every couple of years—usually odd-numbered ones—one of its international touring companies returns to where it all began, the Vieux-Port, and sets up the familiar blue-

and-yellow tent for a summer of sold-out shows. ☎*514/790–1245 or 800/361–4595* ⊕*www.cirquedusoleil.com.*

CLASSICAL MUSIC

For a city its size, there are a remarkable number of opportunities for fans of classical music to get their fill in Montréal. The Orchestre Métropolitain du Grand Montréal, or the MSO (Montréal Symphony Orchestra) as it's known in the Anglophone community, is undoubtedly the best-known local orchestra on the international stage, but if the opportunity presents itself, classical music enthusiasts would be wise to check out the McGill Chamber Orchestra, which generally performs at the architecturally stunning and acoustically perfect Pollack Concert Hall on McGill University's downtown campus.

★ **I Musici de Montréal.** Arguably the best chamber orchestra in Canada, I Musici, under the direction of Yuli Turovsky, performs at Place des Arts and Pollack Hall, but its music is best suited to Tudor Hall atop the Ogilvy department store. ✉*934 rue Ste-Catherine Est* ☎*514/982–6037, tickets 514/982–6038* ⊕*www.imusici.com.*

Orchestre Métropolitain du Grand Montréal. During their regular season, October–April, the Orchestre Métropolitain performs at Place des Arts with a focus on the promotion of Canadian talent. ✉*486 rue Ste-Catherine Ouest* ☎*514/598–0870* ⊕*www.orchestremetropolitain.com.*

FodorśChoice **Orchestre Symphonique de Montréal.** When not on tour or in the recording studio, Montréal's internationally renowned symphony orchestra plays at the Salle Wilfrid-Pelletier at Place des Arts. The orchestra also gives holiday and summer concerts in Basilique Notre-Dame-de-Montréal and pop concerts at the Arena Maurice Richard, which is part of the Stade Olympique. For their free summertime concerts, check the *Gazette* listings. ☎*514/842–9951* ⊕*www.osm.ca.*

Pollack Concert Hall. McGill University's concert hall presents concerts not only by **I Musici** but also by the **McGill Chamber Orchestra**, the **Montréal Chamber Orchestra**, and the **Société de Musique Contemporaine.** ✉*555 rue Sherbrooke Ouest, Square Mile* ☎*514/398–4547* Ⓜ*McGill.*

Spectrum. The Spectrum is a large yet intimate concert hall that primarily books contemporary bands but also serves as a select performance spot during the Jazz Festival and Montréal's FrancoFolies. ✉*318 rue Ste-Catherine Ouest, Downtown* ☎*514/861–5851* ⊕*www.spectrumdemontreal.ca* Ⓜ*St-Laurent.*

Théâtre St-Denis. The 2,500-seat, second-largest auditorium in Montréal (after Salle Wilfrid-Pelletier in Place des Arts), stages a wide range of pop-music concerts performed in English and French, including recent performances by Elvis Costello, folk singer Rita MacNeil, and Québécois rock icon Dan Bigras. ✉*1594 rue St-Denis, Quartier Latin* ☎*514/849–4211* ⊕*www.theatrestdenis.com* Ⓜ*Berri-UQAM.*

DANCE

Traditional and contemporary dance companies thrive in Montréal, though many take to the road or are on hiatus in summer.

Agora de la Danse. This important downtown performance and rehearsal space is affiliated with the Université du Québec à Montréal dance faculty. ✉ *840 rue Cherrier Est, Downtown* ☎ *514/525–1500* ⊕ *www. agoradanse.com* Ⓜ *Sherbrooke.*

Les Ballets Jazz de Montréal. Les Ballets Jazz has done much to popularize modern dance through its free performances at the open-air Théâtre de Verdure in Parc Lafontaine. Performances are also held at Place des Arts and Agora de la Danse. ☎ *514/982–6771* ⊕ *www.bjmdanse.ca.*

Fondation de Danse Margie Gillis. Margie Gillis, one of Canada's most exciting and innovative soloists, works with her own company and guest artists to stage performances at Place des Arts, Agora de la Danse, and other area venues. ☎ *514/845–3115* ⊕ *www.margiegillis.org.*

Les Grands Ballets Canadiens. Québec's premier ballet company performs at Place des Arts. Its seasonal offerings mix such classics as *Romeo and Juliet* and *The Nutcracker* with more contemporary fare. The company also hosts performances by visiting international troupes. ☎ *514/849– 8681* ⊕ *www.grandsballets.qc.ca.*

LaLaLa Human Steps. Casablanca-born choreographer Édouard Lock founded LaLaLa to explore the boundaries of modern dance. The popular troupe has a heavy international schedule, but also performs at Place des Arts and at Montréal festivals. ☎ *514/277–9090* ⊕ *www. lalalahumansteps.com.*

Montréal Danse. Lavish sets and dazzlingly sensual choreography have helped make Montréal Danse one of Canada's most popular contemporary repertory companies. They have a busy touring schedule, but also regularly perform at Place des Arts, Agora de la Danse, Théâtre de Verdure, and elsewhere. ☎ *514/871–4005* ⊕ *www.montrealdanse.com.*

O Vertigo. O Vertigo stages innovative, contemporary performances. ☎ *514/251–9177* ⊕ *www.overtigo.com.*

Place des Arts. Montréal's main concert facility acts as a favorite venue for visiting large-scale productions. ✉ *175 rue Ste-Catherine Ouest, Downtown* ☎ *514/842–2112* ⊕ *www.pda.qc.ca* Ⓜ *Place-des-Arts.*

Tangente. Between September and June, Tangente holds weekly performances of experimental dance at Agora de la Danse. Tangente also acts as an archive for contemporary dance and experimental performance art and fosters national and international exchanges. ☎ *514/525–5584* ⊕ *www.tangente.qc.ca.*

FILM

Although many of the cinemas that once lined rue Ste-Catherine have closed down in recent years to make way for new, stadium-seating megaplexes like the AMC Forum 22, Montrealers remain uniquely privileged in the variety of cinema-going experiences available. Ranging from the ultramodern, uber-hip, Ex-Centris theater on the Main to the gorgeous art deco confines of the majestic Imperial theater on Bleury Street downtown, various venues offer locals the opportunity to enjoy the numerous domestic productions released each year by the province's thriving French-language film industry in addition to the standard Hollywood fare consistently shown at the megaplexes.

AMC Forum 22. Once the home ice of the Montréal Canadiens, the AMC Forum's 22 screens feature plenty of Hollywood biggies, but often host foreign-language and independent productions as well. The complex includes several restaurants and coffee shops, a bar, a poolroom, and a gift shop. ✉ *2313 rue Ste-Catherine Ouest, Downtown* ☎ *514/904–1274* Ⓜ *Atwater.*

Cinémathèque Québécoise. Montréal's Museum of the Moving Image has a collection of 28,000 Québécois, Canadian, and foreign films, as well as a display of equipment dating from the early days of cinema. ✉ *335 blvd. de Maisonneuve Est, Quartier Latin* ☎ *514/842–9763* ⊕ *www.cinematheque.qc.ca* Ⓜ *Berri-UQAM.*

CinéRobothèque. Cinephiles can use a robot to help them browse through the National Film Board of Canada's collection of 8,200 documentaries, dramas, short features, and animated flicks. ✉ *1564 rue St-Denis, Quartier Latin* ☎ *514/496–6887* ⊕ *www.nfb.ca/cine robotheque* Ⓜ *Berri-UQAM.*

Ex-Centris. Cinema buffs looking for the best in independent productions—both Canadian and foreign—head for Ex-Centris. A pleasant 15-minute walk from the Mont-Royal Métro station, it's worth a visit if only to see the huge rotating clock in the lobby and its bathrooms with their reflective metal walls. Its three comfortable theaters are equipped to screen digital works. ✉ *3536 blvd. St-Laurent, Plateau Mont-Royal* ☎ *514/847–2206* ⊕ *www.ex-centris.com* Ⓜ *Sherbrooke.*

Famous Players Paramount. This major theater complex has two IMAX theaters in addition to 15 regular screens—all showing the latest Hollywood blockbusters. ✉ *707 rue Ste-Catherine Ouest, Downtown* ☎ *514/842–5828* ⊕ *www.famousplayers.com* Ⓜ *Peel.*

Grande Bibliothèque. Montréal's new library has 18 screening stations where you can view some of the 1,000 films in its collection. ✉ *475 blvd. de Maisonneuve Est, Quartier Latin* ☎ *514/873–1100* ⊕ *www.banq.qc.ca* Ⓜ *Berri-UQAM.*

Impérial. Since being renovated in 2002, the sumptuous decor dating back to the golden age of cinema has been retained at Montréal's oldest and most distinguished movie theater. It currently screens foreign and independent productions. ✉ *1432 rue Bleury, Downtown* ☎ *514/848–0300* Ⓜ *Place-des-Arts.*

OPERA

Although the genre doesn't generally attract the same size crowds as, say, the Montréal Symphony Orchestra, local opera buffs will tell you that the quality of productions the one major opera company in town presents each year is second to none.

L'Opéra de Montréal. L'Opéra de Montréal stages five productions a year at Place des Arts and features opera workshops as well as an annual benefit performance. ☎ *514/985–2258* ⊕ *www.operademontreal.com.*

THEATER

There are at least 10 major French-language theater companies in town, some of which enjoy international reputations. The choices for Anglophones are more limited.

★ **Centaur Theatre.** Montréal's best-known English-language theater company stages everything from frothy musical revues to serious works by Eugène Ionesco, and prominently features works by local playwrights. Its home is in the former stock-exchange building in Vieux-Montréal. ✉*453 rue St-François-Xavier, Vieux-Montréal* ☎*514/288–3161 or 514/288–1229* ⊕*www.centaurtheatre.com* Ⓜ*Place-d'Armes.*

Leanor and Alvin Segal Theatre. English-language classics like *The Odd Couple* or *The Diary of Anne Frank* can be seen at this center for the arts both for Montréal as a whole and for the Jewish community in particular. ✉*5170 chemin de la Côte Ste-Catherine, Côte-des-Neiges* ☎*514/739–2301 or 514/739–7944* ⊕*www.saidyebronfman. org* Ⓜ*Côte-Ste-Catherine.*

Mainline Theater. Operated by the same people who present the Montréal Fringe Festival every summer, the Mainline opened in early 2006 to serve the city's burgeoning Anglo theater community and has been going strong ever since. ✉*3997 St-Laurent, Plateau Mont-Royal* ☎*514/849–3378* ⊕*www.montrealfringe.ca* Ⓜ*St-Laurent.*

Monument-National. The highly regarded National Theatre School of Canada—or the École Nationale de Théâtre du Canada—supplies world stages with a steady stream of well-trained actors and directors. It works and performs in the historic and glorious old theater that has played host to such luminaries as Edith Piaf and Emma Albani. (Québec's first feminist rallies in the early 1900s also took place here.) Graduating classes perform professional-level plays in both French and English. The theater also plays host to an assortment of touring plays, musicals, and concerts. ✉*1182 blvd. St-Laurent, Downtown* ☎*514/871–2224 or 800/361–4595* ⊕*www.monument-national.qc.ca* Ⓜ*St-Laurent.*

Théâtre Denise Pelletier. The Pelletier, with an objective to introduce younger audiences to theater, puts on French-language productions in a beautifully restored Italianate hall. It's a 15-minute walk from the Métro station. ✉*4353 rue Ste-Catherine Est, Hochelaga-Maisonneuve* ☎*514/253–8974* ⊕*www.denise-pelletier.qc.ca* Ⓜ*Joliette.*

Théâtre Outremont. Inaugurated in 1929, the theatre rapidly became a local favorite, and had its heyday in the '70s before it fell into disarray. After reopening its doors in the early '90s, the theatre has regained much of its steam, offering mostly threatre and live music acts. ✉*1248 av. Bernard, Outremont* ☎*514/495–9944* ⊕*www.theatreoutremont. ca* Ⓜ*Outremont.*

Théâtre de Quat'Sous. This cerebral theater puts on modern and experimental plays in French. ✉*100 av. des Pins Est, Downtown* ☎*514/845–7277* ⊕*www.quatsous.com* Ⓜ*Sherbrooke.*

Fodor'sChoice **Théâtre du Nouveau Monde.** In this North American temple of French ★ and stage classics, a season's offerings can include works by locals Michel Tremblay and Robert Lepage as well as works by Shakespeare, Molière, Camus, Ibsen, Chekhov, and Arthur Miller. ✉*84 rue Ste-Catherine Ouest, Downtown* ☎*514/866–8667* ⊕*www.tnm. qc.ca* Ⓜ*St-Laurent.*

Théâtre du Rideau Vert. A modern French repertoire is the specialty at this theater. ✉*4664 rue St-Denis, Plateau Mont-Royal* ☎*514/844–1793* ⊕*www.rideauvert.qc.ca* Ⓜ*Mont-Royal.*

Théâtre Jean Duceppe. Named for one of Québec's most beloved actors, this theater makes its home in the smallest and most intimate of the four auditoriums in Place des Arts. It stages major French-language productions and is currently celebrating its 35th season. ✉*175 rue Ste-Catherine Ouest, Downtown* ☎*514/842–2112* ⊕*www.duceppe. com* Ⓜ*Place-des-Arts.*

Théâtre St-Denis. Touring Broadway productions can often be seen, especially in summer, at this multipurpose theater. ✉*1594 rue St-Denis, Quartier Latin* ☎*514/849–4211* Ⓜ*Berri-UQAM.*

Shopping

Market Shopping, Montréal.

WORD OF MOUTH

"Montréal is a shopping mecca, and the best place is in the down-town core. Along Ste. Catherine street you'll find several shopping complexes and tons of smaller unique stores to suit your taste...whatever it may be!"

—aucho53

SHOPPING PLANNER

Hours

Most shops open by 10 am Monday to Saturday and close at 6 PM Monday to Wednesday. Stores stay open until 9 PM on Thursday and Friday, while Saturday has an early close of 5 PM. On Sunday, most downtown shops open noon to 5 PM. Exceptions abound, however. Large chain stores in the downtown core often stay open weeknights until 9. They're joined by many retailers in Le Plateau and Vieux-Montréal in the summer.

The Tax Bite

When the Canadian dollar drops in value against the greenback, U.S. visitors to Canada are in bargain heaven, despite hefty tax rates. You must pay 5 percent in federal tax, called the GST, and another 7.5 percent in Québec tax on most goods and services. Still, even when the Canuck buck trades at par, there are deals on certain homegrown items: furs, fast fashion from local chains, and crafty goods that reflect Montréal's funky side.

Frugal, Funky, or Luxe?

The frugal fashionista will head downtown for fabulous pickings unique to Montréal.

First stop: Simons department store for cheap chic for everyone from teenyboppers to madames on a budget to cool dudes with attitude. Along rue Ste-Catherine and in the underground malls, check out trendy Québécois fashion emporiums including Le Château, Bedo, and Jacob. H&M, Zara, and Mango are also on the path of the penny pincher.

Funky fashionistas will want to hit Mile End and Le Plateau. In Mile End, hipster territory includes General 54, Pre-loved, and Maskarad, with crafty or recycled fashions. Moving down Montréal's beloved Main—Boulevard St-Laurent—check out vintage, decor and design shops. Closer to downtown, Lola & Emily, Scandale, and M0851 are worth the walk. More unique, independent shops line l'avenue Mont-Royal and rue St-Denis.

Montréal's luxury lane runs from Ogilvy up to Holt Renfrew along rue de la Montagne, with designer fashion from Marie Saint Pierre and Andy Thê-Anh lining the route.

The path of luxury continues west along rue Sherbrooke, where you'll find la crème de la crème of international fashion, shoes and lingerie, with shops like Les Créateurs, Mona Moore, and Josephine.

For Foodies Only

If food is your first love, head to Montréal's markets, especially in the bountiful days of the autumn harvest.

Marché Jean-Talon in the north end of the city has an Italian flavor; the surrounding streets are home to some of the finest pizza and café latte anywhere.

Marché Atwater has a glorious indoor hall, packed with eateries, butchers, the marvelous Première Moisson bakery and fine food emporiums.

Updated by
Eva Friede

MONTREALERS *MAGASINENT* **(SHOP) WITH A VENGEANCE,** so it's no surprise that the city has 160 multifaceted retail areas encompassing more than 7,000 stores. The law allows shops to stay open weekdays 9–9 and weekends 9–5. However, many merchants close evenings at 6 Monday through Wednesday; a few close on Sunday. Many hair salons and other service shops close Monday as well. Just about all stores accept major credit cards. Most purchases are subject to a federal goods-and-services tax (GST) of 5% as well as a provincial tax of 7.5%.

This city is one of the fur capitals of the world. If you think you might be buying fur, check with your country's customs officials to find out which animals are considered endangered and cannot be imported. The same caveat applies to Inuit ivory carvings, which cannot be imported into the United States or other countries. If you do buy Inuit art, look for the government of Canada's igloo symbol, which attests to the piece's authenticity.

4

SHOPPING DISTRICTS

Fodor'sChoice
★ **Avenue Laurier Ouest.** Shops and boutiques along the eight blocks between boulevard St-Laurent and chemin de la Côte-Ste-Catherine sell high-end fashions, home furnishings, decorative items, artwork, books, kitchenware, toys and children's items, and gourmet food. There are plenty of restaurants, bars, and cafés in which to rest your feet and check your purchases. The street is about a 15-minute walk from the Laurier Métro station.

★ **Boulevard St-Laurent.** Affectionately known as the Main, St-Laurent has restaurants, boutiques, and nightclubs that cater mostly to an upscale clientele. Still, the area has managed to retain its working-class immigrant roots and vitality to some degree: high-fashion shops are interspersed with ethnic-food stores, secondhand bookshops, and hardware stores. Indeed, a trip up this street takes you from Chinatown to Little Italy. Shoppers flock to the two blocks of avenue Mont-Royal just east of boulevard St-Laurent for secondhand clothing. The street is a 10-minute walk west of the Mont-Royal Métro station. Or you can work your way north from the St-Laurent Métro, taking in the hippest bars and boutiques near Sherbrooke Street West.

Downtown. Montréal's largest retail district takes in rues Sherbrooke and Ste-Catherine, boulevard de Maisonneuve, and the side streets between them. Because of the proximity and diversity of the stores, it's the best shopping bet if you're in town overnight or for a weekend. The area bounded by rues Sherbrooke, Ste-Catherine, de la Montagne, and Crescent has antiques and art galleries in addition to designer salons. Fashion boutiques and art and antiques galleries line rue Sherbrooke. Rue Crescent holds a tempting blend of antiques, fashions, and jewelry displayed beneath colorful awnings. De la Montagne is the corridor of chic, between the high-end Holt Renfrew and Ogilvy department stores, with designer boutiques—including top Québec labels—en route. Rue Ste-Catherine is the main shopping thoroughfare, with most of the chain stores and department stores. To get here, take the Métro to the Peel, McGill, or Guy-Concordia station.

RUE CHABANEL
The garment district, good for inexpensive clothes, leather & linens

OUTREMONT

MILE-END

AVENUE LAURIER OUEST
Eight blocks of fashion, furnishings & gourmet food

THE PLATEAU

BOULEVARD ST-LAURENT
Upscale boutiques, funky eateries, second-hand stores

Parc Lafontaine

ch. de la Côte-Ste-Catherine

Cimetière Mont-Royal

av. du Parc

Voie C. Houde

r. Sherbrooke

Chemin Remembrance

Parc du Mont-Royal

r. Ste-Catherine

r. Notre-Dame

RUE AMHERST
Pricy antiques unlimited

av. Cedar

av. Docteur-Penfield

r. Sherbrooke

DOWNTOWN
Department stores and chains glore

av. Viger

Île Ste-Hélèn

r. Ste-Catherine

autoroute Ville-Marie

Pont de la Concorde

VIEUX-MONTRÉAL
Quirky shops and souvenirs

av. Pierre-Dupuy

Parc Jean-Drapeau

r. Notre-Dame

VICTORIA VILLAGE
Stylish independent boutiques along leafy, pretty streets

Lachine Canal

r. St-Patrick

Fleuve Saint-Laurent

P Flo

Notr Dam

RUE NOTRE-DAME OUEST
A sweet spot for eating & antiquing

Pont Victoria

autoroute Bonaventure

0   1/2 mile

0   500 meters

Rue Amherst. Antiques shops began springing up in the Gay Village in the early 1990s, most of them on rue Amherst between rues Ste-Catherine and Ontario. The area used to be less expensive than rue Notre-Dame, but it's not always the case these days. Use the Beaudry Métro station.

Rue Chabanel. The eight-block stretch of Chabanel just west of boulevard St-Laurent is the heart of the city's garment district. The goods seem to get more stylish and more expensive the farther west you go. For really inexpensive leather goods, sportswear, children's togs, and linens, try the shops at 99 rue Chabanel. Many of the city's furriers have also moved into the area. A few places on Chabanel accept credit cards, but bring cash anyway. If you pay in cash, the price will often include the tax. From the Crémazie Métro station, take Bus 53 north.

Rue Notre-Dame Ouest. The fashionable place for antiquing is a formerly run-down five-block strip of Notre-Dame between rue Guy and avenue Atwater. Most of the action is at the western end of the strip, as are many of the restaurants and cafés that have sprung up to cater to shoppers. The Lionel-Groulx Métro station is the closest.

Victoria Village. The carriage-trade area for wealthy Westmount citizens, who reside on the leafy slopes of Mont-Royal, has morphed into a shopping destination for all Montrealers with an eye for style. Independent boutiques offer distinctive home decor, shoes, gifts, stationery, and fashion along rues Victoria and Sherbrooke, with the epicenter between Victoria and Claremont. Cafés and fine specialty food shops also abound. Vendôme is the closest Métro station.

Vieux-Montréal. The old part of the city has more than its share of garish souvenir shops, but fashion boutiques and shoe stores with low to moderate prices line rues Notre-Dame and St-Jacques, from rue McGill to Place Jacques-Cartier. With gentrification in the west end of the area, high-end fashion boutiques and spas have moved in. The area is also rich in art galleries and crafts shops, especially along rue St-Paul. Use the Place-d'Armes or Champ-de-Mars Métro station.

DEPARTMENT STORES

La Baie. The Bay is a descendant of the Hudson's Bay Company, the great 17th-century fur-trading company that played a pivotal role in Canada's development. La Baie has been a department store since 1891. In addition to selling typical department-store goods, it's known for its duffel coats and signature red, green, and white striped blankets. ✉ *585 rue Ste-Catherine Ouest, Downtown* ☎ *514/281–4422* Ⓜ *McGill.*

Fodor'sChoice **Holt Renfrew.** This upscale department store is Canada's answer to Berg-
★ dorf Goodman. Here's where you get your Prada, Chanel, and Gucci fix, as well as contemporary labels like Theory, Diane Von Furstenberg, and Teenflo. A world design lab showcases avant-garde fashion, including rising Canadian stars. The food at the downstairs café is just as stylish, with bread flown in from the Poilâne bakery in Paris several times weekly. ✉ *1300 rue Sherbrooke Ouest, Downtown* ☎ *514/842–5111* Ⓜ *Peel or Guy-Concordia.*

★ **Ogilvy.** Founded in 1865, Ogilvy boasts a Louis Vuitton boutique, as well as in-house shops from Burberry, Hugo Boss, and others. Check out the Ports 1961 boutique for fashions of great beauty and romance, with a touch of strange. The ground floor has one of the best selections of accessories in the city. A kilted piper regales shoppers each day at noon. ⊠ *1307 rue Ste-Catherine Ouest, Downtown* ☎ *514/842–7711* Ⓜ *Peel.*

Simons. Find the trends du jour at a great price from the youth-oriented labels on the ground floor of this bustling department store. Upstairs, the fare is more mature, ranging from respectable and affordable twin-sets to luxe offerings from the likes of Paul Smith and Alberta Ferretti. The store is also known for its fashion-forward selection of menswear and its excellent sales. ⊠ *977 rue Ste-Catherine Ouest, Downtown* ☎ *514/282–1840* Ⓜ *Peel.*

SHOPPING CENTERS & MALLS

Le Centre Eaton. Eaton Center has a youthful edge, with a huge Levi's outlet and some trendy sporting-goods stores. The five-story mall, the largest in the downtown core, has 175 boutiques and shops and is linked to the McGill Métro station. ⊠ *705 rue Ste-Catherine Ouest, Downtown* ☎ *514/288–3708* Ⓜ *McGill.*

Le Complexe Les Ailes. The Les Ailes flagship store in this complex attached to Le Centre Eaton sells women's clothing and accessories; the other 60 retailers include Tommy Hilfiger and Archambault, a music store. ⊠ *677 rue Ste-Catherine Ouest, Downtown* ☎ *514/285–1080* Ⓜ *McGill.*

Les Cours Mont-Royal. This elegant mall caters to expensive and stylish tastes, but there are plenty of affordable options, too. The more than 80 shops include Club Monaco, DKNY, and Harry Rosen. La crème de la crème of designers—Lanvin, Dolce & Gabbana, and Givenchy—is sold at Ursula B./Giorgio Femme. For daring lingerie, check out Dutch designer Marlies Dekkers's boutique. Feet hurting from all the shopping? Terra Firma, in the basement, stocks stylish comfort shoes. ⊠ *1455 rue Peel, Downtown* ☎ *514/842–7777* Ⓜ *Peel.*

Marché Bonsecours. Inaugurated in the 1840s as the city's principal public market, this neoclassical building now houses boutiques that showcase Québécois, Canadian, and First Nations artwork, clothing, and furniture. The Institut de Design Montréal Gallery boutique is full of intriguing office and home gadgets that make unique gifts. ⊠ *350 rue St-Paul Est, Vieux-Montréal* ☎ *514/872–7730* Ⓜ *Champ-de-Mars.*

Marché Central. You can buy everything from fish to electronic gear, from pasta to high fashion, and from canoes to prescription glasses at this sprawling, million-square-foot outlet complex in the north end of the city. It's hard to get to by public transit, but there are acres of free parking, and it's an easy 10-minute drive from downtown. ⊠ *615 rue du Marché Central, North End* ☎ *514/381–8804* Ⓜ *Crémazie and Bus 100 or 146.*

Place Ville-Marie. Place Ville-Marie is where weatherproof indoor shopping first came to Montréal in 1962. It was also the start of the underground shopping network that Montréal now enjoys. Stylish shoppers head to the 100-plus retail outlets for lunchtime sprees. ✉*Blvd. René-Lévesque and rue University, Downtown* ☎*514/866–6666* Ⓜ*McGill or Bonaventure.*

Les Promenades de la Cathédrale. There are more than 50 shops at this complex directly beneath

FOR SERIOUS SHOPPERS ONLY
Bargain-hunter alert: twice a year—in mid-June and at the end of August—the Main Madness street sale transforms boulevard St-Laurent into an open-air bazaar.

Christ Church Cathedral, including Canada's largest Linen Chest outlet, with hundreds of bedspreads and duvets, plus aisles of china, crystal, linen, and silver. The Anglican Church's Diocesan Book Room sells an unusually good and ecumenical selection of books as well as religious objects. ✉*625 rue Ste-Catherine Ouest, Downtown* ☎*514/845–8230* Ⓜ*McGill.*

SPECIALTY SHOPS

ANTIQUES

Antiquités Curiosités. This shop carries well-priced Victorian-era tables and tallboys, as well as lamps and lighting fixtures. The merchandise is crammed into three rooms spread over two floors. ✉*1769 rue Amherst, Gay Village* ☎*514/525–8772* Ⓜ*Beaudry.*

Antiquités Pour La Table. As the name suggests, this store specializes in making your table look perfect. There's an extensive selection of antique porcelain, crystal, and linens—all impeccably preserved and beautifully displayed. Don't bother coming here to replace missing or broken pieces, though, since most of what's on display arecomplete sets. ✉*902 rue Lenoir, St-Henri* ☎*514/989–8945* Ⓜ*St-Henri.*

Cité Déco. Nostalgic for the good old days? This is just the place to pick up a chrome-and-Arborite dining-room set and an RCA tube radio. It also has art deco furnishings and accessories from the '30s, '60s, and '70s, as well as Danish teak and rosewood furniture. ✉*1761 rue Amherst, Gay Village* ☎*514/528–0659* Ⓜ*Beaudry.*

Grand Central. A heavenly assortment of chandeliers, lamps, and sconces to light up your life in the mellow glow of days gone by. ✉*2448 rue Notre-Dame Ouest, St-Henri* ☎*514/935–1467* Ⓜ*Georges-Vanier.*

Ruth Stalker. She made her reputation finding and salvaging fine pieces of early Canadian pine furniture, but Ruth Stalker has also developed a good instinct for such folk art as exquisitely carved hunting decoys, weather vanes, and pottery. ✉*4447 rue Ste-Catherine Ouest, Westmount* ☎*514/931–0822* Ⓜ*Atwater.*

Viva Gallery. Asian antique furniture and art take center stage at Viva, where you'll find a wide selection of carved tables, benches, and armoires. ✉*1970 rue Notre-Dame Ouest, St-Henri* ☎*514/932–3200* Ⓜ*Lucien-L'Allier.*

ART

Montréal brims with art galleries that present work by local luminaries as well as international artists. The downtown area has a wide choice; Vieux-Montréal is also rich in galleries, most of which specialize in Québécois and First Nations work.

★ **Edifice Belgo.** In a nondescript building, Edifice Belgo is in essence a mall of roughly 20 art galleries showing both established and emerging artists. Galerie Roger Bellemare is one of the best galleries in which to look for contemporary art. Galerie Trois Points showcases the work of Montréal and Québec artists. Both galleries are on the fifth floor. ⊠*372 rue Ste-Catherine Ouest, Downtown* ☎*514/393–9969 Galerie René Blouin, 514/866–8008 Galerie Trois Points* Ⓜ*Place-des-Arts.*

Galerie Art & Culture. Canadian landscapes from the 19th and 20th centuries are the specialty here. ⊠*227 rue St-Paul Ouest, Vieux-Montréal* ☎*514/843–5980* Ⓜ*Place-d'Armes.*

Galerie de Bellefeuille. This Westmount gallery has a knack for discovering important new talents. It represents many of Canada's top contemporary artists as well as some international ones. Its 5,000 square feet hold a good selection of sculptures, paintings, and limited-edition prints. ⊠*1367 av. Greene, Westmount* ☎*514/933–4406* Ⓜ*Atwater.*

Galerie de Chariot. This gallery claims to have the largest collection of Inuit soapstone and ivory carvings in Canada. It also has a wide selection of drawings and beadwork, all of which is government authenticated. ⊠*446 pl. Jacques-Cartier, Vieux-Montréal* ☎*514/875–6134* Ⓜ*Champ-de-Mars.*

★ **Galerie Walter Klinkhoff.** Brothers Alan and Eric Klinkhoff specialize in Canadian historical and contemporary art. ⊠*1200 rue Sherbrooke Ouest, Square Mile* ☎*514/288–7306* Ⓜ*Peel.*

★ **La Guilde Graphique.** The Graphic Guild has an exceptional selection of original prints, engravings, and etchings. ⊠*9 rue St-Paul Ouest, Vieux-Montréal* ☎*514/844–3438* Ⓜ*Champ-de-Mars.*

BOOKS & STATIONERY

Bibliomania. It's possible to find some out-of-print gems among Bibliomania's extensive shelves of secondhand books. The store also sells engravings, postcards, and other printed collectibles. ⊠*460 rue Ste-Catherine Ouest, Room 406, Downtown* ☎*514/933–8156* Ⓜ*Place-des-Arts.*

L'Essence du Papier. With its selection of imported and handmade papers, the Essence of Paper is a reminder that letter writing can be an art form. Here are pens suited to most tastes and budgets, as well as waxes and stamps with which to seal any romantic prose that you might be inspired to produce. There's also a wide selection of place cards, invitations, and journals. ⊠*4160 rue St-Denis, Plateau Mont-Royal* ☎*514/288–9691* Ⓜ*Mont-Royal.*

Indigo. Although it is mainly about books and magazines, this chain has branched out into DVDs, cards, gifts, and housewares. This location also has a large children's section. ⊠*1500 av. McGill College, Downtown* ☎*514/281–5549* Ⓜ*McGill.*

★ **Paragraphe.** Stubbornly independent until 2003, when it was bought out by Archambault, a Montréal chain of music stores, Paragraphe carries the usual selection of best-sellers and thrillers, but also stocks Canadian works and histories. It's a favorite with visiting authors, who stop by to read from their latest releases, as well as Booker Prize winner Yann Martel, who drops in from time to time. ✉ *2220 av. McGill College, Downtown* ☎*514/845–5811* Ⓜ*McGill.*

Renaud-Bray. With 23 branches in Québec—nearly half of them in Montréal—Renaud-Bray is the largest French-language book chain in Canada. Its shops stock best-sellers and thrillers in French and English as well as original works from Europe and Canada. There are also substantial gift, music, and magazine offerings. ✉*5117 av. du Parc, Plateau Mont-Royal* ☎*514/276–7641* Ⓜ*Laurier.*

S. W. Welch. The old books here include meditations on religion and philosophy as well as mysteries and science fiction. ✉*225 rue St-Viateur Ouest, Plateau Mont-Royal* ☎*514/848–9358* Ⓜ*Laurier.*

★ **The Word.** Deep in the McGill University neighborhood, the Word is a timeless shop with sagging shelves that hold used books on art, philosophy, and literature. The owner here still tallies your bill by hand. ✉*469 rue Milton, Downtown* ☎*514/845–5640* Ⓜ*McGill.*

CLOTHING

Abe & Mary's. Talk about destination shopping. For Montrealers, visiting this 7,000-square-foot emporium on an industrial strip in the burbs is like a mini-trip to L.A.—think Kitson or Fred Segal—complete with labels like Alice + Olivia, Eileen Fisher, and M Missoni. A denim bar, shoes, bangles, bags, vintage couture, a café and, naturally, a parking lot complete the offerings. ✉*4175 rue Jean-Talon Ouest, Ville Mont-Royal* ☎ *514/448–6223* Ⓜ*Namur.*

BCBG Max Azria. Max Azria's super-stylish clothing, shoes, and handbags all make a statement. This is the place for dresses, from little sunny frocks to sundown gowns. ✉*1300 rue Ste-Catherine Ouest, Downtown* ☎*514/398–9130* Ⓜ*Peel.*

Bedo. If you want to look fashionable without going broke, this is the place to shop for men's and women's casual wear. ✉*1256 rue Ste-Catherine Ouest, Downtown* ☎*514/866–4962* Ⓜ*Peel.*

Billie. Cool fashion with a gentle touch from a designer turned retailer. The store is light and airy, with perfectly edited collections like Filippa K. and Québec's fine knitwear line, Ça Va de Soi. ✉*141 av. Laurier Ouest, Mile-End* ☎*514/270–5415* Ⓜ*Laurier.*

Buffalo David Bitton. Fans adore the fit and reasonable prices of Montrealer David Bitton's jeans. Aside from denim for men and women, there's a full line of trendy clothes and accessories for the gal about town. ✉*1223 rue Ste-Catherine Ouest, Downtown* ☎*514/845–1816* Ⓜ*Peel.*

Le Château. This Québec chain designs its own line of reasonably priced trendy fashions for men and women. Its flagship store is on rue Ste-Catherine, but it also has a factory outlet at the Marché Central. ✉*1310 rue Ste-Catherine Ouest, Downtown* ☎*514/866–2481* Ⓜ*Peel.* ✉*Marché Central, 1007B1A rue Marché Central, North End* ☎*514/382–4220* Ⓜ*Crémazie and Bus 100 or 146.*

Cuir Danier. Leather fashions for men and women are the specialty of this Toronto-based chain, which designs and manufactures it own lines of jackets, skirts, pants, hats, purses, etc. It has a downtown branch in Place Ville-Marie and a warehouse outlet at Marché Central. ⊠ *1 Place Ville-Marie, Downtown* ☎*514/874–0472* Ⓜ*McGill or Bonaventure* ⊠*Marché Central, 999 rue Marché Central, North End* ☎*514/382– 4220* Ⓜ*Crémazie and Bus 100 or 146.*

Henriette L. For more than 20 years, this designer shop has been offering the chic madames of Outremont some of the finest labels from France. ⊠*1031 av. Laurier Ouest, Outremont* ☎*514/277–3426* Ⓜ*Laurier.*

Indigo. As the name suggests, the main product here is jeans, but casual Ts, dresses, and accessories are also on offer. ⊠*4920 rue Sherbrooke Ouest, Westmount* ☎*514/486–4420* Ⓜ*Vendôme.*

Jacob. Fashionable professional women shop at Jacob for office-appropriate clothes. ⊠*1220 rue Ste-Catherine Ouest, Downtown* ☎*514/861–9346* Ⓜ*Peel.*

James. Casual California chic reigns in this laid-back boutique that caters to the girlie girl. There's always a rack of romantic summer whites. ⊠*4910 rue Sherbrooke Ouest, Westmount* ☎*514/369–0700* Ⓜ*Vendôme.*

Kanuk. This company's owl trademark has become something of a status symbol among the shivering urban masses. These coats and parkas are built to keep an Arctic explorer warm and dry. ⊠*485 rue Rachel Est, Plateau Mont-Royal* ☎*514/527–4494* Ⓜ*Mont-Royal.*

Les Créateurs. Thank retailer Maria Balla for nurturing an inimitable selection of avant-garde design from the likes of Jil Sander, Comme des Garçons, Yohji Yamamoto, and Rick Owens. There's hardly a shop like this anywhere between Montréal and L.A. For the true connoisseur. ⊠*1444 rue Sherbrooke Ouest, Downtown* ☎*514/284–2102* Ⓜ*Guy-Concordia.*

Lola & Emily. The perfect boutique for the undecided woman: Lola's side specializes in the fun and frilly, Emily's in everything in basic black or beige. ⊠*3475 blvd. St-Laurent, Plateau Mont-Royal* ☎*514/288–7598* Ⓜ*St-Laurent.*

Lululemon. Forgot your yoga pants? Heaven forbid! The cult yoga line born in Vancouver has you covered, with three outposts in the city, downtown, on rue St-Denis, and in Westmount. ⊠*1232 rue Ste-Catherine Ouest, Downtown* ☎*514/394–0770* Ⓜ*Peel.*

Lyla. Some of the finest lingerie in the city, from Eres and La Perla for instance, and the staff to find what fits and flatters you, is augmented by recherché fashion from Europe and the U.S. One of the city's best selections of swimsuits—and darling cover-ups—is another reason to stop and shop here. ⊠*400 av. Laurier Ouest, Outremont* ☎*514/271–0763* Ⓜ*Laurier.*

Mains Folles. You'll find tropical-print dresses, skirts, and blouses imported from Bali at this store. ⊠*4427 rue St-Denis, Plateau Mont-Royal* ☎*514/284–6854* Ⓜ*Mont-Royal.*

Mousseline. Trend-worthy styles from France and Italy for women well out of their teens. ⊠*120 av. Laurier Ouest, Mile-End* ☎*514/878– 0661* Ⓜ*Laurier.*

Mimi & Coco. Check out this local collection of basic and lace-trimmed Ts designed in Montréal and made in Italy of super-fine cotton. ✉*201 av. Laurier Ouest, Mile-End* ☎*514/906–0349* Ⓜ*Laurier.*

Parasuco. Montrealer Salvatore Parasuco—inventor of stretch jeans—has been making history in denim ever since he opened his first store in 1975 at the age of 19. He has since spread across the country and into the United States, but his flagship shop—completely refurbished in 2006—is in Montréal. ✉*1414 rue Crescent, Downtown* ☎*514/284–2288* Ⓜ*Guy-Concordia.*

Roots. Quality materials and an approachable, sometimes retro look have made Canada's Roots chain a fashion favorite for the casual, out-doorsy look. Good leatherwear and bags. ✉*1025 rue Ste-Catherine Ouest, Downtown* ☎*514/845–7995* Ⓜ*Peel.*

Space FB. The initials stand for François Beauregard, a Montréal designer whose colourful cotton tops and hip-hugging pants are much loved by the younger crowd. ✉*3632 blvd. St-Laurent, Plateau Mont-Royal* ☎*514/282–1991* Ⓜ*St-Laurent or Sherbrooke.*

Tilley Endurables. The famous Canadian-designed Tilley hat is sold here, along with other easy-care travel wear. ✉*1050 av. Laurier Ouest, Outremont* ☎*514/272–7791* Ⓜ*Laurier.*

TNT. Montréal's latest style mecca boasts almost 200 swoon-worthy labels, including many of the usual suspects—Theory, Velvet and Pucci —and then some: Helmut Lang, Issa, and Majestic. A denim bar, shoes, a rainbow of Ts, and menswear are also on offer. Try the spicy Cubano sandwich at the Java U café on-site while you ponder your purchases. ✉*4100 rue Ste-Catherine Ouest, Westmount* ☎*514/935–1588* Ⓜ*Atwater.*

Tristan. This chain sells contemporary fashions for women and men that appeal to the young professional and just-out-of-university set. ✉*1001 rue Ste-Catherine Ouest, Downtown* ☎*514/289–9609* Ⓜ*Peel.*

U&I. Hipsters flock to this shop on the Main for retailer Eric Toledano's latest finds from Europe. Men and women are equally well served in the double shop with avant-garde lines like Viviennne Westwood, Engineered Garments, and Tiger of Sweden. Look for special pieces from Montréal design darlings Mackage, Yso, and Denis Gagnon. ✉*3650 blvd. St-Laurent, Plateau Mont-Royal* ☎*514/844–8788* Ⓜ*St-Laurent or Sherbrooke.*

Ursula B./Giorgio Femme. Flirty Cavalli, sexy Dolce & Gabbana, and romantic Lanvin make this two-story shop a designer treasure trove. Oh, and don't forget to check out the fabulous sale room upstairs. ✉*Les Cours Mont-Royal, 1455 rue Peel, Downtown* ☎*514/282–0294* Ⓜ*Peel.*

Winners. This discount clothing store has turned shopping into a sport. And now that it carries housewares, leaving empty-handed is even more difficult. Its downtown outlet is on the lowest level of Place Montréal Trust. ✉*1500 av. McGill College, Downtown* ☎*514/788–4949* Ⓜ*McGill.*

CHILDREN'S **Oink Oink.** This piggy store carries fashions as well as toys and books for infants and children. It also stocks clothes for teenagers. It's fun to hear the staff answer the phone. ✉*1343 av. Greene, Westmount* ☎*514/939–2634* Ⓜ*Atwater.*

MEN'S ONLY   **Duo.** DSquared, Dolce, and J. Lindbergh hang side by side in this super-cool menswear shop. ✉*30 rue Prince-Arthur Ouest, Plateau Mont-Royal* ☎*514/848–0880* Ⓜ*St-Laurent or Sherbrooke.*

Harry Rosen. Harry and Lou Rosen's 16-store chain supplies some of the country's best-dressed men with high-end shirts, suits, jackets, and slacks. ✉*Cours Mont-Royal, 1445 rue Peel, Downtown* ☎*514/284–3315* Ⓜ*Peel.*

Henri Henri. Simply the best men's hat store in Canada, Henri Henri has a huge stock of Homburgs, Borsalinos, fedoras, top hats, and derbies, as well as cloth caps and other accessories. Hat prices range from about C$60 to well over C$1,000 for a top-of-the-line Homburg or Panama. ✉*189 rue Ste-Catherine Est, Downtown* ☎*514/288–0109 or 888/388–0109* Ⓜ*St-Laurent.*

Michel Brisson. The go-to place for art directors, architects, and other cool dudes with an eye for European design from Etro or Dries Van Noten. ✉*1012 av. Laurier Ouest, Outremont* ☎*514/270–1012* Ⓜ*Laurier. 384 rue St-Paul, Ouest, Vieux-Montréal* ☎*514/285–1012* Ⓜ*Place-d'Armes.*

L'Uomo. L'Uomo bills itself as the "finest men's store in Canada," and it does, indeed, stock some of the finest European labels—Prada, Bottega Veneta, Loro Piana, Avon Celli, and Kiton, to name a few. ✉*1452 rue Peel, Downtown* ☎*514/844–1008 or 877/844–1008* Ⓜ*Peel.*

Zilli. Is money no object? Here's where snazzy men might pick up a $35,000 deerskin jacket (fur lining included) or yellow alligator shoes. ✉*1472 rue Sherbrooke Ouest, Downtown* ☎*514/935–3777* Ⓜ*Guy-Concordia.*

QUÉBEC DESIGNERS   **Boutique Andy.** Designer Andy Thé-Anh's sexy gowns are a staple of Canadian catwalks, red carpets, and galas. Also find curvy, sophisticated suits and coats, often set off with spectacular fur collars. ✉*Les Cours Mont-Royal, 1455 rue Peel, Downtown* ☎*514/985–9898* Ⓜ*Peel. 2120 rue de la Montagne, Downtown* ☎*514/8424208* Ⓜ*Peel or Guy-Concordia.*

Aime Com Moi. Funky Québécois designers dominate at this women's boutique. ✉*150 av. Mont-Royal Est, Plateau Mont-Royal* ☎*514/982–0088* Ⓜ*Mont-Royal.*

Dubuc. Edgy menswear of superb cut and fine fabric from a talented designer. ✉*4451 rue St-Denis, Plateau Mont-Royal* ☎*514/282–1424* Ⓜ*Mont-Royal.*

Bodybag by Jude. When Nicole Kidman appeared on David Letterman in a zip denim dress from this line, the designer Judith Desjardins' star was set. Hipster territory. ✉*17 rue Bernard Ouest, Mile-End* ☎*514/274–5242* Ⓜ*Laurier.*

Diffusion Griff 3000. This is Anne de Shalla's showcase for leading Québécois fashion designers. ✉*350 rue St-Paul Est, Vieux-Montréal* ☎*514/398–0761* Ⓜ*Champ-de-Mars.*

General 54. Stores like this are what give Mile-End its rep for cutting edge. The clothes—many by local designers—are very feminine and whimsical. ✉*54 rue St-Viateur Ouest, Mile-End* ☎*514/271–2129* Ⓜ*Laurier.*

Harricana. Yesterday's old fur coats and stoles are transformed into everything from car coats and ski jackets to baby wraps and cushions. For summer, vintage scarves become flirty little tops. The recycled furs are sold at dozens of shops, but the best place to see what's available is this combination atelier and boutique. ⊠*3000 rue St-Antoine Ouest, Downtown* ☎*877/894–9919* Ⓜ*Lionel-Groulx.*

M0851. Sleek, supple leather wear and bags from designer Frédéric Mamarbachi have a cult following from Tokyo to Antwerp, and Montréal, of course. ⊠*3526 blvd. St-Laurent, Plateau Mont-Royal* ☎*514/849–9759* Ⓜ*St-Laurent or Sherbrooke.*

Marie Saint Pierre. The doyenne of the Montréal design scene, Marie Saint Pierre interprets her signature pleats and ruffles in silks, jerseys, and mesh to suit the mood of each season. Consider this wearable art—and a must-see for serious fashion fans. ⊠*2081 rue de la Montagne, Downtown* ☎*514/281-5547* Ⓜ*Peel or Guy-Concordia.*

Muse. Designer Christian Chenail's contemporary take on fashion always has a French twist, and his daring black gowns are famed as show-stoppers. ⊠*4467 rue St-Denis, Plateau Mont-Royal* ☎*514/848–9493* Ⓜ*Mont-Royal.*

Revenge. Nearly 40 Canadian and Québécois designers create Revenge's well-crafted original fashions for women. ⊠*3852 rue St-Denis, Plateau Mont-Royal* ☎*514/843–4379* Ⓜ*Sherbrooke.*

Rudsak. Quality leathers and coats for men and women are on trend, and very nicely priced. ⊠*1400 rue Ste-Catherine Ouest, Downtown* ☎*514/399–9925* Ⓜ*Guy-Concordia.*

Scandale. Québécois designer Georges Lévesque loves the female form, and embellishes it with flounces, bustles, and vivid prints. Think cutting edge with a Victorian twist. ⊠*3639 blvd. St-Laurent, Plateau Mont-Royal* ☎*514/842–4707* Ⓜ*Sherbrooke or St-Laurent.*

Shan. Everything you need poolside from swimwear designer Chantal Lévesque. Truly fine fabrics and fit with a soupçon of French flair. ⊠*2150 rue Crescent, Downtown* ☎*514/287–7426* Ⓜ*Peel or Guy-Concordia.*

VINTAGE &
RECYCLED

Boutique Encore. Although best known for its nearly new women's fashions, it also includes the big names for men. ⊠*2165 rue Crescent, Downtown* ☎*514/849–0092* Ⓜ*Peel or Guy-Concordia.*

Eva B. If your fantasy is being a flapper, or if you want to revive the pillbox hat, turn back the clock and perk up your wardrobe with an item from the vast collection sold here. ⊠*2015 blvd. St-Laurent, Downtown* ☎*514/849–8246* Ⓜ*St-Laurent.*

Maskarad. An eclectic mix of old and new set in a bordello-chic shop. Great prices on vintage costume jewelry and furs. ⊠*103 av. Mont-Royal Ouest, Plateau Mont-Royal* ☎*514/844–7676* Ⓜ*Mont-Royal.*

Preloved. Granny's sheets are transformed into a frock, dad's cardigan into a tunic. Recycled clothing is a hit among the hipsters of Mile-End. ⊠*4832 blvd. St-Laurent, Mile-End* ☎*514/499–9898* Ⓜ*Laurier or Mont-Royal.*

FOOD

Marché Atwater. The venerable Atwater Market is a favorite with down-towners looking for fresh produce, specialty meats and sausages, fresh fish, and Québec cheese. The main produce market is outdoors under shelters. Restaurants and shops inside a two-story complex are perfect for rainy-day browsing. ⊠ *138 av. Atwater, Downtown* ☎ *514/937–7754* Ⓜ *Lionel-Groulx.*

Fodor'sChoice **Marché Jean-Talon.** This is the biggest and liveliest of the city's public
★ markets. On weekends in summer and fall, crowds swarm the half-acre or so of outdoor produce stalls, looking for the fattest tomatoes, sweetest melons, and juiciest strawberries. Its shops also sell meat, fish, cheese, sausage, bread, pastries, and other delicacies. The market is in the northern end of the city, but is easy to get to by Métro. ⊠ *7070 rue Henri-Julien, Little Italy* ☎ *514/937–7754* Ⓜ *Jean-Talon.*

Gourmet Laurier. Fine condiments, acres of chocolate and candy, and the best coffee beans in town draw the carriage trade to this Outremont shop. ⊠ *1042 av. Laurier Ouest, Outremont* ☎ *514/274–5601* Ⓜ *Laurier.*

La Vieille Europe. For a taste of the old Main, where generations of immi-grants have come to shop, look no farther than this deli packed with sausages, cold cuts, jams, cheeses, coffee, and atmosphere. ⊠ *3855 blvd. St-Laurent, Plateau Mont-Royal* ☎ *514/842–5773* Ⓜ *St-Laurent or Sherbrooke.*

Milano. One of the largest cheese selections in the city as well as fresh pastas of all kinds are the highlights of this market. An entire wall is devoted to olive oils and vinegars; there's also a butcher and a sizeable produce section. ⊠ *6862 blvd. St-Laurent, Little Italy* ☎ *514/273–8558* Ⓜ *Jean-Talon.*

FURS

Close to 90% of Canada's fur manufacturers are based in Montréal, as are many of their retail outlets. Furriers were traditionally clustered along rue Mayor and boulevard de Maisonneuve in the downtown area, but many have moved to greener pastures in the city's north end. For those wishing to browse, the Gordon Brown Building, at 400 bou-levard de Maisonneuve Ouest (Place-des-Arts Métro), still houses some merchants; many others have moved to 9250 l'avenue du Parc, near rue Chabanel.

Alexandor. Alexandor caters to downtown shoppers. It sells fur-lined cloth coats as well as coats in mink, fox, chinchilla, and beaver. ⊠ *2055 rue Peel, Downtown* ☎ *514/288–1119* Ⓜ *Peel.*

Holt Renfrew. The fur showroom here is perhaps the most exclusive in the city, with prices to match. When Queen Elizabeth II got married in 1947, Holt gave her a priceless Labrador mink. ⊠ *1300 rue Sherbrooke Ouest, Downtown* ☎ *514/842–5111* Ⓜ *Peel or Guy-Concordia.*

Labelle Fourrure. This family business has stayed a fixture on Montréal's fur map for close to a century by adapting to the fashions of the day and offering good service and value for your dollar. ⊠ *6570 rue St-Hubert, Villeray* ☎ *514/276–3701* Ⓜ *Beaubien.*

Salon Élégance, Ogilvy. Luxe furs and shearlings, including extravagant, colorful sheared beavers from Montréal's Zuki. ✉*1307 rue Ste-Catherine Ouest, Downtown* ☎*514/987–8044* Ⓜ*Peel or Guy-Concordia.*

GIFTS

Arthur Quentin. Check out this elegant shop for fine French tableware from Gien and Maintenon, linens, gourmet kitchen gear, and a gift room with designer messenger bags, maps, pens, and notions. ✉*3960 rue St-Denis, Plateau-Mont-Royal* ☎*514/843–7513* Ⓜ *Sherbrooke.*

Ben & Tournesol. Glittering bijoux, fine housewares from Michael Aran and Hermès, vegan leather goods from Montréal's Matt & Nat, and cute toys—Hello Kitty!—are jam-packed in this small Westmount shop. ✉*4915 rue Sherbrooke Ouest, Westmount* ☎*514/481–5050* Ⓜ*Vendôme.*

Desmarais et Robitaille. The local clergy come here to buy vestments, chalices, altar candles, and other liturgical items, but Desmarais et Robitaille also stocks Québécois wood carvings, handicrafts, religious articles, and sacred music. ✉*60 rue Notre-Dame Ouest, Vieux-Montréal* ☎*514/845–3194* Ⓜ*Place-d'Armes.*

L'Empreinte Coopérative. Fine Québec handicrafts are on display here. ✉*272 rue St-Paul Est, Vieux-Montréal* ☎*514/861–4427* Ⓜ*Champ-de-Mars.*

JEWELRY

Aqua Skye. Oodles of baubles, including a selection from Montréal designers. ✉*2035 rue Crescent, Downtown* ☎*514/843–7513* Ⓜ*Peel or Guy-Concordia.*

Birks. Since 1879 Birks has been helping shoppers mark special occasions, whether engagements, weddings, or retirements. ✉*1240 Phillips Sq., Downtown* ☎*514/397–2511* Ⓜ*McGill.*

★ **Bleu Comme Le Ciel.** In France they call costume jewelry bijoux de fantaisie, and that's what you find here: fantasy in a sparkling array of colourful crystal baubles from France. ✉*2000 rue Peel, Downtown* ☎*514/847–1128* Ⓜ*Peel.*

Château d'Ivoire. There are no fakes here, but there is plenty of fantasy. Jewels from Chopard, Mikimoto, and Bulgari; watches from every top line from Cartier to Omega are set in a warren of rooms. ✉*2020 rue de la Montagne, Downtown* ☎*514/845–4651* Ⓜ*Peel or Guy-Concordia.*

Kaufmann de Suisse. Expert craftspeople create the fine jewelry sold here. ✉*2195 rue Crescent, Downtown* ☎*514/848–0595* Ⓜ*Guy-Concordia.*

Les Jardins Tissés. Rare antique gems from India and Afghanistan in this boutique that also sells carpets and antique armoires. ✉*4875 rue Sherbrooke Ouest, Westmount* ☎*514/488–0444* Ⓜ*Vendôme.*

Nee Nah. Charming, romantic, and flowery notions to give and to get, from designers Michal Negrin, Ayala Bar, and others. ✉*1228 av. Greene., Westmount* ☎*514/931–6358* Ⓜ*Atwater.*

LINGERIE

Collange. Lacy goods of the designer variety are sold here. ✉*1 Westmount Sq., Westmount* ☎*514/933–4634* Ⓜ*Atwater.*

Deuxième Peau. A tiny shop tucked away in a basement, Second Skin sells a fine assortment of French lingerie. While you're feeling brave and beautiful, kill two birds with one stone and try on a bathing suit. ✉*4457 rue St-Denis, Plateau Mont-Royal* ☎*514/842–0811* Ⓜ*Mont-Royal.*

Josephine. Indulgent lingerie and swimwear from Chantal Thomass, La Perla, and Huit. ✉*1448 rue Sherbrooke Ouest, Downtown* ☎*514/849–7774* Ⓜ*Guy-Concordia.*

La Senza. This international Québec chain, now allied with Victoria's Secret, is the place to get that fuchsia push-up bra and matching rhinestone-trimmed panty. Basics, too, at reasonable prices. ✉*1133 rue Ste-Catherine Ouest, Downtown* ☎*514/281–0101* Ⓜ*Peel.*

Marlies Dekkers. Strappy bras, panties, and swimwear with a kinky edge from a Dutch designer. ✉*Les Cours Mont-Royal, 1455 rue Peel, Downtown* ☎*514/303–8599* Ⓜ*Peel.*

SHOES

Browns. This local institution stocks fashion footwear and accessories for men and women. As well as the store's own label, it carries DKNY, Chie Mihara, Manolo Blahnik, Miu Miu, and Stuart Weitzman. ✉*1191 rue Ste-Catherine Ouest, Downtown* ☎*514/987–1206* Ⓜ*Peel.*

John Fluevog. The Vancouver shoe designer has a cult following for his funky footwear for men and women. ✉*3857 rue St-Denis, Plateau Mont-Royal* ☎*514/509–1627* Ⓜ*Sherbrooke.*

Mona Moore. Pale-pink walls and a lemon brocade settee create the backdrop for the city's most luxurious selection of women's shoes, featuring such names as Dries Van Noten, Lanvin, and Pierre Hardy. ✉*1446 rue Sherbrooke Ouest, Downtown* ☎*514/842–0662* Ⓜ*Guy-Concordia.*

Rosenstein. All the Christian Louboutin you can imagine plus cashmere from Lucian Pellat-Finet—just in case the Montréal climate gives you a chill. ✉*2148 rue de la Montagne, Downtown* ☎*514/287–7682* Ⓜ*Peel or Guy-Concordia.*

Specchio. Style with substance in an excellent selection of fine footwear for women who like to walk. ✉*2025 rue de la Montagne, Downtown* ☎*514/282–2222* Ⓜ*Peel or Guy-Concordia.*

Tony's. Dedicated to the finely shod foot, Tony's places stylish imports beside elegantly sensible domestic footwear for men and women. ✉*1346 av. Greene, Westmount* ☎*514/935–2993* Ⓜ*Atwater.*

TOYS & GAMES

★ **Cerf Volanterie.** Claude Thibaudeau makes the sturdy, gloriously colored kites sold here. He signs each of his creations and guarantees them for three years. ✉*4019 rue Ste-Catherine Est, Hochelaga-Maisonneuve* ☎*514/845–7613* Ⓜ*Pie-IX.*

Franc Jeu. The antithesis of the big-box toy store, this shop carries Corolle dolls from France, as well as educational toys from Québec's Jouets Boom and Gladius lines. ✉*4152 rue St-Denis, Plateau Mont-Royal* ☎*514/849–9253* Ⓜ*Sherbrooke.*

Jouets Choo-Choo. This shop 20 minutes from downtown sells quality European toys and educational games. ✉*940 blvd. St-Jean, Pointe-Claire* ☎*514/697–7550.*

Sports & Outdoor Activities

5

Rafting on the Lachine River.

WORD OF MOUTH

"Montréal is a great city for bicycling, and bikes can readily be rented. Biking from Parc la Fontaine down to the port and along the Lachine Canal, stopping at Atwater Market for lunch, would be a great way to spend an afternoon. Walking up to the top of Mt. Royal is another outdoorsy activity. There are several kinds of boat rides available, including riding the rapids, and jet boats."

—zootsi

Updated by
Anne Marie
Marko

MOST MONTREALERS WOULD PROBABLY CLAIM they hate winter, but the city is full of cold-weather sports venues—skating rinks, cross-country ski trails, and toboggan runs. During warm-weather months, residents head for the tennis courts, miles of bicycle trails, golf courses, and two lakes for boating and swimming.

AUTO RACING

Grand Prix du Canada. One of only two venues in North America where Formula 1 racing can be witnessed, the Canadian Grand Prix takes place in late June at the Circuit Gilles Villeneuve on Île Notre-Dame, consistently inspiring Montréal's busiest tourist weekend. ☎514/350–4731, 514/350–0000 tickets ⊕www.grandprix.ca.

BIKING

Despite the bitter winters (or perhaps because of them), Montréal has fallen in love with the bicycle. More than 350 km (217 mi) of cycling paths crisscross the metropolitan area, and bikes are welcome on the first car of Métro trains during off-peak hours. Ferries at the Vieux-Port take cyclists to Île Ste-Hélène and the south shore of the St. Lawrence River, where riders can connect to hundreds of miles of trails in the Montérégie region.

Féria de Vélo de Montréal *(Montréal Bike Festival).* Held each year at the end of May and continuing until the beginning of June, the Montréal Bike Festival is the biggest such celebration in North America. Events include a 22-km (14-mi) ride for children and challenge races of 100 km (62 mi) and 150 km (93 mi). It all culminates with as many as 50,000 cyclists taking over the streets for the **Tour de l'Île,** a 50-km (31-mi) night ride along a route encircling the city. ☎514/521–8356 or 800/567–8356 ⊕www.velo.qc.ca.

★ **Lachine Canal.** The most popular cycling trail on the island begins at the Vieux-Port and wends its way to the shores of Lac St-Louis in Lachine. Every summer weekend, guided cycling tours along the Lachine Canal are conducted by **Parks Canada** (☎514/283–6054 or 514/637–7433 ⊕www.pc.gc.ca).

La Maison des Cyclistes. Rent a bike, drop in to sip a coffee at the Bicicletta café, or browse through the cycling maps in the adjoining boutique. ✉1251 rue Rachel Est, Plateau Mont-Royal ☎514/521–8356 ⊕www.velo.qc.ca Ⓜ Mont-Royal.

Le Pôle des Rapides. This network of 100 km (62 mi) of bicycle trails follows lakefronts, canals, and aqueducts. ☎514/364–4490 ⊕www.poledesrapides.com.

Vélo Montréal. The best place to rent bicycles for a tour of Parc Maisonneuve, the Botanical Gardens, and the site of the 1976 summer Olympics is this east-end shop which is located directly on the bike path and near those destinations. ✉3880 rue Rachel Est, Rosemont ☎ 514/259–7272 ⊕www.velomontreal.com Ⓜ Pie-IX.

BOATING

In Montréal you can climb aboard a boat at a downtown wharf and be crashing through Class V white water minutes later.

Lachine Rapids Tours. For an hour-long voyage up the river in a big aluminum jet boat, Lachine Rapids Tours offers daily departures (every two hours) from May through October at a cost of C$60 per person with all gear included. Rafting trips are also available, or you can opt for a half-hour jaunt around the islands in a 10-passenger boat reaching speeds up to 100 KPH (62 MPH). Departures are every half hour between 10 AM and 6 PM from May to October at a cost of C$25 for adults. Trips are narrated in French and English. ☒ 47 de la Commune West, *Clock Tower Pier (for jet-boating) and Jacques Cartier Pier (for speedboating), located at the Old Port of Montréal, Vieux-Montréal* ☎*514/284–9607* ⊕*www.jetboatingmontreal.com* Ⓜ*Champ-de-Mars.*

FOOTBALL

Although there is some football played at the college level in Montréal, the quality pales in comparison to the high-stakes world of American college ball. When Montrealers think football, they think of their cherished Alouettes, who play their home games at the foot of Mont-Royal park in the wonderfully intimate Molson Stadium.

Montréal Alouettes. The 2002 national champions of the Canadian Football League play the Canadian version of the game—bigger field, just three downs, and a more wide-open style—under open skies at McGill University's Percival Molson Stadium from June through October. With ticket prices ranging from C$24.50 (end zones) to C$125 (Super Platinum), it's one of the best sporting deals in town. ☎*514/871–2266 information, 514/871–2255 tickets* ⊕*www.montrealalouettes.com.*

GOLF

Montréal golf enthusiasts have several excellent golf courses available to them, many less than a half-hour drive from downtown.

Tourisme Québec. For a complete listing of the many golf courses in the area, this is the best place to start. ☎*514/873–2015 or 800/363–7777* ⊕*www.bonjourquebec.com.*

Club de Golf Métropolitain Anjou *(Anjou Metropolitan Golf Club).* A clubhouse featuring a steak-house restaurant, a banquet hall, a snack bar, a terrace BBQ grill, and a pro shop with an indoor practice range makes this a top-notch facility—not to mention, of course, their par-72, 18-hole championship golf course (7,005 yards from the gold tees). They also have a slightly less challenging 18-hole executive course (2,751 yards) on their grounds. Rates for 18 holes range from C$18 to C$53, plus C$30 for an electric cart. Getting here is only a 20-minute drive from downtown Montréal. ☒*9555 blvd. du Golf, Anjou* ☎*514/353–5353* ⊕*www.golfmetropolitainanjou.com.*

Golf Dorval. A short car ride from downtown Montréal, Golf Dorval encompasses two 18-hole courses (par 70 and 72), a driving range, and two putting greens. Rates for 18 holes range from C$26 to C$47. A cart is an additional C$33. ☒*2000 av. Reverchon, Dorval* ☎*514/631–4653 (GOLF) for reservations* ⊕*www.golfdorval.com.*

Meadowbrook Golf Club. A somewhat challenging par-75, 18-hole course whose main selling point is its location, Meadowbrook is only a few miles from the heart of downtown Montréal. Rates range from C$20 to C$34 for 18 holes. A cart is C$28. The closest Métro stop is Ville-Marie, although it's quite a distance away. ✉ *8370 Côte St-Luc, Côte St-Luc* ☎ *514/488–6612* ⊕ *www.clubdegolfmeadowbrook.com.*

HOCKEY

Ice hockey is nothing short of an institution in Montréal, the city that arguably gave birth to the sport back in the late 19th century. Although variations of the game are said to have been played in other U.S. and Canadian cities as early as 1800, the first organized game of modern hockey was played in Montréal in 1875, and the first official team, the McGill University Hockey Club, was founded in Montréal in 1880. The city's beloved Montréal Canadiens is the oldest club in the National Hockey League and, as Montrealers will be keen to tell you, one of the most successful teams in North American sports history. The Habs, taken from Habitants, or early settlers, as they are affectionately referred to locally, have won 24 Stanley Cups, although they've been struggling in the standings for several years now and haven't won a cup since the 1992–93 season. Nevertheless, Les Canadiens are a great source of pride to the city's sports fans, and tickets for their local games continue to be a hot commodity.

Montréal Canadiens. The Habs meet National Hockey League rivals at the Centre Bell from October through April (and even later if they make the play-offs). Buy tickets in advance to guarantee a seat. ✉ *1260 rue de la Gauchetière Ouest, Downtown* ☎ *514/989–2841 or 514/790–1245* ⊕ *www.canadiens.com* Ⓜ *Lucien-L'Allier or Peel.*

McGill University Redmen. The Redmen make up in passion what they might lack in polish—especially when they take on their cross-city rivals, the Concordia University Stingers. ✉ *475 av. des Pins Ouest, Downtown* ☎ *514/398–7006* ⊕ *www.redmenhockey.com* Ⓜ *McGill.*

ICE-SKATING

Come the winter months, you don't have to look very far to find an ice-skating rink in Montréal. There are municipally run outdoor—and some indoor—rinks in virtually every corner of the city.

Access Montréal. For information on the numerous ice-skating rinks (at least 195 outdoor and 21 indoor) in the city, it's best to call or check the Web sites listed. Outdoor rinks are open from January until mid-March, and admission is free. The rinks on Île Ste-Hélène and at the Vieux-Port are especially large, but there is a C$4 admission charge to skate at the latter. ☎ *514/872–1111* ⊕ *www.ville.montreal.qc.ca.*

Atrium le Mille de la Gauchetière. You can skate year-round at this glassed-in atrium in a downtown skyscraper. There's disco skating Friday and Saturday nights from October to April, and ice shows are scheduled throughout the year. It's closed Monday from Easter to Thanksgiving. Skate rental is C$5.75 per day. ✉ *1000 rue de la Gauchetière, Downtown* ☎ *514/395–1000, 514/395–0555, or 514/395–1000* ⊕ *www.le1000.com* Ⓜ *Bonaventure.*

JOGGING

Most city parks have jogging paths, and you can also run the trail along the Lachine Canal.

Parc du Mont-Royal. For a panoramic view, head to the dirt track in Parc du Mont-Royal. It's a superb place for a tranquil jog surrounded by nature right in the middle of the city. ☎514/844–4928 ⊕*www. lemontroyal.qc.ca.*

OTHER SPORTS

☺ **Trapezium.** If you've ever longed to run away and join the circus, then the Trapezium can help you fulfill that fantasy. Instructors assess your skill level and then teach you how to fly through the air with the greatest of ease. Even the faint of heart have been known to take the plunge in the center's safe and friendly environment. ✉*2350 rue Dickson, Montréal Est* ☎*514/251–0615* ⊕*www.trapezium.qc.ca* ✆*C$40* Ⓜ*l'Assomption.*

ROCK CLIMBING

If you're planning on scaling any of the considerable mountains in the nearby Laurentian or Eastern Townships regions, you might first want to practice your technique at an indoor climbing center in Montréal.

Allez-Up. With the highest climbing walls in Montréal (48 feet), Allez-Up has 35 top ropes installed and offers more than 75 different routes. It's located on the edge of downtown Montréal in a landmark redbrick building, and rates start at C$13. Hours vary depending on the season, so it's best to call in advance. ✉*1339 rue Shearer, Pointe-St-Charles* ☎*514/989–9656* ⊕*www.allezup.com* Ⓜ*Charlevoix.*

☺ **Escalade Horizon Roc.** Located deep in the heart of the city's east end, Escalade Horizon Roc has expanded to feature more than 27,000 square feet of climbing surfaces, making it the largest climbing center in the world. It's open weekdays 5–11, Saturday 9–6, and Sunday 9–5. ✉*2350 rue Dickson, Montréal Est* ☎*514/899–5000* ⊕*www.horizon roc.com* Ⓜ*l'Assomption.*

SKIING & SNOWBOARDING

You don't have to travel far from Montréal to find good downhill skiing or snowboarding, but you do have to travel. There is a wealth of ski centers in both the Laurentian and Eastern Townships regions with pros and cons to each. The slopes in the Townships are generally steeper and slightly more challenging, but it requires more time to get out to them. Also, the Townships' centers tend to be quieter and more family-oriented, so if it's après-ski action you're looking for, you might prefer heading out to a Laurentian hill like Mont-St-Sauveur where, for many, partying is as much the experience as is conquering the slopes.

As for cross-country skiing, you needn't even leave the city to find choice locations to pursue the sport. There is a network of trails stretching throughout Mont-Royal park, and the Lachine Canal offers a 12-km (7-mi) stretch of relatively flat terrain, making for both a scenic and relatively simple cross-country excursion.

Tourisme Québec. The "Ski-Québec" brochure available from the tourism office has a wealth of information about skiing in and around the city. ☎*514/873–2015 or 800/363–7777* ⊕*www.bonjourquebec.com.*

CROSS-
COUNTRY
Cap-St-Jacques Regional Park. Cross-country trails crisscross most city parks, including Parcs des Îles, Maisonneuve, and Mont-Royal, but the best cross-country skiing on the island is found along the 32 km (20 mi) of trails in the 900-acre Cap-St-Jacques park in the city's west end, about a half-hour drive from downtown. To get to the park via public transportation, take the Métro to the Henri-Bourassa station and then Bus 69 west. ⊠ *20099 blvd. Gouin Ouest, Pierrefonds* ☎ *514/280–6784 or 514/280–6871* Ⓜ *Henri-Bourassa (Bus 69 west).*

DOWNHILL
Mont-Bromont. About a 45-minute drive from downtown Montréal, Mont-Bromont (54 trails, 9 lifts) is the closest Appalachian hill, with a 1,336-foot vertical drop. It's in the Eastern Townships, southeast of the city. ☎ *450/534–2200.*

Mont-St-Bruno. Mont-St-Bruno (19 trails, 4 lifts), on the south shore, has a modest vertical drop of 525 feet, but it includes Québec's biggest ski school and a high-speed lift. It also offers night skiing. ☎ *450/653–3441.*

Mont-St-Sauveur. With a vertical drop of 700 feet, Mont-St-Sauveur (38 trails, 8 lifts) is the closest decent-size ski area in the Laurentian Mountains, the winter and summer playground for Montrealers. It's about an hour's drive northwest of Montréal. ☎ *514/871–0101.*

Parc du Mont-Royal. Within Montréal, "the mountain," as it's familiarly called, is essentially a toboggan run, but its modest slope makes it ideal for beginners and little ones learning to ski.

SOCCER

Although soccer still isn't quite the phenomenon in Montréal that it is elsewhere around the globe, the city has been supporting one professional team, the Montréal Impact, since 1993. A new stadium built expressly for the Impact is scheduled to be completed in 2007, a strong indication of the sport's increasing popularity, and a sign that the team's local owners, the Saputo family, are firmly committed to seeing the sport prosper in Montréal.

Montréal Impact. A consistently strong member of the North American A league, the team plays from mid-May until mid-September at the Stade Saputo and is a great sports bargain. ☎ *514/790–1245 or 514/328–3668* ⊠ *4750 Sherbrooke Est.* ⊕ *www.impactmontreal.com.*

SWIMMING

Most of the city's municipal outdoor pools are open from mid-June through August. Admission is free weekdays and C$2.75 on weekends and holidays.

Bain Schubert. Swimming is free at this renovated art deco pool. ⊠ *3950 blvd. St-Laurent, Plateau Mont-Royal* ☎ *514/872–2587* Ⓜ *Sherbrooke or St-Laurent.*

Parc-Plage l'Île Notre-Dame. The water is always clean at this sandy man-made beach, located just over the water from downtown. To get there by public transit, take Bus 167 from the Métro station. ⊠ *West side of Île Notre-Dame, Île Notre-Dame* Ⓜ *Jean-Drapeau.*

Vieux-Montréal CEGEP. There is a free indoor pool, open noon–8:30 Tuesday through Friday and Saturday 9–4:30, on the campus of this Montréal junior college. ✉*255 rue Ontario Est, Quartier Latin* ☎*514/982–3457* Ⓜ*Berri-UQAM or St-Laurent.*

TENNIS

The City of Montréal maintains public tennis courts in several neighborhood parks around the city. Fees vary from court to court but are generally quite reasonable.

Accès Montréal. The Jeanne-Mance, Kent, Lafontaine, and Somerled parks all have public courts. For details, contact Accès Montréal. ☎*514/872–1111* ⊕*www.ville.montreal.qc.ca.*

WINDSURFING & SAILING

Although people have been sailing it for centuries, and windsurfing it for at least a couple of decades, who would ever have thought in a city where winters can last six months there would be opportunities to actually surf the St. Lawrence River? In 1999, South African champion kayaker and river surfer Corran Addison, a recent immigrant to Montréal, discovered a heretofore unknown yet ever-present 6-foot-tall standing wave that never breaks, thus allowing for an epic ride.

L'École de Voile de Lachine. You can rent sailboards and small sailboats at the Lachine Sailing School, where courses are offered as well. ✉*3045 blvd. St-Joseph, Lachine* ☎*514/634–4326* ⊕*www.ecoledevoilede lachine.com* Ⓜ*Angrignon.*

Where to Eat

The Beaver Club, Downtown Montréal.

WORD OF MOUTH

"There are lots of interesting, moderately priced restaurants in the plateau area, which is centered around St. Denis above Sherbrooke. On Duluth near St. Denis is a string of byob places, most are reasonable and fun. . . ."

—zootsi

Updated by
Joanne Latimer

GOOD RESTAURANTS CAN POP UP just about anywhere in Montréal, and sometimes they appear in the oddest places. Toqué!, for example, long touted as one of the city's best, is on the ground floor of an office tower in the financial district. Still, there are those certain areas—such as rue St-Denis and boulevard St-Laurent between rues Sherbrooke and Mont-Royal—that have long been the city's hottest dining strips, with everything from sandwich shops to high-price gourmet shrines.

The bring-your-own-wine craze started on rue Prince-Arthur and avenue Duluth, two lively pedestrian streets in the Plateau that still specialize in good, relatively low-cost meals. Most downtown restaurants are clustered between rues Guy and Peel on the side streets that run between boulevard René-Lévesque and rue Sherbrooke. Some interesting little cafés and restaurants have begun to spring up in the heart of the antiques district along rue Notre-Dame Ouest near avenue Atwater. Vieux-Montréal, too, has a good collection of restaurants, most of them clustered on rue St-Paul and Place Jacques-Cartier.

Wherever you go to eat, be sure to watch for such Québec specialties as veal from Charlevoix, lamb from Kamouraska, strawberries from Île d'Orléans, shrimp from Matane, lobster from the Îles-de-la-Madeleine, blueberries from Lac St-Jean, and cheese from just about everywhere.

When you dine out, you can usually order à la carte, but make sure to look for the table d'hôte, a two- to four-course package deal. It's usually more economical, often offers interesting specials, and may also take less time to prepare. If you want to splurge on time and money, consider a *menu dégustation,* a five- to seven-course tasting menu executed by the chef. It generally includes soup, salad, fish, sherbet (to cleanse the palate), a meat dish, dessert, and coffee or tea. At the city's finest restaurants, such a meal for two, along with a good bottle of wine, can cost more than C$200 and last four hours.

Menus in many restaurants are bilingual, but some are only in French. If you don't understand what a dish is, don't be shy about asking; a good server will be happy to explain. If you feel brave enough to order in French, remember that in French an *entrée* is an appetizer, and what Americans call an entrée is a *plat principal,* or main dish.

Dinner reservations are highly recommended for weekend dining.

WHERE TO EAT PLANNER

Hours

Montréal restaurants keep unpredictable schedules. Some close Sundays, some close Mondays, some never close. Call ahead. Kitchens generally stop taking orders at 10 or 11 pm, but eateries in the Old Port can remain open later in the summer, as do hot spots in the Plateau and Mile End. Downtown locations tend to focus on lunch, so they close earlier. Brunch is over by 3 pm.

What to Wear

Dress up! This is no time to wear your comfortable airport clothes. Women in Montréal take pride in their appearance, which features heels, pretty scarves, dresses, and jewelry. What about men? The standard uniform for hipsters is a fashionable shirt with dark jeans or dress pants. No running shoes, please. Men should also wear a jacket for restaurants in the $$$ range and above.

Prices

Long live the table d'hôte! This cost-cutting special is a regular feature at many Montréal restaurants. Chefs enjoy changing the three-course special on a daily or weekly basis, so it never gets boring. Tip: up-scale restaurants serve elaborate lunch menus at cut-rate prices, while some eateries have early bird prix-fixe deals. When it comes time to pay, it is not a "given" that you can use your debit card. Many destinations on the Plateau and elsewhere only accept cash or credit.

WHAT IT COSTS AT DINNER

¢	$	$$	$$$	$$$$
under C$8	C$8–C$12	C$13–C$20	C$21–C$30	over C$30

Price per person for a median main course or equivalent combination of smaller dishes.

Eating Out Strategy

Where should we eat? With hundreds of Montréal eateries competing for your attention, it may seem like a daunting decision. Here's an 80-plus selection of the city's best restaurants—from the hippest burger joints to the finest French dining this side of Paris.

Children

Since smoking was banned in restaurants, it's more common to see kids in bistros, brasseries and even up-scale dining rooms. Many of the eateries reviewed in this chapter are appropriate for families and are marked with a ☺ symbol.

Reservations

Pity the fool who doesn't plan ahead for a weekend meal. Reservations are key. Call at least three nights ahead for busy bistros. Because Montrealers eat quite late, it's possible to arrive unannounced before 7 pm and get a table—if you're lucky.

Smoking

Smoking is prohibited in all enclosed public spaces in Montréal, including restaurants and bars.

BEST BETS FOR MONTREAL DINING

With thousands of restaurants to choose from, how will you decide where to eat? Fodor's writers and editors have selected their favorite restaurants by price, cuisine, and experience in the Best Bets lists below. In the first column, Fodor's Choice properties represent the "best of the best" in every price category.

Fodor's Choice ★

Au Pied de Cochon, p. 118

Brioche Lyonnaise. p. 119

La Croissanterie Figaro, p. 121

La Rapière, p. 114

Schwartz's Delicatessen, p. 125

Toi Moi et Café, p. 126

Best By Price

¢

Binerie Mont-Royal, p. 118

Le Taj, p. 115

Mr. Steer, p. 116

St-Viateur Bagel & Café, p. 125

$

Alep, p. 118

Brioche Lyonnaise, p. 119

Café Souvenir, p. 119

Chalet Barbecue, p. 113

Chez Doval, p. 119

Rotisserie Panama, p. 125

Schwartz's Delicatessen, p. 125

$$

Bistro Boris, p. 126

L'Express, p. 123

Leméac, p. 122

m:brgr, p. 116

Pintxo, p. 124

Rumi, p. 125

$$$

Au Pied de Cochon, p. 118

Bonaparte, p. 127

Brasserie Brunoise, p. 113

Club Chasse et Pêche, p. 128

Mythos Ouzerie, p. 124

Rosalie, p. 116

$$$$

La Chronique, p. 121

Moishe's, p. 124

Nuances, p. 117

Toqué!, p. 129

Trinity Estiatoria, p. 117

Best By Cuisine

CAFÉS

Claude Postel, p. 127

La Croissanterie Figaro, p. 121

Les Gâteries, p. 123

Olive + Gourmando, p. 128

Toi Moi et Café, p. 126

FRENCH

Bonaparte, p. 127

Chez l'Épicier, p. 127

L'Express, p. 123

Narcisse Bistro Bar à Vin, p. 128

Nuances, p. 117

La Rapière, p. 114

GREEK

Milos, p. 123

Mythos Ouzerie, p. 124

Trinity Estiatoria, p. 117

ITALIAN

Da Emma, p. 128

Il Mulino, p. 120

Tre Marie, p. 126

Le Petit Italien, p. 122

STEAK

Moishe's, p. 124

Queue de Cheval, p. 116

Mr. Steer, p. 116

VEGETARIAN

Chu Chai, p. 120

Le Commensal, p. 115

Crudessence, p. 120

Best By Experience

BRUNCH

Café Souvenir, p. 119

Kaizen, p. 117

Senzala, p. 125

Toi Moi et Café, p. 126

HOT SPOTS

L'Express, p. 123

Joe Beef, p. 114

Koko, p. 121

Lab, p. 121

LATE-NIGHT DINING

Da Emma, p. 128

Leméac, p. 122

Rotisserie Panama, p. 125

MOST ROMANTIC

Chez l'Épicier, p. 127

Club Chasse et Pêche, p. 128

Verses, p. 129

SINGLES SCENE

L'Assommoir, p. 122

Globe, p. 120

Lab, p. 121

Med Grill, p. 123

DOWNTOWN & CHINATOWN

$$$$ ✕**Beaver Club.** This grand old institution is now contemporary, with
CONTINENTAL tapestry banquettes and a brown, beige, and cream color scheme. It's
still pretty sumptuous, with wing chairs, starched linens, an impeccable
staff, and a menu that relies on such classics as roast beef, grilled chops,
poached salmon, and Cornish hens. The bar serves the best martini
in the city. ✉*Fairmont Le Reine Elizabeth, 900 blvd. René-Lévesque
Ouest, Downtown* ☎*514/861–3511 Jacket and tie* ☐*AE, D, DC,
MC, V* ⊘*Closed Sun. and July. No dinner Mon., no lunch Sat. or Aug.*
Ⓜ*Bonaventure.* ✢ *5D*

$$$ ✕**Bistro Gourmet.** Yogi Berra's immortal line—"Nobody goes to that
FRENCH restaurant anymore, it's too crowded"—could easily be applied to Chef
Gabriel Ohana's tiny yellow and blue room. It's usually so packed that
service can be slow, especially on weekends. But that's because the
food is worth the wait. Try the house specialties: flank steak and rack
of lamb with herbs. ✉*2100 rue St-Mathieu, Downtown* ☎*514/846–
1553* ☐*MC, V* ⊘*No lunch weekends* Ⓜ*Guy-Concordia.* ✢ *5B*

$$$ ✕**Brasserie Brunoise.** Juicy steak frit is the backbone of this adapted
FRENCH Parisian brasserie. Adapted how? The menu has French classics—duck
confit and Lyonnaise salad—alongside unexpected treats like shepherd's
pie, Moroccan lamb shank, and red pepper penne. Long, wooden banquet tables make it homey, but the Brunoise isn't as noisy as some
brasseries, so it attracts couples and business diners who want to chat.
Warning: there are big screens for sporting events, so make your dinner
reservation around the hockey schedule. ✉*1012 rue de la Montagne,
Downtown* ☎*514/933–3885* ⚑*Reservations recommended* ☐*AE,
MC, V* ⊘*Closed Sun.* No weekend lunch Ⓜ*Lucien L'Allier.* ✢ *5C*

$$$ ✕**Café Ferreira.** A huge mural of antique pottery fragments decorates
PORTUGUESE the pale-yellow walls of this high-ceiling room—an elegant setting for
its "haute" version of Portuguese cuisine. Chef Marino Tavares helms
the open-concept kitchen, which is renowned for its roasted black cod,
its traditional soup made with kale and sausage, and its seared tuna. An
excellent meal is also made from appetizers like giant shrimp tempura
and grilled octopus. ✉*1446 rue Peel, Downtown* ☎*514/848–0988*
☐*AE, MC, V* ⊘*No lunch Sat.* Ⓜ*Peel.* ✢ *4D*

$$$ ✕**Cavalli.** The young and the beautiful like to sip cocktails by Cavalli's
ITALIAN big front window, which in summer is open to the passing scene on
busy rue Peel. The interior—a black illuminated bar, green and pink
velvet chairs, and blond-wood paneling—makes an enticing backdrop.
The food is Italian, mostly, with Asian influences. Chefs Ross Gur-
reri and Frank Gioffre marinate the Chilean sea bass in miso, and
serve their mac 'n' cheese with truffles. Models order the endive salad.
✉*2040 rue Peel, Downtown* ☎*514/843–5100* ⚑*Reservations essential* ☐*AE, DC, MC, V* ⊘*No lunch weekends* Ⓜ*Peel.* ✢ *4D*

$ ✕**Chalet Barbecue.** Fast-food restaurants across Canada sell what
SOUTHERN they call "Montréal-style barbecued chicken." The claims are laugh-
able. For the real thing, head to Chalet Barbecue and line up with
the cabbies, truck drivers, and local families for crispy, spit-barbecued
chicken served with a slightly spicy, gravylike sauce and mountains of
french fries. You can eat in—call the decor rustic vinyl—or order your

chicken to go. ✉*5456 rue Sherbrooke Ouest, Notre-Dame-de-Grace* ☎*514/489–7235* ▤*MC, V* Ⓜ*Vendôme.* ✛*5A*

$$$
ITALIAN

✕**Da Vinci.** If you're a hockey fan, book a table near the front of Da Vinci's Victorian dining room and keep an eye on the door. If you're lucky, you might spot hot-shot players like Saku Koivu or Alexei Kovalev of the Montréal Canadiens dropping in for roast veal tenderloin or crab-stuffed ravioli. Freshly renovated with white, square chairs and modern art, you can still expect the discreet service and generous portions that have made Da Vinci an after-practice and after-game favorite for decades. When ordering, however, keep in mind just how much professional hockey players earn these days. ✉*1180 rue Bishop, Downtown* ☎*514/874–2001* ⌕*Reservations essential* ▤*AE, DC, MC, V* ⊘*Closed Sun.* Ⓜ*Guy-Concordia.* ✛*5C*

$$–$$$
INDIAN

✕**Devi.** Devi's chefs cater to the true aficionados who know there's more to food of the Asian subcontinent than hot, hotter, and scalding— although some of their less subtly spiced dishes (the lamb vindaloo, for example) can still take your breath away. Favorite dishes of middling intensity include the new bhatti murg tikka (chicken) and the Manchurian cauliflower. And for the romantic, the setting is classy-exotic, with jeweled lanterns and raw-silk hangings. ✉*1450 rue Crescent, Downtown* ☎*514/286–0303* ▤*AE, DC, MC, V* ⊘*No lunch Sun.* Ⓜ*Guy-Concordia or Peel.* ✛*5C*

$$$$
FRENCH

✕**Guy and Dodo Morali.** In the best French tradition, Guy runs the kitchen and wife Dodo handles the front room, although Guy wanders out occasionally to chat with customers and listen to complaints and compliments. The decor's classic —pale yellow walls hung with impressionist prints and photos of Paris—as is the cooking. The daily table-d'hôte menu is the best bet, with openers such as lobster bisque followed by sweetbreads with mushrooms or lobster poached with champagne. For dessert, try the tarte tatin (apples and caramel with crème anglaise). In summer, diners spill out onto a little terrace on rue Metcalfe. ✉*Les Cours Mont-Royal, 1444 rue Metcalfe, Downtown* ☎*514/842–3636* ⌕*Reservations essential* ▤*AE, DC, MC, V* ⊘*Closed Sun.* Ⓜ*Peel.* ✛*4D*

$$$
CONTEMPORARY
Fodor's Choice
★

✕**Joe Beef.** Dining at Joe Beef is a little like being invited to a dinner party by a couple of friends who just happen to be top-notch chefs. David MacMillan and Frédéric Morin were pioneers of Montréal's modern dining scene until they got tired of living on the edge and opened this little restaurant to rediscover the joy of cooking. Everything written on the chalkboard menu is simple and good, from the oysters to organic rib steak. If the booths in Joe Beef are full, move to Liverpool House, their restaurant right next door. ✉*2491 rue Notre-Dame Ouest, Downtown* ☎*514/935–6504* ⌕*Reservations essential* ▤*AE, DC, MC, V* ⊘*Closed Sun. and Mon. No lunch* Ⓜ*Lionel-Groulx.* ✛*6B*

$$$–$$$$
FRENCH
Fodor's Choice
★

✕**La Rapière.** The musketeer D'Artagnan came from southwestern France, as do most of this elegant restaurant's specialties. Indulge in goose cassoulet, rack of lamb, or Dover sole. For dessert there's nougat ice with custard, crème brûlée, or an excellent cheese plate. The room itself is soothing, with terra-cotta-color walls, tapestries, and stained-glass windows. Children receive special attention from the chef, who is a good sport about their limited palates. ✉*Sun Life Building, 1155 rue Metcalfe, Downtown* ☎*514/871–8920* ♨*Reservations essential* 🚫*AE, DC, MC, V* ⊘*Closed Sun; Closed July 20–Aug. 17; No lunch Sat.* Ⓜ*Peel.* ✛ *5D*

$$$ ✕**Le Caveau.** Among the towers of downtown is this Victorian house
FRENCH where buttery French sauces and creamy desserts have survived the onslaught of nouvelle cuisine. The restaurant takes its name from its warm and comfortable cellar, but if you don't like low ceilings, there's plenty of room upstairs amid the sculptures and paintings on the upper two floors. Main courses might include salmon, tuna and beef tartar, or rack of lamb crusted with bread crumbs, mustard, garlic, and herbs. A flexible children's menu, rare in restaurants of Le Caveau's caliber, is available. ✉*2063 av. Victoria, Downtown* ☎*514/844–1624* 🚫*AE, DC, MC, V* ⊘*No lunch weekends* Ⓜ*McGill.* ✛ *4D*

$$ ✕**Le Commensal.** You don't have to be a vegetarian to like Le Com-
VEGETARIAN mensal. Even members of the steak-frites crowd drop in occasionally to sample the salads, couscous, and meatless versions of such favorites as lasagna and shepherd's pie that this Montréal-grown chain dishes out. The food is served buffet style and sold by weight. There are at least seven outlets on the island, all of them big and bright with modern furniture; the nicest is on the second floor of a downtown building with windows overlooking busy, fashionable rue McGill College. ✉*1204 rue McGill College, Downtown* ☎*514/871–1480* 🚫*AE, DC, MC, V* Ⓜ*McGill* ✉*1720 rue St-Denis, Quartier Latin* ☎*514/845–2627* Ⓜ*Sherbrooke* ✉*5199 ch. de la Côte-des-Neiges, Plateau Mont-Royal* ☎*514/733–9755* Ⓜ*Côte-des-Neiges.* ✛ *4D*

$$$ ✕**Le Paris.** Nothing has changed much at Le Paris since the Poucant
FRENCH family opened it in 1950. And why should it? Every city needs a faded bistro with big tables, age-dimmed paint, and honest, soulful French food like grilled *boudin* (blood sausage), calves' liver, and roast chicken. It's the kind of place that makes you want to take your shoes off and relax, and maybe ask the regular at the next table what he recommends. If you do, chances are he'll suggest you start with the *brandade de morue*—a kind of spread made with salt cod, mashed potatoes, garlic, and cream—served with green salad. And to finish? How about stewed rhubarb or *île flottante* (meringue floating in a sea of custard)? ✉*1812 rue Ste-Catherine Ouest, Downtown* ☎*514/937–4898* 🚫*DC, MC, V* ⊘*Closed Sun.* Ⓜ*Guy-Concordia.* ✛ *5C*

$$ ✕**Le Taj.** The focus is the cuisine of northern India, less spicy and more
INDIAN delicate than that of the south. Tandoori ovens seal in the flavors of the grilled meat and fish. It's noteworthy that a new vegetarian tandoori platter was added to the menu, among the vegetarian choices like *thali*—one vegetable entrée, lentils, and basmati rice—and *saag paneer,* spicy white cheese with spinach. A nine-course lunch buffet costs C$12.95, and an "Indian feast" is C$38. ✉*2077 rue Stanley, Downtown* ☎*514/845–9015* 🚫*AE, MC, V* ⊘*No lunch Sat.* Ⓜ*Peel.* ✛ *4D*

$$ ✕**Maison Kam Fung.** Kam Fung is no place for a romantic tête-à-tête, but
CHINESE it's a great place to go with a gang of friends for a noisy dim sum feast. From 7 AM until 3 PM waiters clatter up and down the aisles between

6

tables, pushing a parade of trolleys bearing such treats as firm dumplings stuffed with pork and chicken, stir-fried squid, and barbecued chicken feet. In the evening you can order Cantonese and Szechuan dishes until 10 pm. The Peking duck does not require advanced notice! ⊠ *1111 rue St-Urbain, Chinatown* ☎ *514/878–2888* ⊟ *AE, DC, MC, V* Ⓜ *Place-d'Armes.* ✛ *4F*

$$$
CANADIAN
✕ **m:brgr.** New to the scene in 2008, this is a hip place to build a specialty burger with toppings like apple-wood bacon, grilled pineapple, and goat cheese. Even highfalutin foodies admit that m:brgr is a cut above, with designer mac 'n' cheese (served with truffle carpaccio, if you want) and Angus beef hot dogs. Surrounded by panoramic murals of Montréal, students, families, and young couples share dipping sauces, sweet potato fries, and fresh-baked cookies for dessert. ⊠ *2025 rue Drummond, Downtown* ☎ *514/906–2747* ⊟ *AE, MC, V* ✛ *4C*

$
STEAK
✕ **Mr. Steer.** Why mess with a winning formula? Brisk service, vinyl booths, and juicy, almost spherical hamburgers served slightly *saignant* (rare) with heaps of curled "Suzie Q" french fries. For 50 years, locals have been chowing down on steer burgers at this unpretentious spot in the downtown shopping district, near the major cinemas. Steak, too, is available at reasonable prices. What's new? The veggie burgers, made from mushrooms and chickpeas (not soy). ⊠ *1198 rue Ste-Catherine Ouest, Downtown* ☎ *514/866–3233* ⊟ *MC, V* Ⓜ *Peel.* ✛ *5D*

$$$$
CHINESE
✕ **Orchidée de Chine.** Diners feast on such dishes as baby bok choy with mushrooms, spicy spareribs, feather-light fried soft-shell crabs with black-bean sauce, and tender strips of beef served with bell peppers and fried basil leaves. The cream-and-yellow, glassed-in dining room has a great view onto a busy, fashionable sidewalk; a more intimate room is in the back. ⊠ *2017 rue Peel, Downtown* ☎ *514/287–1878* ⚑ *Reservations essential* ⊟ *AE, DC, MC, V* ☉ *Closed Sun. No lunch Sat.* Ⓜ *Peel.* ✛ *4D*

$$$$
STEAK
✕ **Queue de Cheval.** The white-aproned chefs toiling away under the 20-foot-wide copper canopy look more like pagan priests engaged in some arcane ritual than cooks grilling slabs of dry-aged, prime beef on a huge open grill. The meat is sold by the pound, and all accompaniments are extra, so the crowd is pretty much limited to people whose wallets are as thick as the steaks—say, 1½ to 3½ inches. "Go big or stay home" is Queue de Cheval's motto, so don't say you weren't warned. Herringbone brick walls and wide windows create an atmosphere that's half stable, half château. Cigar smoking is permitted, if not encouraged. Start your evening with a vodka martini on the veranda, where mistresses and testosterone make for a heady mix. ⊠ *1221 blvd. René-Lévesque Ouest, Downtown* ☎ *514/390–0090* ⊟ *AE, D, DC, MC, V* Ⓜ *Peel.* ✛ *5C*

$$$
FRENCH
✕ **Rosalie.** Rosalie's long granite bar and leather chairs are all very chic, but it's the big *terrasse* out front that draws the crowds on late summer afternoons. And the litchi martinis should get some credit. The thirtysomething professionals who pour in after work often stay for an early supper by Chef Gabriel Campopiano before heading out on the town. Try the braised veal cheeks or the octopus appetizer. ⊠ *1232 rue*

Where to Refuel Around Town

Grabbing a decent, quick bite in a food-mad city like Montréal is pretty easy—and can give you a good, inexpensive sampling of typical French Canadian cuisine.

For local flavor, try either La Belle Province or Lafleur fast-food restaurants, two popular Québec casse croute (snack bars) chains offering up the very finest in authentic poutine.

Several steps up the fast-food chain are the Barbecue St-Hubert restaurants for Montréal-style chicken with crispy french fries and spicy gravy, and Chez Cora restaurants for sumptuous and—if you stick to the fruity side of the menu—healthful breakfasts.

For a picnic lunch, two local bakery chains—Première Moisson and Pain Doré—make terrific sandwiches on really good fresh bread. (All is good, here.)

---

de la Montagne, Downtown ☎*514/392–1970* ▤*AE, MC, V* Ⓜ*Guy-Concordia.* ✛ *5C*

$$$$
SEAFOOD
✕ **Trinity Estiatoria.** Well-dressed guests enter through Aegean blue doors and sweep up marble stairs to view the 300-seat new taverna below—alive with lavish displays of fish on ice, an open kitchen solarium, and a pond in the middle. Like a prosperous villa in Santorini, the air crackles with good-natured activity. But it's not all show. Chef John Zoumis's platters of grilled meat and fish (try the wild sea bass) keep everyone happy before they retire to the Moroccan-style lounge behind sheer curtains. Bragging rights: Sommelier Theo Diamantis' wine cellar of private Greek imports won a Wine Spectator award. ✉*1445 rue Drummond, Downtown* ☎*514/787–4648* ☖*Reservations essential* ▤*AE, D, DC, MC, V* ☾*No lunch weekends* Ⓜ*Stanley.* ✛ *5C*

THE ISLANDS

$$$$
FRENCH
✕ **Nuances.** If you hit the jackpot on one of the slot machines downstairs, you'll have no trouble paying the bill at the Casino de Montréal's premier restaurant. Gracious and warm, the staff guides dinner guests to romantic tables by the windows, which offer the best view of Montréal's twinkling skyline. Refreshed by a makeover, Nuances looks and feels like a boutique hotel, with cushy white seats and back-lit paintings. Now the decor fits with the fancy cuisine by executive chef Jean-Pierre Curtat, who goes so far as to make his own butter. Warm lobster salad and Alaskan cod are just two of the kitchen's specialties. ✉*1 av. du Casino, Île Notre-Dame* ☎*514/392–2708* ☖*Reservations essential* ▤*AE, DC, MC, V* ☾*No lunch* Ⓜ*Jean-Drapeau.* ✛ *6G*

MONT-ROYAL & ENVIRONS

$$$
JAPANESE
✕ **Kaizen.** If you like a little drama with your sushi, Kaizen's black-clad waitresses, floor-to-ceiling blue curtains, and glassed-in wine cellar certainly add a dash of theater to dinner. It's a buzz-filled place that attracts the kind of well-dressed patrons who can't bear to leave their

cell phone and Blackberry at home. The sushi, maki, lambas, sashimi, and seafood soups are all well above average, and the Kobe beef is just daring enough to be interesting without being intimidating. There's a new weekend brunch with hard-to-find fresh soba noodles. ⊠*4075 rue Ste-Catherine Ouest, Westmount* ☎*514/932–5654* ⚂*Reservations essential* ⊟*AE, MC, V* Ⓜ*Atwater.* ✛ *5A*

$$$
CONTEMPORARY

✕**Tavern on the Square.** The corporate crowd sips martinis at the bar, while well-dressed young moms entertain their toddlers on the *terrasse.* This easygoing bistro has a daytime clientele devoted to the goat-cheese salads, Thai chicken, and Asian curries, while the evening crowd comes for updated Italian classics like "mac 'n' cheese" with bacon and bread crumbs. Business diners gravitate toward the veal and New York sirloin steak. ⊠*1 Westmount Sq., Westmount* ☎*514/989–9779* ⊟*AE, DC, MC, V* ☉*Closed Sun. No lunch Sat.* Ⓜ*Atwater.* ✛ *5A*

THE PLATEAU & ENVIRONS

$$
MIDDLE EASTERN

✕**Alep.** Bring your entire clan to Alep, where the music, plants, ivy, and stone-wall construction encourage relaxation. Graze on the *mouhamara* (pomegranate and walnuts), *sabanegh* (spinach and onions), *fattouche* (salad with pita and mint), and *yalanti* (vine leaves stuffed with rice, chickpeas, walnuts, and tomatoes). For an Armenian flavor, try the salad with cumin and flefle. Kebabs, pronounced "kababbs," dominate the main courses. ⊠*199 rue Jean-Talon Est, Little Italy* ☎*514/270–6396* ⊟*MC, V* ☉*Closed Sun. and Mon.* Ⓜ*Jean-Talon or de Castelnau.* ✛ *1D*

$$$
CANADIAN
Fodor's Choice
★

✕**Au Pied de Cochon.** Whatever you do, don't let your cardiologist see Martin Picard's menu; if he spots the pigs' feet stuffed with foie gras, he's liable to have a stroke, and he won't be too happy about the pork hocks braised in maple syrup, either, or the *oreilles-de-crisse* (literally, Christ's ears)—crispy, deep-fried crescents of pork skin that Picard serves as appetizers. But it's foie gras that Picard really loves. He lavishes the stuff on everything, including hamburgers and his own version of poutine. Oddly enough, the trendy crowd that packs his noisy brasserie every night doesn't look particularly chubby. In summer, they gravitate to the seafood platters, chatting about Picard's television show on the Food Network, "The Wild Chef." ⊠*536 av. Duluth, Plateau Mont-Royal* ☎*514/281–1114* ⚂*Reservations essential* ⊟*AE, D, DC, MC, V* ☉*Closed Mon. No lunch* Ⓜ*Sherbrooke or Mont-Royal.* ✛ *2F*

¢
CANADIAN

✕**Binerie Mont-Royal.** That rarest of the city's culinary finds—authentic Québecois food—is the specialty at this tiny restaurant. Sit at the long counter and make your way through bowls of stew made with meatballs and pigs' feet, various kinds of tourtière, and pork and beans. It's cheap, filling, and charming. ⊠*367 av. Mont-Royal Est, Plateau Mont-Royal* ☎*514/285–9078* ⊟*No credit cards* ☉*No dinner weekends* Ⓜ*Mont-Royal.* ✛ *1E*

$$$
FRENCH

✕**Bistro Bienville.** You probably know people whose dining rooms are larger than the Bistro Bienville. Twenty people will fill it, and that includes a handful sitting at the counter overlooking the postage-sized kitchen, where a couple of very young and very enthusiastic chefs cheerfully crank out reasonably priced versions of such classics as calamari, sweetbreads, and roast duck. Dishes are sized (and priced) so that two make a meal. ⊠*4650 rue de Mentana, Mont-Royal* ☎*514/509–1269* ⌕*Reservations essential* ▤*AE, D, DC, MC, V* ⊘*Closed Sun.–Mon. No lunch Sat.* Ⓜ *Mont-Royal.* ✛*1F*

$$
BRASSERIE
✕**Brasserie Les Enfants Terribles.** With its cavernous corner spot on Outremont's trendy av. Bernard, sophisticated yet playful decor, and artfully prepared comfort food, Les Enfant Terribles packs 'em in at all hours. The menu at this brasserie-with-a-twist, owned and run by native-born Montrealer Francine Brûlé, is a mix of high-class cuisine and comfort food favorites: beef tartare with truffle oil; fish and chips; roasted salmon with tomato, mango, and basil salsa; and mac 'n' cheese. While the food is the main attraction, take notice of the interior decor: A lane from an old bowling alley was transformed into the bar, the metal chairs are from an area school, and a demolished barn's faded wood lines the walls. As for the photos on the menu and clear thumbprints infused on the glasses? Those are from Brûlé's very own enfants terribles. ⊠*1257 Bernard Ouest, Outremont, Montréal* ☎*514/759–9981* ▤*AE, MC, V.* ✛*2B*

$$
CAFÉ
Fodor'sChoice
★
✕**Brioche Lyonnaise.** You'll have to go a long way to find a better butter brioche—and try saying that three times quickly—than the one at the Brioche Lyonnaise. Order one along with a steaming bowl of café-au-lait (please don't call it a latte—not here), and you've got a breakfast fit for a king. Come back in the afternoon to try one of the butter-and-cream-loaded pastries in the display case. Heartier fare is available at lunch and dinner, and the place stays open until midnight. The atrium in the back and a *terrasse* are open when the weather is nice. ⊠*1593 rue St-Denis, Quartier Latin* ☎*514/842–7017* ▤*AE, MC, V* Ⓜ*Berri-UQAM.* ✛*3F*

¢–$
CAFÉ
✕**Café Souvenir.** From media moguls to Olympic medalists, you'll find them here, nibbling crêpes with Chantilly cream or hauling on double espressos. Weekend brunch is the signature meal at this Parisian-style eatery, where omelets and croque matins comes with generous mounds of fresh fruit. Diners exchange sections of The New York Times and check their Blackberries, happy to chat at the breakfast bar or at the bistro tables. For a casual evening meal, regulars rave about the hamburgers, the quesadillas and the cesar salad with chicken. ⊠*1261 rue Bernard O., Outremont* ☎*514/948-5259* ▤*AE, MC, V* Ⓜ*Outremont or Parc* ✛*2B*

$$
THAI
✕**Chao Phraya.** The huge front window of this bright, airy restaurant decorated with subtle Asian accents overlooks fashionable rue Laurier. Customers come for such classics as crispy spinach, chicken with peanut sauce, crunchy *poe pia* (tightly wrapped spring rolls), *pha koung* (grilled-shrimp salad), and fried halibut in a red curry sauce with lime juice. For Thai food, it's a bit pricey, but reliable. ⊠*50 rue Laurier Ouest, Laurier* ☎*514/272–5339* ⌕*Reservations essential* ▤*AE, DC, MC, V* ⊘*No lunch* Ⓜ*Laurier.* ✛*3C*

$$
PORTUGUESE
✕**Chez Doval.** Chez Doval is a neighborhood restaurant with a split personality. If you're looking for a little intimacy, book a table in the softly lighted dining room by the main entrance; if you're looking for some-

6

thing a little more raucous—guitar music, maybe a friendly argument about sports or politics—try the tavern on the far side. Foodwise, it doesn't really matter where you sit. The chicken, sardines, grouper, and squid—all broiled à-la-Portugaise on an open grill behind the bar—are succulent, simple, and good. Good prices attract artsies from afar. ⊠ *150 rue Marie-Anne Est, Plateau Mont-Royal* ☎ *514/843–3390* ☐ *AE, MC, V* Ⓜ *Mont-Royal.* ✛ *1E*

$$ ✕ **Chu Chai.** Vegetarians can dine well in any Thai restaurant, as veg-
VEGETARIAN etable dishes abound. But chefs at the rigorously vegan Chu Chai also prepare meatless versions of such classics as calamari with basil, duck salad with pepper and mint leaves, fish with three hot sauces, and beef with yellow curry and coconut milk, substituting soy and *seitan* (a firm, chewy meat substitute made from wheat gluten) for the real thing. Don't leave without trying the miam kram (coconut, ginger, nuts, and lime) appetizer. ⊠ *4088 rue St-Denis, Plateau Mont-Royal* ☎ *514/843– 4194* ⚭ *Reservations essential* ☐ *AE, DC, MC, V* Ⓜ *Sherbrooke or Mont-Royal.* ✛ *2E*

$$ ✕ **Crudessence.** Hippies and health nuts rejoiced at the opening of this
VEGETARIAN casual, raw food counter near Jean Mance Park. Open for lunch and dinner, Crudessence promises that its tasty tamales, curry roles, spring rolls, and zucchini lasagna are organic, vegetarian, and raw. Sit at the recycled wooden bar and sip smoothies made of sesame or almond milk. If the weather is nice, take a chair on the sidewalk and watch circus practice in the park. ⊠ *105 rue Rachel Ouest, Plateau Mont-Royal* ☎ *514/510–9299* ☐ *Interact only* ☽ *No dinner Mon.* Ⓜ *Mont-Royal.* ✛ *2D*

$$$ ✕ **Globe.** There's a persistent rumor that some people actually go to the
CONTEMPORARY Globe for Chef Alex Rolland's powerful plates of food. No, they don't just order up braised bison or crab ravioli to rubberneck for celebrities and ogle pretty patrons. Copious seafood platters and suckling pig dishes are almost enough to make us forget that George Clooney once fell for a barmaid here. Since then, Leonardo DiCaprio and Steven Spielberg have been spotted chowing down in Globe's square-shaped booths. ⊠ *3455 blvd. St-Laurent, Plateau Mont-Royal* ☎ *514/284– 3823* ☐ *AE, DC, MC, V* ☽ *No lunch* Ⓜ *Sherbrooke.* ✛ *3E*

$$ ✕ **Ian Perreault.** Part food bar, part take-out counter, Ian Perreault is an
CONTEMPORARY up-scale commissary in the entrance of the grand old Theatre Outrem-
★ ont. With its hot pink lamps, Baroque mirrors and flocked tapestry, it's easy to get distracted from the superior quality of the chef's prêt-a-manger dinners. (Most meals require re-heating or a small amount of finishing). Ravioli and risotto dishes sell out fast, as do the prepared lamb, duck and chicken dinners. At the counter, order a soup, sandwich or salad to eat on the outdoor patio. Try a pot of the chef's homemade preserves, like spicy ketchup with dates, or pickled onions in vanilla Bourbon. Parking is brutal outside the theatre, so be prepared to walk a distance from the car. ⊠ *1248 rue Bernard O., Outremont* ☎ *514/948- 1248* ☐ *MC, V* ☽ *Closed Sunday and Monday.* Ⓜ *Outremont* ✛ *1D*

$$$ ✕ **Il Mulino.** No longer "rustic," Il Mulino has a fresh decor that matches
ITALIAN its kitchen's uncompromising standards. This upscale, family-run trat-toria in Little Italy was made over with chocolate-brown chairs, white

linens, and marble. All the better to enjoy the comfort food, such as roasted baby goat, roasted lamb, risotto, gnocchi, and antipasti. Wine lovers are impressed by the 250-label cellar of private imports. ✉ *236 rue St-Zotique Est, Little Italy* ☎ *514/273–5776* ⚑ *Reservations essential* ▤ *AE, DC, MC, V* ⊘ *Closed Sun. and Mon.* Ⓜ *Beaubien.* ✛ *1G*

$$$
CONTEMPORARY

✕ **Koko.** Wear your slinkiest dress and heels when heading to Koko, perched atop Hôtel Opus. The decor at this hopping new restaurant says it all—black-velvet curtains, silver sofas, black-leather benches, flocked pillows, twinkling chandeliers, and baroque mirrors. The vibe is "cheery urban goth," with table accents in bamboo to foreshadow the Asian-inspired cuisine—spicy masala lobster, curried lentil hash, and shrimp toast. Outside, on the airy terrace, black-and-white sectional couches harbor tourists and locals seeking refreshment with an option to flirt. ✉ *10 rue Sherbrooke Ouest, Quartier Latin* ☎ *514/657–5656* ▤ *AE, DC, MC, V* ⊘ *No lunch* Ⓜ *St-Laurent.* ✛ *3E*

$
CONTEMPORARY

✕ **Lab.** Home of celebrity mixologists Fabien Maillard and Sam Dalcourt, Lab is the perfect showcase for their flare bartending skills. Wearing vests, silk ties and silver arm bands, this duo whips up original cocktails, like the Vanilla Twist Collins and the Lab Potion, in the comfort of their speakeasy-style bar. With great aplomb, over 80 cocktails are mixed at the bar—bottles flying—while Quebec's Schoun beer is steadily consumed by knowing locals who can't find it anywhere else in town. Perched on wood-and-leather stools, clients make easy conversation without yelling over softly piped classic rock music. ✉ *1351 rue Rachel E. H2J 2K2, Plateau Mont-Royal* ☎ *514/544-1333* ▤ *MC, V* Ⓜ *Sherbrooke* ✛ *1G*

$$$
CONTEMPORARY

✕ **La Chronique.** It's a pretty place with scarlet walls and black-and-white pictures, but people don't come to Chef Marc de Canck's little 36-seat restaurant for the ambience or for the crowd; they come, quite simply, for the food. Without fuss or fanfare, De Canck has been cranking out the city's most adventurous dishes ever since he opened in 1995. The man doesn't seem capable of compromise or playing safe. His work seamlessly blends lightened French fare with Japanese, Chinese, and Creole touches. Starters like sashimi salmon rubbed with coarsely ground pepper, coriander, and mustard seed might precede veal sweetbreads with chorizo or panfried mahimahi with thin slices of eggplant filled with goat cheese. To spend hours savouring the food, order the prix-fixe meals—five courses are C$72, and seven courses are C$100. ✉ *99 rue Laurier Ouest, Mile-End* ☎ *514/271–3095* ⚑ *Reservations essential* ▤ *AE, DC, MC, V* ⊘ *No weekend lunch* Ⓜ *Laurier* ✛ *3C.*

$–$$
CAFÉ
Fodor's Choice
★

✕ **La Croissanterie Figaro.** Famous for its wrap-around patio and Parisian vibe, La Croissanterie is comfortable inside its 100-year old corner building. It's hard to know which architectural detail to admire first—the Art Deco chandelier, the Art Nouveau bar imported from Argentina, the "gilded" tables, the copper vats, the stained glass or the wood work. It's fun to sit and stare at the antique décor, while local television actors nibble the homemade croissants and nurse big bowls of café au lait. Although this is a full bistro, serving three meals every day of the week, it shines brightest in the morning, serving the Special Bonjour croissant with ham and cheese and hearty sandwiches. ✉ *5200*

6

rue Hutchison H2V 4B3, Outremont ☎514/278-6567 ⊟*AE, MC, V* Ⓜ*Outremont* ⊹ *1D*

$–$$
FRENCH
★
✕ **La Moulerie.** This bustling French brasserie focuses its efforts on mussels, luring in local media personalities with the all-white décor, banquet-style tables and the chef's weekly special. But stick to the namesake dish, which comes with a choice of 24 sauces. For over 20 years, diners have been torn between the butter sauce, the curry-ginger sauce and the tomato sauce with mustard. Weekend brunch is a draw, especially in the summer when the wrap-around patio is a prime mingling location. Try the eggs benedict with a side order of crepes. ⊠*1249 rue Bernard O., Outremont* ☎514/273-8132 ⌕*Reservations essential* ⊟*AE, MC, V* Ⓜ*Outremont or Parc* ⊹ *2B*

$$$
CONTEMPORARY
✕ **L'Assommoir.** The cocktail menu originally put this hip bistro on the map, drawing crowds for creative martinis (think cucumber and basil), and now the food holds its own. House specialties are ceviche—the menu lists over 10 variations of raw fish "cooked" in citrus—and heaps of grilled meat and fish served on wooden chopping blocks. Young partiers like the cafeteria-style tables, where they mingle over ginger-beer cocktails and tapas. ⊠*112 rue Bernard Ouest, Mile-End* ☎514/272–0777 ⊟*AE, MC, V* ⊙*No lunch Mon.–Wed.* Ⓜ*St-Laurent and Bus 55.* ⊹ *1D*

¢–$
CANADIAN
✕ **Le Glacier Bilboquet.** Families and couples with dogs congregate on warm summer nights at Bilboquet, where the "artisanal" ice cream recipes are prepared by hand. Real cream and real milk are the star ingredients, while the sorbets are 80% fruit puree. There's always a line up outside, but the wait is never long because everyone pays with cash—house rule. What's the hottest flavours? Classic vanilla and chocolate, or mango and raspberry sorbet in a waffle cone. If you don't fee like something sweet, there are sandwiches and vegetarian salads. ⊠*1311 rue Bernard O. H3N 1V7, Outremont* ☎514/276-0414 ⊟ *No credit cards, no debit* ⊙*Closed January 1st to March 15th* Ⓜ*Outremont* ⊹ *2B*

$–$$
FRENCH
★
✕ **Leméac.** Enlivening a popular street corner in Outremont, this French bistro creates good karma by heating its outdoor terrace for eight months of the year. The other winning move is its late-night special: between 10pm and midnight, get the table d'hôte for only $22, with a choice of 10 starters and 10 main dishes. Regulars gravitate toward the veal liver, the beef tartar and the hanger steak—all served with ceremonial aplomb on white linen table clothes. It's no secret that the fries at Leméac are world class, as is the weekend brunch. ⊠*1045 rue Laurier O., Outremont* ☎514/270-0999 ⌕*Reservations essential* ⊟ *MC, V* Ⓜ*Outremont*

$$–$$$
ITALIAN
★
✕ **Le Petit Italien.** Three key factors conspire to make this a great date spot: flattering lighting over intimate tables for two; late-night hours seven days a week; and the savory comfort food comes at reasonable prices. The longest wall of this modern bistro is lined, to dramatic effect, with glass mason jars of the house tomato sauce, reminding diners that everything served at Le Petit Italien is lovingly prepared from scratch. One bite of the mezza lune pasta, served with smoked salmon and mascarpone mouse, and you're a believer. Same goes for the buon-

gustaio pasta dish, enriched with chicken, raisins and white wine sauce. For a memento, take home a jar of the house tomato sauce for $10, or spend another $2 and get the exceptionally tasty bolognaise sauce. ⊠ *1265 rue Bernard O., Outremont* ☎*514/278-0888* ⚑*Reservations essential* ⊟*AE, MC, V* Ⓜ*Parc or Outremont* ✛ *2B*

$ ⤫ **Les Gâteries.** Many writers and artists take their morning espresso in
CAFÉ this comfortable little café facing Square St-Louis. Such local favorites as bagels, muffins, maple-syrup pie, and toast with *cretons* (a coarse, fatty kind of pâté made with pork) share space with baguettes and croissants. It's not well known, but Les Gâteries serves beer and wine, too. ⊠ *3443 rue St-Denis, Plateau Mont-Royal* ☎*514/843–6235* ⊟*AE, MC, V* Ⓜ*Sherbrooke.* ✛ *3F*

$$ ⤫ **L'Express.** Mirrored walls and noise levels that are close to painful on
BISTRO weekends make L'Express the closest thing Montréal (and maybe even Canada) has to a Parisian bistro. Service is fast, prices are reasonable, and the food is good, even if the tiny crowded tables barely have room to accommodate it. Chef Joel Chapoulie's steak tartare with french fries, salmon with sorrel, and calves' liver with tarragon are marvelous. Jars of gherkins, fresh baguettes, and aged cheeses make the pleasure last longer, as do the reasonably priced bottles of imported French wine. ⊠ *3927 rue St-Denis, Plateau Mont-Royal* ☎*514/845–5333* ⚑*Reservations essential* ⊟*AE, DC, MC, V* Ⓜ*Sherbrooke.* ✛ *2F*

$$$ ⤫ **Maestro S.V.P.** Regulars belly up to the glass oyster bar and stay put.
SEAFOOD Owner Ilene Polansky imports them from all over the world—the oysters that is, not the regulars—so you can compare the subtle differences between, say, a delicate little bivalve from Kumamoto Japan and a big meaty Kawakawa from New Zealand. A free lesson in shucking techniques comes with the order. Famous guests, from Leonard Cohen to Laura Linney, sign their oyster shells and Polansky displays them in a frame. If oysters aren't your thing, don't despair: Polansky also serves poached salmon and the inevitable *moules et frites* (mussels and french fries). ⊠ *3615 blvd. St-Laurent, Plateau Mont-Royal* ☎*514/842–6447* ⊟ *MC, V* ☽*No lunch weekends* Ⓜ*Sherbrooke.* ✛ *3E*

$$$ ⤫ **Med Grill.** Dining in the Med Grill is a little like dining in a fishbowl,
CONTEMPORARY which might not appeal to everyone. But if you want to see and be seen, it's pretty hard to beat a set of floor-to-ceiling windows big enough for an automobile showroom. (Tip: to look your best, dress to match the cherry-red walls.) But the Med's not all show and no eat. The food— red snapper, grilled tuna, and pan seared filet mignon, for example, and a spectacular molten-chocolate cake—looks as delectable as the crowd. Looking for a great vodka martini? The Med Grill bar is a weekend hotspot for anything served in a martini glass. ⊠ *3500 blvd. St-Laurent, Plateau Mont-Royal* ☎*514/844–0027* ⚑*Reservations essential* ⊟*AE, MC, V* ☽*No lunch* Ⓜ*Sherbrooke.* ✛ *3E*

$$$$ ⤫ **Milos.** Don't let the nets and floats hanging from the ceiling fool you:
SEAFOOD Milos is no simple taverna—a fact reflected in the prices, which some argue are exorbitant. The main dish is usually the catch of the day grilled over charcoal and seasoned with parsley, capers, and lemon juice. Fish are priced by the pound (C$23–C$32) and often displayed, along with the vegetables, in the restaurant's colourful, open-market

interior. There is a lunch special (priced at C$20.09 to match the current calendar year) to commemorate the recent Olympics in Athens. ✉*5357 av. du Parc, Mile-End* ☎*514/272–3522* ⌚*Reservations essential* ▭*AE, D, DC, MC, V* ⊘*No lunch weekends* Ⓜ*Laurier* ✢ *3B*.

$$$
STEAK

✕**Moishe's.** The motto says it all: "There is absolutely nothing trendy about Moishe's." Yet, this is a place to be seen, enjoying your largess and ordering a bone-in fillet. If you want a thick, marbled steak, perfectly grilled—preceded perhaps by a slug of premium single-malt Scotch—you've found the right clubhouse. Members of the Lighter family, who have been operating Moishe's since 1938, offer other dishes, such as lamb and fish, but people come for the beef, which the family ages in its own lockers. ✉*3961 blvd. St-Laurent, Plateau Mont-Royal* ☎*514/845–3509* ▭*AE, DC, MC, V* Ⓜ*St-Laurent.* ✢ *2E*

$$$
GREEK

✕**Mythos Ouzerie.** Scores of fun-seeking diners come to this brick-lined semibasement every weekend to eat, drink, and be merry in a delightfully chaotic atmosphere. The food—moussaka, plump stuffed grape leaves, braised lamb, grilled squid—is grilled on "real wood charcoal" and it's always good, but go Thursday, Friday, or Saturday night, when the live and very infectious bouzouki music makes it impossible to remain seated. Or dine on the upper floor and watch the merriment below. ✉*5318 av. du Parc, Mile-End* ☎*514/270–0235* ▭*AE, DC, MC, V* Ⓜ*Laurier.* ✢ *3B*

$$
CHINESE

✕**Om.** Be careful; stepping into Om's saffron-scented calm from the noise and tumult of boulevard St-Laurent can be startling enough to give you the bends. Walls the color of the Dalai Lama's robes provide the backdrop for such traditional Tibetan dishes as *momos* (beef, shrimp, or cheese dumplings), *churu* (soup with blue cheese and lamb), and the fiery and sweet chicken chili. There's also an extensive list of Indian dishes, like curry lamb and butter chicken. ✉*4382 blvd. St-Laurent, Plateau Mont-Royal* ☎*514/287–3553* ▭*AE, MC, V* ⊘*Closed Mon.* Ⓜ*Mont-Royal.* ✢ *1D*

$$
SPANISH

✕**Pintxo.** You don't dine at Pintxo—you graze. And what a lovely pasture it is, too, with bare brick walls, white tablecloths, and a welcoming fireplace. Pintxos (pronounced "pinchos") are the Basque version of tapas, tiny two-bite solutions to the hunger problem, best enjoyed with a good beer or a glass of chilled sherry. There are about 15 of them on the menu every night, ranging from tiny stacks of grilled vegetables to more substantial dishes, such as duck tartar, octopus, and the crowd-pleasing strawberry gazpacho. If creating your dinner one bite at a time doesn't appeal, there are more normal-size dishes on the menu, such as black cod and beef cheeks braised in wine. ✉*256 rue Roy Est, Plateau Mont-Royal* ☎*514/844–0222* ⌚*Reservations essential* ▭*AE, DC, MC, V* C*No lunch Sat.–Tues.* Ⓜ*Sherbrooke.* ✢ *2E*

$$$
MIDDLE
EASTERN

✕**Restaurant Daou.** Heaven knows that singer Céline Dion could afford to fly her lunch in from Beirut on a chartered jet, but when she and hubby René Angelil—whose parents were both Syrians—are in town, this is where they come to get Lebanese food. The decor is nothing to write home about, but the marinated chicken breast, hummus with ground meat, stuffed grape leaves, and delicately seasoned kebabs attract plenty of Middle Eastern expatriates and native-born Montrealers. ✉ *519 rue Faillon, Villeray* ☎*514/276–8310* ▭*AE, MC, V* 🕒*Closed Mon.* Ⓜ*Parc.* ✛ *1D*

$$ ✕**Rotisserie Panama.** Some of the best grilled meat in Montréal is what
GREEK attracts big, noisy crowds to the Rotisserie Panama. The chicken and
crispy lamb chops are excellent, as is the new grilled red snapper and
sea bass. Extended families come on the weekend for the roasted baby
lamb. Prices won't empty your wallet. ✉ *789 rue Jean-Talon Ouest,*
Mile-End ☎*514/276–5223* ▭*AE, MC, V* Ⓜ*Parc or Acadie.* ✛ *1D*

$–$$ ✕**Rumi.** With a menu inspired by the ancient spice route, Rumi attracts
MIDDLE a mix of chatty travelers, students and foodies who appreciate meats
EASTERN cooked in Moroccan tagines. Starting with Persian black tea, diners proceed to little dishes of hodja (puréed eggplant) and wali (feta
with basil) eaten with Uzbecki-style naan bread or pita bread baked
in the traditional taboon oven. Dahl soup is a best-seller, as is the
lamb shank, lamb patties and the tangy salmon tagine. Candles on the
wooden tables make for a cozy night-time atmosphere, which is calm
and festive, as Chef Ali Ashitian presides in the open kitchen. ✉*5198*
rue Hutchison Outremont ☎*514/2490-1999* ▭*MC, V* 🕒*Closed Mon.*
Ⓜ*Outremont or Parc* ✛ *3B*

$ ✕**Schwartz's Delicatessen.** Schwartz's has no frills. The furniture's shabby,
AMERICAN the noise level high, and the waiters are—well, trying harder to be
Fodor's Choice pleasant these days. The cooks do such a good job of curing, smoking,
★ and slicing beef brisket that even when it's 20 below zero locals line up
outside to get a seat at the city's most famous deli and order a sandwich
thick enough to dislocate jaws. (Both Angelina Jolie and Halle Berry
couldn't resist the medium-fat sandwich on rye). Avoid lunch and dinner hours, and when you do get in, don't ask for a menu; there isn't
one. Just order a smoked meat on rye with fries and a side order of
pickles. If you're in a rush, use the take-out counter next door. ✉*3895*
blvd. St-Laurent, Plateau Mont-Royal ☎*514/842–4813* ⬧*Reserva-*
tions not accepted ▭*No credit cards* Ⓜ*Sherbrooke.* ✛ *2E*

$$ ✕**Senzala.** Two homey locations serve tasty Brazilian fare, including
BRAZILIAN such specialties as *feijoada* (a stew of pork, black beans, cabbage, and
oranges). But brunch—served Thursday to Sunday—is what the locals
line up for. Familiar foods like bacon and eggs are served with a tropi-
cal touch alongside fried plantains and fruit kebabs. There's also a
great selection of fruity smoothies. Bring the weekend newspaper in
case you have to wait in line. ✉*177 rue Bernard Ouest, Mile-End*
☎*514/274–1464* Ⓜ*St-Laurent* ✉*1218 rue de la Roche, Plateau*
Mont-Royal ☎*514/521–1266* Ⓜ*Mont-Royal* ▭*AE, MC, V* 🕒*No*
lunch Mon.–Wed. ✛ *1D, 1F*

¢ ✕**St-Viateur Bagel & Café.** Even expatriate New Yorkers have been
CAFÉ known to prefer Montréal's light, crispy, and slightly sweet bagel to its
Fodor's Choice heavier Manhattan cousin. (The secret? The dough is boiled in honey-
★ sweetened water before baking.) St-Viateur's wood-fired brick ovens
have been operating since 1959. With coffee and smoked salmon, these
bagels make a great breakfast. ✉*1127 av. Mont-Royal Est, Mile-End*
☎*514/528–6361* ▭*No credit cards* Ⓜ*Laurier.* ✉*263 rue St-Via-*
teur Ouest, Plateau Mont-Royal ☎*514/276–8044* ▭*No credit cards*
Ⓜ*Mont-Royal.* ✛ *1F*

6

$$ ✕ **Thai Grill.** Behold, a 10-foot gold statue of Buddha! He's right in the
THAI   middle of the room, presiding over the scrumptious Pad Thai dishes, mussaman curry with beef, sautéed chicken with cashews, onions, and dried red peppers, plus the ever popular *gai hor bai toey* (chicken in pandanus leaves and served with a black-bean sauce). All the cooks are Thai, so this is the real deal. ✉ *5101 blvd. St-Laurent, Plateau Mont-Royal* 📞 *514/270–5566* 🖃 *AE, DC, MC, V* Ⓜ *Laurier.* ✛ *1D*

$$ ✕ **Toi Moi et Café.** Film producers and poets congregate at this cor-
CAFÉ   ner café-bistro, sitting on the terrace to sip award-winning espresso.
Fodor's Choice   Although there's a hearty lunch and dinner menu of salads and grilled
★   meat, brunch is the big draw. It features soft-boiled eggs with strips of toast for dipping, fruit, and cheese. Regular breakfast is served seven days a week, so you can get a morning meal throughout the week. Try the Baklava Coffee topped with toasted almonds and honey. ✉ *244 rue Laurier Ouest, Mile-End* 📞 *514/279–9599* 🖃 *AE, DC, MC, V* Ⓜ *Laurier.* ✛ *1D*

$$ ✕ **Tre Marie.** When a young man from Montréal's Italian community
ITALIAN   meets someone he thinks he might get serious about, this is where he often takes her. The stucco walls and dark-wood trim give the place a little class, and the food is like Mama's—veal stew, for example, and veal tripe with beans and tomato sauce. And if you're really hungry, there's a three-pasta dish that could feed a family of four. ✉ *6934 rue Clark, Little Italy* 📞 *514/277–9859* 🍽 *Reservations essential* 🖃 *AE, DC, MC, V* ⊘ *Closed Sun. and Mon.* Ⓜ *de Castelnau.* ✛ *1D*

¢–$ ✕ **Yannick Fromagerie.** With an aroma to announce its vocation, this
CANADIAN   cheese shop is the go-to destination for the city's top chefs and cheese aficionados. Yannick Achim carries 400 varieties, buying from local dairies and stocking an astonishing international selection. Witness the look of surprise on shoppers' faces when they find Monte da Vinha sheep's milk cheese from Portugal or raw milk cheese from Compton, Quebec. Expect to be engaged in conversation by other cheese lovers, who eagerly trade advice on building the perfect after-dinner cheese plate. ✉ *1218 rue Bernard O. H2V 1V6, Outremont* 📞 *514/279-9376* 🖃 *AE, MC, V* ⊘ *Closed Monday* Ⓜ *Outremont* ✛ *2B*

VIEUX-MONTRÉAL

$$$$ ✕ **Aix Cuisine du Terroir.** Planters of fresh flowers and semicircular ban-
CONTEMPORARY   quettes provide a little privacy for romantic couples splurging on veal roasted in port wine or caramelized leek and onion tart. But summertime guests must make the trek up to the rooftop terrace for creative cocktails and intense flirtation. Bring your business cards. ✉ *711 Côte de la Place d'Armes, Vieux-Montréal* 📞 *514/904–1201* 🍽 *Reservations essential* 🖃 *AE, D, DC, MC, V* Ⓜ *Place-d'Armes.* ✛ *5F*

$$ ✕ **Bistro Boris.** Behind the restored facade of a burned-out building is
FRENCH   one of the best alfresco dining areas in the city. Like a magical forest, the tree-shaded *terrasse* draws crowds to sip kiwi-infused Caipi Saki or glasses of Plozner ($8). Outdoor tables fill up quickly, but those sitting inside are heartened by the new glass wall looking onto the terrace and sidewalk. Clients on both sides of the wall wash down

French dishes of duck and rabbit with goblets of exclusive Italian rosé and over 20 varieties of wine by the glass. ⊠*465 rue McGill, Vieux-Montréal* ☎*514/848–9575* ⌂*Reservations essential* ⊟*AE, DC, MC, V* Ⓜ*Square-Victoria.* ✛ *5E*

\$\$\$
CONTEMPORARY

✕**Bonaparte.** Book a table in one of the front window alcoves and watch the calèches clatter by over the cobblestones as you dine. You can order à la carte—try the tuna and mushroom ravioli—but the restaurant's best deal is the six-course tasting menu, which includes such classics as lobster bisque flavored with anise, and breast of duck cooked with maple syrup and berries. Don't be intimidated by the number of courses, because portions are generally smaller than main-menu versions. Their delivery is gently paced by one of the city's most professional staffs. Regulars and guests from afar, including Madonna and tennis star Roger Federer, are no doubt charmed by host Michael Banks, a leading tastemaker and bon vivant in the Old Port. Upstairs is a small inn. ⊠*443 rue St-François-Xavier, Vieux-Montréal* ☎*514/844–4368* ⌂*Reservations essential* ⊟*AE, DC, MC, V* ⊘*No lunch weekends* Ⓜ*Place-d'Armes.* ✛ *5F*

\$\$
POLISH

✕**Café Stash.** On chilly nights many Montrealers come here for sustenance—for borscht, pierogies, or cabbage and sausage—in short, for all the hearty specialties of a Polish kitchen. Live piano music on weekends is the perfect accompaniment for roasted wild boar or Wiener schnitzel. Seating is on pews from a chapel and at tables from an old convent. ⊠*200 rue St-Paul Ouest, Vieux-Montréal* ☎*514/845–6611* ⊟*AE, MC, V* Ⓜ*Place-d'Armes.* ✛ *5F*

\$\$\$
FRENCH
Fodor's Choice
★

✕**Chez l'Épicier.** There is, indeed, an épicier (grocery) at the front of this stone-and-brick walled eatery. Browse through shelves of comestibles, like bottles of Chef Laurent Godbout's basil and lemongrass strawberry jams, before inspecting the menu of French fusion classics. Printed on brown paper bags, the menus are boho, but the tables have crisp white linens and there's nothing down-market about the creative dishes: frogs'-leg fritters, red tuna in a peanut crust, and rabbit with eggplant caviar. This is the kind of quiet place you go to canoodle with an old flame or new conquest. ⊠*311 rue St-Paul Est, Vieux-Montréal* ☎*514/878–2232* ⊟*AE, DC, MC, V* ⊘*No lunch weekends* Ⓜ*Place-d'Armes.* ✛ *5F*

\$\$
CAFÉ
★

✕**Claude Postel.** Hordes of hungry clerks and lawyers line up at lunchtime for fast, ready-made meals. Conversation is hushed and urgent over paninis, plates of smoked salmon, and braised veal. The bistrolike dining room is comfortable and welcoming if you want to eat in, but you can also nosh at the outside tables or take your sandwich—on excellent crusty bread—and eat it alfresco at the Vieux-Port, a couple of blocks south. Mid-afternoon hunger pangs? Stock up on the celebrated chocolate truffles or French tarts. In the summer, you won't be able to resist the intensely flavored gelato-style ice cream. Doors closes at 7 PM. ⊠*75 rue Notre-Dame Ouest, Vieux-Montréal* ☎*514/844–8750* ⊟*MC, V* Ⓜ*Place-d'Armes.* ✛ *5F*

\$\$\$
CONTEMPORARY
Fodor's Choice
★

✕**Club Chasse et Pêche.** Don't fret—this isn't a hangout for the local gun-and-rod set. The name—which means Hunting and Fishing Club—is an ironic reference to the wood-and-leather decor Chef Claude Pelletier inherited from the previous owners. He's jazzed it up, though, to reflect his innovative style, but the entrance is still one of the most discrete in town. Impeccable service has made this a favorite with the city's serious foodies. They sip glasses of German Riesling on the new summer terrace, set in a garden across the street. Try Pelletier's seared scallops or braised piglet with risotto. ✉ *423 rue St-Claude, Vieux-Montréal* ☎ *514/861–1112* ⌂ *Reservations essential* ▤ *AE, DC, MC, V* ⊘ *Closed Sun. and Mon. No lunch Sat.* Ⓜ *Champ-de-Mars.* ✛ *5F*

$$$ ╳ **Da Emma.** The cellar of what used to be Montréal's first women's
ITALIAN   prison hardly sounds like the ideal setting for an Italian restaurant, but fear not: Mama Emma's cooking is satisfying enough to drive out any lingering ghosts from those sad days. The place's stone walls and heavy beams make an ideal, catacomb-like setting for such Roman special-ties as roasted lamb with grilled vegetables, mushroom pasta, and tripe in tomato sauce. The covert local also serves harried celebrities like Johnny Depp and John Travolta—repeat customers who retire to the terrace and private garden with their families. ✉ *777 rue de la Com-mune Ouest, Vieux-Montréal* ☎ *514/392–1568* ▤ *AE, D, DC, MC, V* ⊘ *No lunch Sat.* Closed Sun. Ⓜ *Square-Victoria.* ✛ *6E*

$$ ╳ **Magnan.** Everyone from dockworkers to executives comes to this
STEAK   tavern in a working-class neighborhood for the unbeatable roast beef and steaks. The salmon pie is a delightfully heavy filler that makes great picnic fare. In summer Magnan adds Québec lobster to its menu, and turns its parking lot into an outdoor dining area. Excellent beer from several local microbreweries is on tap. The style is upscale warehouse, with TV sets noisily tuned to sports. ✉ *2602 rue St-Patrick, Pointe St-Charles* ☎ *514/935–9647* ▤ *AE, DC, MC, V* Ⓜ *Charlevoix.* ✛ *6B*

$$$ ╳ **Méchant Boeuf.** If you have a yen for the past as it never really
ECLECTIC   was, Hôtel Nelligan's casual dining room trades on nostalgia with a 1980s sound track and such comfort-food favorites as braised pork, beer-can chicken, and the mighty Méchant hamburger. The food may be humble, but the atmosphere is cheeky and chic, with an interior waterfall, brick walls, and an illuminated bar. ✉ *124 rue St-Paul Ouest, Vieux-Montréal* ☎ *514/788–4020* ▤ *AE, D, DC, MC, V* Ⓜ *Place-d'Armes.* ✛ *5F*

$$$ ╳ **Narcisse Bistro Bar à Vin.** A dramatic floor-to-ceiling, glassed-in wine
FRENCH   cellar serves as a visual focal point in this airy bistro inside the Auberge du Vieux-Port. Upscale diners appreciate the classic French cuisine and the expansive wine list, with many labels served by the glass at surprisingly reasonable prices. In the summer, knowing locals eat on the rooftop terrace for an excellent view of the annual Montréal fire-works festival. What do they order? Duck breast with maple syrup and the mushroom-stuffed raviolis. ✉ *93 rue de la Commune Est, Vieux-Montréal* ☎ *514/392–1649* ⌂ *Reservations recommended* ▤ *AE, DC, MC, V* ⊘ *No lunch weekends* Ⓜ *Place-d'Armes.* ✛ *5F*

$ ╳ **Olive + Gourmando.** Successful hipsters arrive at lunchtime, en masse,
CAFÉ   to wait for a table at this bustling bakery and sandwich shop. Owners Dyan Solomon and Éric Girard have a romantic backstory straight out of a movie: they fell in love while working the bread ovens at up-scale Toqué! before opening going out on their own. Fittingly, movie stars like Benjamin Bratt, Ethan Hawke, and the late Heath Ledger have

been spotted here nibbling paninis, fig scones, chocolate brioches, and foccacia bread. Wait for a seat, then order your sandwiches at the back; get your pastries at the side counter. ✉ *351 rue St-Paul Ouest, Vieux-Montréal* ☎*514/350–1083* ▭*Interact only* ⊘*Closed Sun. and Mon.* Ⓜ*Square-Victoria.* ✛ *5E*

$$

BISTRO

✕**Pub St-Paul.** Sometimes you just want to get away from all the reverential foodie talk, slump into a comfortable chair in a big noisy bistro, and wash down a steak and a heap of frites with a good draft beer. If there's room and time, you might want to follow that with a slab of apple pie or a big lump of blueberry cheesecake. When that mood hits, this is the place—and it comes with stone walls, big wooden beams, an inviting new bar and, on weekends, live entertainment. There's also a children's menu. ✉*124 rue St-Paul Est, Vieux-Montréal* ☎*514/874–0485* ▭*AE, DC, MC, V* Ⓜ*Place-d'Armes.* ✛ *5F*

$$$$

CONTEMPORARY

Fodor'sChoice

★

✕**Toqué!** Toqué is slang for "just a little mad," as in Chef Normand Laprise's insistence on using fresh, local ingredients from the best providers. Located on the ground floor of a glass tower, this celebrated bastion of fine dining attracts government rainmakers and the expense-account crowd. The menu changes daily, depending on what Laprise finds at the market, but foie gras, duck, and wild venison are staples. Some clients wouldn't consider ordering anything but the seven-course tasting men. Chit-chat at the tables revolves around Laprise's latest award and how lucky everyone is to have gotten a reservation. ✉*900 pl. Jean-Paul-Riopelle, Vieux-Montréal* ☎*514/499–2084* ⚭*Reservations essential* ▭*AE, DC, MC, V* ⊘*Closed Mon. and 2 weeks over Christmas. No lunch* Ⓜ*Square-Victoria or Place-d'Armes.* ✛ *5E*

$$$$

ECLECTIC

✕**Vauvert.** Black walls and twinkling lights makes Vauvert sound more like the setting for a Halloween party or Avril Lavigne's wedding than a place for a seriously romantic tête-à-tête, but somehow the "goth chic" works. It suits Chef Pascal Leblond's bold take on classics, such as filet mignon and perfectly bronzed guinea hen. Leblond earns points with picky Italian clients for his seafood pasta and risotto dishes. Another way to try Vauvert is to order room service at the Hotel St. Paul. ✉*355 rue McGill, Vieux-Montréal* ☎*514/867–2823* ▭*AE, DC, MC, V* Ⓜ*Square-Victoria.* ✛ *6E*

$$$$

CONTEMPORARY

Fodor'sChoice

★

✕**Verses.** The setting—a stone-walled room overlooking the hubbub of rue St-Paul—is the most romantic in the Old City. And the food is poetic—especially the Chilean sea bass, the tuna with green papaya, and the seared foie gras with sun-dried cherry sauce. But the reason for this restaurant's name is that it's housed on the ground floor of Hôtel Nelligan, named after the Romantic Québecois poet Émile Nelligan. For a main course, try the braised lamb shank with steel-cut oats. Wash it all down on the rooftop terrace with a pitcher of Verses' signature drink, clear sangria. ✉*Hôtel Nelligan, 100 rue St-Paul Ouest, Vieux-Montréal* ☎*514/788–4000* ⚭*Reservations essential* ▭*AE, DC, MC, V* Ⓜ*Place-d'Armes.* ✛ *5F*

6

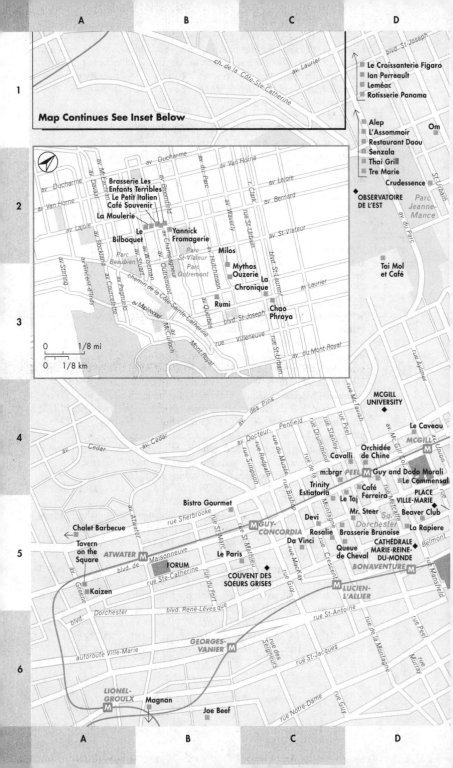

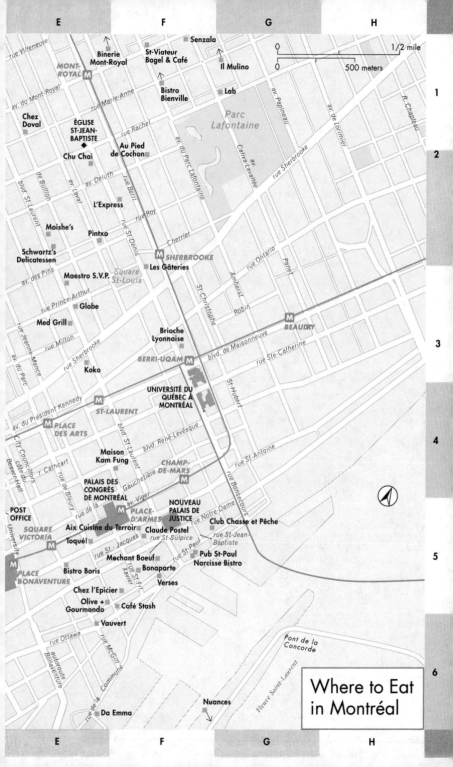

Where to Eat in Montréal

Where to Stay

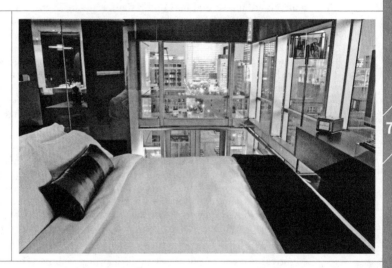

Opus Hotel, Downtown Montréal.

WORD OF MOUTH

"I would personally prefer to stay in a downtown location . . . rather than in Old Montréal. That part of the city has more restaurants, bars, etc. and is less touristy. However, as others have noted, Old Montréal might feel more romantic."

—Vttraveler

Updated by
Joanne Latimer

MONTRÉAL HAS A WIDE VARIETY of accommodations, from the big chain hotels you'll find in every city to historic inns, boutique hotels, and bargain-rate hostels. You can sleep in the room where Liz Taylor and Richard Burton got married or book a bed in an 18th-century stone inn where George Washington didn't sleep but Benjamin Franklin did.

Keep in mind that during peak season (May through August), finding a bed without making reservations can be difficult. From mid-November to early April rates often drop, and throughout the year many hotels have two-night, three-day, double-occupancy packages at substantial discounts.

Most of the major hotels—the ones with big meeting rooms, swimming pools, and several bars and restaurants—are in the downtown area, which makes them ideal for those who want all the facilities along with easy access to the big department stores and malls on rue Ste-Catherine, the museums of the Golden Square Mile, and nightlife on rues Crescent and de la Montagne. If you want something a little more historic, consider renting a room in one of the dozen or so boutique hotels that occupy the centuries-old buildings lining the cobbled streets of Vieux-Montréal. Most of them offer all the conveniences along with the added charm of stone walls, casement windows, and period-style furnishings.

If, however, your plans include shopping expeditions to avenue Mont-Royal and rue Laurier with maybe a few late nights at the jazz bars and dance clubs of Main Street and rue St-Denis, then the place to bed down is in one of the Plateau Mont-Royal's small but comfortable hotels. Room rates in the area tend to be quite reasonable, but be careful: the hotels right in the middle of the action—on rue St-Denis for example—can be a little noisy, especially if you get a room fronting the street.

Montréal is a city of pockets with distinct personalities. The downtown core provides more of a universal lodging experience, via chain hotels, while the Old Port and The Plateau have unique auberges and boutique hotels. Expect lots of exposed brick walls and original hardwood floors.

One final note about safety—you can unclench in Montréal. Crime is nearly a non-issue in tourist areas. Locals and tourists use the metro in the evening without clutching their pocket books and praying. If the weather's nice, feel free to stroll back to your hotel from the theatre or the bistro.

WHERE TO STAY PLANNER

Family Travel

Sure, bring the kids! Most of the chain hotels—Hilton, for example—have great pools. Avoid smaller auberges, however, because noise travels and the charming ambience isn't exciting enough for the little ones. Hotels in the Old Port are popular with families because they're near the iSci Centre and the bike path.

Does Size Matter?

For a major city, the hotel rooms in Montréal are generous. Budget rooms and auberges are the exception, with rooms measuring less than 300 square feet. Otherwise, expect standard sizes of about 400–600 square feet.

Services

Most hotels are wired, with a business centre in the lobby. Smaller auberges may not have televisions and air-conditioning, but often have Wi-Fi. Bath tubs, plush bath robes, and fluffy white duvets are popular here for winter comfort. Bigger hotels have day spas and health clubs, as well as some of the city's finest restaurants.

Prices

Aside from the Grand Prix and the Jazz Festival, it's possible to get a decent hotel room in high season for $200 to $300. Take advantage of Web-only deals and ask about promotions.

WHAT IT COSTS FOR LODGING				
¢	$	$$	$$$	$$$$
under C$75	C$75–C$125	C$126–C$175	C$176–C$250	over C$250
Prices are for a standard double room in high season.				

Lodging Strategy

How can you choose between boutique hotels, stately chateaus, and cozy inns? Whether you prefer chic lofts or four-poster beds, you'll find what you want in this 40-plus selection of the city's best accommodations. "Auberge" is the French word for "inn," signaling a smaller, less corporate property.

Need a Reservation?

Montréal is always hosting a festival or an international convention, so the hotels are consistently booked. This takes tourists by surprise. Many of the quaint auberges have a small number of rooms, so they fill up fast. It's necessary to book months ahead for the Jazz Festival, the World Film Festival, and the Grand Prix.

Parking

Parking is a sore point in Old Montréal. Expect to pay heftily for valet service. Elsewhere, there is often parking available under the large-scale hotels. This is a blessing in winter, when you don't want to shovel snow and de-ice your car. If possible, avoid taking your car.

7

BEST BETS FOR MONTRÉAL LODGING

Fodor's offers a selective listing of quality lodging experiences in every price range, from the city's best budget beds to its most sophisticated luxury hotels. Here, we've compiled our top recommendations by price and experience. The very best properties—in other words, those that provide a particularly remarkable experience in their price range—are designated in the listings with the Fodor's Choice logo.

Fodor's Choice ★

Auberge les Passants
du Sans Soucy, p. 148
Hôtel Opus, p. 143
Hôtel Nelligan, p. 146
Loews Hôtel Vogue, p. 140
Le Place d'Armes, p. 149
W Montréal, p. 148

Best by Price

¢

Auberge Alternative, p. 150
McGill Student Apartments, p. 142

$

Hôtel Anne ma soeur Anne, p. 145
Hôtel Terrasse Royale, p. 143
Manoir Ambrose, p. 141

$$

Auberge de la Place Royale, p. 150

Hôtel de L'Institut, p. 144

$$$

Auberge Bonaparte, p. 150
Château Versailles, p. 141
Delta Montréal, p. 141
Hilton Montreal Bonaventure, p. 139

$$$$

Hôtel Opus, p. 143
Hôtel Gault, p. 145
Hôtel St. Paul, p. 146
Loews Hôtel Vogue, p. 140
Le Place d'Armes Hôtel & Suites, p. 149
Le Saint-Sulpice, p. 147

Best by Experience

BEST CELEBRITY RETREAT

Loews Hôtel Vogue, p. 140

Le Saint-Sulpice, p. 147

BEST HOTEL BAR

Hôtel Nelligan, p. 146
Hôtel Opus, p. 143
Le Place d'Armes Hôtel & Suites, p. 149

BEST FOR ROMANCE

Auberge de la Place Royale, p. 150
Auberge du Vieux-Port, p. 148
Auberge Les Passants du Sans Soucy, p. 148

BEST B&BS

Auberge Bonaparte, p. 150
Casa Bianca, p. 145
Pierre du Calvet, p. 147

BEST GRAND DAME HOTELS

Hôtel XIX Siècle, p. 147
Le St. James, p. 146
Ritz-Carlton, p. 138

BEST HIPSTER HOTELS

Hôtel Gault, p. 145
Hôtel St. Paul, p. 146
W Montréal, p. 148

BEST INTERIOR DESIGN

Hôtel Gault, p. 145
Le Germain, p. 139
Hôtel Opus, p. 143
W Montréal, p. 148

BEST POOLS

Delta Montréal, p. 141
Hilton Montréal Bonaventure, p. 139

BEST BUILDING ARCHITECTURE

Hôtel Gault, p. 145
Le St. James, p. 146
Hôtel St. Paul, p. 146
W Montréal, p. 148
Le Place d'Armes, p. 149

BEST NEW HOTELS

Casa Bianca, p. 145
Hôtel Le Crystal, p. 137

BEST SINGLES SCENE

Auberge Alternative, p. 150
Hôtel Nelligan, p. 146
W Montréal, p. 148

WHERE SHOULD I STAY?

	Neighborhood Vibe	Pros	Cons
Vieux-Montréal	Horse-drawn carriages, boutique hotels, and historic architecture; very touristy.	Quaint; easy access to bike paths; nice to walk along the waterfront.	It's quiet at night outside the hotel lobbies; parking is scarce.
Downtown & Chinatown	Mostly business travelers flock here for big-name hotel chains, central location, and garage parking.	Near museums; shopping; easy access to the metro; tons of hotel options.	Traffic congestion can be unpleasant; not as many dining options as other neighborhoods.
The Plateau & Environs	Scattered auberges and B&Bs host the artsy crowd and academics.	Stumbling distance to the best bistros and pubs; unique boutiques.	Limited metro access; limited hotel selections.
Mount-Royal & Environs	Only a few hotels are in this quiet section of the city.	Unhurried pace; lots of green space; lower rates.	Limited metro access and very few dining options.

DOWNTOWN & CHINATOWN

$$$$ ☷ **Le Centre Sheraton.** Full of conventioneers and university kids from upscale schools, the lobby bar is a magnet for local businesspeople grabbing a drink before heading home to the suburbs. The morning crowd shares newspapers at the in-house Starbucks café. If that's not your idea of a holiday, stay away, but if you don't mind the action, the location is right in the heart of downtown, and the blandly decorated rooms are large and airy. Those on higher floors have big windows that overlook the mountain or the St. Lawrence River. **Pros:** new digital hub in lobby has big-screen televisions and computer stations; good gym; downtown location; close to the Bell Centre for hockey and concerts. **Cons:** a favorite with bus tours and school groups; no in-hotel access to the Métro. ⊠ *1201 blvd. René-Lévesque Ouest, Downtown,* ☎ *514/878–2000 or 800/325–3535* ⊕ *www.sheraton.com/lecentre* ➥ *785 rooms, 40 suites* ⌂ *In-room: refrigerators, Ethernet (fee). In-hotel: public Wi-Fi, 2 restaurants, room service, bar, pool, gym, concierge, laundry service, parking (fee)* ▤ *AE, D, DC, MC, V* ⏏ *EP* Ⓜ *Bonaventure or Peel* ⊕ *5D.*

$$$$ ☷ **Hôtel Le Crystal.** Every room feels like a penthouse in this airy new boutique hotel with floor-to-ceiling windows. Filled with 131 luxury suites, Le Crystal pampers travelers with spa-style bathrooms, rain showers, and separate soaking tubs. Like the lobby, suites feature chocolate brown accents, warm wood, and black leather tub chairs. You'll drift off to sleep on the pillow-top queen bed with 300 thread-count linens and silk duvets. Start your day with a trip to the 9,000-square-foot fitness center and Izba Spa on the 12th floor for a "banya" Russian scrub or a session on the treadmill. Some guests come specifically to get a little Botox and see the plastic surgeon at the hotel's private surgical clinic. **Pros:** extraordinary views; saltwater pool; outdoor whirlpool hot tub; private surgical clinic. **Cons:** lofty rates. ⊠ *1100 de la Montagne, Downtown* ☎ *514/861–5550* ⊕ *www.hotellecrystal.com* ➥ *131 suites*

7

♿In-room: safe, kitchen, DVD, Ethernet, Wi-Fi. In-hotel: restaurant, room service, bar, pool, gym, spa, laundry service, concierge, public Internet, public Wi-Fi, parking (fee), some pets allowed ⊟AE, MC, V ⦿| *EP* ✠ *5D.*

$$$$ ▦ **Le Marriott Château Champlain.** At the southern end of Place du Canada stands this 36-floor skyscraper with distinctive half-moon windows that give it a Moorish look. Some argue that it resembles a cheese grater. These distinctive windows give the rooms wonderful views of Mont-Royal to the north and the St. Lawrence River to the south and east. Although the 1960s exterior seems to call out for retro decoration, the public areas, including the comfortable Bar Le Senateur, are elegant and French traditional in style. Upon entry, all eyes are drawn upwards to the gold domed ceiling. Bedrooms are cozy rather than large, with white downy comforters on the new beds. Convenient underground passageways connect the hotel with the Bonaventure Métro station and Place Ville-Marie. **Pros:** expansive views and parkside location. **Cons:** a favorite for parties and receptions—especially with the high-school-prom crowd in the spring. ⊠*1050 rue de la Gauchetière Ouest, Downtown,* ☎*514/878–9000 or 800/200–5909* ⊕*www.marriott.com* ⤵*611 rooms, 33 suites* ♿*In-room: Wi-Fi. In-hotel: 2 restaurants, room service, bar, pool, gym, concierge, laundry service, parking (fee), no-smoking building* ⊟*AE, DC, MC, V* ⦿|*BP* Ⓜ*Bonaventure* ✠ *5D.*

$$$$ ▦ **Ritz-Carlton Montréal.** Montréal's grandest hotel in the Golden Mile is closing its doors from June 2008 until Summer 2009 to rebuild—not to remodel, not to update, but to totally rebuild. This massive undertaking, costing $100 million, will keep the hotel's famed interior courtyard, but create 130 new luxury rooms and suites. (That should stop all the whining about The Ritz's small rooms!). While the original Ritz set the standard in stately decor, the new Ritz will triumph in its modernity. Expect the same level of personal service: your shoes are shined, there's fresh fruit in your room, and everyone greets you by name, which is probably why guests have included such luminaries as Elizabeth Taylor and Richard Burton, who were married here in 1964. **Pros:** the new building will be a conversation piece; lives up to Ritz standards of luxury and service; great shopping within a five-minute walk. **Cons:** poor Métro access. ⊠*1228 rue Sherbrooke Ouest, Square Mile,* ☎*514/842–4212 or 800/363–0366* ⊕*www.ritzmontreal.com* ⤵*419 rooms, 47 suites* ♿*In-room: safe, Wi-Fi. In-hotel: restaurant, room service, bar, gym, concierge, public Wi-Fi, laundry service, parking (fee), some pets allowed (fee)* ⊟*AE, DC, MC, V* ⦿|*EP* Ⓜ*Peel or Guy-Concordia* ✠ *4C.*

$$$ ▦ **Fairmont Le Reine Elizabeth.** John Lennon and Yoko Ono staged their "bed in for peace" in Room 1742 of this hotel in 1969. Rooms are modern, spacious, and spotless, with lush carpeting and richly textured fabrics. Think chocolate-brown and shades of cream. The suite-level floors (20 and 21) have business services, and the Gold floors (18 and 19) have their own elevator, check-in, and concierge. The hotel is the site of many conventions. **Pros:** chic gym, easy access to trains, Métro, and the Underground City; excellent afternoon tea. **Con:** lobby is as

busy as a train station. ✉ *900 blvd. René-Lévesque Ouest, Downtown,* ☎ *514/861–3511 or 800/441–1414* ⊕ *www.fairmont.com* ⟿ *937 rooms, 100 suites* ♿ *In-room: refrigerator (some), high-speed Internet. In-hotel: 2 restaurants, tea salon, room service, 2 bars, pool, gym, concierge, laundry service, executive floor, public Wi-Fi (fee), parking (fee), no-smoking rooms, some pets allowed (fee)* ▤ *AE, D, DC, MC, V* ⟨○⟩ *EP* Ⓜ *Bonaventure* ✛ *5D.*

$$$ 🏨 **Hilton Montréal Bonaventure.** After a $15 million renovation, the interior—with dark-wood furniture, downy bedding, granite counter tops, and Cuisinart coffeemakers—will make you forget the Brutalist concrete facade. Thankfully, the design team knew not to touch the 2½ acres of rooftop gardens and the open-air year-round swimming pool, which sets the Hilton apart from the usual run of corporate hotels and makes it a great place to take the family. High-tech cardio machines fill the new 24-hour gym, while plans are being laid for a Nordic spa. Conventioneers and tourists like the location—right on top of the Place Bonaventure exhibition center with easy access to the métro and the Underground City. **Pros:** each and every room has a view of the rooftop garden; swimming pool. **Cons:** full of conventioneers. ✉ *900 rue de la Gauchetière, Downtown,* ☎ *514/878–2332 or 800/267–2575* ⊕ *www. hilton.com* ⟿ *395 rooms, 15 suites* ♿ *In-room: safe, refrigerator, Ethernet. In-hotel: 2 restaurants, room service, bar, pool, gym, concierge, laundry service, public Wi-Fi, parking (fee), no-smoking rooms, some pets allowed* ▤ *AE, D, DC, MC, V* ⟨○⟩ *EP* Ⓜ *Bonaventure* ✛ *5D.*

$$$ 🏨 **Hôtel le Germain.** What was once a dowdy, outdated downtown office building is now a sleek, luxurious boutique hotel. In a coup, it lured Chef Daniel Vézina from Québec City to run the knock-out new restaurant, called Laurie Raphaël. Well-fed, guests drift upstairs to earth-tone rooms, which showcase Québec-designed bedroom and bathroom furnishings in dark, dense tropical woods. Leather armchairs add a traditional feel. All rooms have individual sound systems and huge flat-screen TVs; some have grand views of Mont-Royal or the skyscrapers along avenue du Président-Kennedy. If you need more space, there is also a pair of two-story apartments. **Pros:** Chef Daniel Vezina in the restaurant; quiet location in the heart of downtown; near McGill University. **Con:** on a charmless urban street. ✉ *2050 rue Mansfield, Downtown,* ☎ *514/849–2050 or 877/333–2050* ⊕ *www.hotelgermain. com* ⟿ *99 rooms, 2 suites* ♿ *In-room: refrigerator, Wi-Fi. In-hotel: restaurant, room service, bar, gym, concierge, laundry facilities, laundry service, parking (fee), no-smoking floor, some pets allowed* ▤ *AE, DC, MC, V* ⟨○⟩ *CP* Ⓜ *Peel or McGill* ✛ *4D.*

$$$ 🏨 **Hôtel le Square-Phillips et Suites.** The location is certainly majestic: King Edward VII entertains the pigeons in the square across the street, and La Baie department store, St. Patrick's Basilica, and Christ Church Cathedral are all within 200 yards of the front door. After a busy day of shopping and museum-hopping, you can take a relaxing swim in the glassed-in pool on the rooftop or just take in the views from the sundeck. All the rooms and suites have fully equipped kitchens, but you might not get a chance to use them because it's easier to find a restaurant than a grocery store anywhere near here. The art deco

7

building itself was designed by Ernest Cormier (1885–1980) and was converted into a hotel with a rooftop sundeck in 2004. **Pros:** great in-room kitchen facilities; excellent rooftop sunbathing; good shopping nearby. **Cons:** not much nightlife nearby. ⊠ *1193 rue Square-Phillips, Downtown,* ☎ *514/393–1193 or 866/393–1193* ⊕ *www. squarephillips.com* ↝ *80 rooms, 80 suites* ⚒ *In-room: kitchen, Wi-Fi. In-hotel: pool, laundry facilities, parking (fee)* ⊟ *AE, DC, MC, V* ⊧⊙⊧ *CP* Ⓜ *McGill* ⊹ *5E.*

$$$ 🖺 **Hyatt Regency Montreal.** The Hyatt is *the* place to stay during the International Jazz Festival in July—if you're a jazz fan, that is. The 12-story hotel, built at the northern end of Complexe Desjardins shopping mall, overlooks the Place des Arts plaza where most of the festival's free concerts are staged. It's a good location the rest of the year, too. The Musée d'Art Contemporain is across the street and Chinatown is a block away (you can walk to both via the Underground City if it's raining) and the restaurants of rue St-Denis and boulevard St-Laurent are within walking distance. **Pros:** great location for shoppers and concert lovers, and good access to the Underground City. **Cons:** dark, catacomb-like public spaces; lackluster service. ⊠ *1255 rue Jeanne-Mance, Downtown,* ☎ *514/982–1234 or 800/361–8234* ⊕ *www.montreal. hyatt.com/property* ↝ *605 rooms, 30 suites* ⚒ *In-room: refrigerator (some), dial-up, Wi-Fi. In-hotel: restaurant, bar, pool, gym, spa, laundry service, parking (fee), no-smoking floor* ⊟ *AE, D, DC, MC, V* ⊧⊙⊧ *EP* Ⓜ *Place-des-Arts or Place-d'Armes* ⊹ *4E.*

$$$ 🖺 **Loews Hôtel Vogue.** Montréal's first boutique hotel has bragging rights.
Fodor's Choice It's where such stars as George Clooney, Julia Roberts, and Michael
★ Douglas come to stay and play. The lobby bar with its big bay window overlooking rue de la Montagne is a favorite for martinis after work, but for something a little quieter you can sip your predinner drinks by the big fireplace in the lobby lounge. Guest rooms are luxurious, with striped silk upholstered furniture and beds draped with lacy duvets. Canopy beds give many rooms a romantic touch. The bathrooms have whirlpool baths, televisions, and phones. The location—a five-minute walk from Holt Renfrew and other high-end boutiques—makes it an ideal base for serious shoppers. **Pros:** cocktails with a view in the lobby bar; fancy Kruger espresso machines in the rooms; good celebrity-spotting. **Cons:** standard rooms are small, considering the price. ⊠ *1425 rue de la Montagne, Downtown,* ☎ *514/285–5555 or 800/465–6654* ⊕ *www.loewshotels.com* ↝ *126 rooms, 16 suites* ⚒ *In-room: Wi-Fi. In-hotel: restaurant, room service, bar, gym, concierge, children's programs (ages 1–18), laundry service, parking (fee), some pets allowed* ⊟ *AE, D, DC, MC, V* ⊧⊙⊧ *EP* Ⓜ *Peel* ⊹ *5C.*

$$ 🖺 **Hôtel du Fort.** In a residential neighborhood known as Shaughnessy Village, Hôtel du Fort is close to shopping at the Faubourg Ste-Catherine and Square Westmount and just around the corner from the Canadian Center for Architecture. All rooms here have good views of the city, the river, or the mountain. Wood furniture and pleasantly plump sofas fill the large, airy rooms, which have spacious bathrooms. Breakfast is served in a charming lounge. **Pros:** quiet building, big rooms. **Con:** off the beaten path, near a seedy section of rue Ste-Catherine. ⊠*1390 rue du Fort, Shaughnessy Village,* ☎*514/938–8333 or 800/565–6333* ⊕*www.hoteldufort.com* ⬦*103 rooms, 24 suites* ⌂*In-room: safe, kitchen, Wi-Fi. In-hotel: gym, laundry service, parking (fee), no-smoking rooms* ⊟*AE, DC, MC, V* ⦿*EP* Ⓜ*Atwater or Guy-Concordia.*

$$ ⊞ **Delta Montréal.** With a huge baronial chandelier and gold carpets, the two stories of public space at the Delta look a bit like a French château. Government employees cycle through regularly, attracted by the rooms' pleasing proportions, the mahogany-veneer furnishings, and windows that overlook the mountain or downtown. The hotel has a complete exercise and swimming facilities, featuring a saltwater pool and plush towels. The Cordial bar serves lunch on weekdays. **Pros:** comfy new mattresses and mod white bedding; very kid-friendly; close to McGill University. **Cons:** no hip factor. ⊠*475 av. du Président-Kennedy, Downtown,* ☎*514/286–1986 or 877/286–1986* ⊕*www. deltamontreal.com* ⬦*456 rooms, 4 suites* ⌂*In-room: refrigerator (some, ethernet, Wi-Fi. In-hotel: 2 restaurants, room service, bar, pool, gym, spa, concierge, children's programs (ages 1–13), laundry service, parking (fee), no-smoking floor, some pets allowed (fee)* ⊟*AE, D, DC, MC, V* ⦿*EP* Ⓜ*McGill or Place-des-Arts* ✛ *4D.*

$$ ⊞ **Château Versailles.** The two elegant mansions that make up this luxury hotel were built at the turn of the 20th century, and have high ceilings and plaster moldings. The sumptuous furnishings throughout reflect the Beaux-Arts architecture. The marble fireplaces in many of the guest rooms and public rooms still work—a treat on chilly evenings. **Pros:** elaborate Continental buffet-style breakfast with fruit, cheeses and/or pâté; huge rooms with fireplaces; easy access to museum district. **Cons:** located at busy intersection; has no in-hotel Métro access. ⊠*1659 rue Sherbrooke Ouest, Square Mile,* ☎*514/933–3611 or 888/933–8111* ⊕*www.versailleshotels.com* ⬦*63 rooms, 2 suites* ⌂*In-room: safe, refrigerator, Wi-Fi. In-hotel: room service, bar, gym, concierge, laundry service, parking (fee), no-smoking rooms* ⊟*AE, DC, MC, V* ⦿*CP* Ⓜ*Guy-Concordia* ✛ *4B.*

$$ ⊞ **Holiday Inn Select.** From the two pagodas on the roof to the well-tended garden in the lobby, this Chinatown hotel is full of surprises. The hotel sits catercorner to the Palais des Congrès convention center and is a five-minute walk from the World Trade Center. An executive floor has a range of business facilities. Its restaurant, Chez Chine, serves excellent Chinese food. The hotel has a small gym, but you also have access to a plush private health club downstairs with a whirlpool, saunas, a billiards room, and a bar. **Pros:** great access to Chinatown and convention centre. **Cons:** noisy location, and the shops in the entrance mall are a bit dowdy. ⊠*99 av. Viger Ouest, Chinatown,* ☎*514/878–9888 or 888/878–9888* ⊕*www.yul-downtown.hiselect.com* ⬦*235 rooms, 6 suites* ⌂*In-room: Wi-Fi. In-hotel: restaurant, bar, pool, gym, spa, laundry service, parking (fee), no-smoking rooms, refrigerator* ⊟*AE, D, DC, MC, V* ⦿*EP* Ⓜ*Place-d'Armes* ✛ *4F.*

$ ⊞ **Manoir Ambrose.** Staying at the Manoir Ambrose is like staying with an eccentric relative who just happens to have a couple of mansions halfway up the southern slope of Mont-Royal and just a few hundred yards from some of the best shopping in Canada. Despite its grand past, the Manoir is more homey than luxurious, like a comfortable pair of slippers. Within a few hours, manager Toni Carriero and her cheery staff will have you feeling as if you've lived in the Golden Square Mile all your life. Carriero recently jazzed up the Continental breakfast with copious baskets of fruit on the buffet. The two-room family suite is a great deal at C$150 a night. **Pros:** homey atmosphere and Golden Square Mile location for a fair price. **Cons:** no elevator, parking can be very difficult. ⊠*3422 rue Stanley, Square Mile,* ☎*514/288–6922* ⊕*www.manoirambrose.com* ➶*22 rooms, 20 with private bath, 2 with shared bath* ⌂*In-room: Wi-Fi. In-hotel: laundry service, no-smoking building* ☰*AE, MC, V* Ⓞ*CP* Ⓜ*McGill* ✛ *4C.*

¢   ⌂**Hostelling International.** Young travelers from around the world, as well as a smattering of families and adventurous older wanderers, flock to Hostelling International's Montréal branch. With its red awnings and friendly café-bar, it resembles a small European hotel. Thirsty travelers will be pleased to learn that the bar area expanded this year and carries more brands of beer. There are same-sex dorm rooms that sleep 4, 6, or 10 people and 20 private rooms suitable for couples or small groups. If you're not Canadian, you must have a Hostelling International membership to stay here (C$35 for two years). There are kitchen facilities and lockers for valuables. Reserve early for summer lodging. **Pros:** sweet price for a downtown location near the Bell Centre and nightlife of rue Crescent. **Cons:** noisy. ⊠*1030 rue Mackay, Downtown,* ☎*514/843–3317, 866/843–3317* ⊕*www.hostellingmontreal. com* ➶*226 beds* ⌂*In-room: no a/c (some), no TV, Wi-Fi. In-hotel: restaurant, laundry facilities, no-smoking rooms* ☰*AE, DC, MC, V* ⓄEP Ⓜ*Lucien-L'Allier* ✛ *5C.*

¢   ⌂**McGill Student Apartments.** From mid-May to mid-August, while McGill students are on summer recess, you can stay in the school's new hotel-style residences off campus or in university dorm rooms. Pick the dorms if you want to stroll around the grassy, quiet campus in the heart of the city. You can use the school swimming pool and gym facilities for a fee. The university cafeteria is open during the week, serving breakfast and lunch. Be sure to book early. **Pros:** new hotel-style residences are more private; inexpensive, big rooms (some halfway up Mont-Royal); access to McGill's extensive athletic facilities. **Cons:** shared baths in dorms, institutional decor, and a somewhat battered look. ⊠*3935 rue University, Square Mile,* ☎*514/398–5200* ⊕*www. mcgill.ca/residences* ➶*1,000 rooms without bath* ⌂*In-room: kitchen (some), Wi-Fi (some), access to cafeteria, pool (fee), gym (fee). In-hotel: restaurant, pool, gym, computer lab with high-speed Internet, parking (fee), no-smoking buildings* ☰*MC, V* ☉*Closed mid-Aug.–mid-May* ⓄCP Ⓜ*McGill* ✛ *3D.*

¢   ⌂**YWCA.** One block from rue Ste-Catherine, this lodging is open to both men and women, contrary to popular belief. It's near dozens of restaurants, museums, nightclubs, and attractions. The auberge floor, where the rooms have sinks and shared baths, is very popular with budget travelers. The more expensive—but still very reasonable—hotel floor has large, well-maintained rooms with private baths. It's particularly popular with couples and with businesswomen. **Pros:** earnest and unpretentious. **Cons:** not so chic. ✉ *1355 blvd. René-Lévesque Ouest, Downtown,* ☎514/866–9941 ⊕*www.ydesfemmesmtl.org* ⋙*63 rooms, 30 with bath* ⚿*In-room: TV, dial-up (some). In-hotel: restaurant, public Wi-Fi (some)* ▤*MC, V* ¶⃝*EP* Ⓜ*Lucien-L'Allier* ✛ *5C.*

MONT-ROYAL & ENVIRONS

$ ▦**Hôtel Terrasse Royale.** At first blush, the location looks remote. But the Oratoire St-Joseph and Parc Mont-Royal are just a walk away and the busy local neighborhood—Côte-des-Neiges—is full of little markets and ethnic restaurants where you can dine cheaply and well. Getting downtown is no problem, either: the Côte-des-Neiges Métro is just across the street. The hotel itself is clean and comfortable, and the rooms all have kitchen facilities. **Pros:** practical kitchens; lively, multilingual neighborhood; easy access to Métro. **Cons:** noisy, grubby lobby. ✉*5225 chemin de la Côte-des-Neiges, Mont-Royal,* ☎*514/739–6391 or 800/567–0804* ⊕*www.terrasse-royale.com* ⋙*56 rooms* ⚿*In-room: safe, kitchen, Wi-Fi. In-hotel: parking (fee)* ▤*AE, D, DC, MC, V* ¶⃝*EP* Ⓜ*Côte-des-Neiges* ✛ *1A.*

¢ ▦**Université de Montréal Residence.** The university's student housing accepts visitors from early May to mid-August. Rooms are simple, but clean and well maintained. It's on the opposite side of Mont-Royal from downtown and Vieux-Montréal, but next to the Edouard-Montpetit Métro station. You have access to the university's extensive pool and gym facilities for C$7 a day. **Pros:** great athletic facilities for a nominal fee; easy access to Mont-Royal and the Oratoire St-Joseph; good opportunity to practice French. **Cons:** spartan rooms; remote from downtown; largely French unilingual staff. ✉*2350 blvd. Edouard-Montpetit, Mont-Royal,* ☎*514/343–6531* ⊕*www.resid.umontreal. ca* ⋙*800 rooms, 200 with bath* ⚿*In-room: refrigerator. In-hotel: pool, gym, laundry facilities, parking (fee)* ▤*MC, V* ⊘*Closed late Aug.–early May* ¶⃝*EP* Ⓜ*Université-de-Montréal or Edouard-Montpetit* ✛ *1A.*

THE PLATEAU & ENVIRONS

$$$$ ▦**Hôtel Opus.** One of the chicest and sleekest hotels on St-Laurent,
Fodor'sChoice the Opus is across the street from such hot spots as the Globe and the
★ Med Grill. International jetsetters love the uncompromisingly modern interior—exposed concrete ceilings, tile floors, and stainless-steel furnishings with splashes of vibrant reds, greens, and oranges. The result could be called minimalist-plus. A popular perk among Java connoisseurs is the Keurig coffee machine in each room. Outside, the hotel's exterior is striking—one half is an art-nouveau classic from 1915; the other is a brick-and-concrete contemporary completed in 2004. In the evening, the mirror-walled breakfast room opening onto St-Laurent becomes a popular lounge, Suco, dispensing cocktails and tapas. But knowing hipsters head up to the new Koko terrace restaurant and bar to lounge on low sofas and sip Mojos (gin, green tea, mint, lime). **Pros:**

classic art-deco building; luxury rooms; maid service twice per day; hot location for nightlife. **Cons:** congested street and iffy parking. ✉ *10 rue Sherbrooke Ouest, Quartier Latin,* ☎ *514/843–6000 or 866/744–6346* ⊕ *www.opusmontreal.com* ⌨ *122 rooms, 14 suites* ♿ *In-room: refrigerator, high-speed Internet. In-hotel: 2 restaurants, public Wi-Fi, room service, gym, hair salon, sauna, bar, concierge, dry cleaning, laundry service, parking (fee), some pets allowed, no-smoking rooms* ▭ *AE, DC, MC, V* �ⓄⒸ*CP* Ⓜ*St-Laurent* ⟠ *3E.*

$$$ ⌂**Auberge de la Fontaine.** Winner of the city's Prix Ulysse in 2008 for best three-star hotel, this turn-of-the-20th-century residence overlooks Parc Lafontaine and one of the city's major bicycle trails. Housed in two adjoining old homes, it looks a little staid on the outside, but the interior is what Montrealers would call *branché*—or just a little zany. One wall of your room might be bare brick, for example, another purple, and the ceiling might be green. But somehow it all works. Some rooms have whirlpool baths, and a few have private balconies with views of the park. A copious Continental breakfast is served in the dining room, and you are free to use the little ground-floor kitchen and help yourself to snacks from the refrigerator. **Pros:** plush, white bathrobes in every room; parkside location on a bicycle trail; some of the city's trendiest restaurants and night spots are nearby. **Cons:** some rooms are quite small and not very well soundproofed. ✉ *1301 rue Rachel Est, Plateau Mont-Royal,* ☎ *514/597–0166 or 800/597–0597* ⊕ *www.aubergedelafontaine.com* ⌨ *18 rooms, 3 suites* ♿ *In-room: Wi-Fi. In-hotel: guests' kitchen, parking (no fee), no-smoking rooms, no elevator* ▭ *AE, DC, MC, V* ⓄⒸ*CP* Ⓜ*Mont-Royal* ⟠ *1F.*

$$ ⌂**Hôtel de l'Institut.** People rave about the unbeatable location on Square St-Louis and the great views of the St. Lawrence River from the balconies, but what sets this hotel apart is the charming service. It occupies two floors of the Institut de Tourisme et d'Hôtellerie du Québec, an internationally known school that trains students seeking careers in the hospitality industry. Working in the hotel is an integral part of their education, and as a result you're cared for by squads of smiling, eager-to-please young people in crisp uniforms. Students also staff the bar and the ground-floor restaurant (where student chefs sharpen their skills in the kitchen. **Pros:** Québécois cuisine; rooms with balconies; earnest, friendly service. **Cons:** when phoning reception, expect to be put on hold; earnest doesn't always mean polished. ✉ *3535 rue St-Denis, Quartier Latin,* ☎ *514/282–5120 or 800/361–5111 Ext. 1* ⊕ *www.ithq.qc.ca* ⌨ *40 rooms, 2 suites* ♿ *In-room: Wi-Fi. In-hotel: restaurant, bar, concierge, parking (fee), no-smoking rooms* ▭ *AE, DC, MC, V* ⓄⒸ*BP* Ⓜ*Sherbrooke* ⟠ *3F.*

$ ⌂**Auberge le Jardin d'Antoine.** Patterned wallpaper and antique-reproduction furniture give this small hotel plenty of charm, but its best selling point is its location right on rue St-Denis, among the Quartier Latin's trendy restaurants, cinemas, and poutine joints. Budget travelers mingle on the front terrace, watching the street traffic. Some rooms open onto a narrow, brick-paved terrace. Breakfast is served in a pleasant, stone-walled dining room in the basement. **Pros:** new, secure luggage room in the lobby for late departures; located on one of the liveliest stretches of rue St-Denis. **Cons:** Victorian doll-house decor in some rooms feels dated; the lively location means that it can be noisy. ⊠*2024 rue St-Denis, Quartier Latin,* ☎*514/843–4506 or 800/361–4506* ⊕*www.aubergelejardindantoine.com* ⌨*25 rooms* ♿*In-room: DVD (some), Wi-Fi. In-hotel: no elevator, no-smoking building* ▤*AE, D, MC, V* ⦿*CP* Ⓜ*Berri-UQAM* ⌖ *3F.*

$ 🏠**Casa Bianca Bed & Breakfast.** An ode to French Renaissance Revival architecture, this renovated maison d'hôte built in 1912 is impressive, covered with white glazed tiles. Quiet and uncluttered, the entrance boasts the mansion's original terra-cotta fountain, hard wood floors, and fancy moldings. Are those Corinthian columns in the master suite? Yes they are. There is no extraneous furniture, thus keeping the spotlight on the architectural glory. Rooms are painted stark white, featuring broad, low beds. Claw-foot tubs and porcelain sinks—the taps say "hot" and "froid"—bring a smile to hipster guests. All bedding is organic, as are the Continental breakfast and in-house cleaning products. **Pros:** dripping with style; facing Mount Royal and public tennis courts (fee). **Cons:** there are only five rooms, so book early. ⊠*4351 Ave. de L'Esplanade, Plateau Mont-Royal* ☎*514/312–3837 or 866/775–4431* ⊕*www.casabianca.ca* ⌨*3 rooms, 2 suites* ♿*In-room: no phone, Wi-Fi. In-hotel: no elevator, concierge, parking (fee), no-smoking building* ▤ *MC, V* ⦿*CP* Ⓜ*Mont-Royal* ⌖ *2D.*

$ 🏠**Hôtel Anne ma soeur Anne.** Staying at Anne ma soeur Anne is a little like having your own *pied-à-terre* in the Plateau Mont-Royal, especially if you book a back room with a view over the little tree-shaded garden (worth every penny of the extra cost). The built-in furniture adds to the effect: tip up your Murphy bed and you have a living room right on rue St-Denis. The rooms all have kitchenettes—coffeemakers, sinks, microwaves, and toaster ovens—but every morning the staff delivers fresh coffee and a croissant to your room. Nibble your pastry while inspecting the paintings of hockey players and jazz musicians hung in the hall. **Pros:** great morning croissants, delightfully friendly staff, and lovely garden—all in the heart of Plateau Mont-Royal's nightlife. **Cons:** there is a daunting number of stairs to climb outside; the bustling street scene right outside can be noisy. ⊠*4119 rue St-Denis, Plateau Mont-Royal,* ☎*514/281–3187 or 877/281–3187* ⊕*www.annemasoeuranne.com* ⌨*15 rooms, 2 suites* ♿*In-room: high-speed Internet, Wi-Fi. In-hotel: no elevator* ▤*AE, MC, V* ⦿*CP* Ⓜ*Mont-Royal* ⌖ *2E.*

VIEUX-MONTRÉAL

$$$$ 🏠**Hôtel Gault.** The street is lined with gaslights and the facade dates
Fodor'sChoice from the 1800s, but this boutique hotel looks like something out of
★ a modern-design magazine. Witness the yellow sectional couch in the lobby. Each loft-style room is different: some have tile-and-concrete floors brightened by boldly patterned geometric rugs; others have sleek, blond-wood furnishings and contrasting rough-brick walls. All have CD and DVD players (you can rent movies from a library of classics and indie film titles downstairs). Bathrooms have freestanding modern tubs and heated tile floors. In the summer, ask for a room on the fifth

7

floor, where there are private terraces. Pros: airy, expansive rooms. Cons: a bit hard to find. ⊠*449 rue Ste-Hélène, Vieux-Montréal,* ☎*514/904–1616 or 866/904–1616* ⊕*www.hotelgault.com* ⇩*22 rooms, 8 suites* ⟁*In-room: safe, refrigerator, DVD, Ethernet, dial-up. In-hotel: restaurant, room service, bar, gym, laundry service, public Wi-Fi, parking (fee), no-smoking rooms, some pets allowed* ⊟*AE, D, MC, V* †⊙†*CP* Ⓜ*Square-Victoria* ✛ *5E.*

$$$$ **⊞ Hôtel Nelligan.** Verses by Émile Nelligan, Québec's most passionate
Fodor's Choice poet, decorate the stone and brick walls of this ultraromantic hotel on
★ fashionable rue St-Paul. The hotel, just a block south of the Basilique Notre-Dame-de-Montréal, was dramatically expanded in 2007, and now occupies four adjoining buildings from the 1850s. Some suites have terraces with views of the river; others overlook the four-story, brick-walled atrium. At the pub-style bar, Méchant Bœuf, make sure to snag a table near the window overlooking rue St-Paul and watch the world hustle by. And for breakfast with a view of the Old City and the harbor, try the rooftop terrace. Complimentary wine and cheese are served every evening. Pros: rooftop lounge and restaurant have great views of the old city; lively bar right on rue St-Paul; romantic ambience. Cons: not well suited for small children. ⊠*106 rue St-Paul Ouest, Vieux-Montréal,* ☎*514/788–2040 or 877/788–2040* ⊕*www. hotelnelligan.com* ⇩*105 rooms, 28 suites, penthouse* ⟁*In-room: safe, Ethernet. In-hotel: 2 restaurants, room service, bar, gym, concierge, laundry service, parking (fee), no-smoking building* ⊟*AE, D, DC, MC, V* †⊙†*CP* Ⓜ*Place-d'Armes* ✛ *5F.*

$$$$ **⊞ Hôtel Le St. James.** In 2006 Madonna took over this lavishly fur-
Fodor's Choice nished luxury hotel, which quietly pampers European nobility, the
★ business elite, and Hollywood moguls. They can be spotted having high tea in the grand salon (between 2:30 and 5:30 PM) or reading in the clubby library. Dripping with Old World charm, Le St. James was once the Mercantile Bank of Canada. That explains why a former boardroom has 20-foot ceilings and lovingly restored murals of hydroelectric dams and waterfalls. Guest rooms include large marble bathrooms with separate tubs and showers, and have Bang & Olufsen sound systems; some rooms have gas fireplaces. The hotel restaurant XO revamped the menu to feature modern Italian cuisine, served in the sweeping, main banking hall. Pros: civility reigns; great in-room sound systems; decadently luxurious bathrooms; stateliest lobby in the city. Cons: rue St-Jacques is a very quiet street after 6 PM. ⊠*355 rue St-Jacques, Vieux-Montréal,* ☎*514/841–3111 or 866/841–3111* ⊕*www.hotellestjames.com* ⇩*23 rooms, 38 suites, 1 apartment* ⟁*In-room: Wi-Fi. In-hotel: restaurant, room service, bar, gym, spa, concierge, laundry service, parking (fee), some pets allowed* ⊟*AE, D, DC, MC, V* †⊙†*EP* Ⓜ*Square-Victoria* ✛ *5F.*

$$$$ **⊞ Hôtel St. Paul.** Stark white walls and huge shuttered windows give the "sky rooms" in this converted 19th-century office building in Vieux-Montréal a light, ethereal feel. The "earth rooms" are decorated in richer, darker colors. All have separate sitting areas with sleek leather furniture. There's no danger of being horrified by busy paintings on the walls, because the St. Paul keeps the focus on its silk, stone, and raw-

metal decor accents. Repeat customers, including A-listers like Cate Blanchett and Brendan Fraser, appreciate the panoramic views of the Old Port's architecture and the hotel's overall serenity. **Pros:** decorator's delight; lobby fireplace. **Cons:** poor location for night life. ⊠*355 rue McGill, Vieux-Montréal,* ☎*514/380–2222 or 866/380–2202* ⊕*www. hotelstpaul.com* ⇆*96 rooms, 24 suites* ⌂*In-room: refrigerator, Ethernet, dial-up. In-hotel: restaurant, room service, bar, gym, concierge, laundry service, public Wi-Fi, parking (fee), no-smoking rooms* ⊟*AE, D, DC, MC, V* ⏐○⏐*BP* Ⓜ*Square-Victoria* ✢ *5E.*

$$$$ 🏨**Hôtel XIXe Siècle.** You'd think that crystal chandeliers, 14-foot ceilings, and opulent Second Empire moldings would make the Hôtel XIXe Siècle the exclusive preserve of romantic couples and dowager duchesses, but its location in the middle of the financial district and a block from the city's convention center makes it a favorite with business travelers as well. Determined to stay fresh, this Victorian hotel re-fitted the lobby with new, high-back leather chairs and benches. Clients rave about the new mirrored doors separating the beds from the salons inside the suites. **Pros:** opulent decor; big high-ceilinged rooms, room service from Bistro Boris. **Cons:** service can be stoic; rue St-Jacques is deadly dull after 6 pm. ⊠*262 rue St-Jacques Ouest, Vieux-Montréal,* ☎*514/985–0019 or 877/553–0019* ⊕*www.hotelxixsiecle.com* ⇆*45 rooms, 14 suites* ⌂*In-room: Wi-Fi. In-hotel: bar, parking (fee)* ⊟*AE, D, DC MC, V* ⏐○⏐*BP* Ⓜ*Square-Victoria* ✢ *5F.*

$$$$ 🏨**Pierre du Calvet** AD **1725.** Merchant Pierre du Calvet—a notorious republican and Freemason—entertained Benjamin Franklin behind the stone walls of this elegant 18th-century home in Vieux-Montréal. Today it's a B&B luxuriously decorated with antique furnishings and Oriental rugs. The new flat-screen televisions are appropriately sized (small) to maintain the rooms' unplugged tranquillity. With its revamped menu, the Filles du Roy restaurant now specializes in fine Québécois cuisine, such as roasted duck, rack of lamb, and smoked veal. The glassed-in garden, filled with flowers and potted plants, is a great place for breakfast. **Pros:** garden setting for breakfast; opulent antiques. **Cons:** no room service; not suited for kids. ⊠*405 rue Bonsecours, Vieux-Montréal,* ☎*514/282–1725 or 866/282–1725* ⊕*www.pierreducalvet. ca* ⇆*1 room, 8 suites* ⌂*In-room: Wi-Fi. In-hotel: restaurant, no elevator, laundry service, parking (fee), no-smoking rooms* ⊟*AE, D, DC, MC, V* ⏐○⏐*BP* Ⓜ*Champ-de-Mars* ✢ *5G.*

$$$$ 🏨**Le Saint-Sulpice.** The Basilique Notre-Dame-de-Montréal is next door, and the comfortable lobby lounge and bar open onto a courtyard garden that's one of the rare green spots in Vieux-Montréal's stony landscape. The lodgings—huge suites with queen-size beds piled high with feather duvets, new plasma televisions, granite kitchen counters, glass bathroom sinks, and casement windows that actually open—are in a structure built in 2002 to blend in with the rest of the neighborhood; the 24-hour gym and business center are in an adjoining 19th-century building. Some suites have fireplaces and balconies. **Pros:** private garden; excellent celebrity-spotting; easy access to the Basilique Notre-Dame de Montréal. **Cons:** church bells on Sunday morning may disturb late sleepers. ⊠*414 rue St-Sulpice, Vieux-Mon-*

7

tréal, ☎*514/288–1000 or 877/785–7423* ⊕*www.lesaintsulpice.com*
⬆*108 suites* ⟡*In-room: safe, kitchen, high speed Internet, Wi-Fi. In-hotel: restaurant, room service, gym, spa, concierge, laundry service, parking (fee), no-smoking building, some pets allowed (fee)* ▤*AE, MC, V* ⦿|*BP* Ⓜ*Place-d'Armes* ✛ *5F.*

$$$$ ⊡ **W Montréal.** This ultraluxurious chain opened its first Canadian hotel
Fodor's Choice   here in 2004, and introduced Montréal to its famed slogan: "Whatever,
★   whenever service." Want rose petals in your bathtub at 3 AM? Just call. The hotel is housed in the old Bank of Canada building, but you'd never know it once you walk through those whooshing sliding doors into the modern lobby. The bright, airy guest rooms are decorated in various shades of gray highlighted with electric-blue pinstripes. Faux-fur throws on the beds allude to Montréal's commercial past, and the bathrooms have deep, square tubs and sinks. The mezzanine-level Plateau bar is popular with local professionals, while the late-night Wunder Bar attracts supermodels and A-list celebrities—from Snoop Dog and Josh Hartnett to Team Ferrari during the Grand Prix. Penthouse suites feature wraparound terraces and 12-foot ceilings. **Pros:** guests feel like rock stars; huge sexy bathrooms; fastest room service in town; friendly desk staff. **Cons:** no breakfast included. ⊠*901 Square Victoria, Vieux-Montréal,* ☎*514/395–3100* ⊕*www.whotels.com/montreal* ⬆*152 rooms, 30 suites* ⟡*In-room: safe, refrigerator, DVD, dial-up (fee), Wi-Fi (fee). In-hotel: restaurant, room service, 2 bars, gym, spa, concierge, executive floors, some pets allowed* ▤*AE, D, DC, MC, V* ⦿|*EP* Ⓜ*Square-Victoria* ✛ *5E.*

$$$ ⊡ **Auberge les Passants du Sans Soucy.** Daniel Soucy and Michael Banks,
Fodor's Choice   two of the friendliest and most urbane hosts you're likely to run into,
★   will go out of their way to make you feel like a house guest rather than a customer—if you're lucky enough to snag one of their 10 rooms, that is. Some regulars would rather delay their vacation than stay anywhere else. And no wonder: the hotel lobby doubles as an art gallery, and the rooms have brass beds, stone walls, exposed beams, whirlpool baths, and lots of fresh-cut flowers. For breakfast there are selections such as salmon omelets and French toast, all served in front of a fireplace that's full of flowers in summer and crackling logs in winter. This classy auberge was the first of its kind in the Old Port when it opened back in 1986, and all subsequent properties struggle to live up to its standard. **Pros:** exquisitely personal service and easy access to area's best museums. **Cons:** rooms need to be booked far in advance, and parking is a hassle. ⊠*171 rue St-Paul Ouest, Vieux-Montréal,* ☎*514/842–2634* ⊕*www.lesanssoucy.com* ⬆*8 rooms, 1 suite* ⟡*In-room: Wi-Fi. In-hotel: no elevator, laundry service, no-smoking building* ▤*AE, MC, V* ⦿|*BP* Ⓜ*Square-Victoria or Place-d'Armes* ✛ *5F.*

$$$ ⊡ **Auberge du Vieux-Port.** Stone and brick walls, brass beds, and exposed beams make this auberge a magnet for romantics. Casement windows overlook either fashionable rue St-Paul or the Vieux-Port, and on warm summer nights you can sip white wine on the rooftop terrace and watch the fireworks competitions. A full breakfast is served in Narcisse, the hotel's French bistro and wine bar on the main floor. Ask the concierge about the nearby lofts and apartments to rent—housekeeping and

room service included—if you have an extended family or an extended stay. Pros: rooftop terrace has unobstructed views of the harbor, as well as easy access to Vieux-Port and rue St-Paul. Cons: occasional bouts of street noise can be heard in rooms on rue St-Paul side. ⊠*97 rue de la Commune Est, Vieux-Montréal,* ☎*514/876–0081 or 888/660–7678* ⊕*www.aubergeduvieuxport.com* ↩*27 rooms* ⌂*In-room: safe, Wi-Fi. In-hotel: restaurant, room service, concierge, laundry service, parking (fee), no-smoking rooms, some pets allowed (fee)* ▭*AE, DC, MC, V* ⏺*BP* Ⓜ*Place-d'Armes or Champ-de-Mars* ⟣ *5E.*

$$$ 🛏 **Inter-Continental Montréal.** On the edge of Vieux-Montréal, this modern luxury hotel is part of the Montréal World Trade Center, a block-long retail and office complex. The 26-story brick tower is softened a bit with fanciful turrets and pointed roofs. Freshly remodeled rooms make you forget the old pastel walls and frumpy chairs. The new focus is on leather and suede bed fixtures, topped with tan and white bedding. Heavy drapes pull back to reveal floor-to-ceiling windows overlooking downtown or Vieux-Montréal and the waterfront. Bathrooms have separate marble tubs and showers. Le Continent restaurant serves fine international cuisine. A footbridge links the hotel's main building with the 18th-century Nordheimer Building, which houses many of its public rooms. Pros: easy underground access to shopping and nightlife. Cons: business oriented (the convention center is across the street) and a bit stuffy. ⊠*360 rue St-Antoine Ouest, Vieux-Montréal,* ☎*514/987–9900 or 800/361–3600* ⊕*www.montreal.interconti.com* ↩*334 rooms, 23 suites* ⌂*In-room: refrigerator, Ethernet, dial-up, Wi-Fi. In-hotel: 3 restaurants, room service, bar, pool, gym, concierge, laundry service, parking (fee)* ▭*AE, D, DC, MC, V* ⏺*EP* Ⓜ*Square-Victoria or Place-d'Armes* ⟣ *5E.*

$$$ 🛏 **Le Place d'Armes Hôtel & Suites.** Three splendidly ornate commercial
Fodor's Choice buildings dating from the Victorian era were merged in 2005 to cre-
★ ate Vieux-Montréal's largest boutique hotel. The high-ceiling guest rooms—some with exposed brick or stone walls—combine old-fashioned grandeur with sleek modern furnishings. The large bathrooms are tiled in black granite and white marble. The 2,000-square-foot spa includes the city's first *hammam*, or Middle Eastern–style steam bath. A rooftop bar and restaurant serves sandwiches and grilled entrées at lunch, and there's a hipster lobby bar, Suite 701, where complimentary wine and cheese are served every evening. The Basilique Notre-Dame-de-Montréal is just across the square, and the Palais des Congrès is nearby. Pros: houses the best spa in town, and has easy access to the sights of Vieux-Montréal. Cons: late sleepers may be disturbed by the noontime Angelus bells at the Basilique Notre-Dame-de-Vieux-Montréal. ⊠*55 rue St-Jacques, Vieux-Montréal,* ☎*514/842–1887 or 888/450–1887* ⊕*www.hotelplacedarmes.com* ↩*83 rooms, 52 suites* ⌂*In-room: refrigerator, safe, Wi-Fi. In-hotel: 2 restaurants, room service, 2 bars, gym, spa, concierge, laundry service, parking (fee)* ▭*AE, DC, MC, V* ⏺*BP* Ⓜ*Place-d'Armes* ⟣ *5F.*

$$$ 🛏 **Springhill Suites.** This modern all-suites hotel with plenty of amenities fits seamlessly into one of the narrowest and oldest streets of Vieux-Montréal. The rooms are plain, but large and comfortable, with

pastel walls and nondescript modern furniture. This is the perfect compromise for those seeking modern amenities in antique surroundings. Busy rue St-Paul is a block south, the Vieux-Port is a five-minute walk, and Place Jacques-Cartier is three blocks east. **Pros:** big rooms and underground parking—both rarities in Vieux-Montréal—and just far enough from rue St-Paul to be quiet. **Cons:** difficult access on a narrow street and poor views. ✉ *445 rue St-Jean-Baptiste, Vieux-Montréal,* ☎ *514/875–4333 or 888/287–9400* ⊕ *www.springhillsuites.com* ⟳ *124 suites* ⬦ *In-room: Ethernet, dial-up. In-hotel: restaurant, room service, hot tub, gym, spa, laundry service, public Internet, public Wi-Fi, parking (fee), refrigerator* ⊟ *AE, D, DC, MC, V* ⦿| *BP* Ⓜ *Champ-de-Mars* ⊹ *5F.*

$$ ── ── ──

$$ ▦ **Auberge Bonaparte.** One of the finest restaurants in Vieux-Montréal, Auberge Bonaparte has converted the upper floors of its 19th-century building into an inn. Clubby and distinguished, with trompe-l'oeil wooden paneling at the entrance, it makes guests feel like they're in a private library. Wrought-iron or Louis Philippe–style furnishings fill the rooms, some of which have double whirlpool baths. The rooms in the rear (some with balconies) have views over the private gardens of the Basilique Notre-Dame-de-Montréal. Breakfast is served in your room. **Pros:** marble fireplace in the clubby new bar, quiet location, perfect for theater lovers—the Centaur Theatre is next door. **Cons:** downstairs restaurant can be a bit noisy on weekends. ✉ *447 rue St-François-Xavier, Vieux-Montréal,* ☎ *514/844–1448* ⊕ *www.bonaparte.ca* ⟳ *30 rooms, 1 suite* ⬦ *In-room: Wi-Fi. In-hotel: restaurant, room service, bar, concierge, public Wi-Fi, parking (fee), no-smoking building* ⊟ *AE, D, DC, MC, V* ⦿| *BP* Ⓜ *Place-d'Armes* ⊹ *5F.*

$$ ▦ **Auberge de la Place Royale.** What was once a 19th-century rooming house is now a waterfront B&B overlooking the Vieux-Port. A magnificent wood staircase links the floors of this stone building, where Leonard Cohen canoodled with Suzanne in Room 202. Antiques and reproductions furnish the spacious guest rooms, some of which have whirlpool tubs. A full breakfast is served either on a sidewalk terrace on warm sunny days or in a dining room when it cold or wet. The service is very attentive. **Pros:** wonderful views of the Vieux-Port; attentive service; pleasant sidewalk restaurant. **Cons:** parking is difficult. ✉ *115 rue de la Commune Ouest, Vieux-Montréal,* ☎ *514/287–0522* ⊕ *www.aubergeplaceroyale.com* ⟳ *6 rooms, 6 suites* ⬦ *In-room: dial-up, Wi-Fi (some). In-hotel: restaurant, no elevator, laundry service, public Wi-Fi, parking (fee), no-smoking rooms* ⊟ *AE, MC, V* ⦿| *BP* Ⓜ *Place-d'Armes* ⊹ *5F.*

¢ ▦ **Auberge Alternative.** The name says it all. You won't find any expense-account fat cats in the breakfast room sipping the fair-trade coffee and checking the stock prices. Instead you'll find earnest, young, and young-at-heart travelers from all over the world and North America—the kind of people who often speak French or try to and are eager to plunge into the local scene. They're also the kind of people who take the time to find really cheap lodgings in really desirable areas. You can get a very basic but clean room for C$55 or a dorm bed for as little as C$20. All guests can use the kitchen facilities, and sign up for the new classes offered in photography, circus arts, and voice. **Pros:** inexpensive, friendly, and attracts an interesting crowd of travelers. **Cons:** cramped and a bit rustic. ⊠*358 rue St-Pierre, Vieux-Montréal,* ☎*514/282–8069* ⊕*www.auberge-alternative.qc.ca* ⊅*7 dorms, 1 room* ♿*In-hotel: laundry facilities, public Internet, public Wi-Fi, no elevator* ⊟*MC, V* ⦿*BP* Ⓜ*Square-Victoria* ✛ *5E.*

7

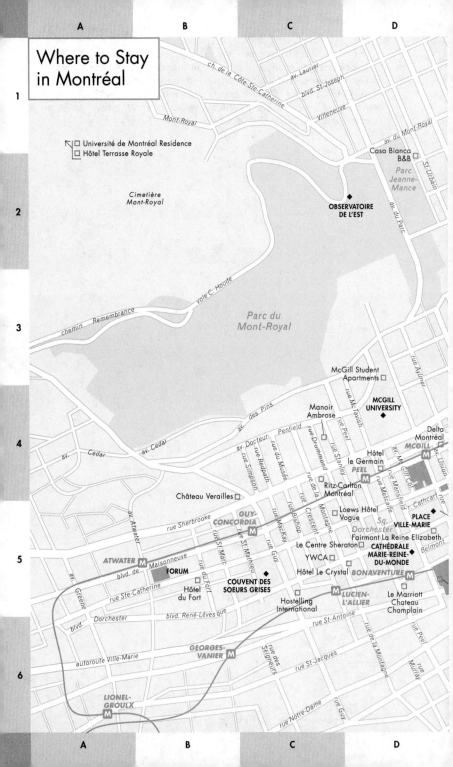

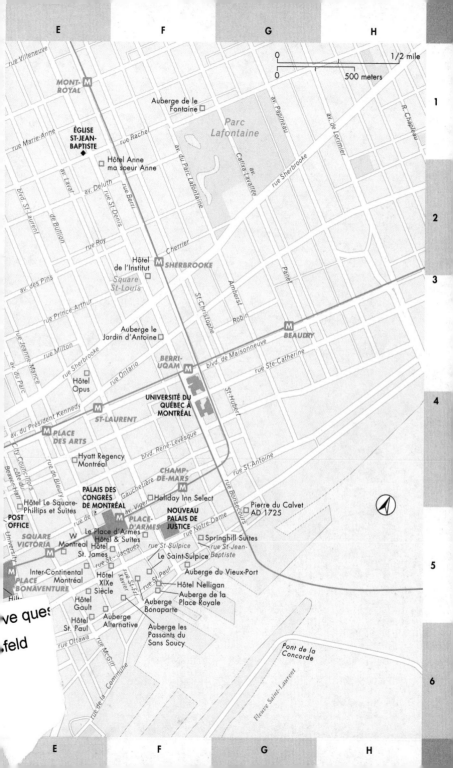

Québec City

Quartier Petit-Champlain in Lower Town.

WORD OF MOUTH

"We enjoyed a horse and carriage tour of Québec City. It was reasonably priced (our carriage was a four-seater) and our tour guide was quite knowledgeable about the history of the city."

—boots08

"I have to admit kids are excited re Québec—they are pretending they're going to Paris."

—alanf

8

www.fodors.com/forums

WELCOME TO QUÉBEC CITY

Traditional stone houses located in the heart of Old Québec City.

TOP REASONS TO GO

★ **Visit Château Frontenac:** Even if you're not staying at Québec City's most famous landmark, make sure to pop in to see the lobby, check out the shops, and take a tour.

★ **Stroll around Vieux-Québec:** Spend at least a day exploring the streets of the Old City—and don't miss a ride on the funicular for fabulous views of the St. Lawrence River.

★ **Explore La Citadelle:** You don't have to be a history buff to enjoy standing atop Québec City's highest perch, which is the largest fortified base in North America.

★ **Recreate on the Plains of Abraham:** From cross-country skiing and sledding in winter to picnicking and in-line skating in summer, this huge park is the place to be for outdoor fun.

★ **Attend Carnival de Québec:** This winter festival stretches over three weekends in January and February, and it's all about playing in the snow from morning until night. Highlights include a canoe race and a snow sculpture contest.

1 Upper Town. Sweeping views of the Laurentians in the distance can be seen from here, where the Château Frontenac sits on the jutting cliff above the Old City below, like the top layer of a wedding cake.

2 Lower Town. A maze of cobblestone streets with tucked-away cafés and creperies characterizes Basse-Ville, but there's a modern flair thrown in, as converted warehouses have become hip boutiques and art galleries.

3 The Fortifications. The 3-mile long wall that encircles Vieux-Québec is a site unto itself—which includes La Citadelle, the star-shaped structure that's built at city's highest point.

GETTING ORIENTED

Upper Town (Haute-Ville) and Lower Town (Basse-Ville) make up the Old City (Vieux-Québec). You can walk from one to the other, or take a ride on the funicular that runs between them. Streets in both these areas are not in a grid, so a map is essential. Outside the walls, the main street is the Grand Alleé, which approaches the Old City from the east.

4 Outside the Walls.
There's an entire city to explore beyond Vieux-Québec that many visitors never get to see. Rue St-Jean, Avenue Cartier, and the Grand Alleé all have restaurants, shops, and nightlife well worth checking out.

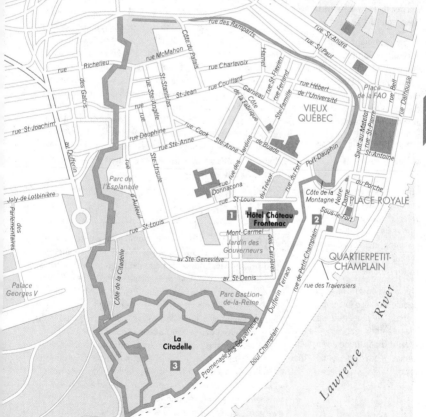

QUÉBEC CITY PLANNER

Getting Around

By far the best way—and in some places the only way—to explore Québec City is on foot. Top sights, restaurants, and hotels are within or near Old Québec, which takes up only 11 square km (4 square mi).

The area is not flat, so walking takes a bit of effort, especially if you decide to walk to the Upper Town from the Lower Town.

Helpful city maps are available at visitor-information offices, the best of which is on the public square in front of the Château Frontenac. A car is necessary only if you plan to visit outlying areas.

When to Go

Although summer here is the most popular time to visit, when there's a general relaxed vibe as its residents soak up the warmth and festivals galore, seeing the city in winter shows its true colors.

The thing to know about the people who live in Québec City is that they don't hole up once the weather gets cold—they revel it in, all bundled in their parkas, ready to go out on the town.

Getting Here

Montréal and Québec City are linked by Autoroute 20 on the south shore of the St. Lawrence River and by Autoroute 40 on the north shore. On both highways, the ride between the two cities is about 240 km (149 mi) and takes about three hours. U.S. I–87 in New York, U.S. I–89 in Vermont, and U.S. I–91 in New Hampshire connect with Autoroute 20, as does Highway 401 from Toronto. Driving northeast from Montréal on Autoroute 20, follow signs for Pont Pierre-Laporte (Pierre Laporte Bridge) as you approach Québec City. After you've crossed the bridge, turn right onto boulevard Laurier (Route 175), which becomes the Grande Allée. If you're flying in, Jean Lesage International Airport is about 19 km (12 mi) northwest of downtown. Driving into town, take Route 540 (Autoroute Duplessis) to Route 175 (boulevard Laurier), which becomes Grande Allée and leads right to Vieux-Québec. The ride takes about 30 minutes. Taxis are available immediately outside the airport exit near the baggage-claim area. A ride into the city costs about C$30. VIA Rail, Canada's passenger rail service, has service between Montréal and Québec City. Trains run four times daily on weekdays, three times daily on weekends. The trip takes less than three hours and costs C$76.35 one-way.

Making the Most of Your Time

Seeing the Old City is a must, even if you're here only on a day-trip. Start in Lower Town at Place Royal, an impressive square with houses topped with Normandy-style roofs. When you get tired, take the funicular for a ride-with-a-view to Upper Town, where you'll land in front of the Château Frontenac. While in Upper Town, spend time strolling along Terrace Dufferin, a wide boardwalk that runs parallel to the river, and from which you'll see the Laurentian Mountains. Reserve at least a half-day for La Citadel, located at the end of Terrace Dufferin. More time in Québec City affords you the chance to see what's outside the Old City's walls. Two top choices include wandering along the Grand Allée, packed with boutiques and restaurants, or heading to the western part of the city to check out urbane St-Roch.

Updated by
Joanne Latimer,
Anne Marie
Marko, and
Paul Waters

NO TRIP TO FRENCH-SPEAKING CANADA is complete without a visit to romantic Québec City. There's a definite European sensibility here, and you'll feel farther from home than you are, walking down cobblestone streets and stopping in small shops selling everything from pastries and artisanal cheese to antiques and art.

The heart of the city is Vieux-Québec (Old Québec), which is divided between the Haute-Ville (Upper Town) and the Basse-Ville (Lower Town). Upper Town, still enclosed by stone ramparts with mounted cannons, was the home of the wealthy and the powerful, while lower orders scrabbled for a living on the narrow streets along the edge of the St. Lawrence River. The old distinctions, however, no longer apply, and today Old Québec is a small, dense, well-maintained neighborhood steeped in four centuries of French, English, and Canadian history and tradition. The city's finest 17th- and 18th-century buildings are here, as are its best parks and monuments. Because of the fortified city's immaculate preservation, Old Québec was designated a UNESCO World Heritage Site in 1985.

But the Old City is just a part of the Québec City experience. Québec City is hilly, so plan accordingly. Use the funicular (a kind of elevator), off Dufferin Terrace, between Upper and Lower Town to avoid the climb. There are cabs to take you back and forth as well. Outside the city walls there are plenty of interesting areas a short walk or bus ride away, such as St-Roch, just west of the Old City, with its grand square, artsy galleries, and funky shops. Or walk down avenue Cartier in the area known as Montcalm, southwest of the Old City, for high-end shopping of all kinds, as well as the Halles Petit Cartier market.

8

UPPER TOWN

Home to many of the city's most famous sites, Upper Town also offers a dramatic view of the St. Lawrence River and the surrounding countryside. It's where you'll find historic institutions and, of course, rue St-Jean's bars, cafés, and shops, along with hotels and bed-and-breakfasts.

Like the Citadel, most of the many elegant homes that line the narrow streets in Upper Town are made of granite cut from nearby quarries in the 1800s. The stone walls, copper roofs, and heavy wooden doors on the government buildings and high-steepled churches in the area also reflect the Upper Town's place as the political, educational, and religious nerve center of both the province and the country during much of the past four centuries.

MAIN ATTRACTIONS

⑬ **Basilique Notre-Dame-de-Québec** *(Our Lady of Québec Basilica)*. François de Laval, the first bishop of New France, and his successors once ruled a diocese that stretched all the way to the Gulf of Mexico. Laval's original cathedral burned down and has been rebuilt several times, but the current basilica still has a chancel lamp that was a gift from Louis XIV, the Sun King himself. The church's somber, ornate interior

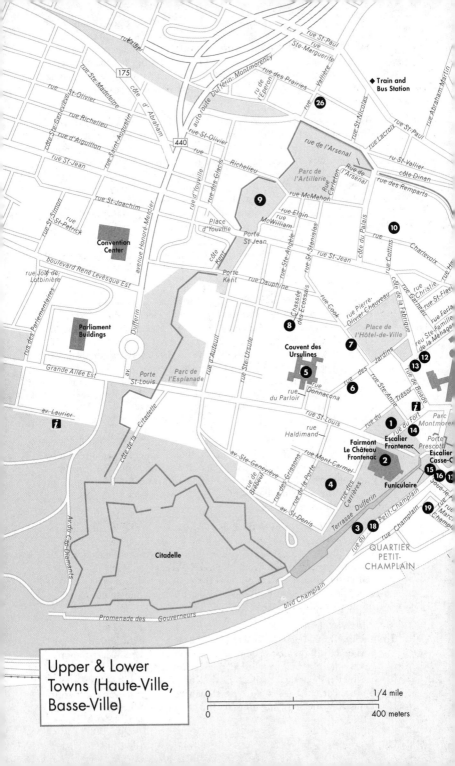

Upper & Lower Towns (Haute-Ville, Basse-Ville)

◆ Train and Bus Station

Parc de l'Artillerie

Couvent des Ursulines

Fairmont Le Château Frontenac

Escalier Frontenac

Escalier Casse-C

Funiculaire

Citadelle

Parliament Buildings

Convention Center

Place d'Youville

Porte St-Jean

Porte Kent

Porte St-Louis

Porte Prescott

Place de l'Hôtel-de-Ville

Parc de l'Esplanade

Parc Montmoren

QUARTIER PETIT-CHAMPLAIN

Promenade des Gouverneurs

0   1/4 mile

0   400 meters

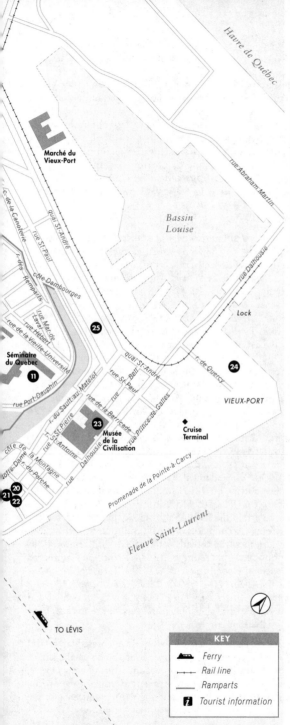

8

includes a canopy dais over the episcopal throne, a ceiling of painted clouds decorated with gold leaf, and richly colored stained-glass windows. The large crypt was Québec City's first cemetery; more than 900 bodies are interred here, including 20 bishops and four governors of New France. Samuel de Champlain may be buried near the basilica: archaeologists have been searching for his tomb since 1950. There are information panels that allow you to read about the history of this church. Or, if you prefer, guided tours are available. The centre d'animation François-de-Laval uses videos and pictures to illustrate the life of Québec's first bishop and founder of the Canada's Catholic Church. ⊠16 rue de Buade, Upper Town ☎418/692–2533 church ⊕www.patrimoine-religieux.com ☜Basilica free, guided tour C$2, crypt C$2 ⊙Mid-Oct.–Apr., daily 8–4; May–mid-Oct., weekdays 7:30–4, weekends 7:30–5.

❺ Couvent des Ursulines (*Ursuline Convent*). Adolesecnt girls still study at the Ursuline convent on rue Donnacona, as they have since 1639 when the place was founded by French nun Marie de l'Incarnation and laywoman Madame de la Peltrie. The convent has many of its original walls intact and houses a little chapel and a museum. The **Chapelle des Ursulines** (*Ursuline Chapel* ⊠10 rue Donnacona, Upper Town ☎No phone ☜Free ⊙Chapel May–Oct., Tues.–Sat. 10–11:30 and 1:30–4:30, Sun. 1:30–4:30) is where French general Louis-Joseph Montcalm was buried after he died in the 1759 battle that decided the fate of New France. In September 2001 Montcalm's remains were transferred to rest with those of his soldiers at the Hôpital Général de Québec's cemetery, at 260 boulevard Langelier. The exterior of the Ursuline Chapel was rebuilt in 1902, but the interior contains the original chapel, which took sculptor Pierre-Noël Levasseur from 1726 to 1736 to complete. The votive lamp was lighted in 1717, and has never been extinguished. The **Musée des Ursulines** (⊠12 rue Donnacona, Upper Town ☎418/694–0694 ☜C$6 ⊙Museum May–Sept., Tues.–Sat. 10–noon and 1–5, Sun. 1–5; Oct.–Apr., Tues.–Sun. 1–4:30) was once the residence of Madame de la Peltrie. The museum provides an informative perspective on 120 years of the Ursulines' life under the French regime, from 1639 to 1759. It took an Ursuline nun nine years of training to attain the level of a professional embroiderer; the museum contains magnificent pieces of ornate embroidery, such as altar frontals with gold and silver threads intertwined with semiprecious jewels. In the lobby of the museum is the **Centre Marie-de-l'Incarnation** (⊠10 rue Donnacona, Upper Town ☎418/694–0413 ⊙Feb. –Nov., Mon. 10–11:30, Tues.–Sat. 10–11:30 and 1:30–4:30, Sun. 1:30–4:30; closed Dec.; open by request only Jan.), a center with an exhibit and books for sale on the life of the Ursulines' first superior, who came from France and co-founded the convent.

❷ Fairmont Le Château Frontenac. Québec City's most celebrated landmark, this imposing turreted castle with a copper roof stands on the site of what was the administrative and military headquarters of New France. It owes its name to the Comte de Frontenac, governor of the French colony between 1672 and 1698. Considering the magnificence of the

Fodor'sChoice
★

château's location overlooking the St. Lawrence River, you can see why Frontenac said, "For me, there is no site more beautiful nor more grandiose than that of Québec City." Samuel de Champlain was responsible for Château St-Louis, the first structure to appear on the site of the Frontenac; it was built between 1620 and 1624 as a residence for colonial governors. In 1784 Château Haldimand was constructed here, but it was demolished in 1892 to make way for Château Frontenac, built as a hotel a year later. The Frontenac was remarkably luxurious at that time: guest rooms contained fireplaces, bathrooms, and marble fixtures, and a special commissioner purchased antiques for the establishment. The hotel was designed by New York architect Bruce Price, who also worked on Québec City's Gare du Palais (rail station) and other Canadian landmarks. The addition of a 20-story central tower in 1925 completed the hotel. It has accumulated a star-studded guest roster, including Queen Elizabeth and Ronald Reagan as well as Franklin Roosevelt and Winston Churchill, who met here in 1943 and 1944 for two wartime conferences. Guides dressed in 19th-century-style costumes conduct tours of the luxurious interior. ⊠*1 rue des Carrières, Upper Town* ☎*418/691–2166* ⊕*www.fairmont.com* ☜*Tours C$8.50* ⊙*Tours May–mid-Oct., daily 10–6 on the hr; mid-Oct.–Apr., weekends noon–5 or on demand. Reservations essential.*

❻ Holy Trinity Anglican Cathedral. The first Anglican cathedral outside the
★ British Isles was erected in the heart Québec City Upper Town in 1804. Its simple, dignified facade is reminiscent of London's St. Martin-in-the-Fields. The cathedral's land was given to the Récollet fathers (Franciscan monks from France) in 1681 by the king of France for a church and monastery. When Québec came under British rule, the Récollets made the church available to the Anglicans for services. Later, King George III ordered construction of the present cathedral, with an area set aside for members of the royal family. A portion of the north balcony is still reserved exclusively for the use of the reigning sovereign or his or her representative. The church houses precious objects donated by George III. The cathedral's impressive rear organ has 3,058 pipes. On Sunday morning the cathedral has traditional English bell ringing. The bells were restored in time to ring in Québec City's 400th anniversary in 2008. ⊠*31 rue des Jardins, Upper Town* ☎*418/692–2193* ☜*Free* ⊙*Mid-May–June, daily 9–6; July and Aug., daily 9–8; Sept.–mid-Oct., weekdays 10–4; mid-Oct.–mid-May, services only; morning services year-round in English daily at 8:30, and Sun. also at 11 AM, in French at 9:30 AM.*

❹ Jardin des Gouverneurs *(Governors' Park).* In this small park just south
Fodor'sChoice of the Château Frontenac stands the **Wolfe-Montcalm Monument,** a
★ 50-foot-tall obelisk that is unique because it pays tribute to both a winning (English) and a losing (French) general. The monument recalls the 1759 battle on the Plains of Abraham, which ended French rule here. British general James Wolfe lived only long enough to hear of his victory; French general Louis-Joseph Montcalm died shortly after Wolfe, with the knowledge that the city was lost. On the south side of the park is **avenue Ste-Geneviève,** lined with well-preserved Victorian houses dating from 1850 to 1900. Several have been converted to inns.

Québec City History

Québec City was founded by French explorer Samuel de Champlain in 1608, and is the oldest municipality in the province of Québec. In the 17th century the first French explorers, fur trappers, and missionaries came here to establish the colony of New France.

French explorer Jacques Cartier arrived 1535, but it was Champlain who founded "New France" some 70 years later, and built a fort on the banks of the St. Lawrence on a spot that is today called Place Royale.

The British were persistent in their efforts to dislodge the French from North America, but the colonists of New France built forts and other military structures, such as a wooden palisade (defensive fence) that reinforced their position on top of the cliff. It was Britain's naval supremacy that ultimately led to New France's demise. After capturing all French forts east of Québec, General James Wolfe led a British army to Québec City in the summer of 1759.

After a months-long siege, thousands of British soldiers scaled the heights along a narrow cow path on a moonless night. Surprised to see British soldiers massed on a farmer's field so near the city, French General Louis-Joseph Montcalm rushed out to meet the British in what became known as the Battle of the Plains of Abraham. The French were routed in the violent 20-minute conflict, which claimed the lives of both Wolfe and Montcalm. The battle marked the death of New France and the birth of British Canada.

British rule was a boon for Québec City. Thanks to more robust trade and large capital investments, the fishing, fur-trading, shipbuilding, and timber industries expanded rapidly. As the city's economic, social, religious, and political sectors developed and diversified, the quality of people's lives also greatly improved.

Wary of new invasions from its former American colonies, the British also expanded the city's fortifications. They replaced the wooden palisades with a massive cut-stone wall and built a star-shaped fortress. Both works are still prominent in the city's urban landscape.

The constitution of 1791 established Québec City as the capital of Lower Canada, a position it held until 1840, when the Act of Union united Upper and Lower Canada and made Montréal the capital. When Canada was created in 1867 by the Act of Confederation, which united four colonial provinces (Québec, Ontario, New Brunswick, and Nova Scotia), Québec City was named the province's capital city, a role it continues to play. In Québec, however, the city is known officially as *"la capitale Nationale,"* a reflection of the nationalist sentiments that have marked Québec society and politics for the past 40 years.

❾ Parc de l'Artillerie *(Artillery Park)*. Nineteenth-century British officers ★ certainly knew how to party in style, if the ornate china and regimental silver glittering in the beautifully restored officers' mess in this national historic site are anything to go by. They and their families didn't live too badly, either, as you'll see if you visit the gardens and rooms of the restored **Officers' Quarters,** all decorated in the style of the 1830s. In July and August you can sample a taste (literally) of life in the lower ranks by trying a piece of chewy "soldier's bread" baked in an outdoor oven, or watch a reenactor in a French uniform of the 18th century demonstrate shooting with a flintlock musket. Artillery Park's four buildings all have long histories. The Officers' Quarters, for example, were built 1817, and the officers' is housed in the Dauphin Redoubt, which, as the name suggests, was originally built in 1712 to house the French garrison and to guard the St. Charles River and the port. The British took it over in 1759, and from 1785 until 1871 it served as the mess for the officers of the Royal Artillery Regiment. The old iron foundry houses a magnificent scale model of Québec City. ⊠*2 rue d'Auteuil, Upper Town* ☎ *888/773–8888 or 418/648–4205* ⊕*www. parkscanada.gc.ca* ⬛*C$3.95* ⊙*Apr., April–Oct., daily 10–5.*

❶ **Place d'Armes.** For centuries, this square atop a cliff has been used for parades and military events. Upper Town's most central location, the plaza is bordered by government buildings; at its west side stands the majestic **Ancien Palais de Justice** (Old Courthouse), a Renaissance-style building from 1887. The plaza is on land that was occupied by a church and convent of the Récollet missionaries (Franciscan monks), who in 1615 were the first order of priests to arrive in New France. The Gothic-style **fountain** at the center of Place d'Armes pays tribute to their arrival. ⊠*Rues St-Louis and du Fort, Upper Town.*

❸ **Terrasse Dufferin.** This wide boardwalk with an intricate wrought-iron guardrail has a panoramic view of the St. Lawrence River, the town of Lévis on the opposite shore, Île d'Orléans, and the Laurentian Mountains. It was named for Lord Dufferin, governor of Canada between 1872 and 1878, who had this walkway constructed in 1878. Dufferin Terrace is currently a dig site, scheduled to be completed by 2008, as archaeologists from Parks Canada work to uncover the remains of the château, which was home to the governors from 1626 to 1834, when it was destroyed by fire, and Fort St-Louis. There are 90-minute tours of the fortifications that leave from here. The **Promenade des Gouverneurs** begins at the boardwalk's western end; the path skirts the cliff and leads up to Québec's highest point, Cap Diamant, and also to the Citadelle.

ALSO WORTH SEEING

❼ **Edifice Price.** Styled after the Empire State Building, the 15-story, art deco structure was the city's first skyscraper. Built in 1929, it served as headquarters of the Price Brothers Company, a lumber firm founded by Sir William Price. Don't miss the interior: exquisite copper plaques depict scenes of the company's early pulp and paper activities, and the two maple-wood elevators are '30s classics. ⊠*65 rue Ste-Anne, Upper Town.*

❿ **Musée et Monastère des Augustines de la Miséricorde de Jésus de l'Hôtel-Dieu de Québec** *(Augustinian Monastery and Museum).* Augustinian nuns arrived from Dieppe, France, in 1639 with a mission to care for the sick in the new colony. They established the first hospital north of Mexico, the **Hôtel-Dieu,** the large building west of the monastery. Certainly worth a look is the richly decorated chapel designed by artist Thomas Baillairgé (1829–1932), as well as the vaults, which date to 1659 and were used by the nuns to shelter from British bombardments.

The museum houses an extensive collection of everything from ornately embroidered liturgical vestments to quite terrifying surgical instruments from the 18th century. Extensive renovations on the museum and monastery began in 2008, and were scheduled to finish by the spring of 2009 ⊠*32 rue Charlevoix, Upper Town* ☎*418/692–2492 tours* ✉*Free Tues.–Sat. 9:30–noon and 1:30–5, Sun. 1:30–5.*

STROLLING ON ST-JEAN

Rue St-Jean becomes a pedestrian street for summer at Place d'Youville—that means you'll have to leave your car behind at the public parking lot and walk.

❽ Morrin College. This stately gray-stone building has served many purposes, from imprisoning (and executing criminals) to storing the national archives. Built between 1802 and 1813, it was the city's first British prison, and two cell blocks of half a dozen cells each remain intact, and some are used to house an English-language cultural center. The scaffold used to hang 16 criminals, however, is long gone.

When the jail closed in 1868, the building was converted into Morrin College, one of the city's first private schools, and the **Literary and Historical Society of Québec** moved in. Founded in 1824, this forerunner of Canada's National Archives still operates a public lending library and has a superb collection that includes some of the first books printed in North America. There are historical and cultural talks held in English, as well as tours of the building. Don't miss the library and Victorian College Hall spaces. ⊠*44 rue Chaussée des Ecossais, Upper Town* ☎*418/694–9147* ⊕*www.morrin.org* ✉*Free, C$3 for group tours (minimum five people), C$6 for individual tours* ⊘*Tues. noon–9, Wed.–Fri. noon–4, Sat. 10–4, Sun. 1–4.*

⓬ Musée de l'Amérique Française. A former student residence of the Séminaire de Québec à l'Université Laval (Québec Seminary at Laval University) houses this museum that focuses on the history of the French in North America. You can view about 20 of the museum's 400 landscape and still-life paintings, some from as early as the 15th century, along with French colonial money and scientific instruments. The attached former chapel is used for exhibits, conferences, and cultural activities. There's a great 26-minute film (English subtitles) about Francophones and an accompanying exhibit that details their journey across North America. ⊠*2 côte de la Fabrique, Upper Town* ☎*418/692–2843* ⊕*www.mcq.org* ✉*C$6, free Tues. Nov.–May* ⊘*June 24–early Sept., daily 9:30–5; early Sept.–June 23, Tues.–Sun. 10–5.*

⓮ Musée du Fort. A sound-and-light show reenacts the area's important battles, including the Battle of the Plains of Abraham and the 1775 attack by American generals Arnold and Montgomery. Three permanent expositions on the history of New France—including weapons, uniforms, and military insignia—were recently added. The model of the city—complete with ships, cannons, and soldiers lined up for battle—was recently cleaned and repainted to celebrate its 40th anniversary. A tribute to the museum's founder, Anthony Price, provides insight into

QUÉBEC CITY'S BEST WALKING TOURS

Les Tours Voir Québec leads English-language walking tours of the Old City through the narrow streets that buses cannot enter. A two-hour tour costs C$19.50.

Ghost Tours of Québec gives ghoulish 90-minute evening tours of Québec City murders, executions, and ghost sightings. Costumed actors lead the C$17.50 tours, in English or French, from May through October. Ghost Tours now offers Witchcraft on Tour as well, which is a reenactment of a trial in English, held indoors.

Le Promenade des Écrivains (Writers' Walk) takes you through the Old City, where guide Marc Rochette, a local writer, stops to read passages about Québec City from the works of famous writers that include Melville, Thoreau, Camus, Ferron, and others. The two-hour tours cost C$15 and are given Wednesday and Saturday.

La Compagnie des Six-Associés gives several historical theme-driven walking tours year-round, starting at C$12. A tour-ending drink is included. The themes cover such timeless topics as "Killers and Beggars," "The Lily and the Lion," and "Lust and Drunkenness."

Contacts **La Compagnie des Six-Associés** (✉ *381 des Franciscains, Upper Town* ☎ *418/692–3033* ⊕ *www.sixassocies.com*). **Ghost Tours of Québec** (✉ *85 rue St-Louis, Upper Town* ☎ *418/692–9770* ⊕ *www.ghosttoursofquebec.com*). **Le Promenade des Écrivains** (✉ *1588 av. Bergemont, Upper Town* ☎ *418/264–2772*). **Les Tours Voir Québec** (✉ *12 rue St-Anne, Upper Town* ☎ *418/694–2001* ⊕ *www.toursvoirquebec.com*).

8

this labor of love. ✉ *10 rue Ste-Anne, Upper Town* ☎ *418/692–1759* ⊕ *www.museedufort.com* 💲 *C$8* ⊙ *Feb. and Mar., and Nov. and Dec., Thurs.–Sun. 11–4; Apr.–Oct., daily 10–5; Dec. 26 to the first Sunday after New Year's Day, daily 11–4.*

⑪ Séminaire du Québec. Behind these gates lies a tranquil courtyard surrounded by austere stone buildings with rising steeples; these structures have housed classrooms and student residences since 1663. François de Montmorency Laval, the first bishop of New France, founded Québec Seminary to train priests in the new colony. In 1852 the seminary became Université Laval, the first Catholic university in North America. In 1946 the university moved to a larger campus in suburban Ste-Foy. Today priests live on the premises, and Laval's architecture school occupies part of the building. The on-site **Musée de l'Amérique Française** gives tours of the seminary grounds and the interior in summer. Tours start from the museum, located at 2 côte de la Fabrique. The small Second Empire–style **Chapelle Extérieure,** at the west entrance of the seminary, was built in 1888 after fire destroyed the 1750 original. Joseph-Ferdinand Peachy designed the chapel; its interior is patterned after that of the Église de la Trinité in Paris. ✉ *1 côte de la Fabrique, Upper Town* ☎ *418/692–3981* 💲 *C$5* ⊙ *Tours weekends mid-June–early Sept.; call for tour times.*

LOWER TOWN

Lower Town is the new hot spot, its once-dilapidated warehouses now boutique hotels, trendy shops, chic art galleries, and popular restaurants and bars. It's home to a great diversity of cultural communities, from businesspeople to hip youngsters sipping coffee or beer at cafés. After exploring Place Royale and its cobblestone streets, you can walk along the edge of the St. Lawrence River and watch the sailboats and ships go by, shop at the market, or kick back on a *terrasse* with a Kir Royal. Rue Petit-Champlain also has charming places to stop and listen to street musicians.

In 1608 Champlain chose this narrow, U-shaped spit of land as the site for his settlement. Champlain later abandoned the fortified *abitation* (residence) at the foot of Cap Diamant and relocated to the more easily defendable Upper Town.

MAIN ATTRACTIONS

㉑ Église Notre-Dame-des-Victoires *(Our Lady of Victory Church).* The fortress shape of the altar is no accident; this small but beautiful stone church has a bellicose past. Grateful French colonists named it in honour of the Virgin Mary, whom they credited with helping French forces defeat two British invasions: one in 1690 by Admiral William Phipps and the other by Sir Hovendon Walker in 1711. The church itself was built in 1688, making it the city's oldest, and has been restored twice. Paintings by Van Dyck, Rubens, and Boyermans decorate the walls, and a model of *Le Brezé*, the boat that transported French soldiers to New France in 1664, hangs from the ceiling. The side chapel is dedicated to Ste. Geneviève, the patron saint of Paris. ☒*Place Royale, Lower Town* ☎*418/692–1650* ☒*Free, C$2 for guided tours* ☉*Early May–late Oct., daily 9–5; late Oct.–early May, daily 10–4; closed to visitors during mass (Sun. at 10:30 and noon), marriages, and funerals.*

⑯ Escalier Casse-Cou. The steepness of the city's first iron stairway, an ambitious 1893 design by city architect and engineer Charles Baillairgé, is ample evidence of how it got its name: Breakneck Steps. The 170 steps were built on the site of the original 17th-century stairway that linked the Upper Town and Lower Town. There are shops and restaurants at various levels.

⑲ Maison Chevalier. This old stone house was built in 1752 for ship owner Jean-Baptiste Chevalier. The house's classic French style is one rich aspect of the urban architecture of New France. The walls, chimneys, vaulted cellars, and original wood beams and stone fireplaces are noteworthy. ☒*50 rue du Marché-Champlain, Lower Town* ☎*418/643–2158* ☒*Free* ☉*May–June 23, Tues.–Sun. 10–5; June 24–Oct. 21, daily 9:30–5; Oct. 22–Apr., weekends 10–5.*

⑮ Maison Louis-Jolliet. Louis Jolliet, the first European to see the Mississippi River, and his fellow explorers used this 1683 house as a base for westward journeys. Today it's the lower station of the funicular. A monument commemorating Louis Jolliet's 1672 trip to the Mississippi stands in the park next to the house. The **Escalier Casse-Cou** is at the north side of the house. ✉ *16 rue du Petit-Champlain, Lower Town.*

■ NEED A
BREAK? Beer has been brewed in Québec since the early 1600s, and **L'Inox** (✉ *37 quai St-André, Lower Town* ☎ *418/692–2877*) carries on the tradition with a combination brewpub and museum. Cherry-red columns and a stainless-steel bar contrast with exposed stone and brick walls, blending the old with the new. A large, sunny terrace is open in summer. L'Inox serves many of its own beers, as well as other beverages, alcoholic and not. Food is limited to plates of Québec cheeses or European-style hot dogs served in baguettes. Tours of the brewery are available for groups of eight or more.

㉓ **Musée de la Civilisation** *(Museum of Civilization).* Wedged between narrow streets at the foot of the cliff, this spacious museum with a striking limestone-and-glass facade was artfully designed by architect Moshe Safdie to blend into the landscape. Its campanile echoes the shape of the city's church steeples. Two excellent permanent exhibits at the museum examine Québec's history. "People of Québec, Now and Then" engagingly synthesizes 400 years of social and political history—including the role of the Catholic church and the rise of the separatist movement—with artifacts, time lines, original films and interviews, and news clips. It's a great introduction to the issues that face the province today. The "Nous, les Premières Nations" (Encounter with the First Nations) exhibit looks at the 11 aboriginal nations that inhabit Québec. Several of the shows, with their imaginative use of artwork, video screens, computers, and sound, appeal to both adults and children. ✉ *85 rue Dalhousie, Lower Town* ☎ *418/643–2158* ⊕ *www.mcq.org* ☎ *C$10, free Tues. Nov.–May* ☉ *June 24–early Sept., daily 9–7; early Sept.–mid-Oct., daily 10–5, mid-Oct. –June 24, Tues.–Sun. 10–5.*

⓴ **Place Royale.** The houses that encircle this cobblestone square, with steep Normandy-style roofs, dormer windows, and chimneys, were once the homes of wealthy merchants. Until 1686 the area was called Place du Marché, but its name changed when a bust of Louis XIV was placed at its center. During the late 1600s and early 1700s, when Place Royale was continually under threat of British attack, the colonists moved progressively higher to safer quarters atop the cliff in Upper Town. After the French colony fell to British rule in 1759, Place Royale flourished again with shipbuilding, logging, fishing, and fur trading. The *Fresque des Québécois,* a 4,665-square-foot trompe-l'oeil mural depicting 400 years of Québec's history is to the east of the square, at the corner of rue Notre-Dame and côte de la Montagne. An information center, the **Centre d'Interprétation de Place Royale** (✉ *27 rue Notre-Dame, Lower Town* ☎ *418/646–3167*) includes exhibits and a Discovery Hall with a replica of a 19th-century home, where children can try on period costumes. A clever multimedia presentation, good for kids, offers a brief history of Québec. Admission is C$4, but it's free on Tuesday from November to May. It's open daily 9:30–5 from June 24 to early September; the rest of the year it's open Tuesday–Sunday 10–5.

Fodor's Choice ★

8

OFF THE
BEATEN
PATH

Québec–Lévis Ferry. En route to the opposite shore of the St. Lawrence River on this ferry, you get a striking view of the Québec City skyline, with the Château Frontenac and the Québec Seminary high atop the cliff. The view is even more impressive at night. Ferries generally run every half hour from 6 AM until 6 PM, and then hourly until 2:20 AM; there are additional ferries from April through November.

> **MURAL MANIA**
>
> Watch for the three-dimensional murals painted on walls in Lower Town. There are two spectacular ones in Place Royale. Stroll down Côte de la Montagne and look to your right as you round the final corner. The other one is at the end of Petit-Champlain.

From late June to August you can combine a Québec–Lévis ferry ride with a bus tour of Lévis, getting off at such sights as the star-shaped Fort No. 1, one of three built by the British between 1865 and 1872 to defend Québec. ✉ *Rue Dalhousie, 1 block south of Place de Paris, Lower Town* 📞 *418/644–3704 or 877/787–7483* 🌐 *www.traversiers. gouv.qc.ca* 💲 *$2.70*

⑱ Rue du Petit-Champlain. The oldest street in the city was once the main street of a harbor village, with trading posts and the homes of rich merchants. Today it has pleasant boutiques and cafés, although on summer days the street is packed with tourists. Natural-fiber weaving, Inuit carvings, hand-painted silks, and enameled copper crafts are some of the local specialties that are good buys here.

NEED A
BREAK?

For a respite from the shoppers on rue du Petit-Champlain, take a table outdoors at **Bistrot Le Pape Georges** (✉ *8 rue du Cul-de-Sac, Lower Town* 📞 *418/692–1320* 🌐 *www.papegeorges.com*) and cool off with a drink and creamy, tangy local cheeses and fruit. This stone-and-wood wine bar is also nice indoors; there's folk and chanson music from Thursday to Sunday nights.

⑰ Verrerie La Mailloche. The glassblowing techniques used in this workshop, boutique, and museum are as old as ancient Egypt, but the results are contemporary. In the workshop, master glassblower Jean Vallières and his assistants can answer your questions as they turn 1,092°C (2,000°F) molten glass into works of art. Examples of Vallières's work have been presented by the Canadian government to visiting dignitaries such as Queen Elizabeth and Ronald Reagan. ✉ *58 rue Sous-le-Fort, Lower Town* 📞 *418/694–0445* 🌐 *www.lamailloche.com* 💲 *Free* 🕐 *Mid-June–mid-Oct., daily 9–10; mid-Oct.–mid-June, daily 9:30–5:30.*

㉔ Vieux-Port de Québec *(Old Port of Québec).* If you're looking for nightlife, this is where to find it. But during the day you can stroll along the riverside promenade, where merchant and cruise ships dock. The old harbor dates from the 17th century, when ships brought supplies and settlers to the new colony. At one time this port was among the busiest on the continent: between 1797 and 1897, Québec shipyards turned out more than 2,500 ships, many of which passed the 1,000-ton mark. At the port's northern end, where the St. Charles meets the St. Lawrence, a lock protects the marina in the Louise Basin from the generous Atlantic tides that reach even this far up the St. Lawrence. In the northwest section of the port, the **Old Port of Québec Interpretation Center** (✉ *100 quai St-André, Lower Town* ☎ *418/648–3300*) presents the history of the port in relation to the lumber trade and shipbuilding. At the **Marché du Vieux-Port** (Old Port Market), at the port's northwestern tip, farmers sell fresh produce and cheese, as well as handicrafts. The market, near quai St-André, is open daily 9–5 in summer. Some stalls stay open daily in winter, and the market is all dressed up for the Christmas season. Take a stroll through and taste some refreshing local produce, such as apples and berries.

ALSO WORTH SEEING

㉕ Antiques district. Antiques shops cluster around rues St-Pierre and St-Paul. Rue St-Paul was once part of a business district packed with warehouses, stores, and businesses. After World War I, shipping and commercial activities plummeted; low rents attracted antiques dealers. Today numerous cafés, restaurants, and art galleries have made this area one of the town's more fashionable sections.

㉖ L'Îlot des Palais *(The Palace Block).* This archaeological museum is an exceptional site with a new historical and archeological interpretation center, as well as a multimedia exhibit. More than 300 years of history are laid bare here on the site of the first two residences of New France's colonial administrative officials. The first palace, built as a brewery by Jean Talon in 1669, was turned into a residence in 1685 and destroyed by fire in 1713. In 1716 a second residence was built facing the first. It was later turned into a modern brewery, but the basement vaults that remain house an archaeology exhibit and a multimedia display. ✉ *8 rue Vallière, Lower Town* ☎ *418/691–6092* 💲 *C$3* ⊙ *June 24–early Sept., daily 10–5*; the rest of the year by reservation.

㉗ Place de Paris. An often-ridiculed black-and-white geometric sculpture, *Dialogue avec l'Histoire* (*Dialogue with History*) dominates this square. A 1987 gift from France, the sculpture is on the site where the first French settlers landed. ✉ *Rue Dalhousie, Lower Town.*

THE FORTIFICATIONS

Declared a Canadian historical monument in 1957, the 4½-km-long (3-mi-long) wall is the heart of a defensive belt that circles the Old City. The wall began as a series of earthworks and wooden palisades built by French military engineers to protect the Upper Town from an inland attack following the siege of the city by Admiral Phipps in 1690. Two of the city's three sides have the natural protection of the 295-foot-high facade of Cap Diamant, so the cape itself was studded with cannon batteries overlooking the river.

Over the next century, the French expended much time, energy, and money to shore up and strengthen the city's fortifications. The Dauphine Redoubt, built in 1712, is the only one of 11 such buildings that remains, and is fully restored and open to the public. After the fall of

New France, the British were equally concerned about strengthening the city's defenses. They built an earth-and-wood citadel atop Cap Diamant. During the Napoleonic Wars they added four medieval-looking martello towers to the fortifications. Of the three that remain, two are open to the public. The British also slowly replaced the wooden palisades that surrounded the city with the massive cut-stone wall that has become the city's trademark attraction. Oddly enough, improvement-minded civic leaders planned to tear the walls down in the 1870s, but Lord Dufferin, Canada's governor-general at the time, luckily vetoed that project.

The crowning touch to the city's fortifications came after the War of 1812, with the construction of the cut-stone, star-shaped citadel. An irregular pentagon with two cannon-lined sides facing the river below, the structure earned Québec City its 19th-century nickname "North America's Gibraltar." But it was never tested. Since 1814, relations between Canada and the United States have sometimes been a little tense, but never hostile. When the citadel was finished, the city's fortifications took up one-quarter of the entire city's surface. American naturalist Henry David Thoreau was so struck with the fortress atmosphere of Québec City during a visit in 1850 that he wrote, "A fortified town is like a man cased in the heavy armor of antiquity with a horse-load of broadswords and small arms slung to him, endeavoring to go about his business."

MAIN ATTRACTIONS

❷ La Citadelle *(The Citadel)*. Built at the city's highest point, on Cap Diamant, the Citadel is the largest fortified base in North America still occupied by troops. The 25-building fortress was intended to protect the port, prevent the enemy from taking up a position on the Plains of Abraham, and provide a refuge in case of an attack. Having inherited incomplete fortifications, the British completed the Citadel to protect themselves against French retaliations. By the time the Citadel was finished in 1832, the attacks against Québec City had ended.

FodorśChoice
★

Since 1920 the Citadel has served as a base for Canada's most storied French-speaking military formation, the Royal 22e Régiment (Royal 22nd Regiment), affectionately known across Canada as the Van Doos, from the French "vingt-deux" (twenty-two). Firearms, uniforms, and decorations from the 17th century are displayed in the **Musée Royal 22e Régiment** (Royal 22nd Regiment Museum) in the former powder magazine, built in 1750. If weather permits, you can watch the changing of the guard, a ceremony in which troops parade before the Citadel in red coats and black fur hats, and a band plays. The regiment's mascot, a well-behaved goat, also watches the activity. The queen's representative in Canada, the governor-general, has a residence in the Citadel, which is sometimes open for tours during the summer. ⊠ *1 côte de la Citadelle, Upper Town* ☎*418/694–2815* ⊕*www.lacitadelle. qc.ca* ⊠*C$10* ☼*Apr., daily 10–4; May and June, daily 9–5; July– Labor Day, daily 9–6; Sept., daily 9–4; Oct., daily 10–3; Nov.–Mar., bilingual tour at 1:30 daily. Changing of the guard June 24–Labor Day, daily at 10 AM. Retreat ceremony July and Aug., Fri.–Sun. at 7 PM.*

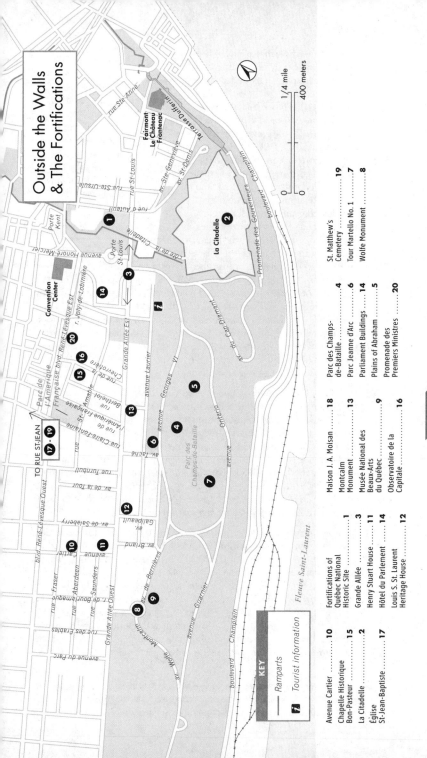

Outside the Walls & The Fortifications

Fairmont Le Château Frontenac

La Citadelle

Convention Center

TO RUE ST-JEAN

1/4 mile
400 meters

Rue Ste-Anne
Terrasse Dufferin
Rue Ste-Ursule
rue St-Louis
av. Ste-Geneviève
av. St-Denis
Porte Kent
avenue Honoré-Mercier
rue d'Auteuil
Côte de la Citadelle
Porte St-Louis
Promenade des Gouverneurs
boulevard Champlain
r. Joly-de-Lobinière
Grande Allée Est
Française blvd. René-Lévesque Est
Parc de l'Amérique
rue de la Chevrotière
rue Berthelot
rue de l'Amérique Française
St-Amable
rue de la Claire-Fontaine
rue Turnbull
av. de la Tour
av. de Salaberry
av. Brland
av. Galipeault
avenue Laurier
avenue Georges VI
avenue Ontario
av. Taché
avenue Cartier
avenue Guarner
avenue Champlain
av. de Bernières
rue des Érables
rue Fraser
rue Aberdeen
rue Saunders
rue de Bourlamaque
Grande Allée Ouest
av. Montcalm
av. Wolfe
Grande Allée Ouest
blvd. René-Lévesque Ouest
Parc des Champs-de-Bataille
Fleuve Saint-Laurent
boulevard Champlain
rue du Cap-Diamant

KEY

— Ramparts

ℹ Tourist information

Avenue Cartier **10**
Chapelle Historique
Bon-Pasteur **15**
La Citadelle **2**
Église
St-Jean-Baptiste **17**

Fortifications of
Québec National
Historic Site **1**
Grande Allée **3**
Henry Stuart House **11**
Hôtel du Parlement **14**
Louis S. St. Laurent
Heritage House **12**

Maison J. A. Moisan **18**
Montcalm
Monument **13**
Musée National des
Beaux-Arts
du Québec **9**
Observatoire de la
Capitale **16**

Parc des Champs-
de-Bataille **4**
Parc Jeanne d'Arc **6**
Parliament Buildings **14**
Plains of Abraham **5**
Promenade des
Premiers Ministres **20**

St. Matthew's
Cemetery **19**
Tour Martello No. 1 ...... **7**
Wolfe Monument **8**

8

1 Fortifications of Québec National Historic Site. In the early 19th century this was a clear space surrounded by a picket fence and poplar trees. What's here now is the **Poudrière de l'Esplanade** (⊠ *100 rue St-Louis, Upper Town* ☎ *418/648–7016* ⊕ *www.parkscanada.gc.ca* 🖼 *C$3.90* ☉ *May–early Oct, daily 10–5.*), the powder magazine (used to store gunpowder) that the British constructed in 1820, and an interpretation center with a multimedia video and a model depicting the evolution of the wall surrounding Vieux-Québec. The French began building ramparts along the city's cliffs as early as 1690 to protect themselves from British invaders. However, the colonists had trouble convincing the French government to take the threat of invasion seriously, and when the British invaded in 1759 the walls were still incomplete. The British, despite attacks by the Americans during the American Revolution and the War of 1812, took a century to finish them. From June 1 to early October, the park can also be the starting point for walking the city's 4½ km (3 mi) of walls. There are two guided tours (C$9.80 each); one starts at the interpretation center and the other begins at Terrasse Dufferin.

> **WORD OF MOUTH**
>
> "You should try to visit La Citadelle, the historic fort that dominates the Upper Town. There are guided tours, and in summer, the Royal 22e Régiment performs the changing of the guard every morning, and on weekends, the beating of retreat ceremony in the evening. The views from the ramparts are outstanding."
>
> —laverendrye

12 Louis S. St. Laurent Heritage House. A costumed maid or chauffeur greets you when you visit this elegant Grande Allée house, the former home of Louis S. St. Laurent, prime minister of Canada from 1948 to 1957. Within the house, which is now part of the federally owned Plains of Abraham properties, period furnishings and multimedia touches tell St. Laurent's story and illustrate the lifestyle of upper-crust families in 1950s Québec City. ⊠ *201 Grande Allée Est, Montcalm* ☎ *418/648–4071* 🖼 *C$10, including house, nearby martello tower, and minibus tour of Plains of Abraham* ☉ *June 24–Labor Day, daily 1–5; early Sept.–June 23, group visits by reservation only.*

13 Montcalm Monument. France and Canada jointly erected this monument honoring Louis-Joseph Montcalm, the French general who gained his fame by winning four major battles in North America. His most famous battle, however, was the one he lost, when the British conquered New France on September 13, 1759. Montcalm was north of Québec City at Beauport when he learned that the British attack was imminent. He quickly assembled his troops to meet the enemy and was wounded in battle in the leg and stomach. Montcalm was carried into the walled city, where he died the next morning. The monument depicts the standing figure of Montcalm, with an angel over his shoulder. ⊠ *Place Montcalm, Montcalm.*

9 ★ Musée National des Beaux-Arts du Québec (*National Museum of Fine Arts of Québec*). A neoclassical Beaux-Arts showcase, the museum has more than 22,000 traditional and contemporary pieces of Québec art. The museum recently unveiled a major permanent exhibit, the Brousseau Inuit Art Collection, containing 150 objects from the past three centuries. That's only a small part of the 5,635 objects collected by Brousseau now in the collection. Portraits by Jean-Paul Riopelle (1923–2002), Jean-Paul Lemieux (1904–90), and Horatio Walker (1858–1938) are particularly notable as well. The museum's dignified building in Parc des Champs-de-Bataille was designed by Wilfrid Lacroix and erected in 1933 to commemorate the 300th anniversary of the founding of Québec. Incorporated within is part of an abandoned prison dating from 1867. A hallway of cells, with the iron bars and courtyard, has been preserved as part of a permanent exhibition on the prison's history. ⊠*1 av. Wolfe-Montcalm, Montcalm* ☎*418/643–2150* ⊕*www.mnba.qc.ca* ☞*Free, special exhibits C$15* ⊙*Sept.–May, Tues. and Thurs.–Sun. 10–5, Wed. 10–9; June–Aug., Thurs.–Tues. 10–6, Wed. 10–9.*

④ Parc des Champs-de-Bataille *(Battlefields Park).* These 250 acres of gently rolling slopes have unparalleled views of the St. Lawrence River. Within the park and west of the Citadel are the Plains of Abraham. In 2009, don't miss the 2,000 reenactors bringing history to life to commemorate the 250th anniversary of the famous Battle of the Plains of Abraham from August 6th to the 9th.

⑥ Parc Jeanne d'Arc. An equestrian statue of Joan of Arc is the focus of
Fodor'sChoice this park, which is bright with colorful flowers in summer. A symbol
★ of military courage and of France itself, the statue stands in tribute to the heroes of 1759 near the place where New France was lost to the British. The park also commemorates the Canadian national anthem, "O Canada"; it was played here for the first time on June 24, 1880. ⊠*Avs. Laurier and Taché, Montcalm.*

⑤ Plains of Abraham. This park, named after the river pilot Abraham Mar-
☾ tin, is the site of the famous 1759 battle that decided New France's fate.
Fodor'sChoice People cross-country ski here in winter and in-line skate in summer. At
★ the **Discovery Pavilion of the Plains of Abraham,** check out the multimedia display, "Odyssey: A Journey Through History on the Plains of Abraham," which depicts 400 years of Canada's history. ⊠*Discovery Pavilion of the Plains of Abraham, 835 av. Wilfrid-Laurier, Level 0 (next to Drill Hall), Montcalm* ☎*418/648–4071 for Discovery Pavilion and bus-tour information* ⊕*www.ccbn-nbc.gc.ca* ☞*Discovery Pavilion C$8 for 1-day pass, bus tour included* ⊙*Discovery Pavilion June 24–Labor Day, daily 8:30–5:30; Labor Day–June 23, weekdays 8:30–5, Sat. 9–5, Sun. 10–5.*

⑧ Wolfe Monument. This tall monument marks the place where the British general James Wolfe died in 1759. Wolfe landed his troops about 3 km (2 mi) from the city's walls; 4,500 English soldiers scaled the cliff and began fighting on the Plains of Abraham. Wolfe was mortally wounded in battle and was carried behind the lines to this spot. ⊠*Rue de Bernières and av. Wolfe-Montcalm, Montcalm.*

8

ALSO WORTH SEEING

Grosse Île National Park. For thousands of immigrants from Europe in the 1800s, the first glimpse of North America was the hastily erected quarantine station at Grosse Île—Canada's equivalent of Ellis Island. During the time Grosse Île operated (1832–1937), 4.3 million immigrants passed through the port of Québec. For far too many passengers on plague-racked ships, particularly the Irish fleeing the potato famine, Grosse Île became a final resting place. Several buildings have been restored to tell the story of the tragic period of Irish immigration. It's necessary to take a boat tour or ferry to visit the park, and you should reserve in advance. **Croisières Le Coudrier** (☎888/600–5554 ⓦ*www.croisierescoudrier.qc.ca*) has tours that depart from Québec City's Old Port, Lévis, Île d'Orléans, and Ste-Anne-de-Beaupré for Grosse Île. Tours cost C\$62.50, which includes admission to the island. **Croisières Lachance** (☎888/476–7734 ⓦ*www.croisiereslachance.ca*) runs a ferry that departs from Berthier-sur-Mer to Grosse Île for C\$41, which includes admission to the island. From Québec City, head south on the Pont Pierre-Laporte (Pierre Laporte Bridge) and follow Autoroute 20 east for about an hour to Berthier-sur-Mer. Follow the signs to the marina. ☎*418/234–8841 Parks Canada, 888/773–8888* ⓦ*www. pc.gc.ca* ✆*C\$44.50, including boat tour or ferry* ☉*May 15–Oct. 15, daily 9–6.*

⑪ Henry Stuart House. If you want to get a firsthand look at how the well-to-do English residents of Québec City lived in a bygone era, this is the place. Built in 1849 by the wife of wealthy businessman William Henry, the Regency-style cottage was bought in 1918 by the sisters Adèle and Mary Stuart. Active in such philanthropic organizations as the Red Cross and the Historical and Literary Society, the sisters were pillars of Québec City's English-speaking community. They also maintained an English-style garden behind the house. Soon after Adèle's death in 1987 at the age of 98, the home was classified a historic site for its immaculate physical condition and the museumlike quality of its furnishings, almost all of them Victorian. Guided tours of the house and garden start on the hour and include a cup of tea. ✉*82 Grande Allée Ouest, Montcalm* ☎*418/647–4347* ✆*C\$7* ☉*June 24–Labor Day, daily 11–4; day after Labor Day–June 23, Sun. 1–5.*

Halles Petit-Cartier (✉*1191 av. Cartier, Montcalm* ☎*418/688–1635*), a small but busy food and shopping mall just a few steps north of the Henry Stuart House on avenue Cartier, has restaurants and shops that sell flowers, cheeses, pastries, breads, vegetables, and candies. You'll find some excellent local cheeses, as well as a few Italian and other European specialties. If you're looking for picnic snacks for a day trip to the Plains of Abraham, plan to fill your basket here and then head up to the park.

⑦ Tour Martello Towers. Of the 16 Martello towers in Canada— four were built in Québec City because the British government feared an invasion after the American Revolution. Tour Martello No. 1, which exhibits the history of the four structures, was built between 1802 and 1810. Tour Martello No. 2, at avenues Taché and Laurier, hosts "Council of

War," a three-hour weekend mystery dinner show with a theme that draws on the War of 1812. Tour No. 3, which guarded the westward entry to the city, was demolished in 1904. Tour No. 4, on rue Lavigueur overlooking the St. Charles River, is not open to the public. ⊠ *South end of Parc Jeanne d'Arc, Montcalm* ☎ *418/648–4071 for information on towers and for Tour No. 2 mystery dinner show* ⌦ *C$10 for day pass to tower and Discovery Pavilion on Plains of Abraham* ⊗ *Daily 10–5* PM.

OUTSIDE THE WALLS

Québec City may be packed with history, but if you look beyond all monuments and old buildings you'll find pockets of trendy restaurants and eclectic boutiques, and even a bit of nightlife. It's hard to miss the buzz along rue St-Jean, and St-Roch, fast becoming the urban heart of the city, has new high-tech businesses, artists' studios, galleries, and cafés popping up regularly. If you're looking for an evening out, this is the place to come, as well as Avenue Cartier, a well-established hot spot for bars, clubs, and pubs that are filled to the brim year-round.

Boulevard Champlain runs from Lower Town all around the southern edge of Québec City, following the St. Lawrence River. It's a beautiful drive, day or night. Above are the cliffs that lead to the Plains of Abraham, and farther on you'll see the Sillery Coves. Any one of the steep hills will take you back toward the main roads that run east–west or the highways that cross north–south: Duplessis, the farthest west; Henri IV; Du Vallon; and Dufferin-Montmorency.

8

MAIN ATTRACTIONS

🔟 **Avenue Cartier.** A mix of reasonably priced restaurants and bars, groceries and specialty food shops, hair salons, and similar stores, Cartier is a favorite lunchtime and after-work stop for many downtown office workers. After business hours the street hums with locals running errands or soaking in sun (and beer) on patios. When darkness falls, the avenue's patrons get noticeably younger. The attraction? A half-dozen nightclubs and pubs that offer everything from cigars and quiet conversation to Latin music and earsplitting dance tunes.

⓯ **Chapelle Historique Bon-Pasteur** *(Historic Chapel of the Good Shepherd).* Charles Baillairgé designed this slender church with a steep sloping roof in 1868. In the ornate baroque-style interior are carved-wood designs elaborately highlighted in gold leaf. The chapel houses 32 religious paintings created by the nuns of the community from 1868 to 1910. In addition to the regular weekday hours below, the chapel is open Sunday between 10 and 1, before and after a musical artists' mass, which begins at 10:45; call ahead on weekdays if you want to visit during this time. ⊠ *1080 rue de la Chevrotière, Montcalm* ☎ *418/522–6221*

📧 *C$2 for tour of chapel; C$15 for classical choral concerts* ⊙ *Weekdays 9–5, weekends by reservation only.*

⑰ Église St-Jean-Baptiste *(St. John the Baptist Church)*. Architect Joseph-
★ Ferdinand Peachy's crowning glory, this church was inspired by the facade of the Église de la Trinité in Paris and rivals the Our Lady of Québec Basilica in beauty and size. The first church on the site, built in 1847, burned in the 1881 fire that destroyed much of the neighborhood. Seven varieties of Italian marble were used in the soaring columns, statues, and pulpit of the present church, which dates from 1884. Its 36 stained-glass windows consist of 30 sections each, and the organ, like the church, is classified as a historic monument. From October 1 to June 23 and outside regular opening hours, knock at the **presbytery** at 490 rue St-Jean to see the church. 📧 *410 rue St-Jean, St-Jean-Baptiste* ☎️ *418/525–7188* ⊙ *June 24–Sept., weekdays 10–4:30, Sun. 9–4.*

❸ Grande Allée. One of the city's oldest streets, Grande Allée was the route people took from outlying areas to sell their furs in town. In the 19th century the wealthy built neo-Gothic and Queen Anne–style mansions here; they now house trendy cafés, clubs, and restaurants. The street actually has four names: inside the city walls it's rue St-Louis; outside the walls, Grande Allée; farther west, chemin St-Louis; and farther still, boulevard Laurier.

⑱ Maison J. A. Moisan. Founded in 1871 by Jean-Alfred Moisan, this store claims the title of the oldest grocery store in North America. The original display cases, woodwork, and tin ceilings preserve the old-time feel. The store sells hand-to-find products from other regions of Québec, including delicious maple-syrup ale. 📧 *699 rue St-Jean, St-Jean-Baptiste* ☎️ *418/522–0685* ⊕ *www.jamoisan.com* ⊙ *Daily 8:30 AM–9 PM.*

NEED A BREAK? **La Piazzeta** (📧 *707 rue St-Jean, St-Jean-Baptiste* ☎️ *418/529–7489*) is all about thin-crust square pizza, and a solid stand-by for a good, affordable meal. It's also an ideal choice if you're traveling with children.

⑯ Observatoire de la Capitale. This observation gallery is atop Edifice Marie-Guyart, Québec City's tallest office building. The gray, modern concrete tower, 31 stories tall, has by far the best view of the city and the surrounding area. 📧 *1037 rue de la Chevrotière, Montcalm* ☎️ *418/644–9841* ⊕ *www.observatoirecapitale.org* 📧 *C$5* ⊙ *Late June–mid-Oct., daily 10–5; mid-Oct.–late June, Tues.–Sun. 10–5.*

⑭ Hôtel du Parlement. The only French-speaking legislature in continen-
★ tal North America, the 125-member Assemblée Nationale du Québec meets behind the stately walls of this Renaissance-style building built between 1877 and 1884. If the Assemblée is sitting (and your French is up to scratch), see if you can get into the visitors gallery to hear heated exchanges between the federalist-leaning Liberals and the secessionist Parti Québécois. Failing that, the buildings themselves, designed by Québec architect Eugène-Étienne Taché, are worth a visit. The facade is decorated with life-sized statues of such important figures of Québec history as Cartier, Champlain, Frontenac, Wolfe, and Montcalm. A

Neighborhood Focus: St-Roch

If you want to be where it's at in Québec City, take a trip to the funky former industrial area St-Roch, bordered by the St-Charles River and the cliff, where artists first flocked about a decade ago. St-Roch's epicenter is Parc St-Roch, with its elongated flower beds and benches around a modern square. Rue St-Joseph is the street for great shopping.

You can pick up a little something for the house at **Villa** (✉ *600 St-Joseph Est* ☎ *418/524–2666*) or **Baltazar** (✉ *461 rue St-Joseph* ☎ *418/524–1991*). For high-end duds, there's **Hugo Boss** (✉ *505 rue St-Joseph Est* ☎ *418/522–5444*) as well as a flurry of smaller boutiques with the latest urban wear.

There's plenty of green public space along boulevard Charest as well as some modern sculpture. Complexe Méduse is an avant-garde arts cooperative that houses multimedia artists, a community radio station, a café, galleries, artists-in-residence, and performance spaces.

St-Roch is also becoming known for its restaurants, such as the luxurious **L'Utopie** (✉ *226½ rue St-Joseph Est* ☎ *418/523–7878*) within walking distance of a night on the town. After dinner, you can boogie down to a live DJ's picks at **Le Boudoir** (✉ *441 rue du Parvis* ☎ *418/524–2777*). Any way you slice it, St-Roch is cutting-edge.

30-minute tour (in English, French, or Spanish) takes in the President's Gallery, the Parlementaire restaurant, the Legislative Council Chamber, and the National Assembly Chamber. Tours may be restricted during legislative sessions. ✉ *Av. Honoré-Mercier and Grande Allée, Door 3, Montcalm* ☎ *418/643–7239* ⊕ *www.assnat.qc.ca* ✉ *Free* ☉ *Guided tours weekdays 9–4:30; late June–early Sept. also open for tours weekends 10–4:30.*

20 **Promenade des Premiers Ministres.** This walk has a series of panels that tell the story (in French) of the premiers who have led the province and their contributions to its development. Because of strong winds, the panels are taken down (usually November–February) in winter. ✉ *Parallel to blvd. René-Lévesque Est between rue de la Chevrotière and the Parliament Buildings, Montcalm.*

19 **St. Matthew's Cemetery.** The burial place of many of the earliest English settlers in Canada was established in 1771, and is the oldest cemetery remaining in Québec City. Also buried here is Robert Wood, the disavowed half-brother of Queen Victoria. Closed in 1860, the cemetery has been turned into a park. Next door is **St. Matthew's Anglican Church,** now a public library. It has a book listing most of the original tombstone inscriptions, including those on tombstones removed to make way for the city's modern convention center. ✉ *755 rue St-Jean, St-Jean-Baptiste* ☎ *No phone.*

8

ALSO WORTH SEEING

OFF THE
BEATEN
PATH

Ice Hotel. At this hotel—the first of its kind in North America—constructed completely of ice and snow, you can tour the art galleries of ice sculptures, get married in the chapel, lounge in the hot tub, have a drink at the bar made of ice, dance in the ice club, then nestle into a bed lined with deerskin. The hotel is open from mid-January to March 31. A night's stay, a four-course supper, breakfast, and a welcome cocktail cost around C$250 per person. ⊠ *Duchesnay Ecotourism Station, 143 Rte. Duchesnay, Ste-Catherine-de-Jacques-Cartier ✚ about 20 mins west of Québec City* ☎ *418/875–4522 or 877/505–0423* ⊕ *www.icehotel-canada.com.*

Parc Aquarium du Québec. Breakfast with the walruses, lunch (carefully) with the polar bears, and spend the afternoon watching the seals do their tricks. When you tire of the mammals, check out the thousands of species of fresh- and saltwater fish in the aquarium's massive, three-level aquatic gallery, or have some hands-on experiences with mollusks and starfish. It is the only aquarium in North America with examples of all five species of cold-water seals. The aquarium is set on a clifftop overlooking the St. Lawrence and Québec City's two main bridges. ⊠ *1675 av. des Hôtels, Ste-Foy* ☎ *866/659–5264 or 418/659–5264* ⊕ *www.sepaq.com/aquarium* ⊠ *C$15.50* ⊙ *Daily 10–5.*

WHERE TO EAT

Most restaurants here have a selection of dishes available à la carte, but more creative specialties are often found on the table d'hôte, a two- to four-course meal chosen daily by the chef. This can also be an economical way to order a full meal. At dinner many restaurants will offer a *menu dégustation* (tasting menu), a five- to seven-course dinner of the chef's finest creations. In French-speaking Québec City, an *entrée,* as the name suggests, is an entry into a meal, or an appetizer. It is followed by a *plat principal,* the main dish. Lunch generally costs about 30% less than dinner, and many of the same dishes are available. Lunch is usually served 11:30 to 2:30, dinner 6:30 until about 11. Tip at least 15% of the bill.

Reservations are necessary for most restaurants during peak season, May through September, as well as on holidays and during Winter Carnival, in January and/or February. In summer, do as the locals do and dine outdoors. Every café and restaurant on the Grande Allée or elsewhere sets up tables outside if it can.

WHAT IT COSTS IN CANADIAN DOLLARS				
¢	$	$$	$$$	$$$$
AT DINNER	under C$8	C$8–C$12	C$13–C$20	C$21–C$30	over $30

Prices are per person for a main course at dinner (or at the most expensive meal served).

BEST BETS FOR QUÉBEC CITY DINING

With thousands of restaurants to choose from, how will you decide where to eat? Fodor's writers and editors have selected their favorite restaurants by price, cuisine, and experience in the Best Bets lists below. In the first column, Fodor's Choice properties represent the "best of the best" in every price category.

Fodor'sChoice ★

Café-Boulangerie Paillard, p. 182
L'Initiale, p. 185
Panache, p. 185
Versa, p. 190

Best By Price

¢

Brulerie Tatum, p. 182
Le Buffet de L'Antiquaire, p. 184
Café-Boulangerie Paillard, p. 181
Chez Victor, p. 188
Le Café Krieghoff, p. 187

$

Casse-Crêpe Breton, p. 182
Chez Cora, p. 188
Le Cochon Dingue, p. 184
Le Commensal, p. 190
Le Parlementaire, p. 189
Thang Long, p. 187

$$

L'Astral, p. 189
Le Café du Monde, p. 186
La Closerie, p. 188

La Fenouillère, p. 188
La Pointe des Amériques, p. 190
Versa, p. 190

$$$

L'Echaudé, p. 185
Largo, p. 185
Louis Hébert, p. 188
Restaurante Michelangelo, p. 189
Le Toast!, p. 185
L'Utopie, p. 186

$$$$

L'Initiale, p. 185
Laurie Raphaël, p. 186
Panache, p. 185

Best By Cuisine

CAFÉS

Brulerie Tatum, p. 182
Café-Boulangerie Paillard, p. 182
Le Cochon Dingue, p. 184
Le Temporel, p. 182

CANADIAN

L'Astral, p. 189
Aux Anciens Canadiens, p. 182

Le Buffet de L'Antiquaire, p. 185
Le Parlementaire, p. 189
Versa, p. 190

CHINESE

L'Elysée Mandarin, p. 183
Thang Long, p. 187

FRENCH

La Closerie, p. 188
L'Echaudé, p. 185
L'Initiale, p. 185
Panache, p. 185
L'Utopie, p. 186

ITALIAN

Il Teatro, p. 189
La Pointe des Amériques, p. 190
Portofino Bistro Italiano, p. 183
Ristorante Michelangelo, p. 189

Best By Experience

BRUNCH

Casse-Crêpe Breton, p. 182
Chez Cora, p. 188
Largo, p. 185

BUSINESS DINING

L'Echaudé, p. 185
Louis Hébert, p. 188
L'Utopie, p. 186

GOOD FOR GROUPS

L'Elysée Mandarin, p. 183
Les Frères de la Côte, p. 183
Thang Long, p. 187

GREAT VIEW

Le Café du Monde, p. 186
La Fenouillère, p. 188
Le Graffiti, p. 189

HOTEL DINING

L'Astral, p. 189
La Closerie, p. 188
Le Fenouillère, p. 188
Le Toast!, p. 185
Panache, p. 185

LATE-NIGHT DINING

Le Café Krieghoff, p. 187
Les Frères de la Côte, p. 183

MOST ROMANTIC

L'Initiale, p. 185
Le Marie Clarisse, p. 186
Panache, p. 185
Le Saint-Amour, p. 183

SINGLES SCENE

Le Café Krieghoff, p. 187
Chez Victor, p. 188
Le Temporel, p. 182
Versa, p. 190

8

UPPER TOWN

CAFÉS

¢–$ ✕ **Brûlerie Tatum.** The Brûlerie is a favorite with students and shoppers, who come for their daily fix as well as for soup, sandwiches, salads, and desserts. The menu expanded this year to include burgers and a range of yummy pasta dishes. But breakfast is the main draw, for the Brûlerie's omelets, crêpes, and such dishes as egg in phyllo pastry with hollandaise sauce and potatoes and fruit. About 40 different types each of coffee and tea are sold here. ⊠*1084 rue St-Jean, Upper Town* ☎*418/692–3900* ▤*AE, D, MC, V* ✧ *2E.*

¢–$ ✕ **Café-Boulangerie Paillard.** Owned by Yves Simard and his partner
Fodor'sChoice Rebecca, originally from Michigan, Wisconsin, this bakery is known
★ for its selection of Viennese pastries, olive bread, and gelato. For a quick, inexpensive bite, there's soup, sandwiches, and pizza. The decor is simple and comfortable, with cafeteria tables at which to mingle. There might be a line while the locals buy their lunch, but it's well worth the wait for the Thai chicken panini with ginger mayo. ⊠*1097 rue St-Jean, Upper Town* ☎*418/692–1221* ⊕*www.paillard. ca* ▤*MC, V* ✧ *2E.*

¢–$ ✕ **Casse-Crêpe Breton.** Crêpes in generous proportions are served in this
★ busy café-style restaurant. From a menu of more than 20 fillings, pick your own chocolate or fruit combinations; design a larger meal with cheese, ham, and vegetables; or sip a bowl of Viennese coffee topped with whipped cream. Many tables surround four round griddles at which you watch your creations being made. Crêpes made with two to five fillings cost less than C$8. This place is popular with tourists and locals alike, and there can be lines to get in at peak hours and seasons. ⊠*1136 rue St-Jean, Upper Town* ☎*418/692–0438* ⌁*Reservations not accepted* ▤*MC, V* ✧ *2E.*

¢ ✕ **Le Temporel.** At this small, crowded, once-upon-a-time smoky café, city dwellers of all sorts—struggling writers, marginal musicians, street-smart bohemians, bureaucrats, businessmen, and busy moms and dads—enjoy the city's best coffee, not to mention its Wi-Fi and the best *croque monsieurs* (open-face French-bread sandwiches with ham, tomato, and broiled cheese), gazpacho, chili, and soups. Good, modestly priced beer and wine are also served. Some patrons start their day here with croissants and coffee at 7 AM and are still here when the place closes at midnight or later on the weekends. ⊠*25 rue Couillard, Upper Town* ☎*418/694–1813* ⌁*Reservations not accepted* ▤*V* ✧ *1F.*

CANADIAN

$$$$ ✕ **Aux Anciens Canadiens.** This establishment is named for a 19th-century book by Philippe-Aubert de Gaspé, who once resided here. The house, dating from 1675, has servers in period costume and five dining rooms with different themes. For example, the *vaisselier* (dish room) is bright and cheerful, with colorful antique dishes and a fireplace. People come for the authentic French-Canadian cooking; hearty specialties include duck in a maple glaze, Lac St-Jean meat pie, and maple-syrup pie with fresh cream. Enjoy a triple treat of filet mignon—elk, bison, and deer—served with a cognac pink-pepper sauce. One of the best

deals is a three-course meal for C$16.95, served from noon until 5:45. ⊠*34 rue St-Louis, Upper Town* ☎*418/692–1627* ⚠*Reservations essential* ☰*AE, DC, MC, V* ⊹ *3F.*

CHINESE

$$ ✕**L'Elysée Mandarin.** A 19th-century home has been transformed into an elegant Chinese mandarin's garden, where you can sip jasmine tea to the strains of soothing Asian music. Owner David Tsui imported stones from China and installed 18 porcelain Buddhas among the rosewood and lacquered panels to emulate his native Yanchao, a city near Shanghai known for training great chefs. Among the restaurant's Szechuan specialties are beef fillets with orange flavoring and crispy chicken in ginger sauce. The crispy duck with five spices is delicious. ⊠*65 rue d'Auteuil, Upper Town* ☎*418/692–0909* ☰*AE, DC, MC, V* ⊹ *3E.*

CONTINENTAL

$$$ ✕**Le Continental.** If Québec City had a dining hall of fame, Le Continental would be there among the best. Since 1956 the Sgobba family has been serving very good traditional dishes. House specialties include orange duckling and filet mignon, flambéed right at your table. Try the appetizer with foie gras, sweetbreads, scampi, and snow crab delicately served on a square glass plate. A staple for this place is the tender, velvety filet mignon "en boîte," flambéed in a cognac sauce at the table and then luxuriously covered in a gravy seasoned with mustard and sage. ⊠*26 rue St-Louis, Upper Town* ☎*418/694–9995* ☰*AE, D, DC, MC, V* ⊹ *3E.*

FRENCH

$$$$ ✕**Le Saint-Amour.** Father-and-son chefs Jean-Luc and Frederic Boulay entice diners with such creations as red-deer steak grilled with a wild-berry and peppercorn sauce, and filet mignon with port wine and local blue cheese at one of the city's most romantic restaurants. Foie gras is the in-house signature delicacy. Sauces are generally light, with no flour or butter. Desserts are inspired; try the tasting plate of seven different kinds of Valhrona chocolate, served with a glass of vanilla-infused milk. The C$95 menu has 10 courses; the C$56 table d'hôte has five. More than 800 wines are available. ⊠*48 rue Ste-Ursule, Upper Town* ☎*418/694–0667* ⊕*www.saint-amour.com* ⚠*Reservations essential* ☰*AE, DC, MC, V* ⊹ *2F.*

$$ ✕**Les Frères de la Côte.** With its central location, Mediterranean influence, and reasonable prices, this busy bistro is a favorite among politicians and the journalists who cover them. Outside tables are alive with bilingual chitchat. The menu, inspired by the south of France, changes constantly, but osso buco and a tender leg of lamb are among the regular choices. If you sit near the back, you can watch the chefs at work. This kitchen is often among those open latest. ⊠*1190 rue St-Jean, Upper Town* ☎*418/692–5445* ☰*AE, D, MC, V* ⊹ *2E.*

ITALIAN

$$ ✕**Portofino Bistro Italiano.** By joining two 18th-century houses, owner Francois Petit helms an Italian restaurant with a bistro flavor. The room is distinctive: burnt-sienna walls, a wood pizza oven set behind

CLOSE UP

Crêpes: A Movable Feast

Crêpes—those delectable, paper-thin pancakes made of flour, eggs, and milk or cream—can be found on menus everywhere. But in Québec City you can order a crêpe in French and know that what you're holding has been part of French gastronomy for centuries.

You'll want to plan your crêpe tour carefully. These little folded-up packages of sweet or savory goodness are quite rich, and so it's not advisable to mix crêpes in the same meal. Your first crêpe of the day can be from the commercial but still yummy **Chez Cora** (✉ 545 rue de l'Église, St-Roch ☎ 418/524–3232), which stays open until 3 PM, so sleep in late and make it brunch. After three hours or so, you'll

be ready for a salad and a decadent fruit- or ice-cream-filled crêpe for dessert at **Casse-Crêpe Breton** (✉ 1136 rue St-Jean, Upper Town ☎ 418/692–0438). Expect to wait in line—even the locals do! Skip the funicular and hit those steps while sightseeing to speed your digestion before heading to **Au Petit Coin Breton** (✉ 1029 St-Jean, Upper Town ☎ 418/694–0758). Here you'll find more traditional gourmet crêpes, filled with seafood, wild boar, ham, or asparagus with béchamel sauce.

Take a deep breath—but not too deep—as you reminisce about all the wonderful crêpes you encountered today. Hemingway would be proud.

a semicircular bar, and caramel tablecloths and chairs. Don't miss the thin-crust pizza and its accompaniment of oils flavored with pepper and oregano. The *pennini all'arrabbiata*—tubular pasta with a spicy tomato sauce—is also good. Save room for the homemade tiramisu. From 3 PM to 7 PM the restaurant serves a beer-and-pizza meal for less than C$11. Guillermo Saldana performs music most days. ✉ 54 rue Couillard, Upper Town ☎ 418/692–8888 ⊕ www.portofino.qc.ca ▭ AE, D, DC, MC, V ⊹ 1F.

LOWER TOWN

CAFÉ

$ ✕ **Le Cochon Dingue.** The café fare at this cheerful chain, whose name translates into the Crazy Pig, includes delicious mussels, *steak frites* (steak with french fries), thick soups, and apple pie with vanilla cream. At the boulevard Champlain location, sidewalk tables and indoor dining rooms artfully blend the chic and the antique; black-and-white checkerboard floors contrast with ancient stone walls. The best-kept secret in Québec City is the full breakfast served here all week. ✉ 46 blvd. Champlain, Lower Town ☎ 418/692–2013 ✉ 6 rue Cul-de-Sac, Lower Town ☎ 418/694–0303 ▭ AE, DC, MC, V ⊹ 3G, 2G.

CANADIAN

¢ ✕ **Le Buffet de L'Antiquaire.** Hearty home cooking, generous portions, and rock-bottom prices have made this no-frills, diner-style eatery a Lower Town institution. As the name suggests, it's in the heart of the antiques district. In summer it has a small sidewalk terrace where you can sit and watch the shoppers stroll by. It's also a good place to sample traditional Québécois dishes such as *tourtière* (meat pie). Desserts, such as the triple-layer orange cake, are homemade and delicious. ⊠*95 rue St-Paul, Lower Town* ☎*418/692–2661* ▤*AE, MC, V* ⊹ *1G.*

FRENCH

$$$$ ✕**Panache.** This restaurant, nestled in the Auberge St-Antoine, has
Fodor's Choice enchanting wooden floors and exposed beams from the building's ware-
★ house days. Chef François Blais has taken traditional French-Canadian cuisine and tweaked it for the modern palate. The menus change with the seasons, but you'll find the duck, roasted on a French spit, any day. A family-owned farm supplies ingredients for the restaurant's recipes. For a true feast, your table can order the Signature Menu, a seven-course meal with wine selections, for C$169 per person. Québec and Canada wines top their list, starting at C$45 a bottle, but they also carry some exclusive imports from Australia, France, and Italy. ⊠*10 rue St-Antoine, Lower Town* ☎*418/692–1022* ▤*AE, DC, MC, V* ⊹ *1G.*

$$$$ ✕**Le Toast!** Le Toast! is the talk of the town. This very chic, very intimate restaurant is in Le Priori hotel on Sault-au-Matelot. Dine under mod light fixtures set against stone and brick walls on big plates of roasted quail, rabbit stuffed with blood sausage, or poached lobster. The three-course meals are $65, while the four-course meals are $75. ⊠*17 rue Sault-au-Matelot, Lower Town* ☎*418/692–1334* ⊕*www.restaurant-toast.com* ▤*AE, DC, MC, V* ⊘*No lunch weekends* ⊹ *1F.*

$$$ ✕**L'Echaudé.** L'Echaudé attracts a mix of businesspeople and tourists because of its location between the financial and antiques districts. The mahogany lobby and green-and-beige interior creates a warm atmosphere, as does the open kitchen. For lunch, try duck confit with fries and fresh salad. Every day there is a meat dish, a fish plate, a steak, and pasta on the menu. Highlights of the three-course brunch are eggs Benedict and tantalizing desserts. The decor is modern, with hardwood floors, a mirrored wall, and a stainless-steel bar with back-lit river stones underneath. ⊠*73 rue Sault-au-Matelot, Lower Town* ☎*418/692–1299* ▤*AE, DC, MC, V* ⊹ *1G.*

$$$ ✕**L'Initiale.** A contemporary setting and gracious service place L'Initiale
Fodor's Choice in the upper echelon of restaurants in this city; it's a member of the
★ Relais & Châteaux group. Widely spaced tables favor intimate dining, and the warm brown-and-cream decor is cozy. But don't rush to your table. Begin your night in the lounge, where you can peruse the menu at your leisure. Chef Yvan Lebrun roasts many of the meats on the menu over a spit: this produces a unique taste, particularly with lamb. The constantly changing menu follows the whims of the chef and the season. Try the *escalope de* foie gras or the lamb. There's also a C$97 eight-course menu dégustation. For dessert, many small treats are arranged attractively on a single plate. After dinner, return to the lounge for your coffee. ⊠*54 rue St-Pierre, Lower Town* ☎*418/694–1818* ▤*AE, DC, MC, V* ⊘*Closed Sun., Mon., and early Jan.* ⊹ *2G.*

$$$ ✕**Largo.** Jazz is what you'll hear and jazzed is what you'll feel at this St-Roch restaurant. Owner Gino Ste-Marie runs a dynamic, evolving gallery and restaurant space that attracts a faithful local clientele. The food is a mix of Mediterranean and Spanish, and on the varied menu

8

you'll find well-done omelets, salads, lamb, and fresh sea fare. Specialties include a bouillabaisse Marseillaise and several tartares. Weekend brunch is popular, and the place to see and be seen is on the custom-made red sofa. If you're here for music, plan to shell out C$25 and arrive an hour before it starts. ✉643 rue St-Joseph Est, St-Roch ☎418/529–3111 ⊕www.largorestoclub.com ⌖Reservations essential ▤AE, MC, V ✛ 2A.

$$$ ✕**L'Utopie.** L'Utopie is a spacious spot for a meal. Sixteen-foot ceilings and slim, potted trees used as table dividers create a calm, modern atmosphere. There's an accent on all things French, with a Mediterranean influence, and chef Stéphane Modat offers highly creative dishes that include his very own smoked salmon and local Angus beef. Other specialties include the grilled tuna, lamb, and foie gras. L'Utopie serves lunch 11 to 2 PM, and supper 6 to 10 PM. ✉226½ rue St-Joseph Est, St-Roch ☎418/523–7878 ▤AE, DC, MC, V ⊘Closed Mon. No lunch weekends ✛ 2A.

$$ ✕**Le Café du Monde.** Next to the cruise terminal in the Old Port, this restaurant has a view to equal its food. The outdoor terrace in front overlooks the St. Lawrence River, while the side *verrière* (glass atrium) looks onto l'Agora amphitheater and the old stone Customs House. Etched-glass dividers, wicker chairs, and palm trees complement the Parisian-bistro-style menu, which includes such classics as steak frites, rotisserie chicken, calamari, and artichoke pudding with smoked salmon. ✉84 rue Dalhousie, Lower Town ☎418/692–4455 ⌖Reservations essential ▤AE, DC, MC, V ✛ 1H.

MODERN CANADIAN

$$$ ✕**Laurie Raphaël Restaurant-Atelier-Boutique.** Local and regional products are at the heart of fine cuisine here. Among Chef Daniel Vézina's creations are duck foie gras with cranberry juice and port, and smoked salmon from Charlevoix with English cucumbers, curry oil, and a maple glaze. There's a C$94 seven-course menu dégustation, with wines to complement each course available by the glass ($55 for wine). If you're seeking adventure, opt for the Chef Chef menu—for C$60 a surprise meal will be delivered to your table. Lunch is $25. If that's not enough, sign up for a private cooking class. Don't miss the exclusive food and product lines available at the Laurie Raphaël boutique. ✉117 rue Dalhousie, Lower Town, ☎418/692–4555 ⊕www.laurieraphael.com ▤AE, D, DC, MC, V ⊘Closed Sun., Mon., and Jan. 1–15 ✛ 1G.

Fodor'sChoice ★

SEAFOOD

$$$ ✕**Le Marie Clarisse.** This restaurant at the bottom of Escalier Casse-Cou is known for unique seafood dishes, such as the superior bouillabaisse or halibut with nuts and honey and scallops with port and paprika. A good game dish is usually on the menu—try the venison and beef duo with berries and sweet garlic. The menu du jour has a choice of about seven main courses; dinner includes soup, salad, dessert, and coffee. Wood-beam ceilings, stone walls, and a fireplace make this one of the coziest spots in town. ✉12 rue du Petit-Champlain, Lower Town

CLOSE UP

A Québec City Cheese Primer

It used to be that all good cheese in Québec City was imported from France—but not anymore. During the last several years there's been a cheese movement, and regional cheese makers have begun producing award-winning aged cheddar and *lait cru* (unpasteurized) cheeses that you won't want to go home without sampling.

Luckily, there are enough cheese shops to keep you cheese shop–hopping all afternoon. Stop by the **Épicerie Européenne** (⊠ *560 rue St-Jean* ☎ *418/529–4847*) in the St-Jean-Baptiste quarter to try some of the lait cru that everyone is raving about. Along the same street, wander through **Épicerie J.A. Moisan** (⊠ *699 rue St-Jean* ☎ *418/522–0685*), another

well-known, well-stocked market, or visit **Aux Petits Délices** (⊠ *1191 av. Cartier* ☎ *418/522–5154*) in the market at Les Halles du Petit Quartier for a large selection of specialty cheeses, along with fruit, breads, crackers, and wine for a picnic on the Plains.

Some good cheeses to watch out for at these shops and others include Bleu Bénédictin from the St-Benoît Abbey, the Île aux-Grues four-year-old cheddar, Portneuf Camembert, or the same region's La Sauvagine, a 2006 top prize winner. There's also a *chèvre noire*, a raw, semifirm goat cheese by Fromagerie Tournevant—wrapped in black wax—that's not to be missed, and the fresh goat cheese La Biquette. If Gouda is your thing, try a piece from Fromagerie Bergeron.

☎ *418/692–0857* ⚞ *Reservations essential* ▤ *AE, DC, MC, V* ⊗ *No lunch weekends Oct.–Apr.* ✚ *2G.*

8

OUTSIDE THE WALLS

ASIAN

$$ ✕**Thang Long.** Low prices and some of the best Asian food in the city ensure this restaurant's popularity. The simple menu of Vietnamese, Chinese, Thai, and Japanese dishes has a few surprises. No one else in town servies *chakis*, for example, which is a tasty fried appetizer of four wrappers filled with shrimp, onions, and sugared potatoes. The General Tao's chicken is outstanding, as is the grilled pork with honey and toasted peanuts. Thang Long doesn't serve any alcohol, but you can bring your own (SAQ, the government liquor store, is two blocks up the hill on rue St-Jean) and sit on the quiet terrace. Chinese lanterns and dark-blue walls and tablecloths decorate this tiny spot. ⊠ *869 côte d'Abraham, St-Jean-Baptiste* ☎ *418/524–0572* ⚞ *Reservations essential* ▤ *MC, V* 🍶 *BYOB* ⊗ *No lunch weekends* ✚ *2C.*

CAFÉ

$ ✕**Le Café Krieghoff.** Modeled after a typical Paris bistro café and named for a Canadian painter who lived just up the street (and whose prints hang on the walls), this busy, noisy restaurant with patios in front and back is a popular place with the locals. Open every day from 7 AM to midnight, Krieghoff serves specialties that include salmon, quiche, "la Toulouse" (big French sausage with sauerkraut), steak with french fries, *boudin* (pig-blood sausage), and "la Bavette" (a French-style minute steak). This place is a big local literary hangout, with great coffee, tea, and desserts. There is a seven-room auberge upstairs now catering to upscale families. ⊠*1089 rue Cartier, Montcalm* ☎*418/522–3711* ▭*DC, MC, V* ✛ *6-A.*

ECLECTIC

$ ✕ **Chez Cora.** Spectacular breakfasts with mounds of fresh fruit are the specialty at this sunny chain restaurant. Whimsy is everywhere, from the plastic chicken decorations to the inventive dishes, often named after customers and family members who inspired them. Try the Eggs Ben et Dictine, which has smoked salmon, or the Gargantua—two eggs, sausage, ham, fruit, pancakes, *cretons* (pâtés), and baked beans. Kids love the Banana Surprise, a banana wrapped in a pancake with chocolate or peanut butter and honey. The restaurant also serves light lunch fare, such as salmon bagels, salads, and club sandwiches. ⊠*545 rue de l'Église, St-Roch* ☎*418/524–3232* ▭*AE, DC, MC, V* ⊘*No dinner* ✛ *2B.*

FAST FOOD

$ ✕ **Chez Victor.** It's no ordinary burger joint: this cozy café with brick and stone walls attracts an arty crowd to rue St-Jean. Lettuce, tomatoes, onions, mushrooms, pickles, hot mustard, mayonnaise, and a choice of cheeses (mozzarella, Swiss, blue, goat, and cream) top the hearty burgers. French fries are served with a dollop of mayonnaise and poppy seeds. Salads, sandwiches, and a daily dessert made fresh by the pastry chef are also available. ⊠*145 rue St-Jean, St-Jean-Baptiste* ☎*418/529–7702* ▭*MC, V* ✛ *4A.*

FRENCH

$$$ ✕ **La Fenouillère.** This restaurant is connected to a standard chain hotel, but there's nothing standard about the cuisine. From a dining room with a view of the pretty Pierre Laporte Bridge, feast on selections from chefs Yvon Godbout and Bernard St. Pierre's constantly rotating table d'hôte. The house specialty is salmon, but veal and other fresh fish are staples, along with the occasional lamb dish. Try anything that comes with the house mango salsa. ⊠*Hotel Best Western Aristocrate, 3100 chemin St-Louis, Ste-Foy* ☎*418/653–3886* ▭*AE, DC, MC, V* ✛ *6-A.*

$$$ ✕ **Louis Hébert.** With its fine French cuisine and convenient location in a 95-year-old home on the bustling Grande Allée, this restaurant has long been popular with many of Québec's top decision makers. Dining areas range from the very public summer terrace to discreet second-floor meeting rooms, a solarium with bamboo chairs, and a cozy dining room with exposed stone walls and warm wood accents. Chef Hervé Toussaint's dazzlers are, along with his rack of lamb, seafood dishes such as shelled lobster, as well as fresh pasta. ⊠*668 Grande Allée Est, Montcalm* ☎*418/525–7812* ▭*AE, D, DC, MC, V* ⊘*No lunch weekends Oct.–Apr.* ✛ *4D.*

$$ ✕ **La Closerie.** Acclaimed chef-owner Jacques LePluart returned from France to relaunch two restaurants, both named La Closerie, in the Hôtel Château Laurier. In the more elegant Grande Table dining room,

rich sauces enhance such dishes as *magret de canard aux cerises séchées* (duck breast with dried-cherry sauce). For dessert, try the delicious white-chocolate mille-feuille with fresh cherries. The kitchen also supplies the slightly less expensive French bistro, serving dishes such as artichoke-heart pizza and salmon fillet. ✉*1220 pl. Georges V Ouest, Montcalm* ☎*418/523–9975* ▭*AE, DC, MC, V* ✛ *5D.*

$$ ✕ **Le Graffiti.** Located in an upscale food mall, this French restaurant with tiny lights covering the ceiling is a good alternative to Vieux-Québec dining. Large windows look out onto avenue Cartier. The seasonal menu lists such dishes as beef tartare, salmon tartare, sweetbreads, and veal medallions with apples in a calvados sauce. The table d'hôte starts at C$28. ✉*1191 av. Cartier, Montcalm* ☎*418/529–4949* ▭*AE, DC, MC, V* ☽*No lunch Sat.* ✛ *6-A.*

ITALIAN

$$$ ✕ **Ristorante Michelangelo.** One of only a handful of eateries outside Italy recognized as genuine Italian restaurants by the Italian government, Michelangelo's has a menu with many succulent meat, pasta, and seafood dishes. The stand-alone building, faced in white stucco, could be confused with a Miami funeral parlor, but that impression is short lived. Inside, the decor is decidedly art deco. Try the house specialties: *côte de veau* (veal cutlets), *escalopes de veau* (veal scallops), and homemade pasta. The restaurant also has the city's largest wine cellar, with some 18,000 bottles. ✉*3111 chemin St-Louis, Ste-Foy* ☎*418/651–6262* ▭*AE, DC, MC, V* ☽*Closed Sun. No lunch Sat.* ✛ *5C.*

$$ ✕ **Il Teatro.** Celebrities show up regularly at this upscale Italian restaurant just outside the St-Jean Gate. The person sitting at the next table may be singing on stage at the adjacent Capitole theater after dinner, or may be in town to promote his or her latest record, film, or play. The drama is enhanced by chocolate-brown curtains and white chairs. Try the salmon tartare, the spaghetti with scampi, or the osso buco *d'agnello alle erbe* (braised lamb shanks with herbs). ✉*972 rue St-Jean, Carré d'Youville* ☎*418/694–9996* ⚖*Reservations essential* ▭*AE, DC, MC, V* ✛ *2D.*

MODERN CANADIAN

$$$ ✕ **L'Astral.** A spectacular view of Québec City is the chief attraction at this revolving restaurant atop the Hôtel Loews Le Concorde. Lowered into olive-green leather chairs, guests smile when they gaze up at the sky painted on the ceiling. Chef Jean-Claude Crouzet makes use of local products—fillet of pork from the Beauce region, or Barbarie duck with honey and Szechuan pepper, turnip confit, and red cabbage with apples. L'Astral offers a nightly buffet for C$46.95 and a Sunday brunch served with a mimosa for $34.95. Watch out for the annual food festivals that enliven the menu. ✉*1225 Cours du Général-de Montcalm, Montcalm* ☎*418/647–2222* ▭*AE, D, DC, MC, V* ✛ *5C.*

$$ ✕ **Le Parlementaire.** Despite its magnificent Beaux-Arts interior and its reasonable prices, the National Assembly's restaurant remains one of the best-kept secrets in town. Chef Réal Therrien prepares contemporary cuisine with products from Québec's various regions. In summer, for example, the three-course lunch menu includes everything from

mini-fondues made with Charlevoix cheese to ravioli made from lobster caught in the Gaspé. Other dishes might include pork from the Beauce region, trout from the Magdalen Islands, and candied-duck salad. The restaurant's typical hours are 8–11 for breakfast and 11:30–2:30 for lunch. Opening hours may change when the National Assembly is in session in fall and spring, so make sure to call ahead. ⊠ *Av. Honoré-Mercier and Grande Allée Est, Door 3, Montcalm* ☎418/643–6640 ⊟*AE, MC, V* ⊘*Closed weekends June 24–Labor Day; closed Sat.–Mon. Labor Day–June 23. Usually no dinner* ⊹ *4D.*

$$ ✕**Versa.** Among the first to revitalize the food scene in St-Roch, Versa's

Fodor'sChoice young-gun chef Christian Veilleux puts a modern twist on comfort

★ food, like updated pogos with sweet sauce and trios of mini basil burgers. The poutine is unlike any other, featuring shredded duck and raw-milk cheese. The decor is sophisticated yet fun, with clubby booths, a back-lit bar, and retro disco ball. Clients chat and canoodle at the big refectory-style table in the middle of the restaurant. The "after work" crowd sips litchi sangria at the oyster bar before enjoying salmon tartare and giant shrimp. Prices are astonishingly affordable. ⊠*432 rue du Parvis, St. Roch* ☎418/523–9995 ⊟*AE, D, DC, MC, V* ⊹ *1B.·*

PIZZA

$ ✕**La Pointe des Amériques.** Adventurous pizza lovers should explore the fare at this bistro. Some pizza combos (like alligator, smoked Gouda, Cajun sauce, and hot peppers) are downright strange. But don't worry—there are more than 27 different pizzas as well as meat and pasta dishes, soups, salads, and Southwestern cuisine. The original brick walls of the century-old building just outside the St-Jean Gate contrast boldly with modern mirrors and artsy wrought-iron lighting. Connected to the downtown restaurant is the Biloxi Bar, which has the same menu and serves seven kinds of the restaurant's own beer, brewed by Archibald Microbrasserie. ⊠*964 rue St-Jean, Carré d'Youville* ☎*418/694–1199* ⊠*2815 blvd. Laurier, Ste-Foy* ☎*418/658–2583* ⊟*AE, DC, MC, V* ⊹ *2D, 4A.*

VEGETARIAN

$ ✕**Le Commensal.** At this upscale cafeteria you serve yourself from an outstanding informal vegetarian buffet and then grab a table in the vast dining room, where brick walls and green plants add a touch of class. Plates are weighed to determine the price. Try to pick light food, as the bill creeps up quickly. Hot and cold dishes, all health conscious in some way, include stir-fry tofu and ratatouille with couscous. ⊠*860 rue St-Jean, St-Jean-Baptiste* ☎*418/647–3733* ⊟*AE, DC, MC, V* ⏰*BYOB* ⊹ *2D.*

WHERE TO STAY

More than 35 hotels are within Québec City's walls, and there is also an abundance of family-run bed-and-breakfasts. Landmark hotels are as prominent as the city's most historic sights; modern high-rises outside the ramparts have spectacular views of the Old City. Another choice is to immerse yourself in the city's historic charm by staying in an old-fashioned inn, where no two rooms are alike. Many hotels were renovated for last year's 400th anniversary celebrations, so this year's travelers benefit from all the upgrades.

Be sure to make a reservation if you visit during peak season (May through September) or during the Winter Carnival, in January and/or February.

During especially busy times, hotel rates usually rise 30%. From November through April, many lodgings offer weekend discounts and other promotions.

WHAT IT COSTS IN CANADIAN DOLLARS					
	¢	$	$$	$$$	$$$$
FOR TWO PEOPLE	under C$75	C$75–C$125	C$126–C$175	C$176–C$250	over $250

Prices are for a standard double room in high season; they exclude 7.5% provincial sales tax, 6% goods-and-services tax (GST), and a C$2.30 city tax.

UPPER TOWN

$$$$ **Fairmont Le Château Frontenac.** Towering above the St. Lawrence
Fodor'sChoice River, the Château Frontenac is a Québec City landmark. Its public
★ rooms—from the intimate piano bar to the 700-seat ballroom reminiscent of the Hall of Mirrors at Versailles—are all opulent. Renovated for the city's 400th anniversary last year, rooms are fresh and elegantly furnished like mini châteaux with gold and green decor touches. (Thankfully, the designers did not try to convert the Frontenac into a hip castle with low couches and Zen gardens). At Le Champlain, classic French cuisine is served by waitstaff in traditional French costumes. This hotel is a tourist attraction in its own right, so the lobby can be quite busy. Reserve well in advance, especially for late June to mid-October. **Pros:** historic aura adds romance; pets are treated like royalty. **Cons:** high foot traffic in public spaces; some rooms are smallish for the price. ⊠*1 rue des Carrières, Upper Town,* ☎*418/692–3861 or 800/441–1414* ⊕*www.fairmont.com* ✎*585 rooms, 33 suites* ⌂*In-room: high-speed Internet. In-hotel: public Wi-Fi, 2 restaurants, room service, bar, pool, gym, concierge, laundry service, executive floor, parking (fee), some pets allowed* ⊟*AE, D, DC, MC, V* ⦾*EP* ✛ *3G.*

$$$ **Hôtel Le Clos St-Louis.** Winding staircases and crystal chandeliers add to the Victorian elegance of this central inn made up of two 1845-era houses. All rooms have antiques or reproductions; some have romantic four-poster or sleigh beds; eight have decorative fireplaces. **Pros:** period decor; cheery breakfast room. **Cons:** Victorian ruffles around the beds won't appeal to young hipsters; no elevator to whisk guests up to their rooms. ⊠*69 rue St-Louis, Upper Town,* ☎*418/694–1311 or 800/461–1311* ⊕*www.clossaintlouis.com* ✎*16 rooms, 2 suites* ⌂*In-room: Wi-Fi. In-hotel: no elevator, parking (fee), no-smoking rooms* ⊟*AE, MC, V* ⦾*CP* ✛ *3F.*

8

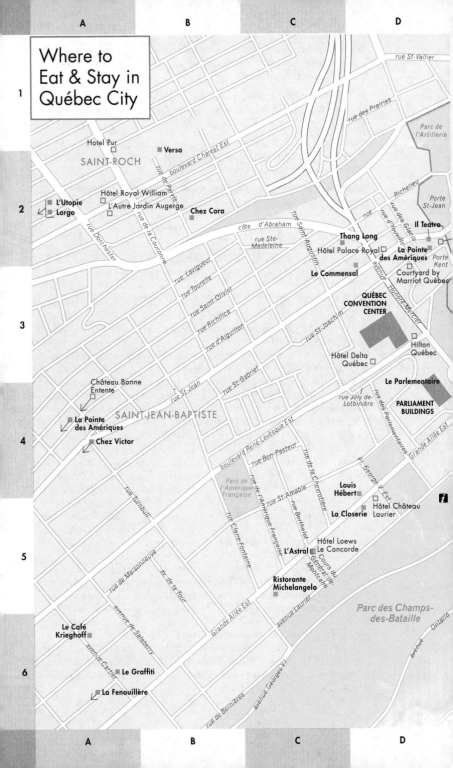

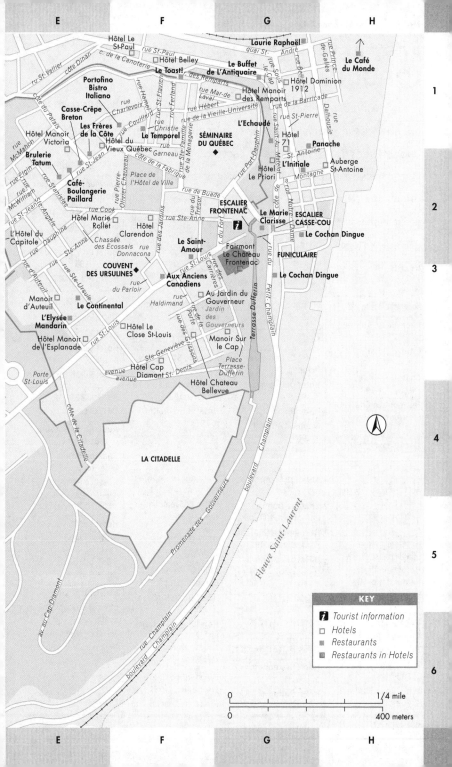

BEST BETS FOR QUÉBEC CITY LODGING

Fodor's offers a selective listing of quality lodging experiences in every price range, from the city's best budget beds to its most sophisticated luxury hotels. Here, we've compiled our top recommendations by price and experience. The very best properties—in other words, those that provide a particularly remarkable experience in their price range—are designated in the listings with the Fodor's Choice logo.

$$$ ⌂**Hôtel Manoir Victoria.** A discreet, old-fashioned entrance leads you into this European-style hotel with an in-house spa. Rooms are decorated simply but elegantly with hardwood furnishings and floral bedspreads. Three rooms and three suites have whirlpool baths and electric fireplaces. You can't beat its location. **Pros:** Indoor parking is a luxury for winter guests. **Cons:** no "wow" factor. ✉*44 côte du Palais, Upper Town,* ☎*418/692–1030 or 800/463–6283* ⊕*www.manoir-victoria. com* ⇌*156 rooms, 3 suites* ⌂*In-room: Ethernet, Wi-Fi, safe (some). In-hotel: public Wi-Fi, 2 restaurants, room service, pool, gym, spa, concierge, laundry service, parking (fee), no-smoking building* ▭*AE, D, DC, MC, V* ⊙*EP* ✛ *1E.*

$$ ⌂**Hôtel Cap Diamant.** An eclectic collection of vintage furniture and ecclesiastical accents—stained glass from a church, a confessional door, even an angel or two—complement the decorative marble fireplaces, stone walls, and hardwood floors at this hotel made up of two adjacent 1826 houses. In the morning you can bring coffee, orange juice, and muffins to your room or dine in a sunroom that overlooks one of the Old City's few gardens. **Pros:** there's a baggage lift. **Cons:** stairs to third-floor rooms are a bit steep. ✉*39 av. Ste-Geneviève, Upper Town,* ☎*418/694–0313 or 888/694–0313* ⊕*www.hcapdiamant.qc.ca* ⇌*12 rooms* ⌂*In-room: no phone, refrigerator, Wi-Fi. In-hotel: no elevator, laundry service, no-smoking building* ▭*MC, V* ⊙*CP* ✛ *3F.*

$$ ⌂**Hôtel Château Bellevue.** Behind the Château Frontenac, this 1898 hotel occupies four heritage homes with the same green roofing. It has comfortable accommodations at reasonable prices in a good location. Guest rooms are modern, with standard hotel furnishings; many have a view of the St. Lawrence River. Rooms vary considerably in size (many are a bit cramped), and package deals are available. The Continental buffet ramps up in high season, with extra goodies like granola bars, muffins, and fruit. **Pros:** fun package deals offered with museums, aquariums, restaurants. **Cons:** smallish rooms lack pizzazz. ✉*16 rue de la Porte, Upper Town,* ☎*418/692–2573 or 800/463–2617* ⊕*www. oldquebec.com/bellevue* ⇌*58 rooms* ⌂*In-room: Wi-Fi, refrigerator (if requested, fee). In-hotel: public Wi-Fi, bar, laundry service, parking (fee)* ▭*AE, D, DC, MC, V* ⊙*CP* ✛ *3F.*

$$ ⌂**Hôtel Clarendon.** Built in 1870, the Clarendon is the oldest operating hotel in Québec City, and it's been refurbished in art deco and art nouveau styles, most notably in the public areas. Some guest rooms have period touches, and some are more modern. Half the rooms have excellent views of Old Québec; the others overlook a courtyard. The new loungy Le Charles-Baillairgé is more contemporary in terms of decor and cuisine than its predecessor, L'Emprise. Small jazz duos perform on weekends. **Pros:** the piano in the lounge attracts merrymakers. **Cons:** rooms need a splash of color to relieve the many shades of beige. ✉*57 rue Ste-Anne, Upper Town,* ☎*418/692–2480 or 888/554–6001* ⊕*www.hotelclarendon.com* ⇌*138 rooms, 5 suites* ⌂*In-room: Wi-Fi. In-hotel: restaurant, room service, bar, parking (fee)* ▭*AE, D, DC, MC, V* ⊙*EP* ✛ *2F.*

8

$$ ⚏ **Hôtel du Vieux Québec.** Visiting students make tracks to this hotel, with its signature red roof and stone walls. It's nicely situated at the end of rue St-Jean, surrounded by stores and restaurants. Rooms are spread over three floors, plus the newest suite in the half-basement, with a king bed and huge flat-screen television. Also popular is the "superior room" with two queen beds and an exposed brick wall. Mingle in the small but lovely lobby library or take a free walking tour in English or French. **Pros:** lively location; breakfast delivered to your door with a weather report. **Cons:** with students come occasional shenanigans. ⌂*1190 rue St-Jean, Upper Town,* ☏*418/692–1850 or 800/361–7787* ⊕*www.hvq.com* ⇆*45 rooms* ♿*In-room: Wi-Fi. In-hotel: restaurant, laundry service, computer stations, parking (fee), no-smoking building, some pets allowed (fee)* ▤*AE, MC, V* ❘◯❘*CP* ✛ *1E.*

$$ ⚏ **Manoir d'Auteuil.** One of the more lavish manors in town, this art deco and art nouveau–style building was converted from a private house into a hotel in the 1950s. An ornate sculpted iron banister wraps up through four floors, and guest rooms blend modern design with the art deco structure. Each room is different; one was once a chapel, and two have a tiny staircase leading to their bathrooms with marble or granite tiles. Two rooms have showers with seven showerheads. Rooms on the fourth floor are smaller but are less expensive and come with great views of the Parliament Buildings. The Edith Piaf room, named for the French singer who used to frequent the hotel, is still a popular hit with some who stay here. Much mingling occurs in the airy lobby and the newly renovated art deco bar. **Pros:** direct view of the Parliament building, close to the convention center, deco charm. **Cons:** midweek business guests do not invite much chitchat in the lobby. ⌂*49 rue d'Auteuil, Upper Town,* ☏*418/694–1173* ⊕*www.manoirdauteuil. com* ⇆*15 rooms, 3 suites* ♿*In-room: Wi-Fi. In-hotel: no elevator, public Wi-Fi, laundry service (fee), parking (fee), no-smoking building* ▤*AE, D, MC, V* ❘◯❘*CP* ✛ *3E.*

$$ ⚏ **Hôtel Manoir de l'Esplanade.** The four 1845 stone houses at the corner of rues d'Auteuil and St-Louis conceal one of the city's good deals: a charming hotel with well-appointed rooms, and an expanded Continental breakfast with fruit, cheese, and yogurt is included. Rooms have an antique feel, with either rich dark-wood furniture or more-modern light-wood furniture, and colors and fabrics vary as well. Some rooms have exposed brick walls, a fireplace, and a glass chandelier. The front rooms, facing St-Louis Gate, are the most spacious. Those on the fourth floor are right under the eaves. **Pros:** ancestral fireplaces and dormer windows add to the charm. **Cons:** central location means some nighttime noise. ⌂*83 rue d'Auteuil, Upper Town,* ☏*418/694–0834* ⊕*www.manoiresplanade.ca* ⇆*36 rooms* ♿*In-room: refrigerator (some), Wi-Fi. In-hotel: no elevator, public Internet, laundry service, no-smoking building* ▤*AE, MC, V* ❘◯❘*CP* ✛ *3E.*

$$ ⛁ **Manoir Sur le Cap.** No two rooms are alike in this elegant 19th-century inn with beautiful views of Governors' Park and the St. Lawrence River. Built in 1837 as a private home, it was severely damaged in 1849 by a major fire in the neighborhood. It was rebuilt the same year by George Mellis Douglas, the medical superintendent at Grosse Île. Rooms are light and airy, with fresh paint, antiques, and hardwood floors. Some have brass beds, brick walls, or small balconies. Note that some bathrooms have only showers and no tubs, and that one room is in the basement. The old stable was converted to a two-level deluxe suite at the side of the hotel. **Pros:** new mattresses this year; more air-conditioning units. **Cons:** no breakfast in high season, quite inexplicably. ⊠ *9 av. Ste-Geneviève, Upper Town,* ☎ *418/694–1987 or 866/694–1987* ⊕ *www.manoir-sur-le-cap.com* ⟻ *11 rooms, 3 suites, 1 apartment* ♿ *In-room: no a/c (some), no phone (some), refrigerator (some), dial-up (some), Wi-Fi (some). In-hotel: no elevator, public Wi-Fi, no-smoking rooms* ⊟ *AE, MC, V* ⍿ *EP* ✢ *3G.*

$ ⛁ **Au Jardin du Gouverneur.** This cream-color stone house with windows trimmed in dark blue is an inexpensive, unpretentious hotel behind the Château Frontenac. Light-wood furnishings and two double beds fill most of the rooms. Stone walls have been exposed, along with old fireplaces in some rooms. The stairs are steep leading up to the fourth floor. **Pros:** sweet staff; carefree ambience. **Cons:** in high season, guests have to schlep to a neighboring restaurant for their breakfast. ⊠ *16 rue Mont-Carmel, Upper Town,* ☎ *418/692–1704 or 877/692–1704* ⊕ *www.quebecweb.com/hjg* ⟻ *16 rooms, 1 suite* ♿ *In-room: no phone, refrigerator (some). In-hotel: no elevator, no-smoking rooms* ⊟ *AE, MC, V* ⍿ *CP* ✢ *3F.*

$ ⛁ **Hôtel Manoir des Remparts.** With its homey furnishings, basic but cheery rooms, and reasonable rates, this serviceable hotel attracts many teachers and travelers who can't bring themselves to stay in a hostel. The two 1830 houses forming this hotel are opposite the wall enclosing Upper Town, only a short walk from Lower Town. Rooms at the front have a view of the port. On the fourth floor, 10 rooms contain sinks and share bathrooms and a TV. **Pros:** good for people who want to escape antiques-filled B&Bs. **Cons:** prices went up a bit this year. ⊠ *3½ rue des Remparts, Upper Town,* ☎ *418/692–2056, 866/692–2056 in Canada* ✉ *manoirdesremparts@sympatico.ca* ⊕ *www.manoirdesremparts.com* ⟻ *34 rooms, 24 with bath* ♿ *In-room: no a/c (some), kitchen (some), refrigerator (some), no TV (some). In-hotel: no elevator, public Wi-Fi, no-smoking building* ⊟ *AE, DC, MC, V* ⍿ *CP* ✢ *1G.*

$ ⛁ **Hôtel Marie Rollet.** In the heart of Vieux-Québec, this intimate little inn built in 1876 by the Ursuline Order has warm woodwork and antiques to match its surroundings. Antique lights and clocks add to the dollhouse charm, as does the Victorian floral bedspreads. Some bathrooms are so tiny the sink is in the bedroom. Steep stairs lead to a rooftop terrace with a garden view. **Pros:** central location; dollhouse charm. **Cons:** steep stairs. ⊠ *81 rue Ste-Anne, Upper Town,* ☎ *418/694–9271 or 800/275–0338* ⊕ *www.hotelmarierollet.com* ⟻ *10 rooms* ♿ *In-room: no phone. In-hotel: no elevator, parking (fee), no-smoking building* ⊟ *AE, MC, V* ⍿ *EP* ✢ *2F.*

8

LOWER TOWN

$$$$ ⊞**Auberge St-Antoine.** A regular on the *Condé Nast Traveler*'s Gold List,
Fodor'sChoice   the Auberge is also a member of the prestigious Relais & Châteaux
★   chain—which isn't easy to join. On the site of a 19th-century maritime
warehouse, this charming hotel incorporates the historic stone walls
of the old building along with artifacts dating to the 1600s, many of
which are encased in glass displays in the public areas and guest rooms.
Antiques and contemporary pieces fill the bedrooms, some with fireplaces, large terraces, or river views. A few rooms have themes, such
as the Capitaine, decorated as a ship-captain's quarters, the Victorian,
or the Garden. Guests can arrange DVD movie screenings at Cinéma
St-Antoine, or work up an appetite in the new gym before dining at the
hotel's restaurant, Panache, which serves fine, updated French-Canadian fare in a rustic setting. **Pros:** free yoga classes on Saturday mornings in the new gym. **Cons:** low vacancy rate means guests must plan
in advance. ⊠*8 rue St-Antoine, Lower Town,* ☎*418/692–2211 or
888/692–2211* ⊕*www.saint-antoine.com* ⟋*83 rooms, 12 suites* ⟁*In-
room: refrigerator, Ethernet, Wi-Fi. In-hotel: restaurant, room service,
bar, gym, concierge, laundry service, public Wi-Fi, parking (fee), no-
smoking building* ▤*AE, DC, MC, V* ⊚*EP, BP* ✥ *2H.*

$$$$ ⊞**Hôtel Dominion 1912.** Sophistication and attention to the smallest
Fodor'sChoice   detail prevail in the modern rooms of this four-star boutique hotel—
★   from the custom-designed swing-out night tables to the white goose-
down duvets and custom umbrellas. Entering the lobby, it's tempting
to sink into a white Montauk couch and never get up. The hotel, which
was built in 1912 as a warehouse, has rooms on higher floors with
views of either the St. Lawrence River or the Old City. **Pros:** designer's
delight. **Cons:** minimal chic decor is perhaps not well suited to families
with small children. ⊠*126 rue St-Pierre, Lower Town,* ☎*418/692–
2224 or 888/833–5253* ⊕*www.hoteldominion.com* ⟋*60 rooms*
⟁*In-room: safe, refrigerator, Ethernet, Wi-Fi. In-hotel: gym, concierge, laundry service, parking (fee), some pets allowed* ▤*AE, DC,
MC, V* ⊚*CP* ✥ *1G.*

$$$ ⊞**Hôtel Le Priori.** A dazzling four-star boutique hotel, Le Priori is nestled
in the Lower Town. The building may be 300 years old, with stone
and brick walls, but the decor is rigorously modern—with custom
leather beds, stainless steel sinks, slate floors, and three-head shower
jets. Suites have fabulous names such as Diva (with private terrace
overlooking Place Royal), and Rolf Benz, and are over 1,000 square
feet. Some have antique bathtubs, kitchens, and working fireplaces. Le
Priori is a member of Epoque hotels. **Pros:** both hot and cold food at
the buffet breakfast. **Cons:** spontaneous trips to Le Priori are curbed
by high occupancy rates. ⊠*15 rue Sault-au-Matelot, Lower Town,*
☎*418/692–3992 or 800/351–3992* ⊕*www.hotellepriori.com* ⟋*20
rooms, 6 suites* ⟁*In-room: refrigerator (some), DVD (some), Wi-Fi.
In-hotel: restaurant, laundry service, parking (fee), no-smoking rooms*
▤*AE, D, DC, MC, V* ⊚*BP* ✥ *2G.*

$$$ ⚟ **Hôtel 71.** This four-star luxury hotel is located in the founding building of the National Bank of Canada. Owners Patrick and Sonia Gilbert also own the neighboring Auberge Saint-Pierre. Rooms have 12-foot-high ceilings and stunning views of Old Québec. Rain-forest showers and surround-sound systems are in every room. **Pros:** outstanding coffee at Café 71, luxurious packages. **Cons:** chic decor might make parents of active kids quite nervous. ✉ *71 rue St-Pierre, Lower Town,* ☎ *418/692–1171 or 888/692–1171* ⊕ *www.hotel71.ca* 🛏 *34 rooms, 6 suites* ⚭ *In-room: safe, Wi-Fi. In-hotel: public Wi-Fi, restaurant, bar, gym, concierge, laundry service, parking (fee), no-smoking rooms* ☰ *AE, MC, V* ⦿|*CP* ⊹ *1G.*

$$ ⚟ **Hôtel Belley.** Modern artwork by local artists is everywhere in this modest little hotel up the stairs above Belley Tavern, a stone's throw from the train station and the antiques district. Built as a private home around 1842, the building has housed various taverns since 1868. The current hotel opened in 1987. Rooms are simple, with exposed brick walls and beamed ceilings. Bathrooms have showers but no tubs. Downstairs, the old-fashioned tin ceilings and modern furniture attract a café crowd. **Pros:** young and friendly tourists hook up at Belley. **Cons:** small capacity means high occupancy. ✉ *249 rue St-Paul, Lower Town,* ☎ *418/692–1694 or 888/692–1694* ⊕ *www.oricom.ca/belley* 🛏 *8 rooms* ⚭ *In-room: refrigerator (some), Wi-Fi. In-hotel: public Wi-Fi, restaurant, laundry service, parking (fee), no elevator* ☰ *AE, MC, V* ⦿|*EP* ⊹ *1F.*

$$ ⚟ **Hôtel Le St-Paul.** Perched at the edge of the antiques district, this basic four-story hotel converted from a 19th-century office building is near art galleries and the train station. Rooms have standard tub chairs, two-tone walls, and wooden headboards. Some rooms have exposed brick walls. **Pros:** baby cots available. **Cons:** underwhelming decor. ✉ *229 rue St-Paul, Lower Town,* ☎ *418/694–4414 or 888/794–4414* ⊕ *www.lesaintpaul.qc.ca* 🛏 *23 rooms, 3 suites* ⚭ *In-room: refrigerator (some), dial-up, Wi-Fi. In-hotel: restaurant, laundry service, no-smoking building* ☰ *AE, DC, MC, V* ⦿|*BP* ⊹ *1F.*

OUTSIDE THE WALLS

$$$$ ⚟ **Château Bonne Entente.** Now a member of Leading Hotels of the
FodorśChoice World, the Château Bonne Entente offers modern simplicity at its fin-
★ est. Its classic rooms were redone in 2008 with white duvets, marble bathrooms, and refinished wood furniture. Urbania—a boutique hotel within the château—offers guests tall ceilings, leather headboards, as well as plasma-screen TVs and bathrooms right out of a design magazine. Urbania has a Zen-like lounge called the Living Rouge, with white couches, chairs, and a red ceiling, where breakfast and coffee are served, and cocktails during happy hour. Espace Terzo is the latest boutique wing, with wood floors and fluffy white bedding. Guests can tee off at nearby La Tempête, and Amerispa runs the luxurious spa. The hotel is 20 minutes from downtown, with free shuttle service June through mid-September. **Pros:** cutting-edge design; heated bathroom floors in Espace Terzo. **Cons:** chic decor not practical for kids without

8

attentive nannies. ✉*3400 chemin Ste-Foy, Ste-Foy,* ☎*418/653–5221 or 800/463–4390* ⊕*www.chateaubonneentente.com* ⌑*120 rooms, 45 suites* ♿*In-room: safe, Ethernet, Wi-Fi, refrigerator. In-hotel: public Wi-Fi, 3 restaurants, bar, pool, gym, spa, concierge, laundry service, airport shuttle (summer), parking (no fee), no-smoking building* ☰*AE, DC, MC, V* ⑩*EP* ✛ *4A.*

$$$ 🖼 **L'Autre Jardin Auberge.** Across the street from the Royal William, this

Fodor's Choice   modern, pleasant inn—with three stars and three CAA diamonds—is
★   owned and operated by a nonprofit organization. In the heart of the burgeoning St-Roch district in downtown Québec, the inn is geared toward the academics, high-tech entrepreneurs, and others who visit the many new office and administrative buildings that surround it. The inn, which has a friendly, helpful staff, has three floors of comfortable rooms and suites with cable TV and Wi-Fi Internet access. Some rooms have therapeutic baths. The breakfast buffet, which includes fair-trade coffee, a variety of breads, fresh croissants, and local cheeses, is served in a dining room in the basement. To meet demand, the dining room was expanded in 2008. In keeping with its owner's aims, there's also a fair-trade shop selling artisanal foods and other items from developing countries. **Pros:** the hotel upgraded its air-conditioning. **Cons:** rooms are a bit spartan. ✉*365 blvd. Charest Est, St-Roch,* ☎*418/523–1790 or 877/747–0447* ⊕*www.autrejardin.com* ⌑*25 rooms, 3 suites* ♿*In-room: Ethernet, Wi-Fi. In-hotel: public Wi-Fi, parking (fee), no-smoking rooms, no elevator* ☰*AE, D, DC, MC, V* ⑩*BP* ✛ *2A.*

$$$ 🖼 **Hilton Québec.** Just opposite the National Assembly, the newly renovated Hilton rises from the shadow of Parliament Hill. The lobby, which can be busy at times, has new chocolate-brown leather couches, a back-lit bar, and dark wood accents. Over 400 rooms were upgraded to "contemporary chic" with fluffy white bedding. Rooms on the upper floors have fine views of Vieux-Québec. The renovation team went all out on the Executive Floor (23rd), with its stunning views of the St. Lawrence and an honor bar from 5 PM to 10:30 PM. **Pros:** direct access to the convention center and a mall. **Cons:** deluxe Continental breakfast is only free on the executive floor; blocky exterior lacks pizzazz. ✉*1100 blvd. René-Lévesque Est, Montcalm,* ☎*418/647–2411, 800/447–2411 in Canada* ⊕*www.hiltonquebec.com* ⌑*529 rooms, 42 suites* ♿*In-room: refrigerator, Wi-Fi. In-hotel: public Wi-Fi, restaurant, room service, bar, pool, gym, concierge, laundry service, parking (fee), no-smoking rooms, some pets allowed* ☰*AE, D, DC, MC, V* ⑩*EP* ✛ *3D.*

$$$ 🖼 **L'Hôtel du Capitole.** This turn-of-the-20th-century structure just outside the St-Jean Gate is a fancy hotel, an Italian bistro, and a 1920s cabaret-style dinner theater (the Théâtre Capitole) all rolled into one. The showbiz theme, with stars on the doors, has attracted Québec celebrities, including Céline Dion. Art deco furnishings fill the small, simple rooms. Painted ceilings have a blue-and-white sky motif, and white down-filled comforters dress the beds. **Pros:** whirlpool tubs and fluffy white towels. **Cons:** lively theatre/hotel complex isn't ideal for cocooning. ✉*972 rue St-Jean, Carré d'Youville,* ☎*418/694–4040 or 800/363–4040* ⊕*www.lecapitole.com* ⌑*39 rooms, 1 suite* ♿*In-*

room: VCR, dial-up, Wi-Fi. In-hotel: public Wi-Fi, restaurant, room service, bar, laundry service, parking (fee) ▭AE, D, DC, MC, V ⦿❘EP ✚ 2D.

$$ ▦**Courtyard by Marriott Québec.** This former bank building exudes a quiet elegance, with stained-glass windows, two fireplaces, and a tiny wood-lined corner bar in the lobby. At the restaurant in back, you can dine around the open kitchen or on the mezzanine. Wood furniture fills the modern rooms, most of which are decorated in blue and beige. The least expensive standard rooms face an office building; those in front have views of the Old City. **Pros:** French gastronomy from Que Sera Sera restaurant's open kitchen; thoughtful facilities like coffeemakers and baby cribs; laundry machines are a bonus. **Cons:** it doesn't inspire a lusty romp. ✉850 pl. d'Youville, Carré d'Youville, ☏418/694–4004 or 866/694–4004 ⊕www.marriott-quebec.com ⤴103 rooms, 8 suites ♿In-room: Ethernet. In-hotel: restaurant, room service, bar, laundry facilities, laundry service, public Wi-Fi, parking (fee), no-smoking building ▭AE, DC, MC, V ⦿❘EP ✚ 2D.

$$ ▦**Hôtel Château Laurier.** Brown leather sofas and wrought-iron chandeliers fill the spacious lobby of this former private house. All rooms have sleigh beds with bedspreads in green, beige, or blue. Those in the newer section are a bit larger; deluxe rooms have fireplaces and double whirlpool baths. In 2007, 92 rooms were added—with urban plasma screens, white linen, and warm wood. Weddings are welcome in the ballroom, and executives in the hotel's 17 meeting rooms. The Château Laurier is rated three diamonds by the CAA. Nearby, the busy Grande Allée is crowded with popular restaurants and trendy bars. **Pros:** updated; rooms for budget travelers. **Cons:** some ambient noise. ✉1220 pl. Georges V Ouest, Montcalm, ☏418/522–8108 or 800/463–4453 🖷418/524–8768 ⊕www.oldquebec.com/laurier ⤴271 rooms, 20 suites ♿In-room: dial-up, Wi-Fi, safe. In-hotel: public Wi-Fi, restaurant, room service, bar, pool, laundry service, parking (fee), no-smoking building ▭AE, D, DC, MC, V ⦿❘EP ✚ 5D.

$$ ▦**Hôtel Delta Québec.** This establishment opposite the Parliament Buildings, part of a Canadian chain, has standard and business-class rooms (the latter come with Continental breakfast and nightly appetizers and drinks on executive floors). Concrete hallways and a rather dreary lobby are less than appealing, but the rooms are large and have undergone a face-lift. Enter the Delta's famous "sanctuary bed" and fresh green marble in the bathrooms. There's also a new health club beside the heated, outdoor pool. The hotel occupies the first 12 floors of a tall office complex next to the convention center; views of Vieux-Québec are limited to the higher floors. **Pros:** kid-friendly environment. **Cons:** feels like a chain hotel. ✉690 blvd. René-Lévesque Est, Montcalm, ☏418/647–1717 or 800/268–1133 ⊕www.deltahotels.com ⤴371 rooms, 6 suites ♿In-room: refrigerator, Ethernet, Wi-Fi. In-hotel: public Wi-Fi, restaurant, room service, bar, pool, gym, laundry service, parking (fee), some pets allowed ▭AE, D, DC, MC, V ⦿❘EP ✚ 3D.

8

$$ **Hôtel Loews Le Concorde.** When Le Concorde was built in 1974, the 29-story concrete structure brought controversy because it supplanted 19th-century Victorian homes. But the hotel's excellent location—on Grande Allée has ensured its longevity. Rooms are larger than average, with ergonomic chairs, Keurig coffee makers, huge windows, and good views of Battlefields Park and the St. Lawrence River. Loews Loves Pets and Loews Loves Kids programs help parents and pet owners relax. **Pros:** central location; toys for kids; treats for pets; plush robes. **Cons:** high-traffic hotel not suited for forbidden trysts. ⊠ *1225 Cours du Général-de Montcalm, Montcalm,* ☎418/647–2222 *or* 800/463–5256 ⊕*www.loewshotels.com* ↩*387 rooms, 19 suites* ♿*In-room: refrigerator, safe, dial-up, Wi-Fi. In-hotel: public Wi-Fi (some), 2 restaurants, room service, bar, pool, gym, concierge, laundry service, parking (fee), some pets allowed* ⊟*AE, D, DC, MC, V* ⏅*EP* ✚ *5C.*

$$ **Hôtel Palace Royal.** A soaring indoor atrium with balconies overlooking a tropical garden, swimming pool, and hot tub lends a sense of drama to this luxury hotel. Its eclectic design makes use of everything from Asian styles to art deco. Elegant rooms with antique gold accents have views of either the Old City or the atrium; some rooms on the seventh floor and up have a view of the St. Lawrence River. **Pros:** soaring atrium adds drama; good packages. **Cons:** the beige decor needs oomph. ⊠*775 av. Honoré-Mercier, Carré d'Youville,* ☎418/694–2000 *or* 800/567–5276 ⊕*www.jaro.qc.ca* ↩*69 rooms, 165 suites* ♿*In-room: refrigerator, high-speed Internet. In-hotel: restaurant, room service, bar, pool, gym, concierge, public Wi-Fi, parking (fee)* ⊟*AE, D, DC, MC, V* ⏅*EP* ✚ *2D.*

$$ **Hôtel Royal William.** Like its namesake, the first Canadian steamship to cross the Atlantic (in 1833), the Royal William brings the spirit of technology and innovation to this hotel designed with the business traveler in mind. Rooms have two phone lines, a fax connection, plus a high-speed Internet port. Renovations in late 2008 added three floors to house 33 new, spacious rooms decorated in the boutique style with bamboo wood floors and sleek kitchenettes. A full American breakfast is now included in all room rates. Five minutes from Vieux-Québec, the hotel is in the "Nouvo St-Roch" district, popular with young artists, academics, and techies. **Pros:** live piano music in the restaurant. **Cons:** banquet hall ambience in the public areas is uninspired; the business travelers aren't big minglers. ⊠*360 blvd. Charest Est, St-Roch,* ☎418/521–4488 *or* 888/541–0405 ⊕*www.royalwilliam.com* ↩*36 rooms, 8 suites* ♿*In-room: safe, refrigerator, Ethernet. In-hotel: restaurant, gym, laundry service, parking (fee), no-smoking room* ⊟*AE, D, DC, MC, V* ⏅*CB* ✚ *2A.*

$ **Hotel Pur.** For choosy travelers with an image to maintain, this new boutique hotel is worthy of your Prada luggage. Hotel PUR is ultra chic, with a mandate for minimalism. Devoted to a color palette of white and gray, the decor is accented with slate tiles and orange Gerbera daisies. While guests love the Zen-like austerity, there's a high comfort factor, thanks to plush bedding, Aveda bath products, and the rooms' capacity for high-tech gadgetry. The pool and spa will open this year (2009), so there's little reason to leave the grounds. You won't believe it used to be a dumpy Holiday Inn. **Pros:** aesthetic perfection; likely to see models, European DJs, and race-car drivers in the lobby. **Cons:** minimal design may not appeal to conservative tastes. ⊠*395 rue de la Couronne, St-Roch* ☎*418/647–2611* ⊕*www.hotelpur.com* ↩*236 rooms, 3 suites* ⚐In-room: safe, refrigerator, Ethernet, Wi-Fi. In-hotel: restaurant, room service, pool, gym, spa, laundry service, concierge, public Internet, public Wi-Fi, parking (fee), some pets allowed ▤AE, DC, MC, V EP ✛ *1A.*

NIGHTLIFE & THE ARTS

Québec City has a good variety of cultural institutions for a town of its size, from its renowned symphony orchestra to several small theater companies. The arts scene changes with the seasons. From September through May a steady repertory of concerts, plays, and performances is presented in theaters and halls. In summer, indoor theaters close, making room for outdoor stages. Tickets for most shows are sold at **Billetech** (⊠*Bibliothèque Gabrielle-Roy, 350 rue St-Joseph Est, St-Roch* ☎*418/691–7400* ⊠*Colisée Pepsi, Parc de l'Expocité, 250 blvd. Wilfrid-Hamel, Limoilou* ☎*418/691–7211* ⊠*Grand Théâtre de Québec, 269 blvd. René-Lévesque Est, Montcalm* ☎*418/643–8131 or 877/643–8131* ⊠*Salle Albert-Rousseau, 2410 chemin Ste-Foy, Ste-Foy* ☎*418/659–6710* ⊠*Théâtre Capitole, 972 rue St-Jean, Carré d'Youville* ☎*418/694–4444* ⊕*www.billetech.com*).

THE ARTS

8

Fodor'sChoice
★

Grande Théâtre de Québec. This is Québec City's main theater, with two stages for concerts, plays, dance performances, and touring companies of all sorts. A three-wall mural by Québec sculptor Jordi Bonet depicts Death, Life, and Liberty. Bonet wrote "La Liberté" on one wall to bring attention to the Québécois struggle for freedom and cultural distinction. ⊠*269 blvd. René-Lévesque Est, Montcalm* ☎*418/643–8131* ⊕*www.grandtheatre.qc.ca.*

DANCE

Grand Théâtre de Québec. Dancers appear at the Bibliothèque Gabrielle-Roy, Salle Albert-Rousseau, and Complexe Méduse. The Grand Théâtre presents a dance series with Canadian and international companies. ⊠*269 blvd. René-Lévesque Est, Montcalm* ☎*418/643–8131* ⊕*www.grandtheatre.qc.ca.*

FILM

There are several multiplexes in town, and the two in Ste-Foy usually have English films. The Cartier is a cozy little space located upstairs from the Brunet drugstore on the corner of Cartier and René-Lévesque. Many films here are in English or subtitled in English. The IMAX theater has extra-large movie screens—educational fare on scientific, historical, and adventure topics—and translation headsets.

Cineplex Odeon Ste-Foy. This multiplex offers all the new releases. ✉*1200 blvd. Duplessis, Ste-Foy* ☎*418/871–1550* ⊕*www.cineplex.com.*

IMAX theater. If the weather turns, this is a great place to bring the kids. ✉*Galeries de la Capitale, 5401 blvd. des Galeries, Lebourgneuf* ☎*418/624–4629.*

MUSIC

Bibliothèque Gabrielle-Roy. This branch of the Québec City Library network hosts plenty of concerts in its **Joseph Lavergne Auditorium** and art exhibits in a space beside it. Tickets may be bought in advance, but are also sold at the door. ✉*350 rue St-Joseph Est, St-Roch* ☎*418/691–7400.*

Colisée Pepsi. Popular music concerts are often booked here. ✉*Parc de l'Expocité, 250 blvd. Wilfrid-Hamel, Limoilou* ☎*418/691–7211.*

Maison de la Chanson. A charming intimate theater, this is a fine spot to hear contemporary Francophone music during the year and take in a play in summer. ✉*Théâtre Petit Champlain, 68 rue du Petit-Champlain, Lower Town* ☎*418/692–4744.*

Fodor'sChoice **Orchestre Symphonique de Québec** (*Québec Symphony Orchestra*).
★ Canada's oldest symphony orchestra, renowned for its musicians and conductor Yoav Talmi, performs at Louis-Frechette Hall in the Grand Théâtre de Québec. ✉*269 blvd. René-Lévesque Est, Montcalm* ☎*418/643–8131.*

THEATER

Most theater productions are in French. The theaters listed below schedule shows from September to April.

In summer, open-air concerts are presented at Place d'Youville (just outside St-Jean Gate) and on the Plains of Abraham.

Carrefour international de théâtre de Québec. This international theatrical adventure takes over several spaces during the month of May: Salle Albert-Rousseau, Grand Théâtre de Québec, Théâtre Périscope (near avenue Cartier), and Complexe Méduse. There are usually at least one or two productions in English or with English subtitles. ☎*418/692–3131 or 888/529–1996* ⊕*www.carrefourtheatre.qc.ca.*

Complexe Méduse. This multidisciplinary arts center is the hub for local artists. Have coffee or a light meal at Café-Bistrot l'Abraham-Martin. ✉*541 St-Vallier Est, St-Roch* ☎*418/640–9218* ⊕*www.meduse.org.*

Grand Théâtre de Québec. Classic and contemporary plays are staged here by the leading local company, le Théâtre du Trident. ✉*269 blvd. René-Lévesque Est, Montcalm* ☎*418/643–8131.*

Salle Albert-Rousseau. A diverse repertoire, from classic to comedy, is staged here. ✉*2410 chemin Ste-Foy, Ste-Foy* ☎*418/659–6710.*

Théâtre Capitole. This restored cabaret-style theater schedules pop music and musical comedy shows. It has been home to Elvis Story and to Night Fever, a musical presentation, complete with dance floors, of music from the disco generation. ✉*972 rue St-Jean, Carré d'Youville* ☎*418/694–4444.*

Théâtre Périscope. The Periscope is a multipurpose theater that hosts about 125 shows a year, staged by several different theater companies. ⊠*2 rue Crémazie Est, Montcalm* ☎*418/529–2183.*

NIGHTLIFE

Québec City nightlife centers on the clubs and cafés of rue St-Jean, avenue Cartier, and Grande Allée. In winter, evening activity grows livelier as the week nears its end, beginning on Wednesday. As warmer temperatures set in, the café-terrace crowd emerges, and bars are active seven days a week. Most bars and clubs stay open until 3 AM.

BARS & LOUNGES

Bar St-Laurent. One of the city's most romantic spots is the Château Frontenac's bar, with its soft lights, a panoramic view of the St. Lawrence, and a fireplace. ⊠*1 rue des Carrières, Upper Town* ☎*418/692–3861.*

Bar Les Voûtes Napoléon. The brick walls and wine cellar–like atmosphere help make Les Voûtes a popular place to listen to Québécois music and sample beer from local microbreweries. ⊠*680 Grande Allée Est, Montcalm* ☎*418/640–9388.*

Le Boudoir. Some say this is Québec's best and classiest bar for singles and younger couples. Wednesday is live band night, Friday there's a guest DJ, Saturday is Latin hot, and Sunday is cabaret. The lower-level dance floor is DJ-powered from Thursday to Sunday, and you'll find all the latest beats. You'll find martinis, including one called Le Boudoir, and finger food, comfort food, and side dishes here, too. ⊠*441 rue du Parvis, St-Roch* ☎*418/524–2777.*

Chez Maurice. This is a bar complex named after the former prime minister, Maurice Duplessis. The crowd is young, the atmosphere racy, provocative, and sexually charged. ⊠*575 Grande Allée Est, 2nd fl., Montcalm* ☎*418/647–2000.*

★ **Cosmos Café.** This trendy restaurant and lively club is located on the ground floor under Chez Maurice. Great chandeliers, art, and loud music await you here. ⊠*575 Grande Allée Est, Montcalm* ☎*418/640–0606.*

L'Inox. A popular Lower Town brewpub, L'Inox serves beers that have been brewed on-site. Some of them, like Transat and Viking, were developed to mark special events. Inside are billiard tables and excellent European-style hot dogs; outside there's a summer terrace. ⊠*37 quai St-André, Lower Town* ☎*418/692–2877.*

Le Pub Saint-Alexandre. The Saint-Alexandre is a popular English-style pub that serves 40 kinds of single-malt scotch and 200 kinds of beer, 25 of which are on tap. ⊠*1087 rue St-Jean, Upper Town* ☎*418/694–0015.*

Les Salons d'Edgar. Perched on the cliff just above the St-Roch district, Les Salons d'Edgar attracts people in their thirties with its eclectic music—everything from salsa beats and tango to jazz and techno. It's closed in July and August. ⊠*263 rue St-Vallier Est, St-Roch* ☎*418/523–7811.*

8

CLUBS

Beaugarte. Named for Humphrey Bogart, this restaurant-bar-discothèque is for dancing, being seen, drinking, and eating. There's a different theme each night—Wednesday you'll find Latin music, Friday night is disco fever. Supper is served from 4 to 11 PM. There's free indoor parking. ✉*2600 blvd. Laurier, Ste-Foy* ☎*418/659–2442.*

Chez Dagobert. There's a little bit of everything—from rock bands to loud disco—here in this large, popular club. Local bands also perform downstairs some nights. ✉*600 Grande Allée Est, Montcalm* ☎*418/522–0393.*

Le Sonar. Electronic music and a trendy vibe have made Le Sonar one of the hottest dance clubs in town. ✉*1147 av. Cartier, Montcalm* ☎*418/640–7333.*

Vogue. Patrons at this second-story dance floor move to techno and pop beats. ✉*1170 rue d'Artigny, Montcalm* ☎*418/529–9973.*

FOLK, JAZZ & BLUES

Bar Le Sacrilèe. Le Sacrilèe has folk music on Thursday and some Friday nights. This place bears its name well, with a couple of church pews and religious icons; it's also located across the street from Église St-Jean-Baptiste. Le Sacrilèe has McAuslin and Boréale products in bottles and on tap, and the special changes daily. ✉*447 rue St-Jean, Montcalm* ☎*418/649–1985.*

Le Chantauteuil. Established in 1968, this restaurant-pub is a hit with the locals. The kitchen sometimes closes early, but people stay late into the evening for drinking and discussion. ✉*1001 rue St-Jean, Upper Town* ☎*418/692–2030.*

Chez Son Père. French-Canadian and Québécois folk songs fill a once-smoky pub on the second floor of an old building in the Latin Quarter. Singers perform nightly. ✉*24 rue St-Stanislas, Upper Town* ☎*418/692–5308.*

SPORTS & THE OUTDOORS

Scenic rivers and nearby mountains (no more than 30 minutes away by car) make Québec City a great place for the sporting life. For information about sports and fitness, contact **Québec City Tourist Information** (✉*835 av. Wilfrid-Laurier, Montcalm* ☎*418/641–6290* ⊕*www.quebecregion. com/eice*). The **Québec City Bureau of Recreation and Community Life** (✉*160, 76th rue E, 4th fl., St-Roch* ☎*418/641–6224* ⊕*www.ville.quebec.qc.ca*) has information about municipal facilities.

Tickets for events can be bought at **Colisée Pepsi** (✉*Parc de l'Expocité, 250 blvd. Wilfrid-Hamel, Limoilou* ☎*418/691–7211*). You can order tickets for many events through **Billetech** (⊕*www.billetech.com*).

BIKING

There are 64 km (40 mi) of fairly flat, well-maintained bike paths on Québec City's side of the St. Lawrence River and an equal amount on the south shore. Detailed route maps are available through tourism offices. The best and most scenic of the bike paths is the one that follows the old railway bed in Lévis. Take the Québec–Lévis ferry to reach the marvelous views along this 10-km-long (6-mi-long) trail. It is now part of the province-wide Route Verte, a government-funded, 4,000-km-long (2,500-mi-long) circuit of long-distance bicycle paths and road routes.

Corridor des Cheminots. Ambitious cyclists appreciate the 22-km-long (14-mi-long) trail that runs from Limoilou near Vieux-Québec to the town of Shannon.

Côte de Beaupré. Paths along the beginning of this coast, at the confluence of the St. Charles and St. Lawrence rivers, are especially scenic. They begin northeast of the city at rue de la Verandrye and boulevard Montmorency or rue Abraham-Martin and Pont Samson (Samson Bridge) and continue 10 km (6 mi) along the coast to Montmorency Falls.

Mont-Ste-Anne. The site of the 1998 world mountain-biking championship and races for the annual World Cup has 150 km (93 mi) of mountain-bike trails and an extreme-mountain-biking park.

BOATING

Parc Nautique de Cap-Rouge. Located at the western tip of Québec City, on the St. Lawrence River, here you can rent canoes and pedal boats. ✉ *4155 chemin de la Plage Jacques Cartier, Cap-Rouge* ☎ *418/641–6148.*

DOGSLEDDING

Aventures Nord-Bec Stoneham. Now located 30 minutes from old Québec City, Aventures will teach you how to mush in the forest. A half-day spent here, which includes initiation, dogsledding, a guided tour of kennels, and a snack, costs C$85 per person. Overnight camping trips, snowmobiling, snowshoeing, and ice fishing are also available. Transportation between Stoneham and your hotel can be provided for C$30 plus taxes per person. ✉ *4 ch. des Anémones, Stoneham* ☎ *418/848–3732* ⊕ *www.traineaux-chiens.com.*

FISHING

Permits are needed for fishing in Québec. Most sporting-goods stores and all Wal-Mart and Canadian Tire stores sell permits. A one-day fishing permit for a nonresident is C$10.25, a three-day permit is C$22.75, a seven-day permit is C$35, and a season permit is C$52 (includes all sport fish except Atlantic salmon).

Gesti-faune. A corporate fishing outfitter, Gesti-faune has two properties within easy driving distance of Québec City. From May to September the company's nature guides organize trout-fishing trips that include food and lodging in private wilderness retreats. Trips, organized from May to September, cost from C$300 to C$500 per day. Reservations are required. The Manoir Brulé's award-winning cookbook is a must-see. It combines succulent recipes with stunning photos of both plates and landscapes for a uniquely practical souvenir of Québec. ☎ *418/848–5424* ⊕ *www.gestifaune.com.*

Latulippe. This store sells permits and also stocks a large amount of fishing equipment. ✉ *637 rue St-Vallier Ouest, St-Roch* ☎ *418/529–0024.*

8

Réserve Faunique des Laurentides. A wildlife reserve with good lakes for fishing, it is approximately 48 km (30 mi) north of Québec City via Route 73. Reserve a boat 48 hours in advance by phone. ☎*418/528–6868, 800/665–6527 fishing reservations* ⊕*www.sepaq.com.*

GOLF

The Québec City region has 18 golf courses, and most are open to the public. Reservations are essential in summer.

Club de Golf de Cap-Rouge. The 18-hole, par-72 course is 25 minutes by car from Vieux-Québec, and is one of the closest courses to Québec City. Eighteen holes are C$100. The women's course is 5,508 yards, the men's (blue) 6,297 yards, and the advanced course is 6,756 yards. ✉*4600 rue St-Felix, Cap-Rouge* ☎*418/653–9381.*

Club de Golf de Mont Tourbillon. A par-70, 18-hole course that covers 6,600 yards, the Mont Tourbillon is 20 minutes from the city by car via Route 73 North (Lac Beauport exit). Eighteen holes are C$45. ✉*55 montée du Golf, Lac Beauport* ☎*418/849–4418.*

Le Saint-Ferréol. This course is a half-hour drive north of Québec City and has one of the best and best-priced 18-hole, par-72 courses (C$39) in the region. The course covers 6,470 yards. ✉*1700 blvd. les Neiges, St-Ferréol-les-Neiges* ☎*418/827–3778.*

HIKING & JOGGING

Bois-de-Coulonge Park. Along with Battlefields Park, Bois-de-Coulonge is one of the most popular places for jogging. ✉*1215 chemin St-Louis, Sillery* ☎*418/528–0773.*

Cartier-Brébeuf National Historic Site. North of the Old City, along the banks of the St. Charles River, you'll be able to keep going along about 13 km (8 mi) of hiking and biking trails. This historic site also has a small museum and a reconstruction of a Native American longhouse. ✉*175 rue de l'Espinay, Limoilou* ☎*418/648–4038.*

ICE-SKATING

The ice-skating season is usually December through March.

Patinoire de la Terrasse. Try the terrace ice rink, adjacent to the Château Frontenac and open November–April, daily 11–11; it costs C$5 to skate with skate rental included, C$2 if you have your own. ☎*418/828–9898.*

Place d'Youville. This well-known outdoor rink just outside St-Jean Gate is open daily November through the end of March, from 8 AM to 10 PM. Skate rental is C$5, and skating itself is free. A locker will run you C$1. ☎*418/641–6256.*

Village Vacances Valcartier. Nighttime skating is an option here, although closing times vary. The price for skating is C$5. ✉*1860 blvd. Valcartier, St-Gabriel-de-Valcartier* ☎*418/844–2200.*

RAFTING

Excursions et Mechoui Jacques Cartier. The Jacques Cartier River, about 48 km (30 mi) northwest of Québec City, has good rafting. The outfitter runs rafting trips on the river from May through October. Tours originate from Tewkesbury, a half-hour drive from Québec City. A half-day tour costs C$50, C$54 on Saturday; wet suits are C$16. You'll find a C$15 printable rebate coupon online at ⊕www.excursionsj-cartier. com. In winter you can slide on inner tubes for about C$22 a day. ✉*978 av. Jacques-Cartier Nord, Tewkesbury* ☎*418/848–7238.*

Village Vacances Valcartier. This center runs rafting excursions on the Jacques Cartier River from May through September. A three-hour excursion costs C$50, plus C$16 to rent a wet suit. Also available are hydro-speeding—running the rapids on surfboards—and quieter family river tours. ✉*1860 blvd. Valcartier, St-Gabriel-de-Valcartier* ☎*418/844–2200.*

SKIING

Brochures offering general information about ski centers in Québec are available from the **Québec Tourism and Convention Bureau** (☎877/266–5687 ⊕*www.bonjourquebec.com*). Thirty-seven cross country ski centers in the Québec area have 2,000 km (1,240 mi) of groomed trails and heated shelters between them; for information, contact the **Regroupement des Stations de Ski de Fond** (☎*418/653–5875* ⊕*www.rssfrq.qc.ca*). The **Hiver Express** (☎*418/525–5191*) winter shuttle runs between major hotels in Vieux-Québec and ski centers. It leaves hotels in Vieux-Québec at 8 and 10 AM for the ski hills and returns at 2:30 and 4:30 PM. The cost is C$23; reserve and pay in advance at hotels.

CROSS-COUNTRY

Le Centre de Randonnée à Skis de Duchesnay. Located north of Québec City, this center has 150 km (93 mi) of marked trails. ✉*143 Rte. de Duchesnay, St-Catherine-de-Jacques-Cartier* ☎*418/875–2711.*

Mont-Ste-Anne. About 40 km (25 mi) northeast of Québec City, you might just find the best cross-country ski center in Canada, if not North America. The training ground for Olympic-level athletes from across the continent, Mont-Ste-Anne has 27 trails: 224 km (139 mi) for classic skiing and 135 km (84 mi) for skating stride. ✉*2000 blvd. du Beaupré, Beaupré* ☎*418/827–4561.*

Parc des Champs-de-Bataille *(Battlefields Park).* You can reach the park from Place Montcalm. It has more than 10 km (6 mi) of scenic, marked, cross-country skiing trails.

Les Sentiers du Moulin. This center is 19 km (12 mi) north of the city, and it has more than 20 marked trails covering 150 km (93 mi). ✉*99 chemin du Moulin, Lac Beauport* ☎*418/849–9652.*

DOWNHILL

Three downhill ski resorts, all with night skiing, are within a 30-minute drive of Québec City.

Le Massif. This resort, just 20 minutes east of Mont-Ste-Anne in Charlevoix and owned by Cirque du Soleil cofounder Michel Gauthier, is the highest skiing mountain in eastern Canada. Le Massif has a vertical drop of 2,526 feet and has 43 trails. ☎877/536–2774 ⊕*www. lemassif.com.*

Mont-Ste-Anne. This is one of the two biggest, most challenging hills in the region, just 40 minutes east of Québec City on the Côte de Beaupré. It has a vertical drop of 2,050 feet, 56 downhill trails, a half-pipe for snowboarders, a terrain park, and 13 lifts. It also has the longest system of brightly lighted night-ski runs in Canada. ⊠*2000 blvd. du Beaupré, Beaupré* ☎*418/827–4561, 800/463–1568 lodging.*

Le Relais. There are 25 trails and a vertical drop of 734 feet at this relatively small ski center, where you can buy lift tickets by the hour. Le Relais is about 20 minutes from downtown Québec City. ⊠*1084 blvd. du Lac, Lac Beauport* ☎*418/849–1851.*

Station Touristique Stoneham. Stoneham is just 20 minutes north of Old Québec. The hill has a vertical drop of 1,380 feet and is known for its long, easy slopes. It has 32 downhill runs and 10 lifts, plus three terrain parks and one super-half-pipe. ⊠*1420 av. du Hibou, Stoneham* ☎*418/848–2411.*

SNOW SLIDES

Glissades de la Terrasse. A wooden toboggan takes you down a 700-foot snow slide that's adjacent to the Château Frontenac. The cost is C$2 per ride per adult and C$1.25 for children under six. ☎*418/829–9898.*

Village Vacances Valcartier. Use inner tubes or carpets on any of 42 snow slides here. Or join 6 to 12 others for a snow-raft ride down one of three groomed trails. You can also take a dizzying ride on the Tornado, a giant inner tube that seats eight and spins down the slopes. Rafting and sliding cost C$23 per day, C$25 with skating. Trails open daily at 10 AM; closing times vary. ⊠*1860 blvd. Valcartier, St-Gabriel-de-Valcartier* ☎*418/844–2200* ⊕*www.valcartier.com.*

SNOWMOBILING

Québec is the birthplace of the snowmobile, and with 32,000 km (19,840 mi) of trails, it's one of the best places in the world for the sport. Two major trails, the 2,000-km (1,250-mi) Trans-Québec Snowmobile Trail and the 1,300-km (806-mi) Fur Traders Tour, run just north of Québec City. Trail maps are available at tourist offices.

Centre de Location de Motoneiges du Québec. Snowmobiles can be rented here near Mont-Ste-Anne, a half-hour drive north of the city, starting at C$50 per person (two to a snowmobile) for an hour, which does not include equipment or gas (roughly C$15–C$20). A daylong rental, including trail permits and equipment, runs C$120 per person, plus taxes. Expect to pay about C$50–C$70 for gas, depending on your speed. ⊠*15 blvd. du Beaupré, Beaupré* ☎*418/827–8478.*

SM Sport. These folks will pick you up from several downtown hotels at prices starting at C$20 per person. Snowmobile rentals begin at C$45 per hour, or C$135 per day, plus tax, C$15 insurance, and the cost of gas. ⊠*113 blvd. Valcartier, Loretteville* ☎*418/842–2703.*

WATER PARKS

Village Vacances Valcartier. This is the largest water park in Canada, with a wave pool, a 1-km (½-mi) tropical-river adventure called the Amazon, 35 waterslides, and a 100-foot accelerating slide on which bathers reach a speed of up to 80 KPH (50 MPH). The park's newest addition is a family attraction called the Pirate's Hideout—on a ship. There's also a winding indoor river in a medieval setting. Admission is C$26.33 a day for those at least 52 inches tall, C$20.18 for those under 52 inches. ⊠*1860 blvd. Valcartier, St-Gabriel-de-Valcartier* ☎*418/844–2200.*

WINTER CARNIVAL

Fodor's Choice ★ **Carnaval de Québec.** The whirl of activities over three weekends in January and/or February includes night parades, a snow-sculpture competition, and a canoe race across the St. Lawrence River. You can participate in or watch just about every snow activity imaginable, from dogsledding to ice climbing. ✉ *290 rue Joly, Québec City* ⊕ *www.carnaval.qc.ca.*

SHOPPING

On the fashionable streets of Old Québec shopping has a European tinge. The boutiques and specialty shops clustered along narrow streets such as rue du Petit-Champlain, and rues de Buade and St-Jean in the Latin Quarter are like trips back in time.

Stores are generally open Monday–Wednesday 9:30–5:30, Thursday and Friday until 9, Saturday until 5, and Sunday noon–5. In summer most shops have later evening hours.

DEPARTMENT STORES

Large department stores can be found in the malls of suburban Ste-Foy.

La Baie. Part of the historic Hudson's Bay Company chain, La Baie carries clothing for the entire family, as well as household wares. ✉ *Place Laurier, Ste-Foy* ☎ *418/627–5959.*

Holt Renfrew. Canada's upscale department store carries furs, perfume, and designer collections for men and women. ✉ *Place Ste-Foy, Ste-Foy* ☎ *418/656–6783.*

Simons. An old Québec City store, Simons used to be the city's only source for fine British woolens and tweeds. Now the store also carries designer clothing, linens, and other household items. ✉ *20 côte de la Fabrique, Upper Town* ☎ *418/692–3630* ✉ *Place Ste-Foy, Ste-Foy* ☎ *418/692–3630.*

SHOPPING MALLS

Galeries de la Capitale. An indoor amusement park with a roller coaster and an IMAX theater attracts families to this 250-store mall. It's about a 20-minute drive from Vieux-Québec. ✉ *5401 blvd. des Galeries, Lebourgneuf* ☎ *418/627–5800.*

Place de la Cité. There are more than 150 boutiques, services, and restaurants at this shopping center. ✉ *2600 blvd. Laurier, Ste-Foy* ☎ *418/657–6920.*

Les Promenades du Vieux-Québec. You'll find high-end items—clothing, perfume, and art—great for packaging as gifts or tucking away as souvenirs of this unique little shopping corner's boutiques. There's also a restaurant and a change bureau. ✉ *43 rue de Buade, Upper Town* ☎ *418/692–6000.*

8

Fodor'sChoice ★ **Quartier Petit-Champlain.** A pedestrian mall in Lower Town, surrounded by rues Champlain and du Marché-Champlain, Quartier Petit-Champlain has some 50 boutiques, local businesses, and restaurants. This popular district is the best area for native Québec wood sculptures, weavings, ceramics, and jewelry. ☎418/692–2613.

SPECIALTY STORES

ANTIQUES

French-Canadian, Victorian, and art deco furniture, clocks, silverware, and porcelain, are some of the rare collectibles found here. Authentic Québec pine furniture, characterized by simple forms and lines, is rare—and costly.

Antiquités Marcel Bolduc. The largest antiques store on rue St-Paul features furniture, household items, old paintings, and knickknacks. ⊠74 rue St-Paul, Lower Town ☎418/694–9558 ⊕www.marcelbolduc.com.

Argus Livres Anciens. Antique books, most of them in French, draw bibliophiles to this store. ⊠160 rue St-Paul, Lower Town ☎418/694–2122.

Gérard Bourguet Antiquaire. You're not likely to find any bargains here, but this shop has a very good selection of authentic 18th- and 19th-century Québec pine furniture. ⊠97 rue St-Paul, Lower Town ☎418/694–0896 ⊕www.gerardbourguet.com.

L'Héritage Antiquité. This is probably the best place in the antiques district to find good Québécois furniture, clocks, oil lamps, porcelain, and ceramics. ⊠109 rue St-Paul, Lower Town ☎418/692–1681.

ART

Aux Multiples Collections. Inuit art and antique wood collectibles are sold here. ⊠69 rue Ste-Anne, Upper Town ☎418/692–1230.

★ **Galerie Brousseau et Brousseau.** High-quality Inuit art is the specialty of this large, well-known gallery. ⊠35 rue St-Louis, Upper Town ☎418/694–1828 ⊕www.sculpture.artinuit.ca.

Galerie Madeleine Lacerte. Head to this gallery in an old car-repair garage for contemporary art and sculpture. ⊠1 côte Dinan, Lower Town ☎418/692–1566 ⊕www.galerielacerte.com.

CLOTHING

Bedo. A popular chain with trendy, well-priced items to round out your work wardrobe, Bedo also has great sales racks to sort through at the end of seasons. ⊠1161 rue St-Jean, Upper Town ☎418/692–0761.

Le Blanc Mouton. Locally designed creations for women, including accessories and jewelry, fill this boutique in Quartier Petit-Champlain. ⊠51 Sous le Fort, Lower Town ☎418/692–2880.

Boutique Flirt. The name of the game is pleasure at this brightly colored boutique where lingerie for men and women cohabit, and fun meets femme fatale. Flirt specializes in hard-to-find sizes. They carry Cristina, Iaia, Parah, Argento Vivo, Simone Perèle, Le Jaby, Prima Donna, and Empreinte. ⊠525 rue St-Joseph Est, St-Roch ☎418/529–5221.

Jacob. A Montréal-based chain, Jacob sells well-priced work and play clothes with a clean, sophisticated edge. ⊠*1160–1170 rue St-Jean, Upper Town* ☎*418/694–0580.*

La Vie Sportive. This sporting-goods store stocks everything from skates to kayaks, plus a large selection of casual wear. It's about a 10-minute drive out of town. ⊠*600 rue Bouvier, Autoroute Félix-Leclerc* ☎*418/623–8368.*

CRAFTS

Les Trois Colombes. Handmade items, including clothing made from handwoven fabric, native and Inuit carvings, furs, and ceramics, are available at this interesting shop. ⊠*46 rue St-Louis, Upper Town* ☎*418/694–1114.*

FOOD

de Blanchet Pâtisserie, Épicerie Fine. Breads, meats, pastries, and a few shelves stocked with hard-to-find specialty items fill this spacious gourmet store. ⊠*435 St-Joseph Est, St-Roch* ☎*418/525–9779* 🖶*418/525–7337.*

La Boîte à Pain. Baker Patrick Nisot offers a selection of baguettes, multigrain breads (pumpernickel, rye), special flavors (olive, tomato and pesto, Sicilian), and dessert breads. Closed Monday. No credit cards are accepted. ⊠*289 St-Joseph Est, St-Roch* ☎*418/647–3666.*

Camellia Sinensis Maison de Thé. This modest space stocks 150 different teas from China, Japan, Africa, and beyond. Sign up for a tea-tasting session on Saturday at 11 AM. Open Tuesday–Sunday. ⊠*624 St-Joseph Est, St-Roch* ☎*418/525–0247* ⊕*www.camellia-sinensis.com.*

FURS

The fur trade has been an important industry here for centuries. Québec City is a good place to purchase high-quality furs at fairly reasonable prices.

Fourrures Richard Robitaille. This furrier has an on-site workshop that produces custom designs. ⊠*329 rue St-Paul, Lower Town* ☎*418/692–9699.*

J. B. Laliberté. In business since 1867, the well-established Laliberté carries men's and women's furs and accessories. ⊠*595 rue St-Joseph Est, St-Roch* ☎*418/525–4841.*

GIFTS

Collection Lazuli. This store carries unusual art objects and jewelry from around the world. ⊠*Place de la Cité, 2600 blvd. Laurier, Ste-Foy* ☎*418/652–3732.*

★ **Point d'Exclamation!** Handcrafted bags, jewelry, hair accessories, paper, notebooks, cards, and paintings by 140 Québécois artisans fill Diane Bergeron's shop. ⊠*762 rue St-Jean, St-Jean-Baptiste* ☎*418/525–8053.*

8

JEWELRY

Pont Briand Joaillier. Louis Perrier sells Québec-made gold and silver jewelry, as well as a selection from other designers. ✉ *48 rue du Petit-Champlain, Lower Town* ☎ *418/692–4633.*

Zimmermann. Exclusive handmade jewelry can be found at this Upper Town shop. ✉ *46 côte de la Fabrique, Upper Town* ☎ *418/692–2672.*

Excursions from Montréal & Québec City

Lake Viceroy in the Laurentians.

WORD OF MOUTH

"If you have a chance then you should drive to Mont Tremblant, 1½ hours north of Montréal. You'll find good walking, hiking and bike trails, and the gondola to the top of the mountain provides gorgeous scenery."

—Syl

EXCURSIONS FROM MONTRÉAL & QUÉBEC CITY

Great grey owl.

TOP REASONS TO GO

★ **Ski at Mont-Tremblant:** For what's arguably some of the very best skiing on the east coast, Mont-Tremblant, only about 60 mi north of Montréal, also has top-notch hotels and restaurants as well as a lively ski village.

★ **Farm-hop on Île d'Orleans:** The "Garden of Québec" is covered with farmland and B&Bs, and makes for the perfect overnight trip from Québec City.

★ **Whale Watch in Tadoussac:** This town, located in the northernmost corner of Charlevoix, has small, white beluga whales—an endangered species—in waters off the coast.

★ **See Basilique Ste-Anne-de-Beaupre:** More than a million people a year make pilgrimages to this church, named after the patron saint of Québec.

★ **Recreate on the Petit-Train-du-Nord:** What was once a busy railroad line through the Laurentians is now a 124-mi stretch of park, where people bike, hike, and ski.

1 The Laurentians. With its ski hills and lakes, this is sheer paradise for those looking for a quick break from the hustle and bustle of urban life. Quaint villages, many steeped in colorful history, line the delightful countryside—all hardly a stone's throw away from the center of Montréal.

2 The Eastern Townships. A favorite ski and sun destination for those looking to get away from it all, although not blessed with quite as many lakes as its sister recreational getaway to the north. Rich with pastoral beauty, charming bed-and-breakfasts, and excellent regional dining, the Townships offer a certain peaceful tranquillity that is uniquely Québec.

3 Côte de Beaupré. Driving along this coast offers views of Île d'Orléans, as well as Montmorency Falls and the famous pilgrimage site, Ste-Anne-de-Beaupré.

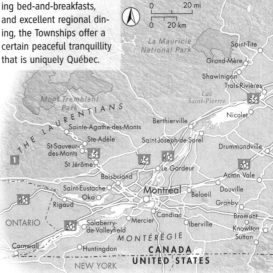

4 Île d'Orléans. This island is called the "Garden of Québec" for all the produce, flowers, and prepared goods that stock restaurants and homes throughout the province. Spend the day here farm-hopping and sampling everything from ice wine to foie gras as you go.

5 Charlevoix. People refer to Charlevoix as the "Switzerland of Québec" due to its terrain of mountains, valleys, streams, and waterfalls. Charlevoix's charming villages line the shore of the St. Lawrence River for about 125 mi.

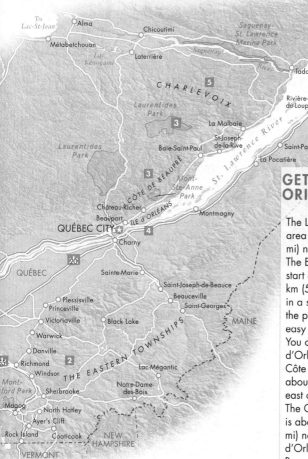

GETTING ORIENTED

The Laurentians resort area begins 60 km (37 mi) north of Montréal. The Eastern Townships start approximately 80 km (50 mi) east of the city in a southern corner of the province. Both are an easy drive from Montréal. You can reach Île d'Orléans and the Côte de Beaupré are about 40 km (25 mi) east of Québec City. The Charlevoix region is about 113 km (70 mi) northeast of Île d'Orléans and Côte de Beaupré, so consider spending the night.

EXCURSIONS FROM MONTRÉAL PLANNER

When to Go

The Laurentians are a big skiing destination in winter, but the other seasons all have their own charms: you can drive up from Montréal to enjoy the fall foliage; to hike, bike, or play golf; or to engage in spring skiing—and still get back to the city before dark. The only slow periods are early November, when there isn't much to do, and June, when the area has plenty to do but is also plagued by black flies. Control programs have improved the situation somewhat.

The Eastern Townships are best in fall, when the foliage is at its peak; the region borders Vermont and has the same dramatic colors. It's possible to visit wineries at this time, but you should call ahead, since harvest is a busy time.

Reservations

Accommodations here range from resort hotels to cozy *auberges* (inns). Many inns—especially in high season—will include two meals, usually breakfast and dinner, in the cost of a night's stay. In addition, hotels and inns often require a minimum two-night stay on weekends in high season, so inquire in advance.

Getting Here

To get to the Laurentians, the major entry points are Ottawa/Hull; U.S. 87 from New York State south of Montréal; U.S. 91 and U.S. 89 from Vermont into the Eastern Townships area; and the Trans-Canada Highway. Autoroute des Laurentides 15 North and Route 117—a slower but more scenic secondary road at its northern end—is another option. Exit numbers on Autoroute 15 are the distance in kilometers from the U.S. border. For the Eastern Townships, take Autoroute 10 Est from Montréal; U.S. 91 from New England, which becomes Autoroute 55 as it crosses the border to the Eastern Townships; Autoroutes Jean-Lesage 20 and Félix-LeClerc 40 between Montréal and Québec; and the scenic Route 138 (called the chemin du Roy between St-Barthélémy and Québec City), which runs from Montréal along the north shore of the St. Lawrence River.

Getting Around

Most people traveling to this region do so by car, making it easy to spend as much or as little time in any given area as desired. However, Québec is in the process of developing the Route Verte, or the Green Route, a 3,600-km (2,230-mi) network of bike trails in the southern part of the province. Many of the trails are currently open for access.

For more information on getting here and around, turn to Travel Smart.

DINING & LODGING PRICES IN CANADIAN DOLLARS				
¢	$	$$	$$$	$$$$
Restaurants				
Under C$8	C$8–C$12	C$13–C$20	C$21–C$30	Over C$30
Hotels				
Under C$75	C$75–C$125	C$126–C$175	C$176–C$250	Over C$250
Restaurant prices are per person for a main course at dinner, excluding tax. Hotel prices are for a standard double room in high season, excluding tax.				

THE LAURENTIANS

Updated by
Anne Marie
Marko

The Laurentians (les Laurentides) are divided into two major regions: the Lower Laurentians (les Basses Laurentides) and the Upper Laurentians (les Hautes Laurentides). But don't be fooled by the designations; they don't signify great driving distances. The rocky hills here are relatively low, but many are eminently skiable, with a few peaks above 2,500 feet. Mont-Tremblant, at 3,150 feet, is the highest.

The P'tit Train du Nord—the former railroad line that is now a 200-km (124-mi) "linear park" used by cyclists, hikers, skiers, and snowmobilers—made it possible to transport settlers and cargo easily to the Upper Laurentians. It also opened up the area to skiing by the early 1900s. Before long, trainloads of skiers replaced settlers and cargo as the railway's major trade. At first a winter weekend getaway for Montrealers who stayed at boardinghouses and fledgling resorts, the Upper Laurentians soon began attracting international visitors.

Ski lodges and private family cottages for wealthy city dwellers were accessible only by train until the 1930s, when Route 117 was built. Today there is an uneasy peace between the longtime cottagers, who want to restrict development, and resort entrepreneurs, who want to expand. At the moment, commercial interests seem to be prevailing. A number of large hotels have added indoor pools and spa facilities, and efficient highways have brought the country even closer to the city—45 minutes to St-Sauveur, 1½–2 hours to Mont-Tremblant.

The resort area truly begins at St-Sauveur-des-Monts (Exit 60 on Autoroute 15) and extends as far north as Mont-Tremblant. Beyond, the region turns into a wilderness of lakes and forests best visited with an outfitter. Guides who offer fishing trips are concentrated around Parc du Mont-Tremblant. To the first-time visitor, the hilly areas around St-Sauveur, Ste-Adèle, Morin Heights, Val Morin, and Val David up to Ste-Agathe-des-Monts form a pleasant hodgepodge of villages, hotels, and inns that seem to blend one into another.

9

OKA

40 km (25 mi) west of Montréal.

Founded in 1721 by the Roman Catholic Sulpician Order, Oka is best known for the cheese produced at nearby Abbaye Cistercienne d'Oka. In the winter months an ice bridge links Oka with Hudson, its sister town just on the opposite shore of Lake of Two Mountains.

For wine lovers, so many apple orchards produce cider around St-Joseph-du-Lac, about a 10-minute drive from Oka, that there's a *Route des Vergers*. This "Orchard Route" lists 39 growers selling all types of cider: dry, sweet, white, and red. Many of the growers have tastings and tours. There's also a winery on the route: La Roche des Brises, whose whites and reds include the portlike *L'été Indien* (Indian Summer).

WHAT TO SEE

Fodor's Choice ★ **Abbaye Cistercienne d'Oka.** In 1887 the Sulpicians donated about 865 acres of their property near the Oka Calvary to the Trappist monks, who had arrived in 1880 from Bellefontaine Abbey in France. Within a decade the monks had built their monastery, one of the oldest North American abbeys. Trappists established the Oka School of Agriculture, which operated until 1960. The monks became famous for their creamy Oka cheese, which is now produced commercially by Corporation de l'Abbaye d'Oka. The abbey store, Magasin de l'Abbaye d'Oka, sells Oka cheese and products from other Québec monasteries, such as chocolate, cheese, and cider. The monks, however, have since relocated to a new monastery in St-Jean de Matha. ⊠*1600 chemin Oka* ☎*450/479–8361* ⊕*www.abbayeoka.com* 🖼*Free* ☾*Call for store hrs.*

Auberge Roches des Brises. You can tour the vineyard (reservations are required), taste the wines for C$5, and dine in the adjacent four-star restaurant serving the best in regional cuisine. Across the road overlooking some of the grape vines is a charming five-room bed-and-breakfast with a spa. It's worth the trip if only to take in the splendor of the exceptionally lovely grounds. ⊠*2007 rue Principale, St-Joseph-du-Lac* ☎*450/472–2722 or 450/472–3477 (restaurant)* ⊕*www.rochedesbrises.com* ☾*Mid-Feb.–Dec.*

☺ **Hudson.** A quick detour on the ferry (C$8.50 one-way) across Lac des Deux-Montagnes brings you to this small town with old homes housing art galleries, boutiques, and Christmas shops. In winter there's an ice bridge: basically a plowed path across a well-frozen lake. Taking a walk across the bridge is a singular experience.

Parc d'Oka. Surrounded by low hills, the park has a lake fringed by a sandy beach with picnic areas and hiking and biking trails. This is a good place for kayaking, canoeing, fishing, and, in winter, snowshoeing and cross-country skiing. There are nearly 900 campsites here. ⊠*2020 chemin Oka* ☎*450/479–8365, 800/665–6527 activities* ⊕*www.sepaq. com* 🖼*C$3.50 plus C$6.25 per car* ☾*Daily 8 AM–8 PM.*

WHERE TO STAY

$$ 🏨 **Hotel du Lac Carling.** The modern but classically furnished hotel is near Lachute (about 40 km [25 mi] northwest of Oka) and on the doorstep to 5,000 acres of wilderness. In addition to a large sports center, 20 km (12 mi) of cross-country ski trails, and an excellent par-72 golf course, there's also an impressive restaurant. The menu includes salmon smoked by the chef. The hotel's rooms are furnished with oil paintings, and antiques line the corridors. The standard rooms are among the largest in the province. Loft suites, with kitchenettes and fireplaces, are entered from the upper floor. **Pros:** lakefront; spectacular grounds; reasonable package deals. **Cons:** rooms could use updating; aside from the pool, there are no significant on-site activities for children. ⊠*2255 Rte. 327 Nord, Grenville-sur-la-Rouge* ☎*450/533–9211 or 800/661–9211* ⊕*www.laccarling.com* 📞*90 rooms, 9 suites* ⚄*In-room: safe, kitchen (some), refrigerator, Wi-Fi. In-hotel: restaurant, room service, bars, golf course, tennis courts, pool, gym, spa,*

The Laurentians (les Laurentides)

beachfront, bicycles, laundry service, no-smoking rooms, some pets allowed ▤*AE, MC, V* ⦾ι*BP.*

ST-JÉRÔME

60 km (37 mi) north of Oka.

Founded in 1834, St-Jérôme is a thriving economic center and cultural hub. The town first gained prominence in 1868, when Curé Antoine Labelle became a pastor of this parish. His most important legacy was the famous P'tit Train du Nord railroad line, which he persuaded the government to build in order to open St-Jérôme to travel and trade.

WHAT TO SEE

Linear Park *(Parc Linéaire).* The P'tit Train du Nord no longer exists, but in 1996 the track was transformed into the 200-km (124-mi) Linear Park. From the moment it opened, the park proved hugely popular. The well-signed trail starts at the former railway station (1 Place de la Gare) in St-Jérôme and is used mostly by cyclists (walkers use it at their peril, because the bikers hurtle by quickly). The path runs all the way to Mont-Laurier in the north. It's flanked by distance markers, so that cyclists can track their progress; some of the old railway stations and historic landmarks along the route have been converted into places where *vélo-touristes* (bike tourists) can stop for a snack. In winter the trail is taken over by cross-country skiers and snowmobilers.

Fodor'sChoice **Parc Régional de la Rivière du Nord.** The trails in this park, created as
★ a nature retreat, lead to the spectacular **Wilson Falls.** The **Pavillon Marie-Victorin** has summer weekend displays and workshops devoted to nature, culture, and history. You can hike, bike, cross-country ski, snowshoe, or snow-slide here. ⊠*750 chemin de la Rivière du Nord* ☎*450/431–1676* ▢*C$5 (summer), C$7 (winter)* ◷*Nov.–May, daily 9–5; June–Oct., daily 9–7.*

Promenade. St-Jérôme's promenade, stretching 4 km (2½ mi), follows the Rivière du Nord from the rue de Martigny bridge to the rue St-Joseph bridge. Descriptive plaques en route highlight episodes of the 1837 Rebellion, a French-Canadian uprising.

SPORTS & THE OUTDOORS

Parachutisme Adrénaline. This parachuting school and flying center, 15 minutes from St-Jérôme, caters to novice and seasoned jumpers alike (C$250–C$275 per person for beginners). ⊠*881 rue Lamontagne, St-Jérôme* ☎*450/438–0855 or 866/306–0855* ⊞*450/438–0585* ⊕*www. paradrenaline.ca.*

ST-SAUVEUR-DES-MONTS

25 km (16 mi) north of St-Jérôme, 63 km (39 mi) north of Montréal.

The town of St-Sauveur encompasses St-Sauveur-des-Monts, a focal point for area resorts. Rue Principale, the main street, has dozens of restaurants serving everything from lamb brochettes to spicy Thai fare.

The narrow strip is so choked with cars and tourists in summer that it's called Crescent Street of the North, after the action-filled street in Montréal. Despite all this development, St-Sauveur-des-Monts has maintained some of its rural character.

Skiing and other snow sports are the main things to do in winter here. Mont-St-Sauveur, Mont-Avila, Mont-Gabriel, and Mont-Olympia all have special season passes and programs, and some ski-center passes can be used at more than one center in the region. Blue signs on Route 117 and Autoroute 15 indicate where the ski hills are.

WHAT TO SEE

☺ **Mont-St-Sauveur Water Park.** Mont-St-Sauveur Water Park keeps children occupied with slides, a giant wave pool, a wading pool, and snack bars. The rafting river attracts an older, braver crowd; the nine-minute ride follows the natural contours of steep hills. On the tandem slides, plumes of water flow through figure-eight tubes. ⊠ *350 rue St-Denis* ☎ *450/227–4671* ⊕ *www.mssi.ca* ⊠ *Full day C$33, after 3 PM C$27, after 5 PM C$19* ⊙ *Early June–mid-June and late Aug.–early Sept., daily 10–5; mid-June–mid-Aug., daily 10–7.*

WHERE TO STAY & EAT

$$ ✕ **Le Bifthèque.** French Canadians flock to this local institution for perfectly aged steaks and other hearty fare. This branch of the chain, in the heart of St-Sauveur, also serves lamb loin with Dijon mustard and trout stuffed with crab and shrimp. Pick up steaks to go at the meat counter if you're staying someplace where you can grill your own. ⊠ *86 rue de la Gare* ☎ *450/227–2442* ▤ *AE, MC, V* ⊙ *No lunch Mon.–Thurs.*

$$ **Relais St-Denis.** A traditional sloping Québécois roof and dormer windows cap this inn, where every guest room has a fireplace. Junior suites have whirlpool baths. They now have a health center and spa on premises. La Treille de Bacchus ($$–$$$$) serves multi-course meals with an emphasis on regional cuisine. **Pros:** walking distance to restaurants, outlet shopping, etc., in St-Sauveur; gourmet French restaurant on premises. **Cons:** there are no activities offered for children. ⊠ *61 rue St-Denis,* ☎ *450/227–4766 or 888/997–4766* ⊕ *www.relaisstdenis. com* ⇆ *18 rooms, 24 suites* ⚘ *In-room: refrigerator, Wi-Fi. In-hotel: restaurant, bar, pool, no-smoking rooms, some pets allowed* ▤ *AE, D, MC, V* ⊚ *CP, MAP.*

SPORTS & THE OUTDOORS

La Vallée de St-Sauveur. This is the collective name for the ski area north of St-Sauveur-des-Monts. The area is especially well known for its night skiing.

Mont-Avila. This mountain has 11 trails (2 rated for beginners, 3 at an intermediate level, and 6 for experts), three lifts, and a 615-foot vertical drop. ⊠ *500 chemin Avila, Piedmont* ☎ *450/227–4671 or 514/871–0101* ⊕ *www.mssi.ca.*

Mont-St-Sauveur. Mont-St-Sauveur has 38 trails (17 for beginning and intermediate-level skiers, 16 for experts, and 5 that are extremely difficult), eight lifts, and a vertical drop of 700 feet. ⊠ *350 ave. St-Denis, St-Sauveur* ☎ *450/227–4671, 514/871–0101, or 800/363–2426* ⊕ *www.mssi.ca.*

Station de Ski Mont-Habitant. Featuring 11 trails (4 rated beginner, 2 difficult, 1 extreme, 4 intermediate), three lifts, and a vertical drop of 600 feet, Ski Mont-Habitant is a choice hill for both novice and intermediate-level skiers. ⊠*12 blvd. des Skieurs, St-Sauveur-des-Monts* ☎*450/227–2637 or 866/887–2637* ⊕*www.monthabitant.com.*

SHOPPING

FodorsChoice **Factoreries St-Sauveur.** Canadian, American, and European manufac-
★ turers sell goods, from designer clothing to household items, at this emporium at reduced prices. The factory-outlet mall has more than 25 stores and sells labels such as Guess, Nike, Jones New York, and Reebok. ⊠*100 rue Guindon, Autoroute 15, Exit 60.* ☎ 800/363-0332 ⊕*www.factoreries.com*

Rue Principale. Fashion boutiques and gift shops adorned with bright awnings and flowers line this popular shopping street.

MORIN HEIGHTS

10 km (6 mi) west of St-Sauveur-des-Monts, 73 km (45 mi) northwest of Montréal.

The town's British architecture and population reflect its settlers' heritage; most residents here speak English. Although Morin Heights has escaped the overdevelopment of neighboring St-Sauveur, there are still many restaurants, bookstores, boutiques, and craft shops to explore.

In summer, windsurfing, swimming, and canoeing on the area's two lakes—Claude and Lafontaine—are popular. You can also head for the region's golf courses (including the 18 holes at Mont-Gabriel) and the campgrounds at Val David and the two lakes, which have beaches. In fall and winter, come for the foliage and the alpine and Nordic skiing.

WHERE TO STAY & EAT

$$$$ ✕ **Auberge Restaurant Clos Joli.** If you're looking for superior French cui-
FodorsChoice sine and are prepared to pay top dollar for the privilege, this family-
★ owned and -operated establishment offers an outstanding gastronomic experience. Award-winning chef Gemma Morin cooks up a wide variety of dishes, but locals will tell you that her legendary venison dishes are to die for. The Sunday brunch is said to be the finest in the Laurentians. ⊠*19 chemin du Clos Joli, J0R 1H0* ☎*450/226–5401or 866/511–9999* ⊕*www.aubergeclosjoli.net* ☰*AE, MC, V* ☉*No lunch.*

$$$ ✕ **Le Petit Prince.** Many locals adore this restaurant in a tiny blue-shingled wood house on a side road near Highway 364 that runs through Morin Heights. Lace curtains on the windows and wood walls accent the bistro-style cuisine. Scallops in Pernod sauce and grilled rib steak are excellent choices. ⊠*139 rue Watchorn,* ☎*450/226–6887* ☰*AE, MC, V* ☉*Closed Mon. and Tues. No lunch.*

$$ ⊞ **Le Flamant et la Tortue.** This charming auberge is set in a beautifully wooded area within striking range of a small, pristine lake. Although the rooms are spartan, they are comfortable, clean, and relatively inexpensive. The outdoor terrace here is one of the most pleasant places to relax in the entire region. **Pros:** enclosed, mosquito-free riverside terrace; tranquil environment; isolated but less than an hour from Montréal; offers an evening of traditional folk music "Soirée Canadienne." **Cons:** small rooms; no a/c. ⊠796 *chemin St-Adolphe,* ☎450/226–2009 *or* 877/616–2009 ⊕*www.aubergeleflamantetlatortue.ca* ⤵*12 rooms* ⏃*In-room: no a/c, no TV. In-hotel: restaurant, bar, no elevator, no-smoking rooms* ⊟*MC, V.*

SPORTS & THE OUTDOORS

Ski Morin Heights. The vertical drop at this ski resort is 656 feet. There are 24 trails, including 8 for beginners, 7 each for intermediate and expert levels, and 1 glade run. The 44,000-square-foot chalet houses eateries, a pub, a day-care center, and equipment rental, but the center doesn't have lodging. ⊠*231 rue Bennett, near Exit 60 off Autoroute 15 Nord* ☎*450/227–2020* ⊕*www.mssi.ca.*

STE-ADÈLE

12 km (7 mi) north of Morin Heights, 85 km (53 mi) north of Montréal.

With a permanent population of more than 10,000, Ste-Adèle is the largest community in the lower part of the Laurentians. A number of government offices and facilities for local residents are here: cinemas, shopping malls, and summer theater (in French). Of interest to visitors are the sports shops, boutiques, restaurants, and family-oriented amusements.

WHAT TO SEE

☺ **Au Pays des Merveilles.** Fairy-tale characters such as Snow White, Little Red Riding Hood, and Alice in Wonderland wander the grounds, playing games with children. Small fry may also enjoy the petting zoo, amusement rides, wading pool, and puppet show. A ride called Le Petit Train des Merveilles (the Marvelous Little Train) is a nod to the historic train that launched the tourism industry in the Laurentians. There are 52 activities, enough to occupy those aged two to nine for about half a day. Check the Web site for discount coupons. The theme park is 100% accessible to wheelchairs. ⊠*3795 rue de la Savane* ☎*450/229–3141* ⊜*450/229–4148* ⊕*www.paysmerveilles.com* ⊠*C$15* ☉*Mid-June–late Aug., daily 10–6.*

WHERE TO STAY & EAT

$$$$ ✕**La Clef des Champs.** The French food served at this romantic restaurant tucked amid trees is quite good. Game dishes, such as medallions of roasted ostrich in a port-infused sauce, grilled venison, or caribou in red-currant marinade, are specialties. Good dessert choices include *gâteaux aux deux chocolats* (two-chocolate cake) and crème brûlée. For C$110 there is a *menu dégustation* (tasting menu) if you're looking to sample a little bit of everything. ⊠*875 chemin Pierre-Péladeau* ☎*450/229–2857* ⊟*AE, DC, MC, V* ☉*Closed Mon. No lunch.*

$$$ ▥**L'Eau à la Bouche.** Superb service, stunning rooms awash with
Fodor'sChoice color, a Nordic spa, and a terrace with a flower garden are high-
★ lights of this charming inn. Guest rooms, some with fireplaces, are

9

decorated in styles that include Victorian, safari, and Inuit. Skiing is literally at your door, since the inn faces Le Chantecler's slopes. The restaurant here ($$$$) interprets nouvelle cuisine with regional ingredients. The menu changes with the seasons, but it has included foie gras with apple-cider sauce, pan-seared large shrimp with fava beans, shiitake mushrooms, and ginger, and roasted thick beef with garlic and rosemary jus. Owner-chef Anne Desjardins, a well-known and highly regarded Québécois personality, offers a two-day cooking course ($575), which includes two working days in the kitchen, one night's lodging, and a table d'hote dinner among other perks (weekends only). **Pros:** outstanding restaurant; stunning outdoor Nordic spa. **Cons:** located uncomfortably close to busy highway; some rooms could use updating. ⊠ *3003 blvd. Ste-Adèle,* ☎ *450/229–2991 or 888/828–2991* ⊕ *www.leaualabouche.com* ⊲ *21 rooms, 1 suite* ♿ *In-room: Wi-Fi. In-hotel: restaurant, bar, pool, no elevator, laundry service, no-smoking rooms* ▤ *AE, DC, MC, V* ⦿ *EP.*

$$ ▦ **Auberge & Spa Beaux Rêves.** Rooms at this rustic Québécois retreat along a riverbank give you plenty of space in which to spread out. The fieldstone building has hardwood floors; furnishings are spare, but all the suites have fireplaces and Jacuzzis. The outdoor hot tub and Finnish sauna are used year-round. Breakfast (brought to your room) and lunch are available, but they no longer serve dinner. **Pros:** offers personalized packages tailored to meet specific needs; all rooms overlook river and have balconies or walk-out terraces. **Cons:** can be noisy due to close proximity to the road; no phone or television in rooms; no pool; no dinner service. ⊠ *2310 blvd. Ste-Adèle,* ☎ *450/229–9226 or 800/279–7679* ⊕ *www.beauxreves.com* ⊲ *6 rooms, 6 suites* ♿ *In-room: no phone, no TV. In-hotel: restaurant, spa, no-smoking rooms, no elevator* ▤ *MC, V* ⦿ *CP.*

$$ ▦ **Le Chantecler.** This favorite of Montrealers is nestled alongside lovely Lac Ste-Adèle. The rooms and chalets, furnished with Canadian pine, have a rustic appeal. Given all the activities here, which include snowshoeing with a trapper as well as cycling races, Le Chantecler is for people looking for an energetic holiday. **Pros:** friendly, helpful staff; lakeside rooms. **Cons:** due to its outstanding reputation, early bookings are highly recommended. ⊠ *1474 chemin Chantecler,* ☎ *450/229–3555 or 888/916–1616* ⊕ *www.lechantecler.com* ⊲ *186 rooms, 29 suites, 7 chalets* ♿ *In-room: a/c, kitchen (some), refrigerator, Wi-Fi. In-hotel: restaurant, room service, bar, golf course, tennis courts, pool, gym, spa, beachfront, bicycles, concierge, children's programs (ages 6 and older), laundry service, no-smoking rooms* ▤ *AE, D, DC, MC, V* ⦿ *EP.*

$$ ▦ **Hôtel Mont-Gabriel.** Built by Josephine Hartford Bryce, whose grandfather founded the A&P grocery chain, the hotel started as a log structure with about a dozen rooms. The site has evolved into a 1,200-acre resort where you can relax in a contemporary room with a valley view or commune with nature in a rustic-style cabin with a fireplace. In winter you can ski out from many rooms. The French cuisine ($$$$) is good, with entrées such as salmon rottolo with balsamic sauce and duck breast with black cherries. **Pros:** beautiful grounds; some rooms with mountain views; some rooms with wheelchair accessibility. **Cons:**

food is good but pricey for what you get. ✉*1699 chemin du Mont-Gabriel (Autoroute 15, Exit 64),* ☎*450/229–3547, 800/668–5253, or 450/229–3547* ⊕*www.montgabriel.com* ⤴*129 rooms, 1 suite, 2 chalets* ⟐*In-room: Wi-Fi. In-hotel: restaurant, room service, bar, golf course, tennis courts, pools, gym, spa, no-smoking rooms* ▤*AE, DC, MC, V* ⍟*EP.*

SPORTS & THE OUTDOORS

GOLF **Club de Golf Chantecler.** This par-72, 18-hole (6,215 yards) course is off Exit 67 of Autoroute 15. Greens fees range from C$31.89 on weekdays to C$39.87 on weekends. ✉*2520 chemin du Club* ☎*450/476–1339 or 450/229–3742* ⊕*www.golflechantecler.com.*

SKIING **Ski Mont-Gabriel.** About 19 km (12 mi) northeast of Ste-Adèle, Mont-Gabriel has 18 superb downhill trails, which are primarily for intermediate and advanced skiers, and seven lifts. The vertical drop is 656 feet. ✉*1501 chemin du Mont-Gabriel, Ste-Adèle* ☎*450/227–1100 or 514/871–0101* ⊕*www.skimontgabriel.com.*

ESTÉREL

15 km (9 mi) north of Ste-Adèle, 100 km (62 mi) north of Montréal.

The permanent population of Estérel is just more than 2,400, but visitors to the Estérel Resort and Convention Centre off Route 370, at Exit 69 near Ste-Marguerite Station, swell the total population throughout the year. Founded in the 1920s on the shores of Lac Dupuis, the 5,000-acre estate was named Estérel by Baron Louis Empain because it evoked memories of his native village in Provence. In 1959 Fridolin Simard bought the property, and Hôtel l'Estérel soon became a household word for Québécois in search of a first-class resort.

WHERE TO STAY & EAT

$$$$ ✕ **Bistro à Champlain.** Its astonishing selection of wines—some 2,000—
FodorsChoice put this bistro on the map. You can tour the cellars, housing 35,000
★ bottles (at last count) with prices from C$28 to C$25,000. The restaurant is in a former general store built in 1864. The C$82 menu dégustation includes a different wine with each of several courses. Fillet of Angus beef in red wine, and pan-fried scallops with tomato and eggplant ratatouille in white wine are typical dishes. ✉*75 chemin Masson, Ste-Marguerite-du-lac-Masson* ☎*450/228–4988 or 450/228–4949* ⊕*www.bistroachamplain.com* ▤*AE, DC, MC, V* ⊙*Summer, Tues.–Sun. from 6 PM; winter, Wed.–Sat. from 6 PM.*

$$ ⌂ **Estérel Resort and Convention Centre.** Dogsledding and an ice-skating disco are two of the more unusual options at this resort, where buses shuttle guests to nearby downhill ski sites. In summer, comfortable air-conditioned rooms have a view of either the lake or the beautiful flower gardens. On weekdays the resort tends to attract groups and conventioneers. Following the lead of the airlines, it offers "name your price" deals on rooms, available only online. Only table d'hôte meals are available at dinner. **Pros:** the wide selection of activities (from dog-sledding to hiking to golf), particularly focusing on activities/pro-

grams for children starting as young as 18 months old. **Cons:** poor desk service; room temperature hard to control; outdated TVs and room furnishings. ⊠*39 blvd. Fridolin Simard,* ☎*450/228–2571 or 888/378–3735* ⊕*www.esterel.com* ⇦*121 rooms, 3 suites* ⚫*In-hotel: restaurant, room service, bar, golf course, tennis court, pool, gym, spa, beachfront, water sports, bicycles, no elevator, laundry service, public Wi-Fi, no-smoking rooms* ▤*AE, DC, MC, V* ⦿*BP.*

VAL DAVID

18 km (11 mi) west of Estérel, 82 km (51 mi) north of Montréal.

Besides being a center for arts and crafts, Val David is a premier destination for mountain climbers, hikers, and campers. Offering several galleries and marvelous art shops, Val David is a renowned cultural village that many Québec artists and artisans call home.

WHAT TO SEE

☾ **Village du Père Noël** *(Santa Claus Village).* At Santa Claus's summer residence kids can sit on his knee and speak to him in French or English. The grounds contain bumper boats, a petting zoo (with goats, sheep, horses, and colorful birds), games, and a large outdoor pool. There is a snack bar, but visitors are encouraged to bring their own food (there are numerous picnic tables). ⊠*987 rue Morin* ☎*819/322–2146 or 800/287–6635* ⊕*www.noel.qc.ca* ▤*C$11.50* ⦿*Early June–late Aug., daily 10–6; Dec. 22–Jan. 6, daily 11–5.*

WHERE TO STAY

$$$ ▦**Hôtel La Sapinière.** This homey, wood-frame hotel overlooks a lake surrounded by fir trees *(sapins* in French). Rooms have country-style furnishings and pastel floral accents, and come with thick terry robes. Some have romantic four-poster beds and fireplaces. The property is renowned for its French nouvelle cuisine ($$$–$$$$): salmon smoked on the premises comes with black-olive tapenade, and bison is cooked in a red-wine sauce with shiitake mushrooms. For dessert, try the mascarpone cheese mousse with berries and a spicy fruit terrine. **Pros:** excellent food at restaurant, lakeside terrace, direct access to popular cycling route "Le P'tit Train du Nord." **Cons:** no Internet access in rooms. ⊠*1244 chemin de la Sapinière,* ☎*819/322–2020 or 800/567–6635* ⊕*www.sapiniere.com* ⇦*44 rooms, 25 suites* ⚫*In-room: refrigerator (some). In-hotel: restaurant, room service, bar, tennis courts, pool, gym, bicycles, laundry service, no-smoking rooms, no elevator* ▤*AE, DC, MC, V* ⦿*MAP.*

SPORTS & THE OUTDOORS

Centre de Ski Vallée-Bleue. Geared toward intermediate and expert skiers, Vallée-Bleue has 17 trails, 4 lifts, and a vertical drop of 365 feet. ⊠*1418 chemin Vallée-Bleue* ☎*819/322–3427 or 866/322–3427* ⊕*www.vallee-bleue.com.*

Mont-Alta. This ski resort has 27 downhill trails—about 40 percent of them for advanced skiers—and one lift. The vertical drop is 584 feet. ⊠*2114 Rte. 117* ☎*819/322–3206* ⊕*www.mont-alta.com.*

SHOPPING

1001 Pots. One of the most interesting events in Val David is this boutique, which showcases the Japanese-style pottery of Kinya Ishikawa—as well as pieces by some 110 other ceramists. The exhibition takes place from mid-July through mid-August. Ishikawa's studio also displays work by his wife, Marie-Andrée Benoît, who makes fish-shaped bowls with a texture derived from pressing canvas on the clay. There are workshops for adults and children throughout the exhibition and there is a tea salon on premises. ⊠ *L'Atelier du Potier, 2435 rue de l'Église* ☎ *819/322–6868* ⊕ *www.1001pots.com* ☯ *July–Aug., daily 10–6; call for hrs in other seasons.*

Atelier Bernard Chaudron, Inc. Atelier Bernard Chaudron sells hand-forged, lead-free pewter objects d'art such as oil lamps, plus hammered-silver beer mugs, pitchers, and candleholders, as well as some crystal. ⊠ *2449 chemin de l'Île* ☎ *819/322–3944 or 888/322–3944* ⊕ *www.chaudron.ca.*

La Verdure. Everything from wood walking sticks to duck decoys and gold, platinum, and silver jewelry is made by the owner, Paul Simard. ⊠ *1310 Dion* ☎ *819/322–7813.*

STE-AGATHE-DES-MONTS

5 km (3 mi) north of Val David, 96 km (60 mi) northwest of Montréal.

The wide, sandy beaches of Lac des Sables are the most surprising feature of Ste-Agathe-des-Monts, a tourist town best known for its ski hills. Water activities include canoeing, kayaking, swimming, and fishing. Ste-Agathe is also a stopover point on the Linear Park, the bike trail between St-Jérôme and Mont-Laurier.

WHERE TO STAY

$ 　**Auberge Watel.** A steep driveway leads up to this white-painted, distinguished hotel overlooking Lac des Sables. Inside, the lounge and restaurant are decorated in a casual country style. Some rooms have a double-size Jacuzzi, a fireplace, and a balcony with a superb view of the lake. You have a choice of either a basic motel-style room or a larger room with pine or wicker furnishings. **Pros:** adjacent to three beaches, close proximity to boutiques and cultural activities in Ste-Agathe. **Cons:** not all rooms have lake view. ⊠ *250 rue St-Venant,* ☎ *819/326–7016 or 800/363–6478* ⊕ *www.watel.ca* ⋗ *25 rooms* ⚲ *In-room: Wi-Fi. In-hotel: restaurant, bar, pool, beachfront, no-smoking rooms, elevator* ▤ *AE, MC, V* ⦿ *MAP.*

¢ ⚠ **Au Parc des Campeurs.** In the woods near a lively resort area, this spacious campground has activities for all age groups, from sport competitions to outings for the kids. There's a sandy beach where you can rent canoes and kayaks and launch your boat from the town's marina. Reservations are recommended. ⚲ *Flush toilets, pit toilets, full hookups, partial hookups, dump station, drinking water, guest laundry, showers, fire pits, picnic tables, food service, electricity, public telephone, general store, swimming (lake)* ⋗ *482 tent sites, 67 RV sites* ⊠ *Lac* *des Sables and Rte. 329,* ☎*819/324–0482 or 800/561–7360* ⊕*www. parcdescampeurs.com* ▤*MC, V* ⊘*Mid-May–Sept.*

SPORTS & THE OUTDOORS

24 Heures de la Voile. Sailing is the favorite summer sport around here, especially during the 24 Heures de la Voile, a weekend sailing competition that takes place in mid-July.

Alouette V and VI. These sightseeing boats offer guided 50-minute tours of Lac des Sables. They leave the dock at least five times a day from mid-May to mid-October and six times a day in July and August. ⊠*Municipal Dock, rue Principale* ☎*819/326–3656 or 866/326–3656* ⊕*www.croisierealouette.com*

MONT-TREMBLANT

★ *25 km (16 mi) north of Ste-Agathe-des-Monts, 100 km (62 mi) north of Montréal.*

Mont-Tremblant, at more than 3,000 feet, is the highest peak in the Laurentians and a major draw for skiers. It's also the name of a nearby village. The resort area at the foot of the mountain (called simply Tremblant) is spread around 14-km-long (9-mi-long) Lac Tremblant. *Ski* magazine consistently rates it among the top ski resorts in eastern North America.

The hub of the resort is a pedestrians-only village that looks a bit like a displaced Québec City. The buildings, constructed in the style of New France, with dormer windows and steep roofs, house pubs, restaurants, boutiques, sports shops, a movie theater, self-catering condominiums, and hotels. A historical town this is not: built for the resort, it may strike you as a bit of Disney in the mountains.

WHAT TO SEE

Fodor'sChoice **Parc National du Mont-Tremblant.** Created in 1894, the park was the
★ home of the Algonquins, who called this area Manitonga Soutana, meaning "mountain of the spirits." Today it's a vast wildlife sanctuary of more than 400 lakes and rivers holding nearly 200 species of birds and animals, including moose, bears, and beavers. In winter its trails are used by cross-country skiers, snowshoers, and snowmobilers. Camping and canoeing are the main summer activities. Entrance to the park is C$3.50; the main entry point is through the town of St-Donat, about 45 minutes north of Mont-Tremblant, via routes 329 and 125. ☎*819/688–2281* ⊕*www.sepaq.com.*

WHERE TO STAY & EAT

$$$$ ✕**Restaurant Le Cheval de Jade.** "The Jade Horse" specializes in French haute cuisine. The elegant dining room has lace curtains, white linens, and ivory china. The food is the real thing—local ingredients and organic produce are used to create classic French fare such as rack of lamb, bouillabaisse, and tiger prawns flambéed with rum and spicy pineapple sauce. Their Discovery menu (C$149) includes wild boar and seared foie gras and their Gastronomic menu (C$176) features snow camp and Matane shrimp cake as well as grilled red tuna fil-

let with raspberry vinaigrette and fine herbs. ✉*688 rue de St-Jovite, Mont-Tremblant* ☎*819/425–5233* ⊕*www.chevaldejade.com* ⚅*Reservations essential* ▤*AE, DC, V* ⊘*Closed Sun.–Mon. No lunch.*

$$$ ✗**Auberge du Coq de Montagne.** This restaurant on Lac Moore (which opens onto a terrace during the summer months), five minutes from the ski slopes, has garnered much praise for its Italian cuisine. Menu offerings include tried-and-true favorites such as veal Marsala and veal *fiorentina* (cooked with spinach and cheese). Hosts Nino and Kay are reputed to be some of the friendliest folks you'll ever meet—and they prepare good food, too! ✉*2151 chemin du Village* ☎*819/425–3380 or 800/895–3380* ⚅*Reservations essential* ▤*AE, MC, V.*

$$$$ ⌗**Hotel Club Tremblant.** Built as a family house in the early 1900s, this building has been a rooming house, brothel, and private club. Now a European-owned hotel, it's just down the lakeside road from the ski station at Mont-Tremblant. The original log-cabin lodge is furnished in a colonial style, with wooden staircases and huge stone fireplaces. Rustic but comfortable, it has excellent facilities. The French restaurant ($$$–$$$$), helmed by award-winning chef Jocelyn Lemieux, is outstanding. Both the main lodge and the split-level condominium complex (with fireplaces, private balconies or patios, and kitchenettes), up the hill from the lodge, have magnificent views of Mont-Tremblant. A complimentary shuttle takes you to the ski hills. **Pros:** Excellent service; beautiful, tranquil grounds. **Cons:** Saturday night buffet can be inconsistent in terms of selection and quality; not within walking distance from town. ✉*121 rue Cuttle,* ☎*819/425–2731 or 800/567–8341* ⊕*www.clubtremblant.com* ⇌*122 suites* ⚭*In-room: no a/c (some), kitchen, dial-up. In-hotel: restaurant, bar, tennis court, pool, gym, spa, beachfront, no elevator, concierge, children's programs (ages 4–16), no-smoking rooms, no elevator, pets allowed* ▤*AE, DC, MC, V* ❢*MAP.*

$$$$ ⌗**Quintessence.** This stone-and-wood all-suites hotel bills itself as the first boutique property in Mont-Tremblant. The quiet, chic Quintessence is on 3 acres along the shore of Lac Tremblant and near the ski slopes. Each suite has a king-size bed, a balcony or patio with lake views, a wood-burning fireplace, a stereo, and a bathroom with a heated marble floor and Jacuzzi. Service, including a ski shuttle and a concierge who can provide firewood, is an emphasis here. **Pros:** very large, elegant rooms ranging from 700 to 1,200 square feet; spectacular views of Lac Tremblant from every suite. **Cons:** very expensive. ✉*3004 chemin de la Chapelle,* ☎*819/425–3400 or 866/425–3400* ⊕*www.hotelquintessence.com* ⇌*30 suites, 1 cabin* ⚭*In-room: a/c, safe, refrigerator, VCR, Wi-Fi. In-hotel: restaurant, room service, bar, pool, gym, spa, concierge, laundry service, no-smoking rooms* ▤*AE, DC, MC, V* ❢*CP.*

$$$$ ⌗**Westin Resort–Tremblant.** The Westin, part of the Tremblant resort town and a short walk from the ski slopes, is plush and polished. Some rooms have fireplaces, most have balconies, and all have kitchenettes. The pathway to the heated saltwater pool and hot tub is also heated, enabling you to use these facilities all winter long. The chic Westin Lounge serves up traditional hearty fare like club sandwiches and

9

pasta, while at the Yamada restaurant ($$$) you can sample sushi in its many forms as well as a wide assortment of Japanese dishes. This is a no-smoking resort. **Pros:** excellent location just steps away from the town center; pets are allowed. **Cons:** too large and corporate to feel truly intimate. ✉ *100 chemin Kandahar,* ☎ *819/681–8000 or 800/937–8461* ⊕ *www.westin.com* ⇒ *55 rooms, 71 suites* ⚐ *In-room: kitchen, dial-up. In-hotel: restaurant, room service, pool, gym, spa, concierge, laundry service, no-smoking rooms, pets allowed* ⊟ *AE, D, DC, MC, V* ⏿ *EP.*

> ## THE GO-TO FOR SPA LOVERS
>
> Relax at the **Spa Nature Le Scandinave Mont-Tremblant** (✉ *4280 Montée Ryan, Mont-Tremblant* ☎ *819/425–5524 or 888/537–2263* ⊕ *www.scandi-nave.com*) by spending a few hours in their Finnish sauna, Norwegian steam bath, or by taking a dip in one of their several outdoor pools. Swedish massage is available, the grounds are delightful, and admission fees are refreshingly reasonable.

$$$ ⌂ **Fairmont Tremblant.** The sporty but classy centerpiece of the Tremblant resort area takes its cues from the historic railroad "castles" scattered throughout Canada. The hotel has wood paneling, copper and wrought-iron details, stained glass, and stone fireplaces. During ski season, guests on the Gold Floor receive complimentary breakfast, evening appetizers, and Internet access. Skiers can zoom off the mountain right into the ground-level deli, near the full-service spa. Elaborate themed buffets are the draw at the Windigo restaurant ($$$$). **Pros:** poolside barbecue during the summer months; pets allowed; easy access to ski hills. **Cons:** nature lovers may be disappointed to find that the hotel is in the center of a fairly busy village and not on more scenic grounds. ✉ *3045 chemin de la Chapelle, Box 100,* ☎ *819/681–7000 or 800/441–1414* ⊕ *www.fairmont.com/tremblant* ⇒ *314 rooms, 61 suites* ⚐ *In-room: kitchen (some), Wi-Fi. In-hotel: restaurant, room service, bar, pools, gym, spa, concierge, laundry service, public Wi-Fi, no-smoking rooms.* ⊟ *AE, DC, MC, V* ⏿ *BP.*

$$$ ⌂ **Le Grand Lodge.** This Scandinavian-style log-cabin hotel is on 13½ acres on Lac Ouimet. Accommodations, from studios to two-bedroom suites, are spacious, with kitchenettes, stone fireplaces, and balconies that overlook the water. The indoor-outdoor café, The Whisky Bar, which serves light dishes, also looks out on the lake. The more-formal Chez Borivage, which has a good wine cellar, specializes in French cuisine. Although the resort attracts a sizable number of business travelers here for conferences, it caters to families as well, with day-care facilities, a game room for teens, and activities that include making summer bonfires on the beach and taffy on the winter snow. **Pros:** friendly staff; good food; peaceful environment; ice rink and ice path in winter; very family-friendly. **Cons:** no pets allowed; no facilities for people with disabilities. ✉ *2396 rue Labelle,* ☎ *819/425–2734 or 800/567–6763* ⊕ *www.legrandlodge.com* ⇒ *11 rooms, 101 suites* ⚐ *In-room: kitchen, dial-up, Wi-Fi. In-hotel: restaurant, bar, tennis courts, pool, gym, spa, bicycles, concierge, laundry service, no-smoking rooms* ⊟ *AE, D, DC, MC, V* ⏿ *EP.*

SPORTS & THE OUTDOORS

Mont-Tremblant. With a 2,131-foot vertical drop, Mont-Tremblant has 94 downhill trails, 13 lifts, and 110 km (68 mi) of cross-country trails. The speedy Duncan Express is a quadruple chairlift; there's also a heated, high-speed gondola. **Versant Soleil** (sunny slope), the area on the other side of the mountain, has a vertical drop of 2,116 feet and 15 trails (including glade skiing) served by a high-speed quad chair that's capable of moving 2,250 people to the summit every hour. Sixty percent of the trails are for advanced or expert skiers only. The remainder are at an intermediate level. ☎ *800/461–8711 or 819/681–3000* ⊕ *www.tremblant.ca.*

THE EASTERN TOWNSHIPS

The Eastern Townships (also known as les Cantons de l'Est, and formerly as l'Estrie) refers to the area in the southeast corner of the province of Québec—bordering Vermont, New Hampshire, and Maine. By early spring the sugar shacks are busy with the new maple syrup. In summer, boating, swimming, sailing, golfing, in-line skating, hiking, and bicycling take over. And every fall the inns are booked solid with visitors eager to take in the brilliant foliage. Fall is also a good time to visit the wineries (although most are open all year). Because of its mild microclimate, the Townships area has become one of the fastest-developing wine regions in Canada, with a dozen of the more than 30 wineries in Québec province.

The Townships were populated by Empire Loyalists fleeing first the Revolutionary War and, later, the newly created United States of America. The Loyalists were followed, around 1820, by the first wave of Irish immigrants (ironically, Catholics fleeing their country's union with Protestant England). Some 20 years later the potato famine sent more Irish pioneers to the Townships. The area became more Francophone after 1850, as French Canadians moved in to work on the railroad and in the lumber industry. During the late 19th century, English families from Montréal and Americans from the border states began summering at cottages along the lakes.

GRANBY

80 km (50 mi) east of Montréal.

Granby, the western gateway to the Eastern Townships, is home to a notable zoo. It also hosts a number of annual festivals: among them are the Festival of Mascots and Cartoon Characters, a great favorite with youngsters and families, and the Granby International, an antique-car competition held at the Granby Autodrome. Both of these are held in July.

WHAT TO SEE

☺ ★ **Jardin Zoologique de Granby** *(Granby Zoo).* One of the biggest attractions in the area, the Granby Zoo houses some 1,000 animals representing 225 species in a naturally landscaped setting and with a focus on education. Zoo zones—from Africa to Oceania—allow you to visit Hippo's River, Gorilla's Valley, Lemur's Island, and more. Youngsters love the shark touch tanks and Amazoo, an aquatic park with turbulent wave pools and rides. At certain times of day keepers demonstrate the acrobatic skills of the birds of prey as well as the clever tricks of the elephants, who perform for the public like old circus pros. The complex includes amusement rides and souvenir shops, as well as a playground and picnic area. ⊠ *525 rue St-Hubert* ☎*450/372–9113 or 877/472–6299* ⊕*www.zoogranby.ca* ⊠*C$29.49* ☉*Mid-May–late June, daily 10–5; late June–end Aug., daily 10–7; Sept. and Oct., weekends only 10–5.*

SPORTS & THE OUTDOORS

Biking is big here. The quiet back roads lend themselves to exploring the region on two wheels, as does the 450-km-long (279-mi-long) network of bike-friendly trails. In the Townships, mountain biking is very popular.

Canada Cup. The mountain-biking season kicks off in late May with the Canada Cup, a 6-km (4-mi) race. ☎*450/534–3333* ⊕*www.cyclisme-bromont.ca.*

l'Estriade. One of the most popular bike and in-line-skating trails (and also the flattest), this 21-km (13-mi) paved trail links Granby to Waterloo.

Masters World Cup. Competitions for serious mountain bikers are held in summer, culminating in early September's Masters World Cup, which attracts competitors from around the world. ☎*450/534–3333* ⊕*www.cyclisme-bromont.ca.*

Montérégiade. This trail runs between Granby and Farnham, and is 21 km (13 mi) long.

La Route Verte *(The Green Route).* This is a province-wide network that is being expanded by leaps and bounds. For details and a map, contact **Vélo Québec** (☎*514/521–8356 or 800/567–8356* ⊕*www.routeverte.com*).

BROMONT

78 km (48 mi) east of Montréal.

The boating, camping, golf, horseback riding, swimming, tennis, biking, canoeing, fishing, hiking, cross-country and downhill skiing, and snowshoeing available here make this a place for all seasons. Bromont has the only night skiing in the Eastern Townships—and there's even a slope-side disco, Le Bromontais. The town also has more than 100 km (62 mi) of maintained trails for mountain bikers.

WHAT TO SEE

☺ **Bromont Aquatic Park.** This water park has more than 23 rides and games, including the Corkscrew and the Elephant's Trunk (where kids shoot out of a model of an elephant's head). Slides are divided into four degrees of difficulty, from easy to extreme (recommended for adults and older children only). Admission includes a chairlift ride to the top of the ski hill. From September through late October it's open only for

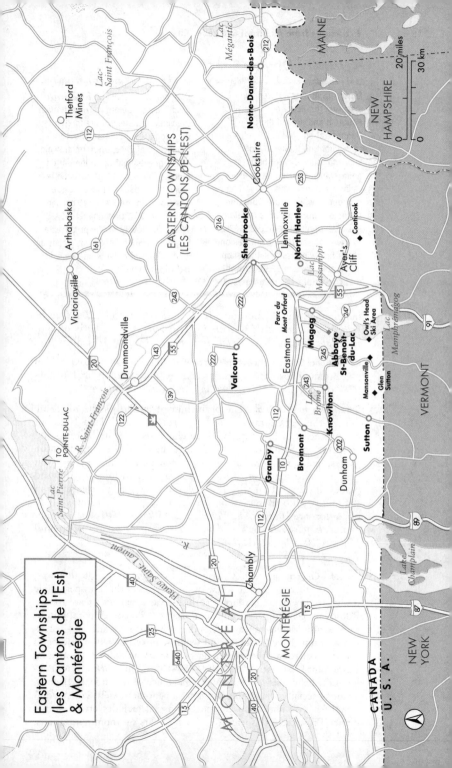

Eastern Townships (les Cantons de l'Est) & Montérégie

MAINE

NEW HAMPSHIRE

VERMONT

NEW YORK

Lac Saint François
Lac Mégantic
Lac Saint-Pierre
Lac Champlain
Lac Memphrémagog
Lac Massawippi
Lac Brome

Thetford Mines
Arthabaska
Victoriaville
Drummondville
Notre-Dame-des-Bois
Cookshire
Sherbrooke
Lennoxville
North Hatley
Coaticook
Ayer's Cliff
EASTERN TOWNSHIPS (LES CANTONS DE L'EST)
Parc du Mont Orford
Magog
Owl's Head Ski Area
Abbaye St-Benoît-du-Lac
Mansonville
Glen Sutton
Sutton
Valcourt
Eastman
Knowlton
Bromont
Granby
Dunham
Chambly
MONTÉRÉGIE
MONTRÉAL
Fleuve Saint-Laurent
R. Saint-François
TO POINTE-DU-LAC

CANADA
U.S.A.

20 miles
30 km

112, 161, 216, 243, 222, 143, 55, 20, 122, 139, 112, 245, 247, 253, 212, 55, 91, 89, 87, 202, 10, 15, 40, 25, 640

A Winery Driving Tour

Dunham. Almost a dozen wineries along the Route des Vins (Wine Route) in and around the town of Dunham, about 20 km (12 mi) south of Bromont on Route 202, offer tastings and tours. Call for business hours, which can be erratic, especially in autumn, when harvesting is under way. **Vignoble Domaine Côtes d'Ardoise** (✉ 879 rue Bruce, Rte. 202, Dunham ☎ 450/295–2020 ⊕ www.cotesdardoise.com) was one of the first wineries to set up shop in the area, back in 1980. **Vignoble de l'Orpailleur** (✉ 1086 Rte. 202,

Dunham ☎ 450/295–2763 ⊕ www.orpailleur.ca.). Before walking through the vineyard here, be sure to stop by the ecomuseum to learn about the production of wine, from the growing of the grapes right up to the bottling process. There's a gift shop, patio restaurant, and daily tastings. **Vignoble Les Trois Clochers** (✉ 341 chemin Bruce, Rte. 202, Dunham ☎ 450/295–2034). This lovely winery produces a dry, fruity white from Seyval grapes as well as several other white, ice, and red wines.

mountain biking. ✉ *Autoroute 10, Exit 78* ☎ *450/534–2200* ⊕ *www.skibromont.com* 🎟 *C$32 with 50% off after 3 PM* ☉ *Early or mid-June–late Aug., daily 10–5; late June–mid-Aug., daily 10–6:30.*

International Bromont Equestrian Competition. Once an Olympic equestrian site, Bromont hosts this equestrian competition every July. ☎ *450/534–0787 or 450/534–3255* ⊕ *www.internationalbromont.org.*

☺ **Safari Aventure Loowak.** The brainchild of butterfly collector Serge Poirier, this park sprawls over 500 acres of wooded land 10 km (6 mi) northeast of Bromont. With an emphasis on team building and cooperation, Safari Loowak has more than 40 different adventure games, including an Indiana Jones–theme guided tour in which you head off into the bush to hunt for treasure and look for downed planes. It's a great hit with little ones, but parents get caught up in the fantasy, too. Reservations are essential. ✉ *475 Horizon blvd., off Autoroute 10, Exit 88, Waterloo* ☎ *450/539–0501* ⊕ *www.safariloowak.qc.ca* 🎟 *C$15 and up per person (4-person minimum)* ☉ *Daily 10–5 by reservation.*

WHERE TO STAY

$$$ 🏨 **Hôtel Château Bromont.** Massages, "electropuncture," algae wraps, and aromatherapy are just a few of the services at this European-style resort. It also includes a large, Turkish-style *hammam* (steam room). Rooms are generally large and comfortable, with contemporary furniture. Sunny Mediterranean colors dress the atrium walls, and center-facing rooms have balconies and window boxes. Greenery and patio furniture surround the swimming pool in the middle of the atrium. Restaurant Les Quatres Canards ($$$–$$$$)—with chef Jacques Poulin at the helm—serves regional cuisine, much of which features duck, an area specialty. The dining room has a panoramic view. For an additional fee, you may choose a meal plan that includes breakfast and dinner. **Pros:** recently spent 1.2 million dollars on room renovations;

outdoor hot tubs; friendly staff. **Cons:** some rooms are on the small side so specify which type of room you want when reserving; windows do not open in rooms that face the hotel interior, and thus can cause rooms to feel claustrophobic. ⊠*90 rue Stanstead,* ☎*450/534–3433 or 800/304–3433* ⊕*www.chateaubromont.com* ⤵*164 rooms, 8 suites* ⌂*In-hotel: 2 restaurants, bar, pools, spa, public Wi-Fi, no-smoking rooms* ▤*AE, D, DC, MC, V* ⍟*EP.*

$$ ⊞**Hôtel Le Menhir.** Set among the rolling hills of the Townships and with great views of the local countryside from every room, this modern hotel is well priced, considering all the amenities available. The indoor pool, sauna, and whirlpool, along with its proximity to some of the best ski hills in the area, make this a great choice for a winter getaway. **Pros:** the outstanding views from each room; friendly staff; proximity to ski hill. **Cons:** lack of an elevator makes it difficult for guests on the upper floors especially with ski equipment and luggage. ⊠*125 blvd. Bromont,* ☎*450/534–3790 or 800/461–3790* ⊕*www.hotellemenhir.com* ⤵*41 rooms* ⌂*In-room: (some) kitchen, Wi-Fi. In-hotel: bar, pool, no-smoking rooms, no elevator* ▤*AE, MC, V.*

SPORTS & THE OUTDOORS

Royal Bromont. This is a superior 18-hole, par-72, bent-grass course. Greens fees are C$25–C$65 and an additional C$33 to rent a cart. ⊠*400 chemin Compton* ☎*450/534–4653 or 888/281–0017* 🖨*450/534–4577* ⊕*www.royalbromont.com.*

Station de Ski Bromont. With 54 trails for downhill skiing (30 of which are lighted for night skiing), Ski Bromont was the site of the 1986 World Cup Slalom. The vertical drop is 1,336 feet, and there are nine lifts. Hiking and mountain biking are popular here in summer and early fall. ⊠*150 rue Champlain* ☎*450/534–2200 or 866/276–6668* 🖨*450/534–4617* ⊕*www.skibromont.com.*

SHOPPING

Shopping for bargains at yard sales and flea markets is a popular weekend activity in the Townships.

Fodor'sChoice ★ **Bromont Five-Star Flea Market.** The gigantic sign on Autoroute 10 is hard to miss. More than 1,000 vendors sell their wares here—everything from T-shirts to household gadgets—each Saturday and Sunday from May to the end of October, 10 AM–6 PM. Shoppers come from Montréal as well as Vermont, just over the border.

SUTTON

106 km (66 mi) southeast of Montréal.

Sutton is a sporty community with craft shops, welcoming eateries, and bars. Surrounded by mountains, the town is best explored on foot; a circuit of 12 heritage sites makes an interesting self-guided walk past the boutiques and the houses built by Loyalists. For a route map with a description of each building and its history, go to the tourist office. It's inside the City Hall building at 11B rue Principale.

WHERE TO STAY & EAT

$$ ✕**Amore Di Pasta.** Offering up sumptuous first-rate pasta dishes, former Montrealers Jessica Kinahan and chef Patrice Lobet are your hosts at this quaint little dining room set along Sutton's main drag. Sit out on their delightful terrace and sample one of Patrice's much-celebrated specialties. Locals will tell you this is one of the best-kept secrets in the Townships, serving exquisite food at relatively moderate prices. Be sure to check out the art adorning the walls and painted on all of Amore Di Pasta's tabletops, all of it created by local artists. ⊠*6 rue Principale Sud* ☎*450/538–2121* ⊟*AE, MC, V* ⊗Closed Wed. *No lunch.*

$ 🏠**Au Diable Vert.** This inn is in one of the most beautiful areas of the province, deep in the heart of the Appalachian Mountains and overlooking the waters of the Missisquoi River. The interior of this early-1900s farmhouse is tastefully decorated with antiques. Lodging options range from luxurious two-bedroom suites to treehouse, rustic and log cabins to prospector tents. Set on 200 acres, Au Diable Vert hosts a wide variety of outdoor activities, including hiking, regular and guided moonlight kayak excursions along the Missisquoi, and horseback-riding lessons (off site). It is also home to the hosts' Scottish Highland Cattle, which are raised free-range for meat. Dogs are allowed at Au Diable Vert, and guests are encouraged to bring them. **Pros:** beautiful, tranquil grounds; friendly staff; on-site activities; variety of lodging choices; in the heart of the mountains. **Cons:** no pool; steep, rocky access road is not for the faint of heart. ⊠*169 chemin Staines,* ☎*450/538–5639* ⊕*www.audiablevert.qc.ca* ✎*3 suites; 8 cabins, 35 campsites* ♿*In-hotel: no elevator* ⊟*AE, MC, V* ⑩*EP.*

SPORTS & THE OUTDOORS

GOLF **Les Rochers Bleus.** You'll need a reservation to golf at this 6,230-yard, par-72, 18-hole course. Its narrow fairways, surrounded by mountains, can be a challenge. Greens fees are C$30–C$40, plus an additional C$26 to rent a cart. ⊠*550 Rte. 139* ☎*450/538–2324 or 800/361–2468* ⊕*www.lesrochersbleus.com.*

HIKING **Au Diable Vert.** Au Diable Vert, which translated means the Green Devil, is a stunningly beautiful 200-acre mountainside site with challenging hiking trails that look out over spectacular scenery. (Glen Sutton, 15 minutes from the village of Sutton, is between the Appalachians and Vermont's Green Mountains; the Missisquoi River runs through the middle.) ⊠*169 chemin Staines, Glen Sutton* ☎*450/538–5639 or 888/779–9090* ⊕*www.audiablevert.qc.ca.*

SKIING **Mont-Sutton.** Known for some of the best snowboarding hills in Québec, Mont-Sutton has 53 downhill trails, a vertical drop of 1,500 feet, and nine lifts. This ski area, one of the region's largest, attracts a die-hard crowd of mostly Anglophone skiers and snowboarders from Québec. Trails plunge and meander through pine, maple, and birch trees. ⊠*671 Maple St. (Rte. 139 Sud)* ☎ *450/538–2545 or 866/538–2545* ⊕*www.montsutton.com.*

SHOPPING

Arts Sutton. This tiny gallery, run by a local nonprofit organization, is dedicated to promoting the works of contemporary regional artists. ⊠ *7 rue Academy* ☎ *450/538–2563* ⊕ *www.artssutton.com.*

Galerie D'Art Les Imagiers. Primarily showcasing the works of 17 local painters and sculptors, Les Imagiers also exhibits work from reputable yet often lesser-known Québécois and international artists. ⊠ *12 rue Principale Sud* ☎ *450/538–1771.*

Rumeur Affamée. Carrying more than 130 kinds of cheese—60 of them produced locally—along with local and imported meats, fresh bread, and spectacular desserts, Rumeur Affamée is a must just for their famous maple-syrup pie, a tasty treat unique to the region. ⊠ *15 rue Principale Nord* ☎ *450/538–1888.*

KNOWLTON (LAC BROME)

101 km (63 mi) southeast of Montréal.

Knowlton is a good stop for antiques, clothes, and gifts. The village is full of high-quality boutiques, art galleries, and interesting little restaurants that have taken residence in renovated clapboard buildings painted every shade of the rainbow. The town also has several factory outlets. Along the shore of Lac Brome, Knowlton is also known for its distinctive Lake Brome ducks, which are found on local menus and celebrated in a food event over several weeks during late September and early October. You can pick up a self-guided walking-tour map at the reception area of Auberge Knowlton.

WHERE TO STAY

$$
Fodor'sChoice
★

Auberge Knowlton. This 12-room inn, at the main intersection in Knowlton, has been a local landmark since 1849, when it was a stagecoach stop. The inn attracts businesspeople, as well as vacationers and locals who like coming to the old, familiar hotel for special occasions. Recently accredited by Agricotours and Vélo Québec, the inn is cyclist-friendly and equipped to meet the needs of those traveling on two wheels (storage, repair kits, etc.). Bistro Le Relais ($$–$$$) serves local wines and cheeses and offers a wide range of duck dishes, including warm duck salad served with gizzards and confit *de canard* all of which can be savored on the terrace during the summer months. **Pros:** within walking distance of everything Knowlton has to offer, including the local beach, charming village with an assortment of antique shops and clothing boutiques; dog-friendly; cyclist-friendly; fine restaurant. **Cons:** on the main road that runs through the town, so not the most scenic location. ⊠ *286 chemin Knowlton, Lac Brome* ☎ *450/242–6886* ⊕ *www.aubergeknowlton.ca* ⊅ *12 rooms* ⌂ *In-room: no a/c (some), dial-up (some), Wi-Fi (some). In-hotel: restaurant, no-smoking rooms, some pets allowed, no elevator* ⊟ *AE, MC, V* ⓘⓄ *EP.*

NIGHTLIFE & THE ARTS

Fodor'sChoice
★

Arts Knowlton. This local theater company stages plays, musicals, and productions of classic Broadway and West End hits. It hosts professional and amateur English-language productions, but has also dabbled in bilingual productions as well as contemporary works by Canadian playwrights. The 175-seat, air-conditioned theater is behind the Knowlton Pub. ⊠*9 Mount Echo Rd.* ☎*450/242–2270 or 450/242–1395* ⊟*450/242–2320* ⊕*www.theatrelacbrome.ca.*

SPORTS & THE OUTDOORS

Golf Inverness. Not far from Knowlton is this 18-hole, par-71 course (6,326 yards) with an elegant clubhouse that dates back to 1915. Greens fees are C$25–C$45, plus an additional C$30 to rent a cart. ⊠*511 chemin Bondville, Rte. 215* ☎*450/242–1595 or 800/468–1595* ⊕*www.golf-inverness.com.*

SHOPPING

Camlen. Cameron and Helen Brown (get it? Cam + len) import gorgeous antiques from China and Eastern Europe and manufacture their own "antiques" using old wood. Their passion for and dedication to the art of furniture making is reflected in their—and their team's—workmanship. They claim to have reinvented the antiques business and, in their own way, they most certainly have. ⊠*110 Lakeside Rd.* ☎*450/243–5785* ⊕*www.camlenantiques.com* ⊘*Daily 10–5:30.*

Rococo. This boutique is owned by U.S.-born Anita Laurent, a former model. Drawing on her many contacts in the fashion world, she buys samples directly from manufacturers and sells her stylish, elegant suits and pants at a fraction of the price charged by large retail stores. ⊠*299 chemin Knowlton* ☎*450/243–6948* ⊘*Daily 10–5:30.*

Fodor'sChoice ★ **Station Knowlton.** Inside an old wrought-iron workshop, colorful Station Knowlton carries locally made gift items, including its own line of homemade soaps and bath salts. The comfortable café here attracts a mix of tourists and locals. ⊠*7 chemin du Mont-Echo* ☎*450/242–5862* ⊕*www.stationknowlton.com* ⊘*Weekdays 11–6.*

Township Toy Trains. Big and small kids visit this delightful shop to check out its stock of trains, dollhouse miniatures, collectable dolls (Reinhard Faelans) and accessories. ⊠*5 chemin du Mont-Echo* ☎*450/243–1881* ⊕*www.townshiptoytrains.com* ⊘*Thurs.–Sun. 10–5.*

VALCOURT

158 km (98 mi) east of Montréal.

Valcourt is the birthplace of the inventor of the snowmobile, and the sport is understandably popular in the Eastern Townships, with more than 2,000 km (1,240 mi) of paths cutting through the woods and meadows.

WHAT TO SEE

Grand Prix Ski-doo de Valcourt. Grand Prix Ski-doo is a three-day event every February with competitions, concerts, and family-oriented festivities. Ticket prices range from C$8 to C$130. ☎*450/532–3443 or 866/532–7543* ⊕*www.grandprixvalcourt.com.*

Fodor'sChoice ★ **Musée Joseph-Armand Bombardier.** This museum displays innovator Bombardier's many inventions, including the snowmobile. It's partly a showcase for Bombardier's products, including Ski-doo snowmobiles, but it also documents the history of snow transportation with interesting facts about winter weather, a topic of import in this corner of the world. As you walk around, you can compare yesteryear's simple modes of snow transportation—loggers working with horses in the woods, Lapps harnessing their reindeer, and so on—shown on photographic backdrops, with today's sleek vehicles. ⊠*1001 av. Joseph-Armand Bombardier* ☎*450/532–5300* ⊕*www.museebombardier.com* ☜*C$7* ☉*May–Labor Day, daily 10–5; closed Mon. Sept.–Jan.*

ABBAYE ST-BENOIT-DU-LAC

Fodor'sChoice
★

132 km (82 mi) southeast of Montréal.

The abbey's bell tower juts above the trees like a fairy-tale castle. Built by the Benedictines in 1912 on a wooded peninsula on Lac Memphrémagog, the abbey is home to some 60 monks who sell apples and sparkling apple wine from their orchards, as well as cheeses: Ermite (which means "hermit"), St-Benoît, and ricotta. Gregorian prayers are sung daily, and some masses are open to the public; call for the schedule. Dress modestly if you plan to attend vespers or other rituals, and avoid shorts. If you wish to experience a few days of retreat, reserve well in advance (a contribution of C$40 per night, which includes meals, is suggested). To get to the abbey from Magog, take Route 112 and follow the signs for the side road (Rural Route 2, or rue des Pères) to the abbey. ⊠*R.R. 2, St-Benoît-du-Lac* ☎*819/843–4080* 🖷*819/868–1861* ⊕*www.st-benoit-du-lac.com* ☉*Store Mon.–Sat. 9–10:45 and 11:45–4:30 (between services).*

PARC DU MONT-ORFORD

115 km (72 mi) east of Montréal.

9

WHAT TO SEE

Orford Arts Centre. Since 1951 thousands of students have come to the center to study and perform classical music year-round. The annual summertime celebration of music and art, Festival Orford, brings classical-music, jazz, and chamber-orchestra concerts to Parc du Mont-Orford. ⊠*3165 chemin du Parc* ☎*819/843–8595, 800/567–6155 in Canada* ⊕*www.arts-orford.org.*

Parc du Mont-Orford. Part of the township of Orford, the Parc is in use year-round, whether for skiing, snowshoeing, camping, golfing, or hiking. ⊠*3321 chemin du Parc* ☎*819/843–6548 or 866/673–6731.*

WHERE TO STAY

$$$ 🏨**Estrimont Suites & Spa.** An attractive complex built of cedar, it has an outdoor Nordic waterfall and is close to ski hills, riding stables, and golf courses. All rooms have fireplaces and private balconies. The restaurant serves regional specialties. There is no smoking anywhere on the premises. **Pros:** very reasonably priced spa packages; excellent place for conferences or business retreats; two outdoor hot tubs in scenic surroundings. **Cons:** only one suite is wheelchair accessible. ⊠*44* *av. de l'Auberge (Rte. 141 Nord),* ☎*819/843–1616 or 800/567–7320* ⊕*www.estrimont.qc.ca* ⟿*91 suites* ☆*In-room: a/c, kitchen, Wi-Fi. In-hotel: restaurant, bar, golf, tennis courts, pools, gym, spa, no-smoking rooms* ▭*AE, DC, MC, V* ⦿*CP.*

MAGOG

118 km (74 mi) east of Montréal.

This bustling town is at the northern tip of Lac Memphrémagog, a large body of water that reaches into northern Vermont. Its sandy beaches are a draw, and it's also a good place for boating, bird-watching, sailboarding, horseback riding, dogsledding, in-line skating, golfing, and snowmobiling. You might even see Memphré, the lake's sea dragon, on one of the many lake cruises—there have been more than 100 sightings since 1816.

The streets downtown are lined with century-old homes that have been converted into boutiques, stores, and eateries—including Japanese and Vietnamese restaurants, fast-food outlets, bistros serving Italian and French dishes, and many others.

WHAT TO SEE

Le Cep d'Argent. The sparkling white wine is particularly good, and the dessert wine, which is similar to a port and flavored with a little maple syrup, goes well with the local cheese. The winery plays a leading role in the annual wine festival that's held in Magog (late August and early September). The guided visit and tasting of four different wines for C$7, or C$15 for the VIP visit, is available only from May to December. ⊠*1257 chemin de la Rivière* ☎*819/864–4441 or 877/864–4441* ⊕*www.cepdargent.com* ⊙*Daily 10–5.*

OFF THE BEATEN PATH

Sucrerie des Normand. One of the oldest, most traditional maple-syrup operations in the Eastern Townships is in Eastman, about 15 km (9 mi) west of Magog. Run by third-generation farmer Richard Normand, the farm is spread over 250 acres of wooded land and includes 10,000 maple trees. You can tour the property in a horse-drawn wagon and watch the "sugaring off" process—from the tapping of trees to the rendering down of the sweet liquid into syrup and sugar. After the tour, Richard and his wife, Marlene (she designs the menus), serve traditional Québécois food in a wood cabin, to the sounds of harmonica and spoons. ⊠*426 chemin Georges Bonnalie, Eastman* ☎*450/297–2659 or 866/297–2659* ⊕*www.hautboisnormand.ca* ⊙*Year-round, call or check the Web site for hours. Reservations required.*

WHERE TO STAY

$$$ ⊡**Ripplecove Inn.** The accommodations, service, and food at the Ripplecove, 11 km (7 mi) south of Magog, are excellent. Bedrooms are elegant, furnished with antiques; colorful walls nicely set off the artwork. Some rooms and suites have lake views. The Table du Chef is an assemblage of local delights that might consist of braised lamb Parmentier, fillet of beef with duck foie gras, honey-roasted pear with onion confit crouton and, for dessert, Guayaquil chocolate mi-cuit 'en cocotte for

C$88 a person. There is also a spa with a variety of treatments. **Pros:** spectacular scenery, one of the finest restaurants in the area. **Cons:** not recommended for those with physical disabilities. ✉ *700 rue Ripplecove, Ayer's Cliff* ☎ *819/838–4296 or 800/668–4296* ⊕ *www.ripplecove.com* ⇨ *3 rooms, 5 suites, 3 cottages In-room: TV, Wi-Fi (some). In-hotel: restaurant, pool, beachfront, water sports, public Internet, no-smoking rooms, no elevator* ▭ *AE, MC, V* ❙❙ *MAP.*

$$ ⚃ **Spa Eastman.** The oldest spa in Québec has evolved from a simple health center into a bucolic haven for anyone seeking rest and therapeutic treatments, including lifestyle and weight-management counseling. Surrounded by 350 acres of rolling, wooded land 15 km (9 mi) west of Magog, the spa itself is an elegant, simple structure that brings to mind the calm of a Japanese garden. Some bedrooms have fireplaces, large balconies, and views of Mont-Orford. Vegetarian dishes, prepared with organic ingredients and produce from the chef's garden, are predominant in the dining room. The assortment of meat dishes accompanied by interesting herbs and sauces, is also organic and from local farms. For a complete head-to-toe spa experience, check out the Hair Spa, featuring a complete range of specialized treatments to revitalize and pamper your hair. **Pros:** perfectly adapted for those seeking a totally relaxing and peaceful respite; with everything on-site, there is no need to leave the premises; wheelchair accessible rooms. **Cons:** no phone or TV might prove too isolating for some. ✉ *895 chemin des Diligences, Eastman* ☎ *450/297–3009 or 800/665–5272* ⊕ *www.spa-eastman.com* ⇨ *43 rooms* ✧ *In-room: no a/c (some), no TV, no phone. In-hotel: restaurant, pool, spa, no kids under 14* ▭ *AE, MC, V* ❙❙ *MAP.*

$ ⚃ **Auberge l'Étoile Sur-le-Lac.** The rooms at this popular inn on Magog's waterfront are modern and have fresh furnishings; the majority have water views and some have fireplaces. Large windows overlooking mountain-ringed Lac Memphrémagog make L'Ancrage restaurant ($$)—which specializes in French cuisine—bright and airy, and dishes ranging from organic pork and veal to caribou and ostrich make it a gourmand's delight. In summer you can eat outside on the terrace overlooking the lake. **Pros:** located directly on Lac Memphrémagog; the popular cycling "Route Verte" is directly accessible from the Auberge; boutiques, restaurants, and bars, theaters of Magog all within comfortable walking distance. **Cons:** not recommended for guests who are looking for isolated, peaceful surroundings. ✉ *1200 rue Principale Ouest, Magog* ☎ *819/843–6521 or 800/567–2727* ⊕ *www.etoile-sur-le-lac.com* ⇨ *52 rooms and suites, 10 condos* ✧ *In-room: a/c, Wi-Fi (some), dial-up. In-hotel: restaurant, pool, spa, bicycles, no elevator* ▭ *AE, DC, MC, V* ❙❙ *CP, MAP.*

NIGHTLIFE & THE ARTS

Magog is lively after dark, with many bars, cafés, bistros, and restaurants catering not only to the local population, but to the numerous tourists and weekend refugees from nearby Montréal who flock here for the exceptional beauty of the surrounding region.

In recent years this formerly depressed textile town has enjoyed something of an economic and cultural rebirth, largely thanks to the tourism industry, but also partially due to the substantial number of artists who have chosen to relocate to this welcoming, and relatively inexpensive, region of the province.

NIGHTLIFE   **Auberge Orford.** A patio bar overlooks the Magog River (you can moor your boat alongside it). Sometimes there's live entertainment, but when musicians aren't around to keep them at bay, flocks of ducks line up alongside the café to beg crumbs from patrons' plates—an entertaining sight in itself. ⊠*20 rue Merry Sud* ☎*819/843–9361.*

Café St-Michel. In a century-old building, this chic pub, outfitted in shades of charcoal and ebony, serves Tex-Mex food, pasta, and local beers. Its patio bar, which is noisy because it's at Magog's main intersection, is a great spot to watch the world go by. Chansonniers (singers) belt out popular hits for a full house on weekends—and every night but Monday in summer. ⊠*503 rue Principale Ouest* ☎*819/868–1062.*

Microbrasserie La Memphré. A pub named after the monster said to lurk in Lake Memphrémagog, La Memphré dates back to the 1800s, when it belonged to Magog's first mayor. Now a microbrewery, it serves Swiss-cheese fondue, sausages with sauerkraut, and panini (pressed sandwiches)—good accompaniments for a cold one. ⊠*12 rue Merry Sud* ☎*819/843–3405.*

THE ARTS   **Le Vieux Clocher de Magog.** One of two former churches converted into theaters by local impresario Bernard Caza (the other is in Sherbrooke), Le Vieux headlines well-known comedians and singers. Most performances are in French. ⊠*64 rue Merry Nord* ☎*819/847–0470* ⊕*www. vieuxclocher.com.*

SPORTS & THE OUTDOORS

GOLF   **Golf Owl's Head.** This course, close to the Vermont border, has some spectacular views. Laid out with undulating fairways, bent-grass greens, and 64 sand bunkers, the 6,671-yard, 18-hole course (par 72), designed by Graham Cooke, is surrounded by mountain scenery. The clubhouse, a stunning timber-and-fieldstone structure with five fireplaces and 45-foot-high ceilings, is a favorite watering hole for locals and visitors alike. Greens fees are C$50–C$60; cart rental costs C$31.01. ⊠*181 chemin du Mont-Owl's Head, Mansonville* ☎*450/292–3666 or 800/363–3342* ⊕*www.owlshead.com.*

Manoir des Sables golf course. This 6,120-yard, 18-hole, par-71 course was built on a sandy base. Lessons start at C$50. Greens fees range from C$30 to C$39, and cart rental is C$29. ⊠*90 av. des Jardins, Magog-Orford* ☎*819/847–4299 or 800/567–3514* ⊕*www.hotelsvillegia.com.*

Orford Le Golf. This venerable course—it was laid out in 1939—is an 18-hole, par-70, 6,287-yard course that winds around forested land; from many of the greens you can see the peak of Mont-Orford. Greens fees are C$15–C$37, and cart rental is C$27. ⊠*3074 chemin du Parc* ☎*819/843–5688* ⊕*www.mt-orford.com.*

SKIING **Owl's Head Ski Area.** On the Knowlton Landing side of Lake Memphrémagog, Owl's Head is great for skiers seeking sparser crowds. It has eight lifts, a 1,772-foot vertical drop, and 44 trails, including a 4-km (2½-mi) intermediate run, the longest such run in the Eastern Townships. ⊠ *40 chemin du Mont-Owl's Head, Rte. 243 Sud; Autoroute 10, Exit 106* ☎ *450/292–3342 or 800/363–3342* ⊕ *www.owlshead.com.*

NORTH HATLEY

134 km (83 mi) east of Montréal.

North Hatley, the small resort town on the tip of Lac Massawippi, has a theater and excellent inns and restaurants. Set among hills and farms, it was discovered by rich vacationers in the early 1900s, and has been drawing visitors ever since.

WHERE TO STAY & EAT

$$$ ✕ **Auberge Le Saint-Amant.** Jean-Claude, the chef-owner, whips up sophisticated fare ($$–$$$$): milk-fed veal sweetbreads with raspberry vinaigrette and capers, lobster ravioli and sautéed shrimp in a saffron sauce, fresh salmon grilled with miso and Damari, and knuckle of lamb in spiced wine jelly are a few examples of the restaurant's French cuisine. A four-course "health menu"—miso soup, salad, a tofu dish, and dessert—is C$34. ⊠ *33 chemin de l'Auberge,* ☎ *819/842–1211* ⊕ *www.aubergelesaintamant.com* ▤ *MC, V* ⦿ *MAP.*

$$ ✕ **Pilsen Pub.** Québec's first microbrewery no longer brews beer on-site, but Massawippi pale and brown ales and a vast selection of microbrews and imports are on tap here. Good pub food—pasta, homemade soups, burgers, and the like—is served in the upstairs restaurant and in the tavern, both of which overlook the water. It can get busy at lunch, so try to get here by noon. ⊠ *55 rue Principale* ☎ *819/842–2971* ⊕ *www.pilsen.ca* ▤ *AE, MC, V.*

$$$–$$$$ ⊡ **Manoir Hovey.** Overlooking Lac Massawippi, this retreat feels like a private estate, with many of the activities included in room rates. Built in 1900, the manor was modeled after George Washington's Mount Vernon. Rooms have a mix of antiques and more modern wood furniture, richly printed fabrics, and lace trimmings; many have fireplaces and private balconies overlooking the lake. The restaurant ($$$$) serves exquisite Continental and French cuisine: try the asparagus with puree of kalamata olives, quinoa, and white truffle oil, the roasted loin of caribou from Nunavut, or the pan-seared fillet of striped bass with Scottish sauce and lardons. There's also a light menu. Home-baked scones, clotted cream, jam, and more than 40 teas and infusions are served at the posh traditional English afternoon tea. **Pros:** voted one of the top hotels in Canada by *Condé Nast Traveler*'s Reader's Choice in 2007; wheelchair accessible. **Cons:** restaurant overpriced. ⊠ *575 chemin Hovey,* ☎ *819/842–2421 or 800/661–2421* ⊕ *www.manoirhovey.com* ⇩ *42 rooms, 5 suites, 1 four-bedroom cottage* ♿ *In-room: a/c, TV, Wi-Fi. In-hotel: restaurant, bars, tennis court, pool, beachfront,*

9

bicycles, public Internet, no-smoking rooms, no elevator ⊟*AE, DC, MC, V* ⏻❙*MAP.*

NIGHTLIFE & THE ARTS

L'Association du Festival du Lac Massawippi. The association presents an annual antiques and folk-art show in July, sponsors classical-music concerts at the Église Ste-Elizabeth in North Hatley on Sunday from late April through December, and presents lively Sunday open-air concerts at Dreamland Park in summer. ☎*819/842–2784.*

Fodor'sChoice **Piggery.** Enriching the Townships' cultural landscape since 1965, this
★ theater that was once a pig barn is still thriving. The venue, which has an on-site restaurant and is nestled in the mountains off a quiet road, often presents new plays by Canadian writers and experiments with bilingual productions. In addition to traditional theater, concerts, musical revues, magic shows, and comedy acts are presented. The season runs mid-May through mid-September. ✉*215 chemin Simard, off Rte. 108* ☎*819/842–2431* ⊕*www.piggery.com.*

SHERBROOKE

130 km (81 mi) east of Montréal.

The region's unofficial capital and largest city, Sherbrooke was founded by Loyalists in the 1790s. This town didn't get its current name, however, until 1818, when it was named for Canadian governor general Sir John Coape Sherbrooke.

On the corner of rues Dufferin and Frontenac is a realistic mural illustrating storefronts and businesses from Sherbrooke's past. Close up, you notice whimsical little details—a bulldog blocking the path of a FossMobile (Canada's first gas-powered automobile, designed by local inventor George Foote Foss); a woman, hair in rollers, yelling at a dog from a balcony; a policeman trying to coax the animal to move out of the way.

WHAT TO SEE

OFF THE BEATEN PATH **La Ferme Martinette.** In the heart of Québec's dairy country, this farm, which doubles as a modest B&B, hosts "sugaring off" parties with traditional menus in March and April. Lisa Nadeau and her husband, Gérald Martineau, have 2,500 maple trees as well as a herd of 50 Holsteins. You can tour the farm in a trailer pulled by the tractor that belonged to Gérald's grandfather, and fill up on the C$22.95 all-you-can-eat traditional meal during the sugaring-off season in March and April or, in the summer months, enjoy a picnic on the lovely grounds. There is also a gift shop on the premises. Coaticook is 32 km (20 mi) south of Sherbrooke. ✉*1728 chemin Martineau, Coaticook* ☎*819/849–7089 or 819/345–7089* ⊕*www.lafermemartinette.com.*

Musée des Beaux-Arts de Sherbrooke. This fine-arts museum has a permanent exhibit on the history of art in the region from 1800 to the present. ✉*241 rue Dufferin* ☎*819/821–2115* ⊕*www.mbas.qc.ca* 🎟*C$7.50* ☉*Tues.–Sun. noon–5; late June–early Sept., 10–5.*

Musée de la Nature et des Sciences. This museum is in what used to be the Julius-Kayser & Co. factory, famous for the silk stockings it made. The elegant building has granite floors and marble stairs, and makes good use of its lofty space. State-of-the-art light and sound effects (the buzzing of mosquitoes may be *too* lifelike) and hands-on displays enhance the exhibits. ✉*225 rue Frontenac* ☎*819/564–3200* or *877/434–3200* ⊕*www.mnes.qc.ca* ⌂*C$7.50* ⊗ *Wed.–Sun. 10–5; late June–early Sept., daily 10–5.*

Sherbrooke Tourist Information Center. The tourist center conducts animated tours, mainly in French, led by costumed actors representing figures from Sherbrooke's past. The history-focused tours, which run weekends from mid-July to late August, are designed for prearranged groups, but individuals can tag along ($25 per person; reservations essential). ✉*785 rue King Ouest* ☎*819/821–1919* ⊕*www.tourismesherbrooke.com.*

WHERE TO STAY & EAT

$$–$$$ ✕**Restaurant au P'tit Sabot.** The adventurous menus here use local ingredients such as wild boar, quail, sweetbreads, venison, and bison in classic French dishes. The serene decor and small dining area (it seats around 35 people) make it a pleasant refuge from the busy and not very attractive shopping mall that houses it. ✉*1410 rue King Ouest* ☎*819/563–0262* ⊟*AE, DC, MC, V.*

¢ ⊡**Bishop's University.** If you're on a budget, these students' residences are a great place to stay mid-May through August. The prices can't be beat, and the location—5 km (3 mi) south of Sherbrooke—is good for touring. The university's lovely grounds have architecture reminiscent of stately New England campuses. The 1857 Gothic-style chapel, paneled with richly carved ash, shows fine local craftsmanship. Reservations for summer are accepted as early as the previous September, and it's a good idea to book far in advance. They also offer special rates for students. **Pros:** reasonably priced accommodations; close to center of town and amenities. **Cons:** dormitory living may not be a desirable option for some travelers. ✉*Rue College, Box 5000, Lennoxville* ☎*819/822–9600 Ext. 2685* or *877/622–4900* ⊕*www.ubishops.ca/ residence/accomodation.html* ⌂*438 rooms without bath, 54 apartments* ⌂*In-room: no a/c, no TV, Ethernet. In-hotel: restaurant, golf course, tennis court, pools, gym* ⊟*MC, V* ⊗ *Closed Sept.–mid-May.*

NIGHTLIFE & THE ARTS

Centennial Theatre. The 600-seat Centennial Theatre is a part of Bishops University and presents a roster of jazz, classical, and rock concerts, as well as opera, dance, mime, and children's theater. ✉*Bishop's University, Lennoxville* ☎*819/822–9600 Ext. 2691, 819/822–9692 box office* ⊕*www.ubishops.ca/centennial.*

Le Vieux Clocher de Sherbrooke. In a converted church, Le Vieux Clocher de Sherbrooke presents music, from classical to jazz, and a variety of theater and comedy shows. ✉*1590 rue Galt Ouest* ☎*819/822–2102* ⊕*www.vieuxclocher.com.*

9

NOTRE-DAME-DES-BOIS

204 km (127 mi) east of Montréal.

With a population of 759 people—as of last count—Notre-Dame-des-Bois remains a sleepy little town surrounded by some of the steepest mountains in the Townships. It's a picturesque part of the world, to be sure, the big tourist draw being the Astrolab observatory atop Mont-Mégantic park.

WHAT TO SEE

Astrolab du Mont-Mégantic *(Mont-Mégantic's Observatory)*. Both amateur stargazers and serious astronomers head to his observatory, located in a beautifully wild and mountainous area. The observatory is at the summit of the Townships' second-highest mountain (3,601 feet), whose northern face records annual snowfalls rivaling any in North America. A joint venture of the University of Montréal and Laval University, the observatory has a powerful telescope, the largest on the East Coast. At the welcome center at the mountain's base, you can view an exhibition and a multimedia show to learn about the night sky. ✉ *Parc Mégantic, 189 Rte. du Parc* ☎ *819/888–2941* ⊕ *astrolab.gtvr.com* ✑ *C$12.40, summit tour C$15.73; additional C$3.50 to enter Parc Mégantic* ⊙ *Mid-May–mid-June, weekends noon–5; mid-June–late Aug., daily noon–4:30 and 8–11; late Aug.–early Oct., weekends noon–5 and 7:30–10:30. Closed Mon. night* ⚠ *Reservations essential.*

WHERE TO STAY

$$
Fodor'sChoice
★
Aux Berges de l'Aurore. This delightful century-old inn is perfectly located less than a minute's drive from the area's primary tourist attractions—Mont Mégantic Provincial Park and the Astrolab housed within it. Sitting at an altitude of 600 feet, surrounded by landscaped gardens and 105 acres of rolling hills, the views to be had at this tiny bed-and-breakfast are nothing short of spectacular. **Pros:** stunning scenery; close proximity to area activities; delicious breakfasts made exclusively from local produce; lots of interesting wildlife in the area, including wolves, moose, and wild cats. **Cons:** compulsory $2 gratuity at breakfast; though close to Mont Mégantic, bear in mind that the population here was under 6,000 residents at last count, and the closest large town is over two hours away; be sure to pack everything you think you might need, because, while truly beautiful, this part of the province is relatively isolated. ✉ *139 Rte. du Parc, Notre-Dame-des-Bois* ☎ *819/888–2715* ⊕ *www.auberge-aurore.qc.ca* ⌨ *3 rooms, 2 suites* ⚿ *In-room: no a/c (some), no TV. In-hotel: no elevator* ▭ *MC, V* ⊙ *Closed mid-Nov.–mid-Dec. and Apr.–mid-May* ⊠ *EP.*

EXCURSIONS FROM QUÉBEC CITY PLANNER

Getting Here

To reach Montmorency Falls, take Route 440 (Autoroute Dufferin–Montmorency) east from Québec City approximately 9½ km (6 mi) to the exit for Montmorency Falls. For Ste-Anne-de-Beaupré, take Route 440 (Autoroute Dufferin–Montmorency) east from Québec City approximately 23 km (14 mi).To get to Île d'Orléans, take Route 440 (Autoroute Dufferin–Montmorency) northeast. After a drive of about 10 km (6 mi) take the Pont de l'Île d'Orléans (a bridge) to the island. The main road, chemin Royal (Route 368), circles the island, extending 67 km (42 mi) through the island's six villages; the route turns into chemin du Bout de l'Île in Ste-Pétronille. To get to Charlevoix from Québec City, take Route 440 (Autoroute Dufferin–Montmorency) northeast and then continue past the Côte de Beaupré on Route 138. From there you'll be able to branch out for destinations such as Petit-Rivière-St-François or Baie-St-Paul. Though a half-hour longer from Québec City, Route 362 between Baie-St-Paul and La Malbaie is more scenic.

Getting Around

Most people traveling to this region do so by car, making it easy to spend as much or as little time in any given area as desired. However, Québec is in the process of developing the Route Verte, or the Green Route, a 3,600-km (2,230-mi) network of bike trails in the southern part of the province.

DINING & LODGING PRICES IN CANADIAN DOLLARS				
¢	$	$$	$$$	$$$$
Restaurants				
Under C$8	C$8–C$12	C$13–C$20	C$21–C$30	Over C$30
Hotels				
Under C$75	C$75–C$125	C$126–C$175	C$176–C$250	Over C$250
Restaurant prices are per person for a main course at dinner, excluding tax. Hotel prices are for a standard double room in high season, excluding tax.				

When to Go

The Côte de Beaupré and Île d'Orléans are spectacular in fall, when you can see the colorful changing leaves and go apple picking. Summer is pleasant for the drive and the chance to picnic along the way. In winter the narrow and more scenic roads can be a bit tougher to maneuver, so you might prefer taking a bus tour with an experienced winter driver.

Charlevoix is full of artists, crafters, and painters in action in summer months, and it's also the perfect time to see the baby beluga whales. Fall is a great time to leaf-peep from the road, the river, or the trail. Sports change with the seasons, and are practiced year-round. In winter there's cross-country skiing, snowshoeing, and ice fishing, among other cold-weather activities.

Reservations

Most of the restaurants on the Côte de Beaupré, Île d'Orléans, and in Charlevoix are open during high season, May to October, so check ahead. Reservations are highly recommended, although off-season it's possible to book a room same-day.

9

Updated by
Anne Marie
Marko

SEVERAL EASY EXCURSIONS FROM QUEBEC City can give you a deeper understanding of this region's history and culture. In addition to the natural beauty of Montmorency Falls and its Manoir Montmorency, experience the calm of rural life on the charming Île d'Orléans, known as "the Garden of Québec," and the historic Beaupré coast. The Charlevoix region's stunning, picturesque landscape is lovely year-round, and in winter visitors flock to the area for a host of outdoor activities.

It's more than well worth crossing the Taschereau Bridge to include Île d'Orléans, but if you have your heart set on only seeing Montmorency Falls it can easily be done in less than a day. A leisurely drive around Île d'Orléans with stops at farms, markets, churches, and craft and antiques shops can be done in an energetic day, though rural inns make it tempting to extend a visit.

While driving along Québec's Côte de Beaupré, you can make several stops to taste maple syrup and honey, and admire local crafts. You'll eventually come to Ste-Anne-de-Beaupré, an immense neo-Roman church that's been the goal of pilgrimages for centuries.

CÔTE DE BEAUPRÉ

As legend has it, when explorer Jacques Cartier first caught sight of the north shore of the St. Lawrence River in 1535, he exclaimed, "*Quel beau pré!*" ("What a lovely meadow!"), because the area was the first inviting piece of land he had spotted since leaving France. Today the Côte de Beaupré (Beaupré Coast), first settled by French farmers, stretches 40 km (25 mi) east from Québec City to the famous pilgrimage site of Ste-Anne-de-Beaupré. Historic Route 360, or avenue Royale, winds its way from Beauport to St-Joachim, east of Ste-Anne-de-Beaupré. The impressive Montmorency Falls lie midway between Québec City and Ste-Anne-de-Beaupré.

WHAT TO SEE

Atelier Paré (Economuseum of Wood Sculpture). This economuseum and workshop represents two centuries of wood sculpture. Visitors may watch artisans at work, tour the outdoor museum, or learn about key personages in Québec's history through the Legend Theatre Workshop. There is a boutique on site as well. ⊠*9269 av. Royale, Ste-Anne-de-Beaupré* ☎*418/827–3992* ⊕*www.atelierpare.com* ✉*Free; new 13-min video presentation in English and French; guided tour C$3* ⊙*June–mid-Sept. 15, daily 9–5; Sept. 15–May 31, Wed.–Sun. 1–4.*

Fodor's Choice **Basilique Ste-Anne-de-Beaupré.** On Route 138, east of Québec City, is the
★   tiny town Ste-Anne-de-Beaupré, named for Québec's patron saint, and each year more than a million pilgrims visit the region's most famous religious site here, dedicated to the mother of the Virgin Mary.

The French brought their devotion to St. Anne (the patron saint of shipwrecked sailors) when they sailed across the Atlantic to New France. According to local legend, St. Anne was responsible over the years for

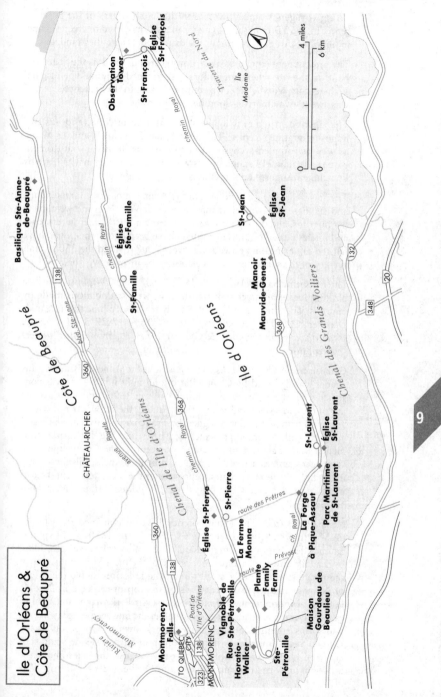

saving voyagers from shipwrecks in the harsh waters of the St. Lawrence. In 1650 Breton sailors caught in a storm vowed to erect a chapel in honor of this patron saint at the exact spot where they landed.

The present neo-Roman basilica, constructed in 1923, is the fifth to be built on the site where the sailors first touched ground. The original 17th-century wood chapel was built too close to the St. Lawrence and was swept away by river flooding.

The gigantic structure is in the shape of a Latin cross, and has two imposing granite steeples. The interior has 22 chapels and 18 altars, as well as rounded arches and numerous ornaments in the Romanesque style. The 214 stained-glass windows, completed in 1949, are by Frenchmen Auguste Labouret and Pierre Chaudière.

Tributes to St. Anne can be seen in the shrine's mosaics, murals, altars, and ceilings. A bas-relief at the entrance depicts St. Anne welcoming her pilgrims, and ceiling mosaics represent her life. Numerous crutches and braces posted on the back pillars have been left by those who have felt the saint's healing powers. The year 2008 marked the 350th anniversary of the shrine, and was celebrated by its many visitors.

The **Musée de Sainte Anne** (☎418/827–6873 🖾C$4), in the basilica parking lot, exhibits church treasures as well as donations made by pilgrims. The museum is open 9–5 daily from early June through mid-October. ✉10018 av. Royale, G0A 3C0☎418/827–3781 ⊕www. ssadb.qc.ca/en/musee.htm 🖾C$2 (free for children 6 and under) ⊘Reception booth daily 9–5. Guided tours June–mid-Oct.

Commemorative Chapel. Across from Basilique Ste-Anne-de-Beaupré, this chapel was designed by Claude Bailiff and built in 1878. It was constructed on the transept of a church built in 1676, and Bailiff made use of the old stones and foundation. Among the remnants is a white-and-gold-trimmed pulpit designed by François Baillargé in 1807 and adorned with a sculpture depicting Moses and the Ten Commandments. **Scala Santa,** a small chapel adjacent to the Commemorative Chapel, resembles a wedding cake. On bended knees, pilgrims climb its replica of the Holy Stairs, representing the steps Jesus climbed to meet Pontius Pilate. ✉Av. Royale ☎No phone ⊘Early May–mid-Oct., daily 8–4:30.

Montmorency Falls. The Montmorency River was named for Charles de Montmorency, viceroy of New France in the 1620s and explorer Samuel de Champlain's immediate commander. The river cascading over a cliff into the St. Lawrence is one of the most beautiful sights in the province—and at 27 stories high, the falls are double the height of Niagara Falls. A cable car runs to the top of the falls in **Parc de la Chute-Montmorency** (Montmorency Falls Park) from late April to early November. During very cold weather the falls' heavy spray freezes and forms a giant loaf-shaped ice cone known to Québécois as the Pain du Sucre (Sugarloaf); this phenomenon attracts sledders and sliders from Québec City. Mid-July to early August, the skies above the falls light up with **Les Grands Feux Loto-Québec** (☎418/523–3389 or

888/934–3473 ⊕*www.lesgrandsfeux.com*), an international competition of fireworks performances set to music. The park also has a historic side. The British general James Wolfe, on his way to conquer New France, camped here in 1759. In 1780 Sir Frederick Haldimand, then the governor of Canada, built a summer home—now a good restaurant called Manoir Montmorency—atop the cliff. The structure burned down, however, and what stands today is a re-creation. The Manoir, open year-round, has a terrace in summertime that offers a stunning view of the falls and river below. ⊠*2490 av. Royale, Beauport* ☎*418/663–3330* ⊕*www.sepaq.com/ct/pcm/en* ⊠*Cable car C$10.50 round-trip, parking C$9.25* ⊙*Cable car daily 8:30* AM*–6:45* PM*, mid-June to late Aug. 8:30* AM*–7:30* PM.

🐾 **Musée de L'Abeille.** Things are buzzing at this economuseum (part of an organization of museums focusing on traditional trades) devoted to bees and honey. A giant glassed-in hive with a tube leading outdoors allows you to take a close look at life inside a beehive. On the bee safari, guides take a hive apart, explaining how it works and how bees behave. You can taste honey made by bees that have fed on different kinds of flowers, from clover to blueberry. The museum is a 10-minute drive east of Montmorency Falls. ⊠*8862 blvd. Ste-Anne, Château-Richer* ☎*418/824–4411* ⊕*www.musee-abeille.com* ⊠*Museum free, bee safari C$4.50* ⊙*Museum open year-round. Call for hours. Bee safari June 15–Labor Day daily, Labor Day–mid-Nov. weekends only.*

Réserve Faunique du Cap Tourmente *(Cap Tourmente Wildlife Reserve).* About 8 km (5 mi) northeast of Ste-Anne-de-Beaupré, more than 800,000 greater snow geese gather here every October and May, with an average of 100,000 birds coming per day. The park harbors hundreds of kinds of birds and mammals, and more than 700 plant species. This enclave on the north shore of the St. Lawrence River also has 18 km (11 mi) of hiking trails; naturalists give guided tours. ⊠*570 chemin du Cap Tourmente, St-Joachim* ☎*418/827–4591* ⊠*C$6* ⊙*Jan.–Oct., daily 8:30–5.*

OFF THE BEATEN PATH

Réserve Faunique des Laurentides. The wildlife reserve, approximately 48 km (30 mi) north of Québec City via Route 175, which leads to the Saguenay region, has good lakes for fishing. It's advisable to reserve a time slot 48 hours ahead by phone or fax. ☎*418/528–6868, 418/890–6527 fishing reservations* 🖷*418/528–8833.*

WHERE TO EAT

$$$ ✗**Auberge Baker.** The best of old and new blend at this restaurant in an 1840 French-Canadian farmhouse built by the owners' ancestors. Antiques and old-fashioned woodstoves decorate the dining rooms, where you can sample traditional Québec fare, from *tourtière* (meat pie) and pork hocks to maple-sugar pie. Or opt for contemporary dishes such as the excellent herbed-and-breaded grilled lamb loin and pastry-wrapped "Ferme d'Oc" goose leg confit and prosciutto. The lower-priced lunch menu is served until 6. Upstairs is a five-room B&B, also decorated in Canadiana; two exterior buildings hold two additional rooms. Château-Richer is 4 km (2½ mi) west of St. Anne's

Basilica. ⊠*8790 av. Royale, Château-Richer* ☎*418/824–4478 or 866/824–4478* ⊕*www.auberge-baker.qc.ca* ⊟*AE, DC, MC, V.*

SPORTS & THE OUTDOORS

Centre de Location de Motoneiges du Québec. Snowmobiles can be rented at Mont-Ste-Anne, starting at C$47 per person (two to a snowmobile) for an hour, which does not include equipment or gas (roughly C$15–C$20). A daylong rental, including trail permits, runs C$126 per person, plus taxes. Expect to pay about C$50–C$70 for gas, depending on your speed and other factors, one being the ever-rising cost of gas. ⊠*15 blvd. Beaupré, Beaupré* ☎*418/827–8478* ⊕*www. locationmotoneiges.com.*

Le Massif. This three-peak ski resort has the longest vertical drop in Canada east of the Rockies—2,526 feet. Owned by Daniel Gauthier, cofounder of Le Cirque du Soleil, the resort has two multi-service chalets at the top and bottom. Five lifts service the 45 trails, which are divided into runs for different levels; the longest run is 4.8 km (2.98 mi). Equipment can be rented on-site. ⊠*1350 rue Principale, Petit-Rivière-St-François* ☎*418/632–5876 or 877/536–2774* ⊕*www. lemassif.com.*

Mont-Ste-Anne. Part of the World Cup downhill circuit, Mont-Ste-Anne is one of the largest resorts in eastern Canada, with a vertical drop of 2,050 feet, 66 downhill trails, two half-pipes for snowboarders, a terrain park, and 13 lifts, including a gondola. Cross-country skiing is also a draw here, with 21 trails totaling 224 km (139 mi). When the weather warms, mountain biking becomes the sport of choice. Enthusiasts can choose from 150 km (93 mi) of mountain-bike trails and 14 downhill runs (and a gondola up to the top). Three bike runs are designated "extreme zones." ⊠*2000 blvd. Beaupré, Beaupré* ☎*418/827–4561 or 800/463–1568* ⊕*www.mont-sainte-anne.com.*

ÎLE D'ORLÉANS

The Algonquins called it Minigo, the "Bewitched Place," and over the years the island's tranquil rural beauty has inspired poets and painters. Île d'Orléans is only 15 minutes by car from downtown Québec City, but a visit here is one of the best ways to get a feel for traditional life in rural Québec. Centuries-old homes and some of the oldest churches in the region dot the road that rings the island. Île d'Orléans is at its best in summer, when the boughs of trees in lush orchards bend under the weight of apples, plums, or pears, and the fields burst with strawberries and raspberries. Roadside stands sell woven articles, maple syrup, baked goods, jams, fruits, and vegetables. You can also pick your own produce at about two-dozen farms. The island, immortalized by one of its most famous residents, the poet and songwriter Félix Leclerc (1914–88), is still fertile ground for artists and artisans.

The island was discovered at about the same time as the future site of Québec City, in 1535. Explorer Jacques Cartier noticed an abundance of vines and called it the Island of Bacchus, after the Greek god of wine. (Today native vines are being crossbred with European varieties at Ste-

Pétronille's fledgling vineyard.) In 1536 Cartier renamed the island in honor of the duke of Orléans, son of the French king François I. Its fertile soil and abundant fishing made it so attractive to settlers that at one time there were more people living here than in Québec City.

About 8 km (5 mi) wide and 35 km (22 mi) long, Île d'Orléans is made up of six small villages that have sought over the years to retain their identities. The bridge to the mainland was built in 1935, and in 1970 the island was declared a historic area to protect it from most sorts of development.

STE-PETRONILLE

17 km (10½ mi) northeast of Québec City.

The lovely village of Ste-Pétronille, the first to be settled on Île d'Orléans, is west of the bridge to the island. Founded in 1648, the community was chosen in 1759 by British general James Wolfe for his headquarters. With 40,000 soldiers and a hundred ships, the English bombarded French-occupied Québec City and Côte de Beaupré.

In the late 19th century the English population of Québec developed Ste-Pétronille into a resort village. This area is considered to be the island's most beautiful, not only because of its spectacular views of Montmorency Falls and Québec City but also for its Regency-style English villas and exquisitely tended gardens.

WHAT TO SEE

Maison Gourdeau de Beaulieu. The island's first home was built in 1648 for Jacques Gourdeau de Beaulieu, the first seigneur (a landholder who distributed lots to tenant farmers) of Ste-Pétronille. Remodeled over the years, this white house with blue shutters now incorporates both French and Québec styles. Its thick walls and dormer windows are characteristic of Breton architecture, but its sloping, bell-shaped roof, designed to protect buildings from large amounts of snow, is typical Québec style. The house is not open to the public. ⊠*137 chemin du Bout de l'Île.*

Plante family farm. Pick apples and strawberries (in season) or buy fresh fruits, vegetables, and apple cider at this family farm. In winter, enjoy maple-sugar treats from the roadside sugar shack. ⊠*20 chemin du Bout de l'Île* ☎*418/828–9603.*

Rue Horatio-Walker. This tiny street off chemin Royal was named after the early-19th-century painter known for his landscapes of the island. Walker lived on this street from 1904 until his death in 1938. At nos. 11 and 13 rue Horatio-Walker are his home and workshop, but they are both closed to the public.

Vignoble de Ste-Pétronille. Hardy native Québec vines have been crossbred with three types of European grapes to produce a surprisingly good dry white wine as well as a red, a rosé, and a locally created ice wine called Vandal. A guided tour of the vineyard includes a tasting. ⊠*1A chemin du Bout de l'Île* ☎*418/828–9554* ⊕*www.vignobleorleans.*

9

com 📷 *Guided tour C$6* 🕐 *Varies by season, best to call for an up-to-date schedule.*

WHERE TO STAY & EAT

$$$ ✕ **La Goéliche.** This English-style country manor, rebuilt in 1996–97 following a fire, is steps away from the St. Lawrence River. Antiques decorate the small but elegant rooms, which all have river views.

> ### HOUSE OF STYLE
>
> The style of houses you'll see in Ste-Pétronille is known as "Regency style," and is marked by their wraparound balconies, four-sided sloped roofs, and colorful shutters.

Classic French cuisine ($$$–$$$$, table d'hôte only in the evening, reservations essential) includes Chef Frédéric Casadei's specialties such as fillet of wapiti with blackcurrant sauce, and cold cantaloupe soup flavored with ice cider and garnished with prosciutto and pancetta. The romantic dining room overlooks the river; an enclosed terrace is open year-round. ✉ *22 chemin du Quai,* 📞 *418/828–2248 or 888/511–2248* 🌐 *www.goeliche.ca* 🟰 *AE, DC, MC, V* ⦿*BP.*

SHOPPING

Chocolaterie de l'Île d'Orléans (✉ *150 chemin du Bout de l'Île* 📞 *418/828–2250*) combines Belgian chocolate with local ingredients to create handmade treats—chocolates filled with maple butter, for example, or *framboisette*, made from raspberries. In summer try the homemade ice creams and sherbets.

ST-LAURENT DE L'ILE D'ORLEANS

9 km (5½ mi) east of Ste-Pétronille.

Founded in 1679, St-Laurent is one of the island's maritime villages. Until as late as 1935, residents here used boats as their main means of transportation. St-Laurent has a rich history in farming and fishing. Work is under way to help bring back to the island some of the species of fish that were once abundant here.

WHAT TO SEE

Église St-Laurent. The tall, inspiring church that stands next to the village marina on chemin Royal was built in 1860 on the site of an 18th-century church that had to be torn down. One of the church's procession chapels is a miniature stone reproduction of the original. ✉ *1532 chemin Royal* 📞 *418/828–2551* 📷 *Free* 🕐 *Mid-June–Oct., daily 9–5.*

La Forge à Pique-Assaut. This forge belongs to the talented local artisan Guy Bel, who has done ironwork restoration for Québec City. He was born in Lyon, France, and studied there at the École des Beaux-Arts. You can watch him and his team at work; his stylish candlesticks, chandeliers, fireplace tools, and other ironwork are for sale. ✉ *2200 chemin Royal* 📞 *418/828–9300* 🌐 *www.forge-pique-assaut.com* 🕐 *June–mid-Oct., daily 9–5; mid-Oct.–May, weekdays 9–noon and 1:30–5.*

Parc Maritime de St-Laurent. This is a former boatyard where craftspeople specializing in boatbuilding practiced their trade. Now you can picnic here and visit the Chalouperie Godbout (Godbout Longboat), which holds a collection of tools used during the golden era of boatbuilding. See fishermen at work trapping eels in tall nets at low tide. ⊠ *120 chemin de la Chalouperie* ☎*418/828–9672* ☒*C$3.50* ⊙*June 24–Labor Day, daily 10–5.*

WHERE TO STAY & EAT

$$$ ✗**Moulin de St-Laurent.** You can dine inside or outside at the foot of the waterfall at this restaurant, converted from an early-18th-century stone mill. Scrumptious snacks, such as quiche and salads, are available on the terrace. Evening dishes include regional salmon and sweetbreads. Stay overnight at one of the Moulin de St-Laurent's chalets, on the edge of the St. Lawrence. There are also lodging packages available from C$420 to C$650. Four chalets are available in winter and seven in summer. ⊠*754 chemin Royal* ☎*418/829–3888 or 888/629–3888* ⊕*www.moulinstlaurent.qc.ca* ☲*AE, DC, MC, V* ⊙*Restaurant closed mid-Oct.–May.*

$$ ☷**Le Canard Huppé.** As the inn's name—the Crested Duck—suggests, its contemporary cuisine ($$–$$$$) usually includes at least one dish with duck, perhaps the rendition with clover honey, fresh thyme, and wild garlic. Chef Philip Rae uses locally raised meat, fish, and fowl. Upstairs, each of the inn's rooms has unusual antiques and original paintings. While the inn is open year-round, the restaurant is closed from November to May. However, when there are guests at the inn during that time period, the restaurant will open for the occasion. **Pros:** ideal spot for gourmands; inventive cuisine; many sights and areas of interest very nearby; good for cyclists. **Cons:** no pool. ⊠*2198 chemin Royal,* ☎*418/828–2292 or 800/838–2292* ⊕*www.canard-huppe.com* ⇄*9 rooms, 1 suite* ⚐*In-room: a/c, refrigerator, Wi-Fi. In-hotel: restaurant, no elevator, public Wi-Fi, parking (no fee), no-smoking rooms* ☲*MC, V* ⊙*Restaurant closed Nov.–May.* ☷*BP.*

9

ST-JEAN

12 km (7 mi) northeast of St-Laurent.

The village of St-Jean used to be occupied by river pilots and navigators. At sea most of the time, the sailors didn't need the large homes and plots of land that the farmers did. Often richer than farmers, they displayed their affluence by building their houses with bricks brought back from Scotland as ballast. Most of St-Jean's small, homogeneous row houses were built between 1840 and 1860.

WHAT TO SEE

Eglise St-Jean. At the eastern end of the village sits a massive granite structure built in 1749, with large red doors and a towering steeple. The church resembles a ship; it's big and round and appears to be sitting right on the river. Paintings of the patron saints of seamen line the interior walls. The church's cemetery is also intriguing, especially if you can read French. Back in the 1700s, piloting the St. Lawrence was a dangerous profession; the cemetery tombstones recall the many lives lost in these harsh waters. ✉*2001 chemin Royal* ☎*418/828–2551* 💳*Free* 🕐*Late May–early Oct., daily 10–5.*

Manoir Mauvide-Genest. St-Jean's beautiful Normandy-style manor was built in 1734 for Jean Mauvide, surgeon to Louis XV, and his wife, Marie-Anne Genest. The most notable thing about this house, which still has its original thick walls, ceiling beams, and fireplaces, is the degree to which it has held up over the years. The house serves as an interpretation center of New France's seigneurial regime, with 18th-century furniture, a multimedia presentation, and tours with guides dressed in 18th-century costumes. ✉*1451 chemin Royal* ☎*418/829–2630* ⊕*www.manoirmauvidegenest.com* 💳*C$6 (non guided tour), C$8 (guided tour)* 🕐*May–Nov., daily 10–5.*

ST-FRANÇOIS

12 km (7 mi) northeast of St-Jean.

Sprawling open fields separate 17th-century farmhouses in St-François, the island's least-toured and most rustic village. This community at the eastern tip of the island was settled mainly by farmers. St-François is the perfect place to visit one of the island's *cabanes à sucre* (maple-sugaring shacks), found along chemin Royal. Stop at a hut for a tasting tour; sap is gathered from the maple groves and boiled until it turns to syrup. When it's poured on ice, it tastes like toffee. The maple-syrup season is from late March through April.

WHAT TO SEE

Eglise St-François. Built in 1734, St-François is one of eight extant provincial churches dating from the French regime. At the time the English seized Québec City in 1759, General James Wolfe knew St-François to be a strategic point along the St. Lawrence. Consequently, he stationed British troops here and used the church as a military hospital. In 1988 a car crash set the church on fire, and most of the interior treasures were lost. A separate children's cemetery stands as a silent witness to the difficult life of early residents. ✉*341 chemin Royal* ☎*419/828–2551* 💳*Free* 🕐*June 24–Sept. 24, daily noon–5.*

Observation Tower. This picnic area with a wooden tower is well situated for viewing the majestic St. Lawrence. In spring and fall wild Canada geese can be seen here. The area is about 2 km (1 mi) north of Eglise St-François on chemin Royal.

STE-FAMILLE

14 km (9 mi) west of St-François.

The village of Ste-Famille, founded in 1661, has exquisite scenery, including abundant apple orchards and strawberry fields with views of Côte de Beaupré and Mont-Ste-Anne in the distance. But it also has plenty of historic charm, with the area's highest concentration of stone houses dating from the French regime.

WHAT TO SEE

Eglise Ste-Famille. This impressive church, constructed in 1749, is the only one in Québec province to have three bell towers at its front. The ceiling was redone in the mid-19th century with elaborate designs in wood and gold. The church also holds a famous painting, *L'Enfant Jésus Voyant la Croix (Baby Jesus Looking at the Cross)*. It was done in 1670 by Frère Luc (Father Luc), sent from France to decorate churches in the area. ✉3915 chemin Royal ☎418/828–2656 ✉Free ⊗Late June–early Sept., daily 11–5.

ST-PIERRE

14 km (9 mi) southwest of Ste-Famille.

St-Pierre, established in 1679, is set on a plateau that has the island's most fertile land. The town has long been the center of traditional farming industries. The best products grown here are potatoes, asparagus, and corn. In 2002 the Espace Félix Leclerc—an exhibit by day and a *boîte à chansons* (combination coffeehouse and bar with live performances) by night—was opened to honor the late singer and songwriter who made St-Pierre his home. If you continue west on chemin Royal, just ahead is the bridge to the mainland and Route 440.

WHAT TO SEE

Eglise St-Pierre. The oldest church on the island dates from 1717. It's no longer used for worship, but it was restored during the 1960s and is open to visitors. Many original components are still intact, such as benches with compartments below where hot bricks and stones were placed to keep people warm in winter. Félix Leclerc, the first Québécois singer to make a mark in Europe, is buried in the cemetery nearby. ✉1249 chemin Royal ☎418/828–9824 ✉Free ⊗May, June and Sept.–Oct., daily 10–5; July and Aug., daily 9:30–5.

La Ferme Monna–L'Isle Ensorceleuse. This family farm has won international awards for its *crème de cassis de l'Île d'Orléans,* a liqueur made from black currants. The farm offers free samples of the strong, sweet cassis or one of its black-currant wines; the tour explains how they are made. In summer you can sample foods made with cassis on a terrace overlooking the river. ✉726 chemin Royal ☎418/828–1057 ✉Free, guided tour C$5 ⊗June–Nov., daily 10–6.

SHOPPING

Poissonnerie Joseph Paquet. The only remaining commercial fisherman on the island smokes his fish and sells it from a tiny shack. You can sample surprisingly tasty smoked eel as well as smoked trout and salmon. Also on sale are fresh and smoked walleye pike and sturgeon, all from the St. Lawrence River. New products include a sturgeon mousse and, a most rare treat—sturgeon *méchoui*: the fish is marinated in salt the traditional way, and then roasted on a spit. ✉2705 chemin Royal ☎418/828–2670 ⊗June 24–Oct. 8, daily 10–6; Oct. 9–June 23, daily 10–5; Jan.–Feb. upon request.

9

CHARLEVOIX

Bordered by the Laurentian Mountains to the north, the Saguenay River to the east, and the St. Lawrence River to the south, the Charlevoix region is famous for awe-inspiring vistas and kaleidoscopes of color that change throughout the day. The region also has rich historical significance for both French Canadians and English Canadians. The "discoverer" of Canada, Jacques Cartier, is believed to have set foot in the area in 1535. More certain is a visit 73 years later by Samuel de Champlain.

New France's first historian, the Jesuit priest François-Xavier de Charlevoix (pronounced sharle-*vwah*), is the region's namesake. The area's first white inhabitants arrived in the early 1700s. Among other things, they developed a small shipbuilding industry that specialized in sturdy schooners called *goélettes,* which were used to haul everything from logs to lobsters up and down the coast in the days before rail and paved roads. In the 19th century, as steamships plied the St. Lawrence, Charlevoix became a popular tourist destination for well-to-do English Canadians and British colonial administrators from Montréal and Québec City. Since then, tourism—and hospitality—has become Charlevoix's trademark.

The region has attracted and inspired generations of painters, poets, writers, and musicians from across Québec and Canada, and became a UNESCO World Biosphere Reserve in 1989. In summer, hiking, fishing, picnicking, sightseeing, and whale-watching are the area's main attractions. Winter activities include downhill and cross-country skiing, ski-dooing (or snowmobiling), ice fishing, dogsledding, and snowshoeing.

BAIE-ST-PAUL

120 km (72 mi) northeast of Québec City.

Baie-St-Paul, one of the oldest towns in the province, is popular with craftspeople and artists. With its centuries-old mansard-roof houses, the village is situated on the banks of a winding river on a wide plain encircled by high hills. Boutiques and a handful of commercial galleries line the historic narrow streets in the town center; most have original artwork and crafts for sale. In addition, each August more than a dozen artists from across Canada take part in the "Symposium of Modern Art." The artists work together to create a giant canvas about the year's theme.

WHAT TO SEE
Centre d'Art Baie-St-Paul. Adjacent to the city's main church, this center displays a diverse collection of works by more than 20 Charlevoix artists. In the tapestry atelier, weavers create traditional and contemporary pieces and demonstrate techniques. ⊠ *4 rue Ambroise-Fafard* 🏛 *418/435–3681* 💬 *Free* 🕙 *Apr.–mid-June, Tues.–Sun. 10–5; late June–early Sept., Tues.–Sun. 10–6; early Sept.–mid-Nov., Tues.–Sun. 10–5; mid-Nov.–Mar., Fri.–Sun. 10–5.*

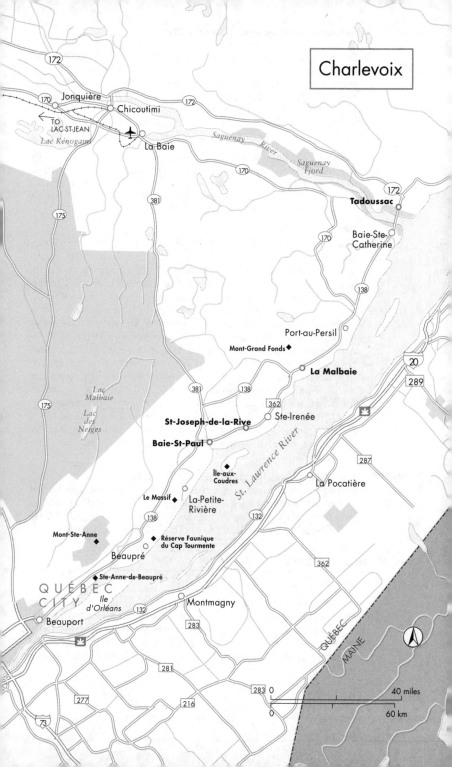

Centre d'Exposition de Baie-St-Paul. The mandate of the exhibition center is to promote modern and contemporary art created by Charlevoix artists from 1920 to 1970. The center is in a modern building that was awarded a provincial architectural prize in 1992. ⊠*23 rue Ambroise-Fafard* ☏*418/435–3681* ⌸*C$4* ⊘ *June 24–early Sept., Tues., Wed., and Sun. 12–5, Thurs.–Sat. noon–9; Sept.–June, Sun. 11–5, Tues.–Fri. 11–5, Sat. 12–6* ⊕*www.centredart-bsp.qc.ca.*

Maison René Richard. Jean-Paul Lemieux, Clarence Gagnon, and many more of Québec's greatest landscape artists have depicted the area. Some of these works are for sale at this gallery that also houses Gagnon's old studio. ⊠*58 rue St-Jean-Baptiste* ☏*418/435–5571* ⌸*Free, C$4 (guided tour)* ⊘*Daily 10–6.*

WHERE TO STAY

$$$ 🖼**Auberge la Maison Otis.** Three buildings in the village center house the calm, romantic accommodations of this inn. Some guest rooms, decorated in traditional or country styles, have whirlpools, fireplaces, and antique furnishings. There are also three apartments. The restaurant ($$$$), in an elegant, Norman-style house that dates to the mid-1850s, serves creative, regionally oriented French cuisine, such as *pintade,* a local fowl, lamb, or Angus beef. Dinner is a five-course, fixed-price affair, but you can also order à la carte. At the Café des Artistes you'll find espresso and Guinness on tap. Food includes European-style pizzas, pasta, and soup. It's a very popular spot. **Pros:** lots of activities available for all age groups on-site or very nearby, reasonable spa packages, opportunity to see original local art works for free. **Cons:** limited wheelchair access. ⊠*23 rue St-Jean-Baptiste,* ☏*418/435–2255 or 800/267–2254* ⊕*www.maisonotis.com* ⤶*29 rooms, 4 suites, 3 apartments* ⌂*In-room: no a/c (some), dial-up. In-hotel: restaurant, bar, pool, no elevator, public Wi-Fi, spa, some pets allowed* ⊟*MC, V* ⍾*MAP.*

▮ EN
ROUTE
From Baie-St-Paul, instead of the faster Route 138 to La Malbaie, drivers can choose the open, scenic coastal drive on **Route 362.** This section of road has memorable views of rolling hills—green, white, or ablaze with fiery hues, depending on the season—meeting the broad expanse of the "sea," as the locals like to call the St. Lawrence estuary.

ST-JOSEPH-DE-LA-RIVE

19 km (12 mi) northeast of Baie-St-Paul.

A secondary road descends sharply into St-Joseph-de-la-Rive, with its line of old houses hugging the mountain base on a narrow shore route. The town has a number of peaceful inns and inviting restaurants. Drive through and see the traces of early town life and the beginning of local industry: an old firehouse and a hydroelectric building that houses a generator dating back to 1928.

WHAT TO SEE

Exposition Maritime *(Maritime Museum).* This small exhibit, housed in an old, still-active shipyard, commemorates the days of the St. Lawrence goélettes, the feisty little schooners that, until the 1950s, were the lifeblood of the region. In the mid-20th century the roads through Charlevoix were little more than rugged tracks. (Indeed, they are still narrow and winding.) Very large families lived in cramped conditions aboard the boats. To modern eyes, it doesn't look like it was a comfortable existence, but the folklore of the goélettes, celebrated in poetry, paintings, and song, is part of the region's strong cultural identity. ✉ *305 pl. de l'Eglise* ☎ *418/635–1131* 🎫 *C$5* ⊙ *Mid-May–mid-June and early Sept.–mid-Oct., weekdays 9–4, weekends 11–4; mid-June–early Sept., daily 9–5.*

Île-aux-Coudres. A free, government-run ferry from the wharf in St-Joseph-de-la-Rive takes you on the 15-minute trip to the island where Jacques Cartier's men gathered *coudres* (hazelnuts) in 1535. Since then, the island has produced many a goélette, and the families of former captains now run several small inns. You can bike around the island and see windmills and water mills, or stop at boutiques selling paintings and crafts such as traditional handwoven household linens. ☎ *418/438–2743 ferry information.*

WHERE TO STAY

$$ 🏨 **Hôtel Cap-aux-Pierres.** One of several properties originally established by the entrepreneurial Dufour family in the 1930s to support their 17 children, the traditional Canadian main building of this hotel has a long veranda with river views. Comfortable accommodations are also available in a motel section, open only in summer. About a third of the rooms have views of the river. The restaurant serves a mix of Québec standards and French cuisine; summer entertainment includes folk dancing on Saturday evening. **Pros:** beautiful environment. **Cons:** hotel rooms fairly unspectacular and motel rooms could use updating. ✉ *444 chemin la Baleine, Île-aux-Coudres, La Baleine* ☎ *888/554–6003 for hotel, 418/438–2711* ⊕ *www.hotelcapauxpierres.com* 🛏 *98 rooms* ☆ *In-room: no a/c (some), dial-up. In-hotel: restaurant, bar, tennis court, pool, spa, no-smoking rooms, some pets allowed* ☰ *AE, D, DC, MC, V* ⊙ *Closed mid-Oct.–Apr.* �🍴EP.

SHOPPING

Papeterie St-Gilles (✉ *354 rue F.A. Savard* ☎ *418/635–2430 or 866/635–2430* ⊕ *www.papeteriestgilles.com*) produces handcrafted stationery using a 17th-century process. The paper factory, which is also a small museum, explains through photographs and demonstrations how paper is manufactured the old-fashioned way. Slivers of wood and flower petals are pressed into the paper sheets, which are as thick as the covers of a paperback book. The finished products—made into writing paper, greeting cards, and one-page poems or quotations—make beautiful, if pricey, gifts.

LA MALBAIE

35 km (22 mi) northeast of St-Joseph-de-la-Rive.

La Malbaie, one of the province's most elegant and historically interesting resort towns, was known as Murray Bay when wealthy Anglophones summered here. The area became popular with American and Canadian politicians in the late 1800s, when Ottawa Liberals and Washington Republicans partied decorously all summer with members of the Québec judiciary. William Howard Taft built the "summer White House," the first of three summer residences, in 1894, when he was the American civil governor of the Philippines. He became the 27th president of the United States in 1908.

Many Taft-era homes now serve as handsome inns, offering old-fashioned coddling with such extras as breakfast in bed, whirlpool baths, and free shuttles to the ski areas in winter. Many serve lunch and dinner to nonresidents, so you can tour the area going from one gourmet delight to the next. The cuisine, as elsewhere in Québec, is genuine French or regional fare.

WHAT TO SEE

Casino de Charlevoix. The casino is one of three gaming halls in Québec (the others are in Montréal and Hull) owned and operated by Loto-Québec. The smallest of the three, it still draws more than 1 million visitors a year—some of whom stay at the Fairmont Le Manoir Richelieu, which is connected to the casino by a tunnel. There are 20 gaming tables and more than 800 slot machines. The minimum gambling age is 18. Photo ID is required to enter the casino. ✉ *183 rue Richelieu, Pointe-au-Pic* ☎ *418/665–5300 or 800/665–2274* ⊕ *www.casino-de-charlevoix.com* ⊗ *Mid-June–Aug., Sun.–Thurs. 9 AM–2 AM, Fri. and Sat. 9 AM–3 AM; Sept.–late-Oct., Sun.–Thurs. 10 AM–1 AM, Fri. and Sat. 10 AM–3 AM.*

Musée de Charlevoix. The museum traces the region's history through a major permanent exhibit called "Appartenances" (Belonging), installed in 2003. Folk art, paintings, and artifacts recount the past, starting with the French, then the Scottish settlers, and the area's evolution into a vacation spot and artists' haven. ✉ *10 chemin du Havre, Pointe-au-Pic* ☎ *418/665–4411* ⊕ *www.museedecharlevoix.ca* ✒ *C$7* ⊗ *June–mid-Oct., daily 9–5.*

OFF THE BEATEN PATH

Poterie de Port-au-Persil. Visiting potters, many from France, study Canadian ceramic techniques at this pottery studio, about 25 km (15½ mi) east of La Malbaie. Classes for amateurs are available from late June through August (by the hour or longer starting at C$12). Half of the bright yellow barn housing the studio is a store, with ceramics and other crafts made by Québec artists. ✉ *1001 rue St-Laurent (Rte. 138), St-Siméon* ☎ *418/638–2349* ⊕ *www.poteriedeportaupersil.com* ⊗ *May–mid-Oct., daily 9–6; off-season, daily 10–4.*

WHERE TO STAY

$$$$ 🏨 **Auberge la Pinsonnière.** An atmosphere of country luxury prevails at this Relais & Châteaux inn, which has an impressive art collection. After a major renovation project in 2006, this five-star inn has fewer, more-luxurious rooms. All have fireplaces and whirlpools, and most have king-size beds. The bathrooms are luxurious, with a sauna or steam shower. Certain rooms have private balconies with glass walls that overlook Murray Bay on the St. Lawrence River. With a 25-foot window and balcony, you'll feel like you're sleeping on the river! The restaurant ($$$$) is excellent, and the auberge has one of the largest wine cellars in North America, housing 12,000 bottles. The haute cuisine doesn't come cheap; the appetizers, including duck foie gras with apple and five-spice chutney, butter-proached Arctic char, and chilled sugarsnap pea soup with shredded snow crab, cost as much as the entrées in other area establishments, but the dining experience is worth the money. **Pros:** friendly staff, the fireplaces in every room, views of Murray Bay, luxurious surroundings in a remote environment. **Cons:** not vegetarian-friendly. ✉*124 rue St-Raphaël, Cap-à-l'Aigle,* ☎*418/665–4431 or 800/387–4431* ⊕*www.lapinsonniere.com* ⤵*18 rooms* ☂*In-room: a/c, safe, refrigerator, Wi-Fi. In-hotel: restaurant, bar, tennis court, pool, spa, beachfront, no elevator, no-smoking rooms* ⊟*AE, MC, V.*

$$$$ 🏨 **Fairmont Le Manoir Richelieu.** Constructed in 1929, this castle-like building and its sweeping grounds underwent a C$100 million restoration in the late 1990s. The restaurants offer a wide range of food, from family fare to haute cuisine. At the clubby after-dinner lounge you can smoke a cigar and sip a single-malt or vintage port. The full-service spa has 22 treatment rooms, and the links-style golf course overlooks the St. Lawrence. A tunnel connects the hotel with the Casino de Charlevoix. A sports facility—including two heated pools and a Jacuzzi outside, and a pool, hot tub, and steam bath indoors—is great for all ages. **Pros:** stunning views, variety of dining options on-site. **Cons:** limited parking space on grounds, rooms could use updating. ✉*181 rue Richelieu, Pointe-au-Pic,* ☎*418/665–3703 or 800/463–2613* ⊕*www. fairmont.com* ⤵*390 rooms, 15 suites* ☂*In-room: safe, refrigerator, Wi-Fi. In-hotel: 3 restaurants, room service, bars, public Wi-Fi, golf course, tennis courts, pool, gym, spa, bicycles, concierge, children's programs (ages 4–12), laundry service, executive floor, no-smoking rooms, some pets allowed* ⊟*AE, DC, MC, V* ⦿*BP.*

$$ 🏨 **Auberge des Peupliers.** About half the guest rooms at this hilltop inn overlook the St. Lawrence River. Accommodations, outfitted in country-style furnishings, are spread among three buildings, including a farmhouse more than two centuries old. A former barn holds more luxurious rooms, some with terraces; a stone house has rooms with fireplaces and balconies. At the restaurant ($$$), chef Dominique Truchon earns high marks for dishes such as Chilean bass and grilled giant shrimp with red quinoa, vegetables, almond, and ginger, among others. For an extra C$70 your lodging can include the evening five-course table d'hôte for two. **Pros:** lounge with fireplace and bar perfect for relaxing; excellent food and service. **Cons:** if spa treatments are not made at time of booking, there may be no availability at time of arrival. ✉*381 rue St-Raphaël, Cap-à-l'Aigle,* ☎*418/665–4423 or 888/282– 3743* ⊕*www.aubergedespeupliers.com* ⇱*22 rooms* ⌂*In-hotel: res- taurant, bar, tennis court, no elevator, no-smoking rooms* ⊟*AE, DC, MC, V* ⊗*No lunch* ⦿*BP.*

THE ARTS

Domaine Forget (✉*5 St-Antoine, Ste-Irenée* ☎*418/452–3535 or 888/336–7438* ⊕*www.domaineforget.com*) is a music and dance acad- emy that has a 604-seat hall in Ste-Irenée, 15 km (9 mi) south of La Malbaie. Fine musicians from around the world, many of whom teach or study at the school, perform during its International Festival. The festival, which runs from mid-June to late August, includes Sunday musical brunches with a variety of music, a buffet lunch, and a view of the St. Lawrence.

SPORTS & THE OUTDOORS

Club de Golf de Manoir Richelieu (✉*181 rue Richelieu, Pointe-au-Pic* ☎*418/665–2526 or 800/665–8082* ⊕*www.fairmont.com*) is a par-71, 6,225-yard, links-style course with 18 holes. Greens fees start at C$50 to C$165 depending on whether you are a hotel guest or a visitor. The resort also has a 9-hole course.

Mont-Grand Fonds (✉*1000 chemin des Loisirs* ☎*418/665–0095 or 877/665–0095* ⊕*www.montgrandfonds.com*), a winter-sports center 10 km (6 mi) north of La Malbaie, has 14 downhill slopes, a 1,105-foot vertical drop, and three lifts. It also has 160 km (99 mi) of cross-coun- try trails. Two trails meet International Ski Federation standards, and the ski center occasionally hosts major competitions. You may also go dogsledding, sleigh riding, ice-skating and tobogganing here.

TADOUSSAC

71 km (44 mi) north of La Malbaie.

The small town of Tadoussac shares the view up the magnificent Saguenay Fjord with Baie-Ste-Catherine, across the Saguenay River. The drive here from La Malbaie, along Route 138, leads past lovely villages and views along the St. Lawrence. Jacques Cartier made a stop at this point in 1535, and from 1600 to the mid-19th century it was an important meeting site for fur traders. Whale-watching excursions and fjord cruises now depart from Tadoussac, as well as from Chicoutimi, farther up the deep fjord.

As the Saguenay River flows from Lac St-Jean south toward the St. Lawrence, it has a dual character: between Alma and Chicoutimi, the once rapidly flowing river has been harnessed for hydroelectric power; in its lower section, it becomes wider and deeper and flows by steep mountains and cliffs en route to the St. Lawrence. Small, white beluga whales, which live here year-round, breed in the lower portion of the Saguenay in summer. The many marine species that live in the conflu- ence of the fjord and the seaway attract other whales, too, such as pilots, finbacks, and humpbacks.

Sadly, the beluga is an endangered species; the whales, with 35 other species of mammals and birds and 21 species of fish, are threatened by pollution in the St. Lawrence River. This has spurred a C$100 million project (funded by the federal and provincial governments) aimed at removing or capping sediment in the most polluted areas, stopping industrial and residential emissions into the river, and restoring natural habitat.

WHAT TO SEE

Centre d'Interprétation des Mammifères Marins. You can learn more about the whales and their habitat at this interpretation center run by members of a locally based research team. They're only too glad to answer questions. In addition, explanatory videos and exhibits (including a collection of whale skeletons) tell you everything there is to know about the mighty cetaceans. ✉ *108 rue de la Cale-Sèche* ☎ *418/235–4701* ⊕ *www.whales-online.net* ✆ *C$8* ⊗ *Mid-May–mid-June and mid-Sept.–mid-Oct., daily noon–5; mid-June–mid-Sept., daily 9–8.*

Parc Marin du Saguenay–St-Laurent. The 800-square-km (309-square-mi) marine park, at the confluence of the Saguenay and St. Lawrence rivers, has been created to protect the latter's fragile ecosystem. ✉ *Park office: 182 rue de l'Église* ☎ *418/235–4703 or 800/463–6769* ⊕ *www.parcmarin.qc.ca.*

WHERE TO STAY

$$$–$$$$ ⬛ **Hôtel Tadoussac.** The rambling white Victorian-style hotel with a red mansard roof is as much a symbol of Tadoussac as the Château Frontenac is of Québec City. The 1942 wood building has retained its gracefulness over the years. The spacious lobby has a stone fireplace and sofas for relaxing. Long corridors lead to country-furnished rooms; half of them overlook the bay, the starting point for whale-watching and fjord tours. Hand-painted murals and wood paneling from the 1852 hotel that originally stood on this site encircle the oldest dining room. **Pros:** they have an ongoing sustainability program and strive to be "green," winning the Three Green Keys award from the Hotel Association of Canada's Green Key Eco-rating program; stunning natural environment; 3 different restaurants to suit tastes and budget. **Cons:** no a/c in rooms. ✉ *165 rue Bord d'Eau,* ☎ *418/235–4421 or 800/561–0718* ⊕ *www.hoteltadoussac.com* ➱ *149 rooms* ♿ *In-room: no a/c. In-hotel: 3 restaurants, bar, mini-golf, tennis court, pool, spa, no-smoking rooms, public Wi-Fi* ▤ *AE, D, DC, MC, V* ⊗ *Closed mid-Oct.–early May* ⍾ *EP.*

9

SPORTS & THE OUTDOORS

The best months for seeing whales are August and September, although some operators extend the season at either end if whales are around. **Croisières AML** (☎ *418/692–1159 or 800/463–1292* ⊕ *www. croisieresaml.com*) offers two- to three-hour whale-watching tours for C$59 for either the Whales and Islands tour or the Whales and Fjord tour. The tours, in Zodiacs or larger boats, depart from Baie-Ste-Catherine and Tadoussac. Fjord tours are also available.

Croisières Dufour (☎ *800/463–5250* ⊕ *www.dufour.ca*) offers daylong cruises combined with whale-watching from Québec City as well as 2¼- and 3-hour whale-watching cruises (C$59) from Baie-Ste-Catherine and Tadoussac. Tours, some of which cruise up the Saguenay Fjord, use Zodiacs or larger boats.

FRENCH VOCABULARY

One of the trickiest French sounds to pronounce is the nasal final n sound (whether or not the n is actually the last letter of the word). You should try to pronounce it as a sort of nasal grunt—as in "huh." The vowel that precedes the n will govern the vowel sound of the word, and in this list we precede the final n with an h to remind you to be nasal.

Another problem sound is the ubiquitous but untransliterable eu, as in bleu (blue) or deux (two), and the very similar sound in je (I), ce (this), and de (of). The closest equivalent might be the vowel sound in "put," but rounded. The famous rolled r is a glottal sound. Consonants at the ends of words are usually silent; when the following word begins with a vowel, however, the two are run together by sounding the consonant. There are two forms of "you" in French: vous (formal and plural) and tu (a singular, personal form). When addressing an adult you don't know, vous is always best.

	ENGLISH	FRENCH	PRONUNCIATION
BASICS			
	Yes/no	Oui/non	wee/nohn
	Please	S'il vous plaît	seel voo play
	Thank you	Merci	mair-**see**
	You're welcome	De rien	deh ree-**ehn**
	Excuse me, sorry	Pardon	pahr-**don**
	Good morning/ afternoon	Bonjour	bohn-**zhoor**
	Good evening	Bonsoir	bohn-**swahr**
	Goodbye	Au revoir	o ruh-**vwahr**
	Mr. (Sir)	Monsieur	muh-**syuh**
	Mrs. (Ma'am)	Madame	ma-**dam**
	Miss	Mademoiselle	mad-mwa-**zel**
	Pleased to meet you	Enchanté(e)	ohn-shahn-**tay**
	How are you?	Comment allez-vous?	kuh-mahn- tahl-ay **voo**
	Very well, thanks	Très bien, merci	tray bee-ehn, mair-**see**
	And you?	Et vous?	ay voo?
NUMBERS			
	one	un	uhn
	two	deux	deuh
	three	trois	twah
	four	quatre	**kaht**-ruh
	five	cinq	sank
	six	six	seess

ENGLISH	FRENCH	PRONUNCIATION
seven	sept	set
eight	huit	wheat
nine	neuf	nuf
ten	dix	deess
eleven	onze	ohnz
twelve	douze	dooz
thirteen	treize	trehz
fourteen	quatorze	kah-torz
fifteen	quinze	kanz
sixteen	seize	sez
seventeen	dix-sept	deez-**set**
eighteen	dix-huit	deez-**wheat**
nineteen	dix-neuf	deez-**nuf**
twenty	vingt	vehn
twenty-one	vingt-et-un	vehnt-ay-**uhn**
thirty	trente	trahnt
forty	quarante	ka-**rahnt**
fifty	cinquante	sang-**kahnt**
sixty	soixante	swa-**sahnt**
seventy	soixante-dix	swa-sahnt-**deess**
eighty	quatre-vingts	kaht-ruh-**vehn**
ninety	quatre-vingt-dix	kaht-ruh-vehn-**deess**
one hundred	cent	sahn
one thousand	mille	meel

COLORS

black	noir	nwahr
blue	bleu	bleuh
brown	brun/marron	bruhn/mar-**rohn**
green	vert	vair
orange	orange	o-**rahnj**
pink	rose	rose
red	rouge	rouge
violet	violette	vee-o-**let**
white	blanc	blahnk
yellow	jaune	zhone

ENGLISH	FRENCH	PRONUNCIATION
DAYS OF THE WEEK		
Sunday	dimanche	dee-**mahnsh**
Monday	lundi	luhn-**dee**
Tuesday	mardi	mahr-**dee**
Wednesday	mercredi	mair-kruh-**dee**
Thursday	jeudi	zhuh-**dee**
Friday	vendredi	vawn-druh-**dee**
Saturday	samedi	sahm-**dee**
MONTHS		
January	janvier	zhahn-vee-**ay**
February	février	feh-vree-**ay**
March	mars	marce
April	avril	a-**vreel**
May	mai	meh
June	juin	zhwehn
July	juillet	zhwee-**ay**
August	août	ah-**oo**
September	septembre	sep-**tahm**-bruh
October	octobre	awk-**to**-bruh
November	novembre	no-**vahm**-bruh
December	décembre	day-**sahm**-bruh
USEFUL PHRASES		
Do you speak English?	Parlez-vous anglais?	par-lay **voo ahn**-glay
I don't speak . . .	Je ne parle pas . . .	zhuh nuh parl pah
French	français	frahn-**say**
I don't understand	Je ne comprends pas	zhuh nuh kohm-**prahn** pah
I understand	Je comprends	zhuh kohm-**prahn**
I don't know	Je ne sais pas	zhuh nuh say **pah**
I'm American/ British	Je suis américain/ anglais	a-may-ree-**kehn**/ ahn-**glay**
What's your name?	Comment vous ap pelez-vous?	ko-mahn voo za-pell-ay-**voo**
My name is . . .	Je m'appelle . . .	zhuh ma-**pell** . . .
What time is it?	Quelle heure est-il?	kel air eh-**teel**
How?	Comment?	ko-**mahn**

ENGLISH	FRENCH	PRONUNCIATION
When?	Quand?	kahn
Yesterday	Hier	yair
Today	Aujourd'hui	o-zhoor-**dwee**
Tomorrow	Demain	duh-**mehn**
Tonight	Ce soir	suh **swahr**
What?	Quoi?	kwah
What is it?	Qu'est-ce que c'est?	kess-kuh-**say**
Why?	Pourquoi?	**poor**-kwa
Who?	Qui?	kee
Where is . . .	Où est . . .	oo ay
the train station?	la gare?	la gar
the subway station?	la station de métro?	la sta-**syon** duh may-**tro**
the bus stop?	l'arrêt de bus?	la-**ray** duh **booss**
the post office?	la poste?	la post
the bank?	la banque?	la bahnk
the . . . hotel?	l'hôtel . . .?	lo-**tel**
the store?	le magasin?	luh ma-ga-**zehn**
the cashier?	la caisse?	la **kess**
the . . . museum?	le musée . . .?	luh mew-**zay**
the hospital?	l'hôpital?	lo-pee-**tahl**
the elevator?	l'ascenseur?	la-sahn-**seuhr**
the telephone?	le téléphone?	luh tay-lay-**phone**
Where are the restrooms?	Où sont les toilettes?	oo sohn lay twah-**let**
(men/women)	(hommes/femmes)	(**oh**-mm/**fah**-mm)
Here/there	Ici/là	ee-**see**/la
Left/right	A gauche/à droite	a goash/a draht
Straight ahead	Tout droit	too drwah
Is it near/far?	C'est près/loin?	say pray/lwehn
I'd like . . .	Je voudrais . . .	zhuh voo-**dray**
a room	une chambre	ewn **shahm**-bruh
the key	la clé	la clay
a newspaper	un journal	uhn zhoor-**nahl**
a stamp	un timbre	uhn **tam**-bruh
I'd like to buy . . .	Je voudrais acheter . . .	zhuh voo-**dray** **ahsh**-tay

ENGLISH	FRENCH	PRONUNCIATION
cigarettes	des cigarettes	day see-ga-**ret**
matches	des allumettes	days a-loo-**met**
soap	du savon	dew sah-**vohn**
city map	un plan de ville	uhn plahn de **veel**
road map	une carte routière	ewn cart roo-tee-**air**
magazine	une revue	ewn reh-**vu**
envelopes	des enveloppes	dayz ahn-veh-**lope**
writing paper	du papier à lettres	dew pa-pee-**ay** a **let**-ruh
postcard	une carte postale	ewn cart pos-**tal**
How much is it?	C'est combien?	say comb-bee-**ehn**
A little/a lot	Un peu/beaucoup	uhn peuh/bo-**koo**
More/less	Plus/moins	plu/mwehn
Enough/too (much)	Assez/trop	a-say/tro
I am ill/sick	Je suis malade	zhuh swee ma-**lahd**
Call a . . .	Appelez un . . .	a-play uhn
doctor	Docteur	dohk-**tehr**
Help!	Au secours!	o suh-**koor**
Stop!	Arrêtez!	a-reh-**tay**
Fire!	Au feu!	o fuh
Caution!/Look out!	Attention!	a-tahn-see-**ohn**

DINING OUT

A bottle of . . .	une bouteille de . . .	ewn boo-**tay** duh
A cup of . . .	une tasse de . . .	ewn tass duh
A glass of . . .	un verre de . . .	uhn vair duh
Bill/check	l'addition	la-dee-see-**ohn**
Bread	du pain	dew pan
Breakfast	le petit-déjeuner	luh puh-**tee** day-zhuh-**nay**
Butter	du beurre	dew burr
Cheers!	A votre santé!	ah vo-truh sahn-**tay**
Cocktail/aperitif	un apéritif	uhn ah-pay-ree-**teef**
Dinner	le dîner	luh dee-**nay**
Dish of the day	le plat du jour	luh plah dew **zhoor**
Enjoy!	Bon appétit!	bohn a-pay-**tee**
Fixed-price menu	le menu	luh may-**new**
Fork	une fourchette	ewn four-**shet**

ENGLISH	FRENCH	PRONUNCIATION
I am diabetic	Je suis diabétique	zhuh swee dee-ah- bay-**teek**
I am vegetarian	Je suis végétarien(ne)	zhuh swee vay-zhay-ta-ree-**en**
I cannot eat . . .	Je ne peux pas manger de . . .	zhuh nuh **puh** pah mahn-**jay** deh
I'd like to order	Je voudrais commander	zhuh voo-**dray** ko-mahn-**day**
Is service/the tip included?	Est-ce que le service est compris?	ess kuh luh sair-**veess** ay comb-**pree**
It's good/bad	C'est bon/mauvais	say bohn/mo-**vay**
It's hot/cold	C'est chaud/froid	Say sho/frwah
Knife	un couteau	uhn koo-**toe**
Lunch	le déjeuner	luh day-zhuh-**nay**
Menu	la carte	la cart
Napkin	une serviette	ewn sair-vee-**et**
Pepper	du poivre	dew **pwah**-vruh
Plate	une assiette	ewn a-see-**et**
Please give me . . .	Donnez-moi . . .	doe-nay-**mwah**
Salt	du sel	dew sell
Spoon	une cuillère	ewn kwee-air
Sugar	du sucre	dew **sook**-ruh
Waiter!/Waitress!	Monsieur!/ Mademoiselle!	muh-**syuh**/ mad-mwa-**zel**
Wine list	la carte des vins	la cart day vehn

MENU GUIDE

FRENCH	ENGLISH
GENERAL DINING	
Entrée	Appetizer/Starter
Garniture au choix	Choice of vegetable side
Plat du jour	Dish of the day
Selon arrivage	When available
Supplément/En sus	Extra charge
Sur commande	Made to order
PETIT DÉJEUNER (BREAKFAST)	
Confiture	Jam
Miel	Honey
Oeuf à la coque	Boiled egg

FRENCH	ENGLISH
Oeufs sur le plat	Fried eggs
Oeufs brouillés	Scrambled eggs
Tartine	Bread with butter

POISSONS/FRUITS DE MER (FISH/SEAFOOD)

Anchois	Anchovies
Bar	Bass
Brandade de morue	Creamed salt cod
Brochet	Pike
Cabillaud/Morue	Fresh cod
Calmar	Squid
Coquilles St-Jacques	Scallops
Crevettes	Shrimp
Daurade	Sea bream
Ecrevisses	Prawns/Crayfish
Harengs	Herring
Homard	Lobster
Huîtres	Oysters
Langoustine	Prawn/Lobster
Lotte	Monkfish
Moules	Mussels
Palourdes	Clams
Saumon	Salmon
Thon	Tuna
Truite	Trout

VIANDE (MEAT)

Agneau	Lamb
Boeuf	Beef
Boudin	Sausage
Boulettes de viande	Meatballs
Brochettes	Kebabs
Cassoulet	Casserole of white beans, meat
Cervelle	Brains
Chateaubriand	Double fillet steak
Choucroute garnie	Sausages with sauerkraut
Côtelettes	Chops
Côte/Côte de boeuf	Rib/T-bone steak
Cuisses de grenouilles	Frogs' legs
Entrecôte	Rib or rib-eye steak
Épaule	Shoulder
Escalope	Cutlet
Foie	Liver
Gigot	Leg

FRENCH	ENGLISH
Porc	Pork
Ris de veau	Veal sweetbreads
Rognons	Kidneys
Saucisses	Sausages
Selle	Saddle
Tournedos	Tenderloin of T-bone steak
Veau	Veal

METHODS OF PREPARATION

A point	Medium
A l'étouffée	Stewed
Au four	Baked
Ballotine	Boned, stuffed, and rolled
Bien cuit	Well-done
Bleu	Very rare
Frit	Fried
Grillé	Grilled
Rôti	Roast
Saignant	Rare

VOLAILLES/GIBIER (POULTRY/GAME)

Blanc de volaille	Chicken breast
Canard/Caneton	Duck/Duckling
Cerf/Chevreuil	Venison (red/roe)
Coq au vin	Chicken stewed in red wine
Dinde/Dindonneau	Turkey/Young turkey
Faisan	Pheasant
Lapin/Lièvre	Rabbit/Wild hare
Oie	Goose
Pintade/Pintadeau	Guinea fowl/Young guinea fowl
Poulet/Poussin	Chicken/Spring chicken

LÉGUMES (VEGETABLES)

Artichaut	Artichoke
Asperge	Asparagus
Aubergine	Eggplant
Carottes	Carrots
Champignons	Mushrooms
Chou-fleur	Cauliflower
Chou (rouge)	Cabbage (red)
Laitue	Lettuce
Oignons	Onions
Petits pois	Peas
Pomme de terre	Potato
Tomates	Tomatoes

Travel Smart
Montréal &
Québec City

GETTING HERE & AROUND

▌ BY AIR

Flying time (gate-to-gate) to Montréal is about 1½ hours from New York, 2½ hours from Chicago, 4 hours from Dallas, and 6 hours from Los Angeles. Flying time to Québec City is about 2 hours from New York, 3 hours from Chicago, 5 hours from Dallas, and 7 hours from Los Angeles.

Trudeau Airport offers self-serve check-in and boarding passes at electronic kiosks throughout the airport. Make sure you arrive at the airport two hours before your flight's scheduled departure.

Security measures at Canadian airports are similar to those in the United States.

Airlines & Airports Airline and Airport Links.com (⊕www.airlineandairportlinks. com) has links to many of the world's airlines and airports.

Airline Security Issues Transportation Security Administration (⊕www.tsa.gov) has answers for almost every question that might come up.

AIRPORTS

For service to Montréal, Montréal–Trudeau International Airport (also known by its previous name, Dorval International Airport, airport code YUL) is 22½ km (14 mi) west of the city. Québec City's Jean Lesage International Airport (YQB) is about 19 km (12 mi) northwest of downtown. Both airports handle domestic and international flights.

Airport Information Aéroports de Montréal (✉1100 blvd. René-Lévesque Ouest, Suite 2100 ☎514/394-7200 ⊕www.admtl. com). **Jean Lesage International Airport** (☎418/640-2600 ⊕www.aeroportde quebec.com). **Montréal–Pierre Elliott Trudeau International Airport** (☎800/465-1213 or 514/394-7377 ⊕www.admtl.com).

▌**TIP**➔Long layovers don't have to be only about sitting around or shopping. These days they can be about burning off vacation calories. Check out www.airportgyms.com for lists of health clubs that are in or near many U.S. and Canadian airports.

GROUND TRANSPORTATION

In Montréal a taxi from Trudeau International to downtown costs about C$35. All taxi companies must charge the same rate for travel between the airport and downtown.

In Québec City private limo service is expensive, starting at C$65 for the ride from the airport into the city. Try Groupe Limousine A-1. Taxis are available immediately outside the airport exit near the baggage-claim area. A ride into the city costs about C$30. Two local taxi firms are Taxi Coop de Québec, the largest company in the city, and Taxi Québec.

La Québécoise shuttles are a much cheaper alternative for getting to and from Trudeau International. Shuttles leave from Montréal Central Bus Station and pick up and drop off passengers at the downtown train station, as well as at major hotels. Shuttles run every 30 minutes from 4 AM to 11:30 PM and cost C$14 one-way, C$24 round-trip.

Montréal Contacts La Québécoise (☎514/842-2281 ⊕www.autobus.qc.ca).

Québec City Contacts Groupe Limousine A-1 (✉160 blvd. des Cedres, Québec ☎418/523-5059 or 866/523-5059). **Taxi Coop de Québec** (✉496 2ᵉ av., Limoilou ☎418/525-5191). **Taxi Québec** (✉975 av. 8ᵉ, Limoilou ☎418/525-8123).

FLIGHTS

Of the major U.S. airlines, American, Continental, Delta, Northwest, United, and US Airways serve Montréal; Continental and Northwest fly to Québec City.

Regularly scheduled flights from the United States to Montréal and Québec City as well as flights within Canada are available on Air Canada and the regional airlines associated with it, including Air Canada Jazz (reservations are made through Air Canada). Air Canada has the most nonstop flights to Montréal and Québec City from some 30 U.S. cities.

Airline Contacts Air Canada (☎888/247–2262 ⊕www.aircanada.ca). **American Airlines** (☎800/433–7300 ⊕www.aa.com). **Continental Airlines** (☎800/523–3273 for U.S. and Mexico reservations, 800/231–0856 for international reservations ⊕www.continental.com). **Delta Airlines** (☎800/221–1212 for U.S. reservations, 800/241–4141 for international reservations ⊕www.delta.com). **Northwest Airlines** (☎800/225–2525 ⊕www.nwa.com). **USAirways** (☎800/428–4322 for U.S. and Canada reservations, 800/622–1015 for international reservations ⊕www.usairways.com).

▌ BY BIKE

Québec is in the process of developing the Route Verte, or the Green Route, a 3,600-km (2,230-mi) network of bike trails covering the southern half of the province, which will eventually link with trails in New England and New York. More than half of the marked trails are already open, and when the project is completed, it will comprise 4,300 km (over 2,600 mi) of bikeways. For information and a map, contact Vélo Québec.

Contact Vélo Québec (☎514/521–8356 or 800/567–8356).

▌ BY BOAT & FERRY

The Québec–Lévis ferry crosses the St. Lawrence River to the town of Lévis and gives you a magnificent panorama of Old Québec. Although the crossing takes 15 minutes, waiting time can increase the trip to an hour. The cost is C$2.65. The first ferry from Québec City leaves daily at 6:30 AM from the pier at rue Dalhousie, opposite Place Royale. Crossings run every half hour from 7:30 AM until 6:30 PM, then hourly until 2:30 AM. From April through November the ferry adds extra service every 10 to 20 minutes during rush hours (7–10 AM and 3–6:45 PM). Schedules can change, so be sure to check the ferry Web site or call ahead.

Boat & Ferry Information Québec–Lévis ferry (☎418/644–3704 Québec City, 418/837–2408 Lévis, 418/837–2408 bilingual service 8:30–4:30 daily ⊕www.traversiers.gouv.qc.ca).

▌ BY BUS

Approximately 10 private bus lines serve the province. Orléans Express is probably the most convenient, as it offers regular service between Montréal and Québec City with a fairly new fleet of clean, comfortable buses. The trip takes three hours.

Limocar, another bus line, serves the ski resorts of the Laurentians and Eastern Townships. Greyhound Lines and Voyageur offer interprovincial service and are timely and comfortable, if not exactly plush. Smoking isn't permitted on any buses.

Bus terminals in Montréal and Québec City are usually efficient operations, with service all week and plenty of agents on hand to handle ticket sales. In villages and some small towns the bus station is simply a counter in a local convenience store, gas station, or snack bar. Getting information on schedules beyond the local ones is sometimes difficult in these places. In rural Québec it's a good idea to bring along a French–English dictionary, although most merchants and clerks can handle a simple ticket sale in English.

Buses from Montréal to Québec City depart daily on the half hour from 5:30 AM to 10:30 PM. Buses run from 6:30 AM to 10 PM on Sunday. A one-way ticket costs about C$50.14, round-trip costs C$77.49. Tickets can be purchased only at terminals. All inter-city bus lines servicing Montréal arrive at and depart from the city's downtown bus terminal, the Station Centrale d'Autobus Montréal, which is built on top of the Berri-UQAM Métro station. The staff has schedule and fare information for all bus companies at the station.

Greyhound's Canada Coach Pass Plus gives you access to Québec as well as the Maritime Provinces. Passes must be purchased in Canada at a Greyhound terminal or online before leaving home. They are an excellent value for travelers who want to wander the highways and byways of the country, packing a lot of miles into a relatively short period of time. However, for occasional day trips (from Montréal to Québec City, for example) they're hardly worth it.

Many bus companies offer discounts if you book in advance, usually either 7 or 14 days ahead. Discounts are also often available for kids (children ages 15 and under can travel for free on most bus lines if tickets are booked three days in advance).

In major bus terminals, most bus lines accept at least some of the major credit cards. Some smaller lines require cash or take only Visa or MasterCard. All accept traveler's checks in U.S. or Canadian currency with suitable identification, but it's advisable to exchange foreign currency (including U.S. currency) at a bank or exchange office. Be prepared to use cash to buy a ticket in really small towns.

Most bus lines don't accept reservations for specific seats. You should plan on picking up your tickets at least 45 minutes before the bus's scheduled departure time.

Bus Information **Central Bus Station** (✉505 blvd. de Maisonneuve Est, Montréal ☎514/842-2281). **Gare du Palais Bus Station** (✉320 rue Abraham-Martin, Québec ☎418/525-3000). **Greyhound**

Lines (☎800/231-2222, 800/661-8747 in Canada ⊕www.greyhound.com). **Limocar** (☎866/692-8899 or 514/842-2281 ⊕www.limocar.ca). **Orléans Express** (☎888/999-3977 or 514/395-4000 ⊕www.orleansexpress.com). **Société de Transport de Montréal** (STM ☎514/288-6287 or 514/786-4636 ⊕www.stcum.qc.ca). **Voyageur** (☎514/842-2281 ⊕www.greyhound.ca).

▌ BY CAR

Montréal is accessible from the rest of Canada via the Trans-Canada Highway, which crosses the southern part of the island as Route 20, with Route 720 leading into downtown. Route 40 parallels Route 20 to the north; exits to downtown include St-Laurent and St-Denis. From New York, take I–87 north until it becomes Route 15 at the Canadian border; continue for another 47 km (29 mi) to the outskirts of Montréal. You can also follow U.S. I–89 north until it becomes two-lane Route 133, which eventually joins Route 10, an east–west highway that leads west across the Champlain Bridge and right into downtown. From I–91 through Massachusetts via New Hampshire and Vermont, you can take Route 55 to Route 10. Again, turn west to reach Montréal.

At the border you must clear Canadian Customs, so be prepared with your passport and car registration. On holidays and during the peak summer season, expect to wait a half hour or more at the major crossings.

Montréal and Québec City are linked by Autoroute 20 on the south shore of the St. Lawrence River and by Autoroute 40 on the north shore. On both highways, the ride between the two cities is about 240 km (149 mi) and takes about three hours. U.S. I–87 in New York, U.S. I–89 in Vermont, and U.S. I–91 in New Hampshire connect with Autoroute 20, as does Highway 401 from Toronto.

Driving northeast from Montréal on Autoroute 20, follow signs for Pont Pierre-Laporte (Pierre Laporte Bridge) as you approach Québec City. After you've crossed the bridge, turn right onto boulevard Laurier (Route 175), which becomes the Grande Allée.

The speed limit is posted in kilometers; on highways the limit is 100 KPH (about 62 MPH), and the use of radar-detection devices is prohibited.

In Québec the road signs are in French, but the important ones have pictograms. Signs with a red circle and a slash indicate that something, such as a left or right turn, is prohibited. Those with a green circle show what is permitted. Parking signs display a green-circled *P* with either the number of hours you can park or a clock showing the hours parking is permitted. It's not unusual to have two or three road signs all together to indicate several different strictures. Keep in mind the following terms: *centre-ville* (downtown), *arrêt* (stop), *détenteurs de permis* (permit holders only), *gauche* (left), *droit* (right), *ouest* (west), and *est* (east).

Drivers must carry owner registration and proof of insurance coverage, which is compulsory in Canada. Québec drivers are covered by the Québec government no-fault insurance plan. Drivers from outside Québec can obtain a Canadian Non-Resident Inter-Provincial Motor Vehicle Liability Insurance Card, available from any U.S. insurance company. The card is accepted as evidence of financial responsibility in Canada, but you're not required to have one. The minimum liability in Québec is C$50,000. If you are driving a car that isn't registered in your name, carry a letter from the owner that authorizes your use of the vehicle.

Your driver's license may not be recognized outside your home country. You may not be able to rent a car without an International Driving Permit (IDP), which can be used only in conjunction with a valid driver's license and which translates your license into 10 languages. Check the AAA Web site for more info as well as for IDPs ($15) themselves.

RENTAL CARS

Rates in Montréal run from about C$34 to C$50 a day for an economy car with air-conditioning and unlimited kilometers. If you prefer a manual-transmission car, check whether the rental agency of your choice offers stick shifts; many agencies in Canada don't.

You must be at least 21 years old to rent a car in Québec, and some car-rental agencies don't rent to drivers under 25. Most rental companies don't allow you to drive on gravel roads. Child seats are compulsory for children ages 5 and under. In Québec, drivers under age 25 often have to pay a surcharge of C$10 a day.

Rentals at the airports near Québec City and Montréal are usually more expensive than rentals elsewhere in the area.

GASOLINE

Gasoline is always sold in liters; 3.8 liters make a gallon. At this writing, gas prices in Canada are fluctuating considerably, ranging from C$1.20 to C$1.50 per liter (this works out to about $1.18 to $1.47 per gallon U.S.). Lead-free gas is called *sans plomb* or *ordinaire* (gas stations don't sell leaded gasoline). Fuel comes in several grades, denoted in Montréal by bronze, silver, and gold colors and in other areas of the province as *regulière* and *supérieure*.

Major credit cards are widely accepted, and often you can pay at the pump. Receipts are provided if you want one—ask for a *facture*.

PARKING

Expect on-street parking in Montréal to be just as difficult as in any major city; your best bet is to leave the car at your hotel garage and take public transportation or a cab. If you must drive, ask your concierge to recommend a garage near your destination. Be extra careful where you park if it snows, to avoid getting towed. Parking in Québec City is much less stressful, although it's also advisable to leave the car at the hotel and walk—especially if you're heading to Vieux-Québec.

The narrow streets of the Old City leave few two-hour metered parking spaces available. However, several parking garages at central locations charge about C$12 a day on weekdays or C$7 for 12 hours on weekends. Main garages are at Hôtel de Ville (City Hall), Place d'Youville, Edifice Marie-Guyart, Place Québec, Château Frontenac, rue St-Paul, and the Old Port.

ROAD CONDITIONS
In Montréal and Québec City the jumble of bicycle riders, delivery vehicles, taxis, and municipal buses can be chaotic. In the countryside at night, roads are lighted at exit points from major highways but are otherwise dark. Roads in the province aren't very good—be prepared for some spine-jolting bumps and potholes, and check tire pressure once in a while. In winter, be aware of changing road conditions: Montréal streets are kept mostly clear of snow and ice, but outside the city the situation deteriorates. Locals are notorious for exceeding the speed limit, so keep an eye on your mirrors.

ROADSIDE EMERGENCIES
Dial 911 in an emergency. Contact CAA, the Canadian Automobile Association, in the event of a flat tire, dead battery, empty gas tank, or other car-related mishap. Automobile Association of America membership includes CAA service.

Emergency Services CAA (☎800/222-4357 or 514/861-7111 ⊕www.caa.ca).

Insurance Information Insurance Bureau of Canada (☎514/288-4321, 877/288-4321 in Québec ⊕www.ibc.ca). **Société de l'assurance automobile du**

Québec (☎800/361-7620, 514/873-7620, or 418/643-7620 ⊕www.saaq.gouv.qc.ca).

RULES OF THE ROAD
By law, you are required to wear seat belts even in the back seat. Infant seats also are required. Radar-detection devices are illegal in Québec; just having one in your car is illegal. Speed limits, given in kilometers, are usually within the 90–110 KPH (50–68 MPH) range outside the cities.

Right turns on red signals are allowed in the province, excluding the island of Montréal, where they're prohibited. Driving with a blood-alcohol content of 0.08% or higher is illegal and can earn you a stiff fine and jail time. Headlights are compulsory in inclement weather. Drivers may use handheld cell phones.

Contact Ministère des Transports du Québec (☎888/355-0511 ⊕www.mtq.gouv.qc.ca).

▌BY CRUISE SHIP

Although many operators offer cruises along sections of the 3,058-km (1,900-mi) St. Lawrence River as it flows from Lake Ontario to the Gulf of St. Lawrence and then the Atlantic Ocean, only three companies offer cabin cruises. Two—Navigation Madeleine (C.T.M.A.) and Relais Nordik—offer cargo cruising between Montréal and the Îles-de-la-Madeleine and between Rimouski and Blanc-Sablon. Celebrity Cruise Lines, Holland America, Regent Seven Seas, and Crystal Cruises all offer cruises departing from the U.S. East Coast, with Montréal and/or Québec City as their final destinations.

Cruise Lines Celebrity Cruises (☎800/647-2251 ⊕www.celebrity.com). **Crystal Cruises** (☎310/785-9300 or 800/446-6620 ⊕www.crystalcruises.com). **Holland America Line** (☎206/281-3535 or 877/932-4259 ⊕www.hollandamerica.com). **Navigation Madeleine (C.T.M.A.)** (☎888/986-3278 or 418/986-3278 ⊕www.ctma.ca). **Regent Seven Seas Cruises** (☎954/776-6123 or 877/505-5370 ⊕www.rssc.com).

▌ BY TRAIN

Amtrak has daily service from New York City's Penn Station to Montréal, although the train sometimes arrives too late to make any connecting trains that evening. Connections are available, often the next day, to Canadian rail line VIA Rail's Canadian routes. The ride takes up to 10 hours, and one-way tickets cost $61 to $75. VIA Rail trains run from Montréal to Québec City often and take three hours. Smoking isn't allowed on these trains.

VIA Rail, Canada's passenger rail service, has service between Montréal and Québec City. The train arrives at the 19th-century Gare du Palais in Lower Town. Trains from Montréal to Québec City and from Québec City to Montréal run four times daily on weekdays, three times daily on weekends. The trip takes less than three hours, with a stop in Ste-Foy. Tickets can be purchased in advance at VIA Rail offices, at the station prior to departure, through a travel agent, or online. The basic one-way fare, including taxes, is C$76.35.

First-class service costs C$142.44 each way and includes early boarding, seat selection, and a three-course meal with wine. One of the best deals, subject to availability, is the round-trip ticket bought 10 days in advance for C$112.81.

To save money, look into rail passes. But be aware that if you don't plan to cover many miles, you may come out ahead by buying individual tickets. The 30-day North American RailPass, offered by Amtrak and VIA Rail, allows unlimited coach-economy travel in the United States and Canada. You can either indicate your itinerary when purchasing the pass or confirm it as you travel. The cost is C$999 late May to mid-October, C$709 at other times. VIA Rail also offers a Canrail pass (for travel within Canada) and a Corridor Pass (for travel anywhere between Windsor, Ontario, and Québec City). Senior citizens (60 and older), children (18 and under), and students are entitled to an additional 10% discount off all rates.

Information Amtrak (☎800/872–7245 ⊕www.amtrak.com). **VIA Rail Canada** (☎888/842–7245 or 514/989–2626 ⊕www.viarail.ca).

Train Information Gare du Palais (✉450 rue de la Gare du Palais, Lower Town ☎No phone).

ESSENTIALS

▌ACCOMMODATIONS

In Montréal and Québec City you have a choice of luxury hotels, moderately priced modern properties, and small older hotels with perhaps fewer conveniences but more charm. Options in small towns and in the country include large, full-service resorts; small, privately owned hotels; roadside motels; and bed-and-breakfasts. Even outside the cities you need to make reservations before you plan to pull into town.

Expect accommodations to cost more in summer than in the colder months (except for places such as ski resorts, where winter is high season). When making reservations, ask about special deals and packages. Big-city hotels that cater to business travelers often offer weekend packages, and many city hotels offer rooms at up to 50% off in winter. If you're planning to visit Montréal or Québec City or a resort area in high season, book well in advance. Also be aware of any special events or festivals that may coincide with your visit and fill every room for miles around. For resorts and lodges, remember that winter ski season is a period of high demand, and plan accordingly. Assume that hotels operate on the European Plan (EP, no meals) unless we specify that they use the Breakfast Plan (BP, with full breakfast), Continental Plan (CP, with Continental breakfast), Full American Plan (FAP, all meals), or Modified American Plan (MAP, breakfast and dinner), or are all-inclusive (AI, all meals and most activities).

APARTMENT & HOUSE RENTALS

The *Gazette* (⊕*www.montrealgazette. com*), Montréal's English-language daily, has the best rental listings in town. *Hour* (⊕*www.hour.ca*), a good weekly free paper in Montréal, also has rental listings.

WORD OF MOUTH

Did the resort look as good in real life as it did in the photos? Did you sleep like a baby, or were the walls paper-thin? Did you get your money's worth? Rate hotels and write your own reviews in Travel Ratings or start a discussion about your favorite places in Travel Talk on www.fodors.com. Your comments might even appear in our books. Yes, you, too, can be a correspondent!

BED & BREAKFASTS

B&Bs can be found in both the country and the cities. For assistance in booking these, be sure to check out B&B Web sites (⊕*www.gitesetaubergesdupassant.com* is an excellent resource for B&Bs throughout the province). Room quality varies from house to house as well, so ask to see a few rooms before making a choice.

Reservation Services Bed & Breakfast.com (☎512/322–2710 or 800/462–2632 ⊕www.bedandbreakfast.com) also sends out an online newsletter. **Bed & Breakfast Inns Online** (☎310/280–4363 or 800/215–7365 ⊕www.bbonline.com). **BnB Finder.com** (☎212/432–7693 or 888/547–8226 ⊕www.bnbfinder.com).

HOME EXCHANGES

With a direct home exchange you stay in someone else's home while they stay in yours. Some outfits also deal with vacation homes, so you're not actually staying in someone's full-time residence, just their vacant weekend place.

Exchange Clubs Home Exchange.com (☎800/877–8723 ⊕www.homeexchange.com); $99.95 for a 1-year online listing. **HomeLink International** (☎800/638–3841 ⊕www.homelink.org); $110 yearly for Web-only membership; $170 includes Web access and two catalogs. **Intervac U.S.** (☎800/756–4663 ⊕www.intervacus.com); $95 for 1-year membership to Intervac USA and Intervac International.

HOTELS

Canada doesn't have a national rating system for hotels, but Québec's tourism ministry rates the province's hotels; the stars are more a reflection of the number of facilities than of the hotel's performance. Hotels are rated zero to three stars, with zero stars representing minimal comfort and few services and three stars being the very best. All hotels listed have private bath unless otherwise noted.

∎ COMMUNICATIONS

INTERNET

Most hotels—even several B&Bs—now have Wi-Fi either in-room or in-hotel. If you're looking for a cybercafé, head to the area around McGill University.

Contacts Cybercafes (⊕ www.cybercafes.com) lists more than 4,000 Internet cafés worldwide.

LANGUAGE

Try to learn a little of the local language. You need not strive for fluency; even just mastering a few basic words and terms is bound to make chatting with the locals more rewarding.

Although Canada has two official languages—English and French—the province of Québec has only one. French is the language you hear most often on the streets here; it is also the language of government, businesses, and schools. Only in Montréal, the Ottawa Valley (the area around Hull), and the Eastern Townships is English more widely spoken. Most French Canadians speak English as well, but learning a few French phrases before you go is useful. Canadian French has many distinctive words and expressions, but it's no more different from the language of France than North American English is from the language of Great Britain.

A phrase book and language-tape set can help get you started.

Fodor's French for Travelers (available at bookstores everywhere) is excellent.

PHONES

The good news is that you can now make a direct-dial telephone call from virtually any point on Earth. The bad news? You can't always do so cheaply. Calling from a hotel is almost always the most expensive option; hotels usually add huge surcharges to all calls, particularly international ones. In some countries you can phone from call centers or even the post office. Calling cards usually keep costs to a minimum, but only if you purchase them locally. And then there are mobile phones (⇨ *below*), which are sometimes more prevalent—particularly in the developing world—than land lines; as expensive as mobile phone calls can be, they are still usually a much cheaper option than calling from your hotel.

CALLING WITHIN CANADA

Pay phones are becoming scarce these days as people rely more heavily on mobile phones. Phone numbers appear just as they do in the U.S., with a three-digit area code followed by a seven-digit number. The area code for Montréal is 514; in Québec City, it's 418.

CALLING OUTSIDE CANADA

The country code for the United States is 1.

MOBILE PHONES

If you have a multiband phone (some countries use different frequencies from those used in the United States) and your service provider uses the world-standard GSM network (as do T-Mobile, Cingular, and Verizon), you can probably use your phone abroad. Roaming fees can be steep, however: 99¢ a minute is considered reasonable. And overseas you normally pay the toll charges for incoming calls. It's almost always cheaper to send a text message than to make a call, since text messages have a very low set fee (often less than 5¢).

If you just want to make local calls, consider buying a new SIM card (note that your provider may have to unlock your phone for you to use a different SIM card) and a prepaid service plan in the destination. You'll then have a local number and can make local calls at local rates. If your trip is extensive, you could also simply buy a new cell phone in your destination, as the initial cost will be offset over time.

■ TIP➜ If you travel internationally frequently, save one of your old mobile phones or buy a cheap one on the Internet; ask your cell phone company to unlock it for you, and take it with you as a travel phone, buying a new SIM card with pay-as-you-go service in each destination.

Contacts Cellular Abroad (☎800/287–5072 ⊕www.cellularabroad.com) rents and sells GMS phones and sells SIM cards that work in many countries. **Mobal** (☎888/888–9162 ⊕www.mobalrental.com) rents mobiles and sells GSM phones (starting at $49) that will operate in 140 countries. Per-call rates vary throughout the world. **Planet Fone** (☎888/988–4777 ⊕www.planetfone.com) rents cell phones, but the per-minute rates are expensive.

▋ CUSTOMS & DUTIES

You're always allowed to bring goods of a certain value back home without having to pay any duty or import tax. But there's a limit on the amount of tobacco and liquor you can bring back duty-free, and some countries have separate limits for perfumes; for exact figures, check with your customs department. The values of so-called "duty-free" goods are included in these amounts. When you shop abroad, save all your receipts, as customs inspectors may ask to see them as well as the items you purchased. If the total value of your goods is more than the duty-free limit, you'll have to pay a tax (most often a flat percentage) on the value of everything beyond that limit.

U.S. Customs and Immigration has pre-clearance services at **Pierre Elliott Trudeau International Airport,** which serves Montréal. This allows U.S.-bound air passengers to depart their airplane directly on arrival at their U.S. destination without further inspection and delays.

American visitors may bring in, duty-free, for personal consumption 200 cigarettes; 50 cigars; 7 ounces of tobacco; and 1 bottle (1.5 liters or 40 imperial ounces) of liquor or wine or 24 355-milliliter (12-ounce) bottles or cans of beer. Any alcohol and tobacco products in excess of these amounts is subject to duty, provincial fees, and taxes. You can also bring in gifts up to a total value of C$750.

Cats and dogs must have a certificate issued by a licensed veterinarian that clearly identifies the animal and vouches that it has been vaccinated against rabies during the preceding 36 months. Certificates aren't necessary for Seeing Eye dogs. Plant material must be declared and inspected. There may be restrictions on some live plants, bulbs, and seeds. You may bring food for your own use, as long as the quantity is consistent with the duration of your visit and restrictions or prohibitions on some fruits and vegetables are observed.

Canada's firearms laws are significantly stricter than those in the United States. All handguns and semiautomatic and fully automatic weapons are prohibited and cannot be brought into the country. Sporting rifles and shotguns may be imported provided they are to be used for sporting, hunting, or competing while in Canada. All firearms must be declared to Canada Customs at the first point of entry. Failure to declare firearms will result in their seizure, and criminal charges may be made. Regulations require visitors to have a confirmed Firearms Declaration to bring any guns into Canada; a fee of C$50 applies, good for one year. For more information, contact the Canadian Firearms Centre.

Information in Montréal and Québec City
Canada Border Services Agency (✉2265 blvd. St-Laurent, Ottawa, ON ☎800/461–9999 in Canada, 204/983–3500, 506/636–5064 ⊕www.cbsa-asfc.gc.ca). **Canadian Firearms Centre** (☎800/731–4000 ⊕www.cfc-cafc.gc.ca).

U.S. Information **U.S. Customs and Border Protection** (⊕www.cbp.gov).

■ EATING OUT

French-Canadian fast food follows the same concept as American fast food, though barbecue chicken is also popular. Local chains to watch for include St-Hubert, which serves rotisserie chicken, and La Belle Province, Lafleur, and Valentine, all of which serve hamburgers, hot dogs, and fries. As an antidote, try the Montréal chain Le Commensal—it's completely vegetarian, and it's excellent.

The restaurants we list are the cream of the crop in each price category. Properties indicated by a ✕🏠 are lodging establishments whose restaurant warrants a special trip.

MEALS & MEALTIMES

Unless otherwise noted, the restaurants listed in this guide are open daily for lunch and dinner.

PAYING

Major credit cards are widely accepted in both Montréal and Québec City.

For guidelines on tipping see Tipping below.

RESERVATIONS & DRESS

Regardless of where you are, it's a good idea to make a reservation if you can. In some places (Hong Kong, for example), it's expected. We only mention them specifically when reservations are essential (there's no other way you'll ever get a table) or when they are not accepted. For popular restaurants, book as far ahead as you can (often 30 days), and reconfirm as soon as you arrive. (Large parties should always call ahead to check the reservations policy.) We mention dress only when men are required to wear a jacket or a jacket and tie.

Online reservation services make it easy to book a table before you even leave home. OpenTable covers most states, including 20 major cities, and has limited listings in Canada, Mexico, the United Kingdom, and elsewhere. DinnerBroker has restaurants throughout the United States as well as a few in Canada.

Contacts DinnerBroker (⊕www.dinnerbroker.com). **OpenTable** (⊕www.opentable.com).

WINES, BEER & SPIRITS

Beer lovers rejoice at the selection available from highly regarded local microbreweries, such as Unibroue (Fin du Monde, U, U2), Brasseurs du Nord (Boréale), and McAuslan (Griffon, St. Ambroise). You may find these and other microbrews bottled in local supermarkets and on tap in bars. The local hard cider P.O.M. is also excellent. Caribou, a traditional concoction made from red wine, vodka (or some other liquor), spices, and, usually, maple syrup, is available at many winter events and festivals throughout the province, such as Québec City's winter carnival. Small bars may also offer the drink in season.

The province's liquor purveyor, SAQ, stocks a wide choice of wines and is also the only place you can buy hard liquor; most SAQ stores are open regular business hours. Supermarkets and convenience stores carry lower-end wines, but they can sell wine and beer until 11 PM all week (long after SAQ stores have closed). The minimum legal age for alcohol consumption is 18.

■ ELECTRICITY

Consider making a small investment in a universal adapter, which has several types of plugs in one lightweight, compact unit. Most laptops and mobile phone chargers are dual voltage (i.e., they operate equally well on 110 and 220 volts), so require only an adapter. These days the same is true of small appliances such as hair dryers. Always check labels and manufacturer instructions to be sure. Don't use 110-volt outlets marked FOR SHAVERS ONLY for high-wattage appliances such as hair-dryers.

Contacts Steve Kropla's Help for World Traveler's (⊕www.kropla.com) has information on electrical and telephone plugs around the world. **Walkabout Travel Gear** (⊕www.walkabouttravelgear.com) has a good coverage of electricity under "adapters."

∎ EMERGENCIES

All embassies are in Ottawa. The U.S. consulate in Montréal is open weekdays 8:30–noon; additionally it's open Wednesday 2–4. The U.S. Consulate maintains a list of medical specialists in the Montréal area.

In Montréal, the main hospital is Montréal General Hospital (McGill University Health Centre). Many pharmacies in Montréal stay open until midnight, including Jean Coutu and Pharmaprix stores. Some are open around the clock, including the Pharmaprix on chemin de la Côte-des-Neiges.

In Québec City, the Centre Hospitalier Universitaire de Québec is the city's largest institution and incorporates the teaching hospitals Pavillon CHUL in Ste-Foy and Pavillon Hôtel-Dieu, the main hospital in Vieux-Québec.

Pharmacie Brunet, north of Québec City in the Charlesbourg district, is open daily 8 AM–10:30 PM. Most outlets of the big pharmacy chains in the region (including Jean Coutu, Racine, Brunet, and Uniprix) are open every day and offer free delivery.

Foreign Embassies & Consulates U.S. Consulate General (⊠1155 rue St-Alexandre, Montréal, QC ☎514/398-9695 ⊠2 pl. Terrasse Dufferin, behind Château Frontenac, Qué-

bec City, QC ☎418/692–2095). **U.S. Embassy** (⊠490 Sussex Dr., Ottawa, ON ☎613/238–5335 ⊕www.ottawa.usembassy.gov).

Hospitals Centre Hospitalier Universitaire de Québec, Pavillon CHUL (⊠2705 blvd. Laurier, Ste-Foy ☎418/656–4141, 418/654–2114 emergencies). **Centre Hospitalier Universitaire de Québec, Pavillon Hôtel-Dieu** (⊠11 côte du Palais, Upper Town ☎418/691–5151, 418/691–5042 emergencies). **Montréal General Hospital (McGill University Health Centre)** (⊠1650 av. Cedar, Downtown ☎514/934–1934 Ⓜ Guy-Concordia).

Late-Night Pharmacies Pharmacie Brunet (⊠Les Galeries Charlesbourg, 4250 1re av., Charlesbourg ☎418/623–1571).

Pharmaprix (⊠1500 rue Ste-Catherine Ouest, Downtown ☎514/933–4744 Ⓜ Guy-Concordia ⊠5038 Sherbrooke Ouest, Notre-Dame-de-Grace ☎514/484–3531 Ⓜ Vendôme ⊠901 rue Ste-Catherine Est, Village ☎514/842–4915 Ⓜ Berri-UQAM ⊠5122 chemin de la Côte-des-Neiges, Côte-des-Neiges ☎514/738–8464 Ⓜ Côte-des-Neiges).

∎ HOLIDAYS

Canadian national holidays are as follows: New Year's Day (January 1), Good Friday (late March or early April), Easter Monday (the Monday following Good Friday), Victoria Day (late May), Canada Day (July 1), Labour Day (early September), Thanksgiving (mid-October), Remembrance Day (November 11), Christmas, and Boxing Day (December 26). St. Jean Baptiste Day (June 24) is a provincial holiday.

∎ HOURS OF OPERATION

Business hours are fairly uniform throughout the province. Businesses don't close on the following Monday when a holiday falls on a weekend.

Most banks in the province are open Monday through Thursday from 10 to 3 and Friday from 10 until 5 or 6. Some banks are open longer hours and on Saturday morning. All banks are closed on national holidays. Most banks (as well as most self-serve gas stations and convenience stores) have automatic teller machines (ATMs) that are accessible around the clock.

Government offices are generally open weekdays 9–5; some close for an hour around noon. Post offices are open weekdays 8–5 and Saturday 9–noon. Postal outlets in city pharmacies—of which there are many in Montréal—may stay open as late as 9 PM, even on Saturday.

Hours at museums vary, but most open at 10 or 11 and close in the evening. Some smaller museums close for lunch. Many museums are closed Monday; some stay open late on Wednesday, often waiving admission.

The days when all churches were always open are gone; vandalism, theft, and the drop in general piety have seen to that. But the major churches in Montréal and Québec City are open daily, usually about 9–6.

Most pharmacies in Montréal and Québec City are open until 10 or 11 PM, but a few stay open around the clock. In the rest of the province, pharmacies are generally open 9–5.

Stores and supermarkets usually are open Monday–Saturday 9–6, although in Montréal and Québec City, supermarkets are often open 7:30 AM–11 PM and some food stores are open around the clock. Most liquor stores are closed Sunday. Shops often stay open Thursday and Friday evenings, most malls until 9 PM. Convenience stores tend to stay open around the clock all week.

▌MAIL

In Canada you can buy stamps at the post office or from vending machines in most hotel lobbies, railway stations, airports, bus terminals, many retail outlets, and some newsstands. If you're sending mail to or within Canada, be sure to include the postal code (a combination of six digits and letters).

The postal abbreviation for Québec is QC.

Within Canada, postcards and letters up to 30 grams cost C$0.52; between 31 grams and 50 grams, the cost is C$0.96; and between 51 grams and 100 grams, the cost is C$1.15. Letters and postcards to the United States cost C$0.96 for up to 30 grams, C$1.15 for between 31 and 50 grams, and C$1.92 for up to 100 grams. Prices include GST (goods and services tax).

International mail and postcards run C$1.60 for up to 30 grams, C$2.30 for 31 to 50 grams, and C$3.75 for 51 to 100 grams.

Visitors may have mail sent to them c/o General Delivery in the town they are visiting, for pickup in person within 15 days, after which time it is returned to the sender.

SHIPPING PACKAGES

Many shops ship purchases home for you; when they do, you may avoid having to pay the steep provincial taxes. By courier, a package takes only a few days, but via regular Canada Post mail, packages often take a week—or longer—to reach the United States. Be sure to address everything properly and wrap it securely.

▌MONEY

Throughout this book, prices are given in Canadian dollars. The price of a cup of coffee ranges from less than C$1 to C$2.50 or more, depending on how upscale or downscale the place is; beer costs C$3 to C$7 in a bar; a smoked-meat sandwich costs about C$5 to C$6; and museum admission can cost anywhere from nothing to C$15.

Prices throughout this guide are given for adults. Substantially reduced fees are almost always available for children, students, and senior citizens.

■TIP➜ Banks never have every foreign currency on hand, and it may take as long as a week to order. If you're planning to exchange funds before leaving home, don't wait till the last minute.

ATMS & BANKS

Your own bank will probably charge a fee for using ATMs abroad; the foreign bank you use may also charge a fee. Nevertheless, you'll usually get a better rate of exchange at an ATM than you will at a currency-exchange office or even when changing money in a bank. And extracting funds as you need them is a safer option than carrying around a large amount of cash.

■TIP➜ PIN numbers with more than four digits are not recognized at ATMs in many countries. If yours has five or more, remember to change it before you leave.

ATMs are available in most bank, trust-company, and credit-union branches across the province, as well as in most convenience stores, malls, and self-serve gas stations.

CREDIT CARDS

Throughout this guide, the following abbreviations are used: **AE**, American Express; **D**, Discover; **DC**, Diners Club; **MC**, MasterCard; and **V**, Visa.

It's a good idea to inform your credit-card company before you travel, especially if you're going abroad and don't travel internationally very often. Otherwise, the credit-card company might put a hold on your card owing to unusual activity—not a good thing halfway through your trip. Record all your credit-card numbers—as well as the phone numbers to call if your cards are lost or stolen—in a safe place, so you're prepared should something go wrong. Both MasterCard and Visa have general numbers you can call (collect if

you're abroad) if your card is lost, but you're better off calling the number of your issuing bank, since MasterCard and Visa usually just transfer you to your bank; your bank's number is usually printed on your card.

If you plan to use your credit card for cash advances, you'll need to apply for a PIN at least two weeks before your trip. Although it's usually cheaper (and safer) to use a credit card abroad for large purchases (so you can cancel payments or be reimbursed if there's a problem), note that some credit-card companies *and* the banks that issue them add substantial percentages to all foreign transactions, whether they're in a foreign currency or not. Check on these fees before leaving home, so there won't be any surprises when you get the bill.

■TIP➜ Before you charge something, ask the merchant whether or not he or she plans to do a dynamic currency conversion (DCC). In such a transaction the credit-card *processor* (shop, restaurant, or hotel, not Visa or MasterCard) converts the currency and charges you in dollars. In most cases you'll pay the merchant a 3% fee for this service in addition to any credit-card company and issuing-bank foreign-transaction surcharges.

Dynamic currency conversion programs are becoming increasingly widespread. Merchants who participate in them are supposed to ask whether you want to be charged in dollars or the local currency, but they don't always do so. And even if they do offer you a choice, they may well avoid mentioning the additional surcharges. The good news is that you *do* have a choice. And if this practice really gets your goat, you can avoid it entirely thanks to American Express; with its cards, DCC simply isn't an option.

Reporting Lost Cards American Express (☎800/528–4800 in the U.S., 336/393–1111 collect from abroad ⊕www.american express.com). **Diners Club** (☎800/234–6377 in the U.S., 303/799–1504 collect from abroad ⊕www.dinersclub.com). **Discover** (☎800/347-2683 in the U.S., 801/902-3100 collect from abroad ⊕www.discovercard.com). **MasterCard** (☎800/627-8372 in the U.S., 636/722-7111 collect from abroad ⊕www.mastercard.com). **Visa** (☎800/847-2911 in the U.S., 410/581-9994 collect from abroad ⊕www.visa.com).

Currency Conversion Google (⊕www.google.com). **Oanda.com** (⊕www.oanda.com). **XE.com** (⊕www.xe.com).

CURRENCY & EXCHANGE

U.S. dollars are accepted in much of Canada, especially in communities near the border. Traveler's checks (some are available in Canadian dollars) and major U.S. credit cards are accepted in most areas.

The units of currency in Canada are the Canadian dollar (C$) and the cent, in almost the same denominations as U.S. currency ($5, $10, $20, 1¢, 5¢, 10¢, 25¢, etc.). The $1 and $2 bill are no longer used in Canada; they have been replaced by $1 and $2 coins (known as "loonies," because of the loon that appears on the coin, and "toonies," respectively).

At this writing, the exchange rate is US$1 to C$1.20.

Bank cards are widely accepted in Québec and throughout Canada. There are many branches of Québec's financial cooperative, La Caisse populaire Desjardins (a "Caisse Pop" as it's locally referred to), as well as bank machines (ATMs), throughout the region.

Even if a currency-exchange booth has a sign promising no commission, rest assured that there's some kind of huge, hidden fee. (Oh…that's right. The sign didn't say no fee.). And as for rates, you're almost always better off getting foreign currency at an ATM or exchanging money at a bank.

▌ PASSPORTS

As of January 1, 2008, all travelers will need a passport or other accepted secure documents to enter or reenter the United States. Naturalized U.S. residents should carry their naturalization certificate. Permanent residents who aren't citizens should carry their "green card." U.S. residents entering Canada from a third country must have a valid passport, naturalization certificate, or "green card."

▌ RESTROOMS

Find a Loo The Bathroom Diaries (⊕www.thebathroomdiaries.com) is flush with unsanitized info on restrooms the world over—each one located, reviewed, and rated.

▌ SAFETY

Montrealers are keen to boast they can walk the streets of their city at any time of day or night without fear of incident. And although both Montréal and Québec City are among the safest cities in North America, travelers should nevertheless be on their guard for pickpockets and other petty criminals, especially when traveling on Montréal's often-crowded Métro system.

▌**TIP→ Distribute your cash, credit cards, IDs, and other valuables between a deep front pocket, an inside jacket or vest pocket, and a hidden money pouch. Don't reach for the money pouch once you're in public.**

Contact Transportation Security Administration (TSA; ⊕www.tsa.gov).

▌ TAXES

A goods and services tax (GST) of 5% applies on virtually every transaction in Canada except for the purchase of basic groceries. In addition to imposing the GST, Québec levies a provincial sales tax of 7.5% on most goods and services as well.

Departing passengers in Montréal pay a C$20 airport-improvement fee that's included in the cost of an airline ticket.

You can get a GST refund on purchases taken out of the country and on short-term accommodations of less than one month, but not on food, drink, tobacco, car or motor-home rentals, or transportation. Rebate forms, which must be submitted within 60 days of leaving Canada, may be obtained from certain retailers, duty-free shops, customs officials, or from the Canada Customs and Revenue Agency. Instant cash rebates up to a maximum of C$500 are provided by some duty-free shops when you leave Canada, and, in most cases, goods that are shipped directly by the vendor to the purchaser's home aren't taxed. Refunds are paid out in U.S. dollars for U.S. citizens. In order to receive a refund, be sure to have all your receipts, barring those for accommodations, validated at Canada Customs before leaving the country. Always save your original receipts from stores and hotels (not just the credit-card receipts), and be sure the name and address of the establishment are shown on the receipt. Original receipts aren't returned, unless you request them. To be eligible for a refund, receipts must total at least C$200, and each receipt must show a minimum purchase of C$50.

Information Canada Customs and Revenue Agency (✉ Visitor Rebate Program, Summerside Tax Centre, 275 Pope Rd., Suite 104, Summerside, PE ☎ 800/668–4748 in Canada, 902/432–5608 ⊕ www.ccra-adrc.gc.ca).

▌ TOURS

In Montreal, from May through October, Amphi Tour sells a unique one-hour tour of Vieux-Montréal and the Vieux-Port on both land and water in an amphibious bus. Bateau-Mouche runs four harbor excursions and an evening supper cruise daily from May through October. The boats are reminiscent of the ones that cruise the canals of the Netherlands—wide-beamed and low-slung, with a glassed-in passenger deck. Boats leave from the Jacques Cartier Pier at the foot of Place Jacques-Cartier in the Vieux-Port.

Gray Line has nine different types of tours of Montréal from June through October and one tour the rest of the year. There are also day trips to Ottawa and Québec City. The company offers pickup service at the major hotels and at Info-Touriste (1001 Square Dorchester).

Gray Line also owns Imperial Tours, whose double-decker buses follow a nine-stop circuit of the city. You can get off and on as often as you like and stay at each stop as long as you like. There's pickup service at major hotels.

In Québec City, Autocar Dupont-Gray Line runs bus tours of the city, departing across the square from the Hôtel Château Laurier (1230 Place Georges V); you can purchase tickets at most major hotels. The company runs guided tours in a minibus as well as tours of Côte de Beaupré and Île d'Orléans, and for whale-watching in Charlevoix. Tours run year-round and cost C$34–C$125. Call for a reservation and the company will pick you up at your hotel.

Croisières AML has day and evening cruises, some of which include dinner, on the St. Lawrence River aboard the MV *Louis-Jolliet*. The 1½- to 3-hour cruises run from May through mid-October and start at C$33 plus tax.

Contacts Amphi Tour (☎ 514/849–5181 ⊕ www.montreal-amphibus-tour.com). **Autocar Dupont-Gray Line** (☎ 418/649–9226, 418/664–0460 or 800/267–8687 ⊕ www. cbaduponttours.com).

Bateau-Mouche (☎ 514/849–9952 or 800/361–9952 ⊕ www.bateau-mouche.com). **Croisières AML** (✉ Pier Chouinard, 10 rue Dalhousie, beside the Québec–Lévis ferry terminal, Lower Town ☎ 418/692–1159 or 800/563–4643 ⊕ www.croisieresaml.

com). **Imperial Tours** (☎877/348–5599 or 514/348–5599).

▌ TIME

Montréal and Québec City are both in the Eastern Standard Time zone. Los Angeles is three hours behind local time and Chicago is one hour behind.

Time Zones Timeanddate.com (⊕www. timeanddate.com/worldclock).

▌ TIPPING

Tips and service charges aren't usually added to a bill in Canada. In general, tip 15% of the total bill. This goes for waiters and waitresses, barbers and hairdressers, and taxi drivers. Porters and doormen should get about C$2 a bag. For maid service, leave at least C$2 per person a day (C$3 to C$5 in luxury hotels).

▌ VISITOR INFORMATION

There are major tourism offices in both Montréal and Québec City.

In Montréal, Centre Info-Touriste, on Square Dorchester, has extensive tourist information on Montréal and the rest of the province of Québec, as well as a currency-exchange service and Internet café. It's open June through early September, daily 8:30–7:30, and early September through May, daily 9–6. The Vieux-Montréal branch is open daily 9–7 between June and September and is otherwise open Wednesday–Sunday 9–5 with a one-hour lunch break 1–2.

Tourisme-Montréal, the city tourist office, doesn't operate an information service for the public, but its Web site has a wealth of well organized information.

In Québec City, the Québec City Region Tourism and Convention Bureau's visitor information centers in Montcalm and Ste-Foy are open June 24–early September, daily 8:30–7:30; early September–mid-October, daily 8:30–6:30; and mid-October–June 23, Monday–Thursday and Saturday 9–5, Friday 9–6, and Sunday 10–4. A mobile information service operates between mid-June and September 7 (look for the mopeds marked with a big question mark).

The Québec government tourism department, Tourisme Québec, has a center open September 3–March, daily 9–6; and April–September 2, daily 8:30–7:30. Tourisme Québec can provide information on specific towns' tourist bureaus.

FODORS.COM CONNECTION

Before your trip, be sure to check out what other travelers are saying in Talk on www. fodors.com.

In the Laurentians, the major tourist office is the Association Touristique des Laurentides, just off Autoroute des Laurentides 15 Nord at Exit 51. The office is open mid-June–August, daily 9–8:30; September–mid-June it's open Saturday–Thursday 9–5 and Friday 9–7. Mont-Tremblant, Piedmont/St-Sauveur, Ste-Adèle, St-Adolphe-d'Howard, Ste-Agathe-des-Monts, St-Eustache, St-Jovite, and Val David have regional tourist offices that are open year-round. Seasonal tourist offices (open mid-June–early September) are in Ferme Neuve, Grenville, Labelle, Lac-du-Cerf, Lachute, Nominique, Notre-Dame-du-Laus, Oka, St-Jérôme, Ste-Marguerite-Estérel, and St-Sauveur.

In the Eastern Townships, year-round regional provincial tourist offices are in Bromont, Coaticook, Granby, Lac-Mégantic, Magog-Orford, Sherbrooke, and Sutton. Seasonal tourist offices (open June–early September) are in Birchton, Danville, Dudswell, Dunham, Eastman, Frelighsburg, Lac-Brome (Foster), Lambton, Masonsville, Pike River, Ulverton, and Waterloo. The schedules of seasonal bureaus are irregular, so it's a good idea to contact the Association Touristique des Cantons de l'Est before visiting. This association also provides lodging information.

At the Beaupré Coast Interpretation Center, in a former convent, guides in costume explain displays on the history of the region. Admission is C$5. The center is open mid-May–mid-October, daily 10–5. The rest of the year, the center is open by reservation only. Québec City Tourist Information has a bureau in Beauport, in Montmorency Falls Park. It's open June 3–mid-October, daily 9–5.

For information about Québec's national parks, contact Parks Canada. Contact the individual park administration about camping in provincial parks. For information on camping in the province's private trailer parks and campgrounds, request the free publication "Québec Camping," from Tourisme Québec.

Agricotours, the Québec farm-vacation association, can provide lists of guest farms in the province.

Contacts **Agricotours** (⊠4545 av. Pierre-de-Coubertin, C.P. 1000, Succursale M, Montréal ☎514/252-3138 ⊕www.agricotours. qc.ca). **Association Touristique des Cantons de l'Est** (⊠20 rue Don Bosco Sud, Sherbrooke ☎819/820-2020 or 800/355-5755 🖶819/566-4445 ⊕www.cantonsdelest. com). **Association Touristique Régionale de Charlevoix** (⊠495 blvd. de Comporté, C.P. 275, La Malbaie ☎418/665-4454 or 800/667-2276 🖶418/665-3811 ⊕www. tourisme-charlevoix.com). **Association Touristique des Laurentides** (⊠14 142 rue de la Chapelle, Mirabel ☎450/224-7007, 450/436-8532, 800/561-6673, 514/990-5625 in Montréal 🖶450/436-5309 ⊕www. laurentides.com). **Beaupré Coast Interpretation Center** (⊠7976 av. Royale, C.P. 40, Château-Richer ☎418/824-3677 🖶418/824-5907 ⊕www.histoire-cotede-beaupre.org). **Canadian Tourism Commission** (☎604/638-8300 ⊕www.travelcanada.

ca). **Centre Info-Touriste** (⊠1001 Square Dorchester, Downtown ☎514/873-2015 or 877/266-5687 ⊕www.bonjourquebec. com Ⓜ Peel or Bonaventure ⊠174 rue Notre-Dame Est, at pl. Jacques-Cartier, Vieux-Montréal Ⓜ Champ-de-Mars). **Parks Canada** (☎418/648-4177 or 888/773-8888 ⊕www.pc.gc.ca). **Québec City Tourist Information** (⊠835 av. Laurier, Montcalm, ☎418/641-6290 ⊕www.quebecregion. com). **Tourisme-Montréal** (☎877/266-5687 ⊕www.tourisme-montreal.org). **Tourisme Québec** (⊠1001 rue du Square-Dorchester, No. 100, C.P. 979, Montréal ☎877/266-5687 or 514/873-2015 ⊕www.bonjourquebec. com).(⊠12 rue Ste-Anne, Place d'Armes, Upper Town ☎877/266-5687 ⊕www. bonjourquebec.com).

INDEX

NOTES

ABOUT OUR WRITERS

Montréal-born Eva Friede, fashion editor at the *Gazette*, is a veteran writer and editor. Ten years ago, the *Gazette* made her an offer she couldn't refuse: leaving the hard news trenches for the wonders of Paris, Milan, and shopping. A natural-born shopper, she chose the fashion beat. She loves a bargain as much as a designer splurge. Okay, a bargain is better. Check out her latest finds in Montréal and beyond on her blog, The Constant Shopper, at www.montrealgazette.com/shopper

Chris Barry is a native Montréaler and freelance journalist who has contributed to scores of publications over the years, not the least being the *Montréal Mirror* where, since 1999, his highly irreverent but hugely popular People column has been published every week. He's currently working on a book documenting his years as a professional rock and roll musician in the 1970s, '80s and '90s.

Anne Marie Marko is a Montréal-based freelance writer/editor. She is a frequent contributor to the *Mirror*, a local arts weekly, and, in recent years, has both written for and edited several tourist/cultural guides for her beloved Montréal and Québec City.

When she's not testing the linens at boutique hotels, Joanne Latimer is covering the lifestyle beat and stealing horses. Her work appears in the *New York Times*, the *Globe & Mail*, *Maclean's*, *enRoute*, *Fashion*, *Wish*, *Strut*, the *Ottawa Citizen*, *ARTnews*, and *Panoramitalia*. She's

a regular contributor to Sweetspot.ca, trolling Montréal for the hottest new spots to get a manicure or a martini. With a background in art history, she began her career reviewing art exhibits before becoming a film reviewer for the *Mirror*. Springboarding into fashion, food, décor, and travel writing, she enjoys getting her passport stamped and seeking out the world's most comfortable traveling shoes.

Paul Waters, a journalist and veteran travel writer, grew up on Canada's east coast. His wife and travel-writing partner, Julie Waters, is a native Montréaler with deep Loyalist roots in Québec's Eastern Townships. They both spent several years living in each of Canada's two metropolises— Toronto and Vancouver—but concluded that neither of those cities can match Montréal for charm, culture, and sheer livability. Paul is on the editorial board of the *Montréal Gazette* and Julie writes for several trade publications.

Brandon Presser comes from a long line of Montréalers. He studied art history at Harvard University and has since worked as a freelance travel journalist writing his way across the globe. Brandon has authored over a dozen guidebooks on a variety of destinations including Thailand, France, the Caribbean, Eastern Europe, Australia, and New England, but always looks forward to coming home to his roots.

DISCARD